GEORGIA & ALABAMA CAMPING

GEORGIA & ALABAMA CAMPING

The Complete Guide to More Than 380 Campgrounds

FIRST EDITION

Marilyn Sue Windle

AVALON
TRAVEL

CPL

FOGHORN OUTDOORS:
GEORGIA & ALABAMA CAMPING
The Complete Guide to
More Than 380 Campgrounds

First Edition
Marilyn Sue Windle

Published by
Avalon Travel Publishing
5855 Beaudry Street
Emeryville, CA 94608, USA

Please send all comments, corrections,
additions, amendments, and critiques to:

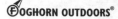

GEORGIA & ALABAMA CAMPING
AVALON TRAVEL PUBLISHING, INC.
5855 BEAUDRY ST.
EMERYVILLE, CA 94608, USA
email: atpfeedback@avalonpub.com
website: www.foghorn.com

Printing History
1st edition—June 2002
5 4 3 2 1

Text © 2002 by Marilyn Sue Windle.
All rights reserved.
Illustrations and maps © 2002 by Avalon Travel Publishing, Inc.
All rights reserved.

Some photos and illustrations are used by permission
and are the property of the original copyright owners.

ISBN: 1-56691-284-9
ISSN: 1532-3838

Editor: Rebecca K. Browning
Series Manager: Marisa Solís
Copy Editor: Jeannie Trizzino
Graphics: Melissa Sherowski
Illustrations: Bob Race
Production: Kirsten Cole, Alvaro Villanueva
Cover Design: Jacob Goolkasian
Map Editors: Naomi Adler Dancis, Olivia Solís
Cartography: CHK America, Kat Kalamaras, Mike Morgenfeld
Index: Beth Polzin
Proofreader: Erika Howsare

Front cover photo: © Shannon Wright

Distributed by Publishers Group West

Printed in USA by Bertelsmann

This book is dedicated to my parents for their

continuing support, even though they'd feel

better if I had a "real" job.

Contents

GEORGIA

ALABAMA

RESOURCES

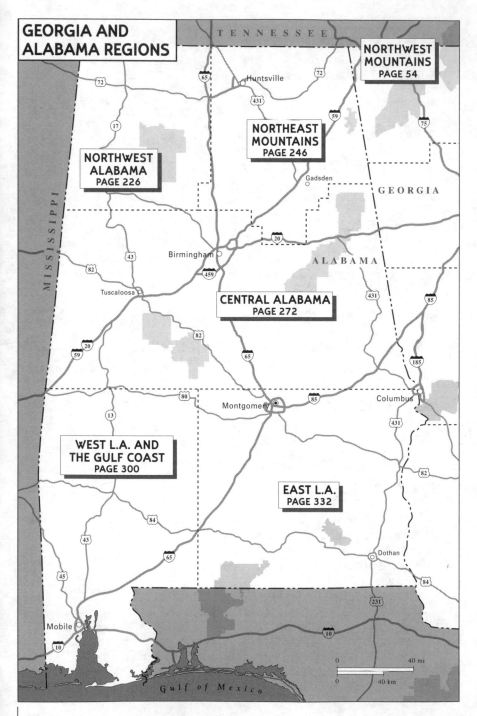

GEORGIA AND ALABAMA REGIONS

TENNESSEE

NORTHWEST MOUNTAINS
PAGE 54

Huntsville

NORTHEAST MOUNTAINS
PAGE 246

NORTHWEST ALABAMA
PAGE 226

Gadsden

GEORGIA

M I S S I S S I P P I

Birmingham

ALABAMA

Tuscaloosa

CENTRAL ALABAMA
PAGE 272

WEST L.A. AND THE GULF COAST
PAGE 300

Montgomery

Columbus

EAST L.A.
PAGE 332

Dothan

Mobile

Gulf of Mexico

0   40 mi
0   40 km

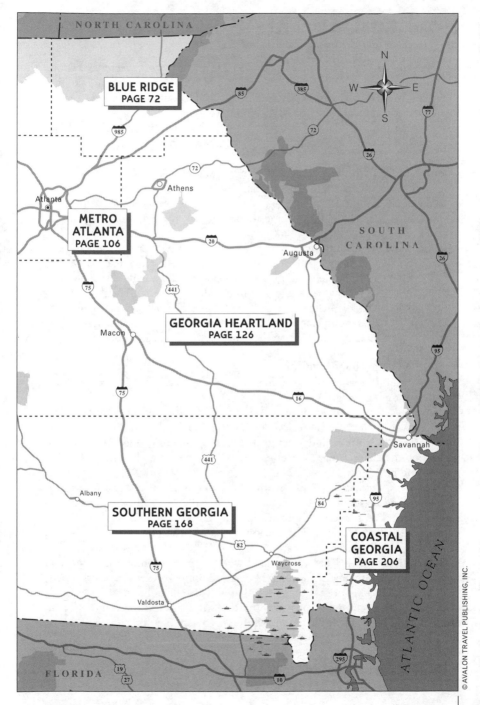

NORTH CAROLINA

BLUE RIDGE
PAGE 72

Athens

Atlanta

METRO
ATLANTA
PAGE 106

SOUTH
CAROLINA

Augusta

Macon

GEORGIA HEARTLAND
PAGE 126

Savannah

Albany

SOUTHERN GEORGIA
PAGE 168

COASTAL
GEORGIA
PAGE 206

Waycross

Valdosta

ATLANTIC OCEAN

FLORIDA

How to Use This Book

Foghorn Outdoors: Georgia & Alabama Camping is divided into 11 regional sections within the two states. Regions in Georgia include Northwest Mountains, Blue Ridge, Metro Atlanta, Georgia Heartland, Southern Georgia, and Coastal Georgia. Regions in Alabama are Northwest Alabama, Northeast Mountains, Central Alabama, West L.A. and the Gulf Coast, and East L.A. Maps at each chapter's beginning show where all the campgrounds in that region are located.

You can search for the ideal campsite in two ways:
1. If you know the name of the specific campground where you would like to stay, or the name of the surrounding geographical area or nearby feature (town, national or state park or forest, mountain, lake, river, etc.), look it up in the index and turn to the corresponding page.
2. If you know the general area you want to visit, you can determine which chapter covers that territory by checking the Georgia and Alabama map. Then turn to the regional map at the beginning of that chapter. Each regional map is broken down into grids, which show by number all the hikes in that chapter. Opposite the map will be a chapter table of contents listing each campground in the chapter by its map number and profile page number. Turn to the corresponding page for complete information on the campground that interests you.

About the Campground Profiles

The practical information you need to plan your trip to each site is broken down into the following categories:

Location— This category provides the general location of the campround by naming its proximity to the nearest major town or landmark. Following this information is a number and letter grid reference to help you locate the campground on the chapter map. The entire entry will be written like this: "Mobile; map 4, grid B8."

Campsites, facilities— This section provides the number of campsites for both tents and RVs and whether hookups are available. Facilities such as restrooms, picnic areas, recreation areas, laundry, and dump stations will be addressed, as well as the availability of piped water, showers, playgrounds, and stores, among others. The campground's pet policy is also mentioned here.

Reservations, fees— This section notes whether reservations are accepted, and the rates for tent sites and RV sites. If there are additional fees for parking or pets, or discounted weekly or seasonal rates, that will also be noted here.

Open—This section also provides the dates that the campground is open. Some campgrounds close during the winter. If you are planning a late spring or early summer trip, call the campground ahead of time to make sure it's open.

Directions— This section provides mile-by-mile driving directions to the campground from the nearest major town.

Contact— This section provides an address, phone number, and Internet address, if available, for the campground.

Trip notes— This section provides a brief overview of the setting, as well as information about the attractions and activities popular at the campground.

About the Icons

The icons in this book are designed to provide at-a-glance information on activities that are available on-site or nearby each campground. Some icons have been selected to also represent facilities available or services provided. They are not meant to represent every activity or service, but rather those that are most significant.

- 🚶 — Hiking trails are available.

- 🚲 — Biking trails or routes are available. This usually refers to mountain biking, although it may represent road cycling as well. Refer to the text for that campground for details.

- 🏊 — Swimming opportunities are available.

- 🎣 — Fishing opportunities are available.

- 🚤 — Boating opportunities are available. Various types of vessels apply under this umbrella activity, including motorboats and personal watercrafts (Jet Skis). Refer to the text for that campground for more detail, including mph restrictions and boat ramp availability.

- 🐕 — Pets are permitted. Campgrounds that allow pets may require an additional fee or that pets be leashed. Campgrounds may also restrict pet size or behavior. Refer to the text for that campground for specific instructions or call in advance.

- 🤸 — A playground is available. A campground with a playground can be desireable for campers traveling with children.

- 🚐 — RV sites are provided.

- ⛺ — Tent sites are provided.

- ♿ — Wheelchair access is provided, as advertised by campground managers. However, concerned persons are advised to call the contact number of a campground to be certain that their specific needs will be met.

About the Maps

The maps in this book are designed to show the general location of campgrounds and are not meant to substitute for more detailed road maps. Readers are advised to take additional maps when heading out to any campground, particularly when venturing into the wilderness.

Acknowledgments

No book of this type could be written without the help and support of many people. I'd like to offer my sincere thanks to all who provided information and advice during the writing of this book, including the many rangers in the state and national parks, Corps of Engineers, and U.S. Forest Service who patiently answered my questions. I'd also like to thank Gautam Bhan of the Sierra Club for his invaluable suggestions for backpackers, and my family and friends for their love and support during the process of writing the book. Special thanks to Betty Baker for her fabulous recipe for Potatoes Wonderful, Starr Johnson for her insights on camping from childhood to adult, Veronica Jones for her bear stories, and Susan Burgin and Vickie Eberlein for providing support and humor throughout the process. Thanks also for the tireless help of Marisa Solís, Mike Ferguson, Jeannie Trizzino, Rebecca Browning, and Mike Morgenfeld of Avalon Travel Publishing.

About Area Codes

Area code changes are becoming a fact of life. As we went to press, BellSouth announced area code changes in both Alabama and Georgia. We've updated the listings where possible, but inevitably we've missed some. Please feel free to contact Avalon Travel Publishing with any omissions or updates.

Our Commitment

We are committed to making *Foghorn Outdoors: Georgia & Alabama Camping* the most accurate, thorough, and enjoyable camping guide to this region. With this well-researched first edition, you can rest assured that every camping spot in this book is accompanied by the most up-to-date information available. However, with the change of seasons, you can bet that some of the fees listed herein have gone up, and that camping destinations may have opened, closed, changed hands, or changed their policies or procedures. It is always a good idea to call the campground ahead of time, but doubly so if you have any special needs, such as wheelchair access, or are traveling with children or pets. The time to find out the pool is closed for renovation is *before* you spend two hours driving to it with hot, cranky kids in the backseat.

If you would like to comment on this book, whether it's to suggest a tent or RV spot we overlooked, or to let us know about any noteworthy experience—good or bad—that occurred while using *Foghorn Outdoors: Georgia & Alabama Camping* as your guide, we would appreciate hearing from you. Please address correspondence to:

Foghorn Outdoors: Georgia & Alabama Camping
Avalon Travel Publishing
5855 Beaudry Street
Emeryville, CA 94608 U.S.A.

email: atpfeedback@avalonpub.com

INTRODUCTION

INTRODUCTION

Growing up along the coast of Florida definitely has its advantages: Merritt Island is beautiful year-round, citrus trees can be found in nearly every backyard, and most of what qualifies as a houseplant in Atlanta thrives outdoors in coastal Florida. It was easy to take for granted the lush beauty around me.

So I had a rude awakening when I moved to Atlanta one January. It was the last day of a five-day ice storm, and the city had been paralyzed with ice and snow. The whole place looked dead. Even the trees were lifeless, except for a few pines.

After living in an area where I was outdoors as much as indoors, I couldn't imagine what people did with their time when near-freezing temperatures kept most within well-insulated walls. Finding myself six hours from the nearest beach also made me think that I'd made a big mistake.

Two things happened that kept me from moving back home: spring arrived, and I took a camping trip.

Spring is unbelievable in Atlanta. In Florida, spring had no real meaning to me beyond something marked on a calendar. In Atlanta, however, spring explodes with so much growth and bloom that the entire city has allergies. If you don't have problems with pollen when you arrive here, you will eventually. It's not unusual for the pollen count to hit 2,000 (over 50 is considered very high) for weeks at a time. This is because everything blooms at the same time, making Atlanta one of the most beautiful cities I've ever seen in the springtime.

When a group of friends suggested a camping trip, my initial reaction was to say no. I'd had some pretty miserable experiences camping as a kid, and didn't ever want to do that again. Besides, when my family went camping, all we ever did was sit in the rain and fish. My friends assured me there'd be no fishing involved, instead a weekend of driving around the mountains looking at the blooming trees and flowers. I decided to go along but never expected to have a good time.

After setting up in our primitive campground, we ate dinner and turned in. Instead of a flat air mattress, we slept on thick, cushy pads. When I woke up the next morning, the only sound I heard was the song of birds. After a leisurely hot breakfast, we piled into one of the cars and headed out to explore the countryside. I'd had no idea there were mountains in Georgia, much less waterfalls. That spring and summer, we explored Amicalola and Anna Ruby Falls, Brasstown Bald, Helen, the Coopers Creek Wildlife Management Area, and Vogel State Park, and each trip was as good as the one before.

As great as those trips were, we were seldom out of a car. When another friend introduced me to hiking that year, I found what I believe to be an ideal combination. Since that year, I've hiked and camped from Key West to the Grand Canyon, and throughout the southeast. When my work schedule permits, I'm out nearly every weekend.

I'm not always able to camp off the beaten path in the woods or mountains, as I'd prefer. Sometimes I'm forced to stop for the night just off the interstate as I head for my ultimate destination. Other times, I'm headed for a city and need an inexpensive place to rest my bones. I've purchased several camping directories, but have never found one that inclusively listed all types of campsites, from backcountry plots to RV resorts with all the amenities.

My two goals in writing this book are: first, to provide the most complete guide possible to this region, and, second, to enhance your camping experience by bringing you the information you need to find that great campsite. I've personally contacted each campground in the book and have made every effort to ensure that what you need to know to choose a site is correct and up to date. Whether you're an experienced camper or would like to be, I hope, as you relax at your campsite and listen to the sounds of nature, you'll feel I've done just that.

CAMPING TIPS

CAMPING OPTIONS FROM BACKPACKS TO BEHEMOTHS

Talk to a dozen campers, and you can end up with twelve different views on what it means to go camping. At one extreme is someone who sees camping as hiking to a remote spot, stretching out on the bare ground, and watching the stars as they fall asleep. Others wouldn't consider going to the woods without a TV and a satellite dish.

Speaking of comfort, if you've been unable to convince your significant other that camping is fun, trying moving up a level. If he or she doesn't like backpacking, try car camping, with lots of foam padding for sleeping comfort. If you've tried car camping and that didn't suit him or her, try renting a pop-up and sleeping in a real bed.

Camping to me is something in between. I wouldn't camp in the open without a tent. I mainly go car camping, but I also camp with friends in their RVs. Though some of my friends think sleeping on the ground is "slumming," the reality is that there's no reason to give up comfort regardless of how you're camping. My camp bed is more comfortable than many I've found in motels. It's just a little closer to the ground.

Although some campgrounds limit campers to either tents or RVs, many have sections for each. There are also plenty of trails in the region where backpacking is the only option. The key is finding the style that suits your taste, your budget, and your comfort level.

Wilderness Etiquette

It never fails. You've hiked in to a spectacular waterfall, taken off your shoes and socks, and splashed in the pool. You're surrounded by lush ferns, hear only birds singing as they flit about the woods, and can't imagine it gets any better. Then you notice the soft drink can floating by some downed wood. Looking more closely, you find plastic bags, gum and candy wrappers, and my personal favorite, one dirty sock.

Walk around any lake, and you'll find broken and discarded fishing tackle. I've seen people flick cigarette butts into the woods, cut across switchbacks, pick or step on wildflowers, throw trash in geysers, and harass wildlife. I wondered for many years if America was just trashier than other cultures, but there are plenty of non-Americans visiting our national parks, and they seem just as likely to trash the nature they traveled to see.

"Enjoy America's country and leave no trace." That's the motto of the Leave No Trace program, and we strongly support it. Promoting responsible outdoor recreation through education, research, and partnerships is its mission. Look for the **Keep It Wild Tips,** developed from the policies of Leave No Trace, sprinkled throughout the book. For a free pocket-size, weatherproof card printed with these policies, as well as information that details how to minimize human impact on wild areas, contact Leave No Trace at P.O. Box 997, Boulder CO, 80306; 303/442-8222 or 800/332-4100; www.lnt.org.

TENT CAMPING

There are two extreme positions on what type of shelter is necessary while camping. At one end are the people who don't use a tent at all or who will use only a bivvy sack, which basically just encloses you and your sleeping bag for bug and rain protection. I think these are the same people who head out for a long weekend carrying not much more than a cup, a knife, and a toothbrush, planning on living off the land for the next three days.

Then there's Betty's husband, Bill. He requires not only a color TV and a VCR, but also a satellite dish in his motor home. Long gone is the pop-up Betty and I used to camp in when she was single. I think if he knew she used to backpack, he'd be horrified.

I'm in the middle between these two extremes. I want the privacy and space a tent provides, but enjoy getting away from the routine of TVs, telephones, and computers when I camp. I also want comfort. After camping for years in tents that made me crawl in the door, I moved up to a model I barely have to incline my head for. I'm fairly tall at five feet, 10 inches, and I don't like having to hunker down to change clothes. I can stand up anywhere inside my tent and not hit my head on the ceiling. One of my friends does graze the top, but he's well over six feet.

That additional height doesn't come without a price, though. You'd never carry this tent on your back. It's strictly for car camping.

Selecting a Tent

Finding the tent that's right for you or your family is important. It doesn't have to be hard, though. Just make sure you ask yourself (or the salesperson at the outfitter) the following questions:

• *How hard is it to put up?* When you're shopping for a tent, you should be able to see it set up on the store floor. Ask the salesperson to show you how to put it up and take it down. If he or she can't handle that, look at another tent. I can set up and take down my dome tent by myself in less than 15 minutes, not including staking out the rain fly. With two people, the time required drops to just over five minutes. That really helps when you arrive at the campground and it starts to rain.

One tent I've seen has an interesting feature: It puts itself up. After unfolding it, you toss it in the air and it pops up into a dome. It doesn't get much easier than that!

• *Is it tall enough?* Once the tent is set up, check the height of the door. I was fine with a low door I had to crawl in until I camped in a friend's pop-up. Think about whether you and your family or friends are willing to crawl in the vestibule, or if you want to be able to walk in.

Next, go inside. Is the tent tall enough for you? Most of the time you're inside, you'll be either sitting or lying down, so it's not a requirement for some people that they can stand upright. It's important to me, but if it's not to you, the shorter models are cheaper and a lot lighter. My first tent was a dome about four feet high in the center. After putting it up, if the location wasn't quite right, I could pick it up with one hand and move it wherever I wanted. I can't do that with my current tent.

• *Is it roomy enough?* As for the size of tent to get, think about how you plan to use it. If you're backpacking, obviously weight will be a deciding factor. Otherwise, add at least one to the number of people who will normally be in your party when you look at how many a tent is supposed to accommodate. A two-person

---

Try Before You Buy

Renting equipment will keep you from making a lot of expensive mistakes. My first tent was so complicated, I needed to read the multi-page instruction manual every time I set it up, not too handy when you arrive at your campsite after dark and find out no one remembered to bring a flashlight. If I had rented it first, I would never have bought it.

Here, then, is the time to find a quality outdoors store in your area. A good outdoors store will usually have a rental department, allowing you to test out equipment and see how it performs. Two of the biggest benefits of the store, though, are the people working there and the quality of the merchandise they sell.

Unless you're an expert on gear, there's no substitute for talking with someone who has actually used the equipment. I economize where possible and buy some things from the camping department of the local discount store, but the clerk who rings me up might have been working in the shoe department last week. I don't expect him or her to be able to tell me how to use a water filter, or to be able to put up or take down a tent. I occasionally will also buy some things from mail order, but for quality gear that will last and perform, even under duress, there is no substitute for a good outdoors store.

Once when shopping for a backpacking stove, I had done my homework and was pretty sure which one I wanted. The salesman demonstrated it for me, and agreed that it was a good product. Just before heading to the register, I asked him if this was the stove he owned. "Oh, no," he said, "This one doesn't work well at higher elevations. I usually camp in the mountains, so I have this one over here." You're not going to get the benefit of that kind of experience at a discount store.

I bought my current tent at REI (see Resources), and spent several hundred dollars for it. On one camping trip, my companion pointed out the tent next door looked a lot like mine, but had a discount store's logo on it. During conversations with our neighbors over the next few days, I learned about all the problems they'd had with theirs. They were planning to replace the tent at the end of that trip, even though they'd only had it a year. At that time, my tent had gotten a lot of use over three years, and still had not a rip or a leak. Plus, my tent has features theirs lacked, such as lots of pockets built into the sides, a truly functional rain fly, and more windows. Was it worth the extra expense? I think so.

On every camping trip I take, I see someone struggling with inferior equipment that doesn't perform reliably or requires constant tinkering to get it to work. Do yourself a favor and buy the best quality gear you can afford, but only after field testing it yourself. You'll save a lot of money in the long run. And then, just in case, don't forget the duct tape. It'll fix almost anything.

---

tent has enough floor space to allow two people to stretch out inside, but it won't hold their gear, and they'd better be pretty friendly.

I'm a bit claustrophobic, so I prefer a larger tent. Plus, I usually bring a friend along when I camp, and always have my dogs and our assorted gear, so I wouldn't consider getting anything smaller than a three-person tent. A four-person size is much more comfortable for me.

• *Will it keep me dry?* Look at the floor, especially by the door. Generally, if the floor is flat and seamed around the edges, you will have a leakage problem eventually. Tent manufacturers solve that problem by extending the floor up the sides an inch or so before hitting a seam. My experience has been, though, that it's easy to trip over this rim when coming in and out of the tent, particularly if you're a dog

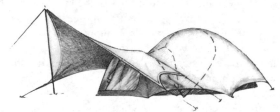

or a child, so consider the height of the rim and who you'll be camping with.

Even though you will be using a ground cloth, get a tent with a double thickness floor. Even if you're careful, you're going to miss some of the rocks at your campsite, and the extra thickness helps protects the floor of the tent.

• *What's the ventilation like?* Other features to look for include the number of windows. Some tents even have a "skylight" at the top that you can unzip to watch the stars. I've never used one for this purpose, as I always have the rain fly on, but it does help a lot with ventilation and temperature control. Camping in the South can get pretty steamy, so the more windows a tent has, the better, especially if you can unzip them in the rain because they're fully covered by the rain fly.

• *Are there any "built-ins"?* My tent has pockets sewn in around the walls that my friend Vickie calls night tables. Some hold small gear like my watch while I sleep, while larger pockets hold objects that would otherwise clutter up the floor space day or night. Pockets near the door hold dog leashes and pooper-scooper bags so they're handy for quick walks down the road, and a flashlight for midnight trips to the comfort station. A small pocket at the door is a good place to stash the keys to the car, so whoever gets up first can get out the stove and get the coffee going.

• *How does it fold up?* One last thing to consider about the tent is how you'll store and transport it. Most are packed in a box they'll never fit back into again. Even if it will, the box would fall apart by your second trip. Your tent may come with a stuff sack, or you can buy one large enough to hold the tent and all its paraphernalia. You need something to hold the tent, poles, stakes, guy lines, and rain fly, or you can end up at your campsite and find you're missing some crucial piece of equipment.

Important Tent Gear

• *Rain fly:* In the mountains of this region, you can count on rain on most camping trips. I consider a functional rain fly to be a necessity. I say functional, because on many tents, particularly ones you find at discount stores, the rain fly doesn't extend far enough down the sides to prevent the tent from getting soaked in a driving rain. No matter what the box says, most tents are more water-resistant than waterproof. Also, if you and your gear are wet when you get into the tent, it's going to get pretty steamy in there if you can't open any of the windows because the rain fly doesn't come down far enough.

The rain fly fulfills another purpose as well. The humidity here in the South is very high. I met Gautam Bhan several years ago when he was teaching a backpacking seminar for the Sierra Club. Because he's an expert at backpacking and gear, I asked him for his advice on rain flies. He pointed out that a rain fly creates a double wall for your tent. During the night, moisture will condense and run down the inside of the fly to puddle on the ground. Without a rain fly, you'll end up with condensation inside the tent.

• *Tent stakes:* While you're considering the rain fly, take a look at the stakes and guy lines that hold it out. Just about everyone will trip over the ropes or stakes at their campsite at some point.

One of the neatest inventions of the last few years has been making stakes that glow in the dark. These are *very* cool. If the store sells them, buy them. Also available is glow-in-the-dark tape you can put on your tent or rain fly, making it a little easier to find in the dark.

Some tent stakes are actually more like long metal nails. Except along the coast, the ground in this region is hard. Metal nails drive into the ground easier and without shattering like the plastic stakes. The problem is, it's easy to lose sight of them after you release the lines, and the plastic colored stakes are much easier to spot. I wouldn't want to step on one of the nails left behind by a previous camper, so I use the stakes. You need to carry extra plastic stakes with you since you'll break them regularly. I sometimes forget to bring a hammer for pounding in the stakes, and end up using rocks. Rocks are very hard on plastic stakes and your knuckles.

• *Ground cover:* Before setting up camp, spread out a ground cloth under the tent. It helps to keep water out and extends the life of your tent as it cuts down on wear and tear on the floor. Fold the ground cloth to be just a tad smaller than the floor of the tent, or water will collect and funnel underneath, eventually leaking inside. You can pick up a tarp at an outdoors or discount store.

While you're looking at tarps, see if they have one that has grommets on the corners. On one particularly stormy trip to the Smokies, I set up an extra tarp that covered my tent and rain fly, and staked it out so we had a protected area outside the door, like an awning. That worked so well I've used it a lot since. You can tie the tarp to surrounding trees to keep it off the top of the tent.

I've seen a lot of people erect a poled dining canopy over their tent, giving them an extra measure of protection from rain and sun. On that same trip to the Smokies, my neighbors put up a screened room enclosing their picnic table. They were the only ones who weren't bothered by June Bugs at dinner.

• *Seam sealant:* Your tent will probably come with a patch kit to repair holes. You'll also want to buy a tube or two of a seam sealer, such as Seam Lock, Seam Grip, or whatever the store sells in that line. Once you've picked out your tent and brought it home, set it up where it can sit for a day or so without getting rained on. Use your ground cloth if you set it up on concrete, like on the basement floor.

Now the fun begins. You want to go over every seam in the tent from the inside with the seam sealer, which is a glue-like substance that will plug all the tiny holes made by sewing your tent together. It's all to the good if the box says the tent was factory seam sealed, but you still need to go over the seams again. As a matter of fact, I do this once a year. You can also go over the seams on the outside of the tent.

When the seam sealer has air-dried for a couple of days, take the tent down and put it away. Put the tent, rain fly, stakes, guy lines, and instructions in the stuff sack, and store it to be ready for your trip.

One Final Tip

When I get home from a trip, I always set up my tent again for a day or so to clean it and let it dry completely. Even if it hasn't rained, condensation and humidity can dampen the tent enough to cause mildew. If your tent mildews, it's trash. You'll never get the smell out.

As I said before, a tent is not where you want to economize. I've used my tent for years with no leaks or tears. I bought it from a good outdoors store, not the camping department of the discount store. The tent poles are shock-corded for quick assembly, meaning an elastic cord through the center connects them and keeps them together. My last tent's poles weren't shock-corded, and I had to match up and connect a bottom, middle, and top section for each pole. Naturally, these three pole parts were not interchangeable.

Selecting a Sleeping Bag

After you select your tent, you need to think about a sleeping pad and bag. Nothing ruins an otherwise good camping trip faster than bad sleep, either because of temperature problems or lack of a comfortable bed. You can survive a night or two of discomfort, but you shouldn't have to, especially on vacation.

I know people who refuse to try camping as adults because they still remember the experience as kids. Most of the horror stories I hear involve sleeping on rocks, sleeping on air mattresses gone flat, trying to sleep while being sucked dry by mosquitoes, and sleeping in the hot confines of a canvas tent. Notice a trend here? Even kids appreciate a good night's sleep. And when we're uncomfortable, even the best of us get cranky.

With the proper sleeping bag and pad, you don't have to sacrifice your sleep to being in the great outdoors. You'll want to consider the following points:

• *Shapes and sizes:* There are two styles of sleeping bags. The first is called a **mummy bag** because of its shape, narrower at the foot than the top. Mummy bags will keep you warmer than rectangular bags because there is less space between you and the bag, so your body has less air to keep warm. If you're cold-natured, or if you do a lot of winter camping, you might want to consider this.

I'm cold-natured, but I'm also way too claustrophobic to be comfortable sleeping in one of those. I prefer a **rectangular bag.** Rectangular bags are roomy. They can also be completely unzipped and laid flat, or can be zipped up with another bag. If you choose a rectangular bag but want to do winter camping, a sleeping bag liner would be a good option.

Sleeping bags come in various sizes, to fit anyone from a child to a large adult. Don't try to get by with a bag that's too large. You'll have a hard time keeping warm if there's too much air for your body to heat between you and the bag.

• *Insulation:* Sleeping bags are rated in temperature degrees. In his backpacking seminars, Gautam believes anything rated at 20 degrees or so is adequate in this region, unless you're planning on doing winter camping. He suggests getting a **sleeping bag liner,** though, which effectively increases the comfort range of your bag. You can also sleep in just the liner on warmer nights. They're easier to clean than the bags, too, another good reason to use them, as liners can usually be tossed in your washer when you get home.

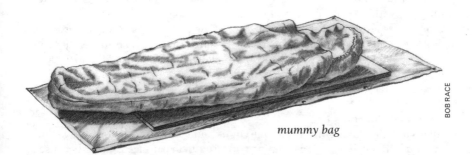

mummy bag

BOB RACE

• *Material:* Sleeping bags are made of various materials from down to the newer, high-tech components. Gautam prefers a down bag because it is lighter and has good loft. Since he does a lot of backpacking, the weight of the bag is very important to him. The biggest problem with down, though, is it's useless if it gets wet. Because of this, his bag is never out of its waterproof stuff sack unless he's inside his tent. Even so, if it's raining and you bring wet clothes into your tent, you can get enough condensation to cause a problem. Down loses all loft and insulating properties when wet.

I object to down for ethical reasons, and so use a bag filled with synthetic stuffing. The synthetic materials insulate even when wet, a nice plus in this region with its high humidity. Plus, they go in the washer and dryer when needed, as opposed to taking a trip to the dry cleaner. Look for bags insulated with Quallofill or Hollofill.

• *Cost:* Sleeping bags range in price from about $20 to well over $300. The cheaper bags are generally "one size fits all," and are made of heavier, less expensive, and less insulating materials. If you only camp during warm weather, the bag fits you in length and width, and weight is not a factor because you never backpack, you can certainly get by with a less expensive bag. Don't shell out serious money on a bag if you haven't tried it out by renting first.

Sleeping bags should not be stored rolled up. Drape your bag over a hanger and stow it in a closet. It will maintain its loft much longer.

Most of the price difference will be based on material, weight, size, and insulating ability. Talking with a knowledgeable salesperson at a good outfitter can help you to pinpoint exactly what you'll need in a bag, and what features are worth paying for. Still, rent the bag first before buying it.

• *Insulation Pads* No matter what bag you buy, you'll be a lot more comfortable if it's lying on a sleeping pad. Though you might think the pad is mainly for comfort from the hard ground, its primary function is to insulate you from the cold. Sleeping pads have improved a lot since the air mattresses I slept on as a child. Those invariably developed slow leaks on the first night of a trip, and the trick was to fall asleep before they were completely flat and you could feel every rock underneath you.

Today's sleeping pads are made of either closed- or open-cell foam. **Closed-cell foam** is a cushion one to several inches thick that can be rolled up. Closed-cell pads are cheaper and can't leak, even if punctured. The disadvantage is that they don't easily compress, and can feel like you're sleeping on a board rather than a cushion. They're just not as comfortable as the open-cell pads. If you get a closed-cell pad, go for the thickest one you can roll and still get in your vehicle. You'll thank me for this later. If you have a small to mid-size car like I do, rather than rolling the pad, lay it flat across the bottom of the trunk, pack in your other gear, then fold it up and over the gear on top. It'll take up much less room.

I prefer **open-cell foam** pads and have a Therm-A-Rest. Open-cell pads self-inflate, a big improvement over the air mattresses of my childhood. They're compressed and rolled for transport, but should be inflated when stored, so they'll attain their full inflation when being used. They come in different lengths, from just enough for your torso and head to full body length. Unless weight restrictions require it, get the full-length model. You'll be much more comfortable, and it'll keep your feet warmer. Also get the widest pad you can afford from a cost and weight perspective. The surface of the pad is slick, as is the outside of your sleeping bag. It doesn't take much to slide off.

Open-cell pads are fairly expensive, particularly when you compare them to the closed-cell pads, but with proper care, you'll use the same one for years, as I have. If you use an open-cell pad, you'll need a patch kit for holes. I've never gotten a hole, but I don't leave home without the patch kit. A hole will render an open-cell pad about as comfortable as a flat air mattress.

Sleeping bags and pads will increase your comfort even if you're camping in a vehicle. On one trip to the desert in June, I was camping in a pop-up and thought the problem would be in staying cool, not keeping warm. I tossed in my sleeping bag almost as an afterthought. I found that after dark, the desert cooled off very quickly, and the additional warmth of the bag was much appreciated.

In a vehicle, a sleeping pad can be even more important to protect you from the cold. Whether you're in a car, van, or the back of a pickup truck, the metal shell of the vehicle will get as cold as the air around it, and, without a pad, so will you.

CAR AND RV CAMPING

I like to go to the RV shows each spring and fall in Atlanta and am always amazed at the variety of options. At most shows, you'll see full pickup campers similar to John Steinbeck's Rocinante, pop-ups, conversion vans, small trailers, motor homes, and what I call conversion buses. Some of the bigger rigs even have Corian countertops in the kitchen and bath, a luxury my house doesn't have. But then, some of these rigs cost about nine times what my home did!

Other options for lower cost vehicle camping include pickup camper shells, vans, minivans, and SUVs. I even know a guy who camps in a station wagon. The biggest problem I've found with sleeping inside an improvised vehicle is temperature control. On one winter trip, the interior of my friend's van stayed nice and cozy from the body heat of two adults and two dogs. By morning, though, the van doors had frozen shut, and the uninsulated floor was so cold it hurt my bare feet. In the summer, there weren't enough windows for good airflow, and the lack of screening made us a little too accessible to the bugs.

If you're a beginning camper, the best advice I can give is to find a dealer in your area that rents gear. Whether you decide you want to rent a tent or rent a vehicle, you'll save a lot of money and frustration by trying before you buy.

When I was a teenager, my family rented a pop-up and drove to the Florida Keys for a week. The rental agent gave us a quick rundown on how to put it up. I remember he said that three teenage girls could put the camper up in 10 minutes. That first night, after two adults and three teenagers had struggled for over an hour, we found the canvas tent top was on upside down.

The lesson to be learned here is to demand that all equipment, purchased or rented, be demonstrated for you before you leave.

BACKPACKING

If you're backpacking, your two main concerns are good boots (see "Footwear" in the "Clothing and Weather Protection" section) and a good pack. Gautam Bhan, who teaches a backpacking seminar for the Sierra Club, recommends buying the best-fitting boots you can afford, and renting the rest of what you'll need. What seems to be a great idea in the store might not work for you on the trail.

Selecting a Pack

Instead of deciding between day or fanny packs, you need to choose between internal and external frame packs. I asked Gautam for recommendations because he teaches beginning backpackers about equipment and is an expert at getting them prepared to hit the trail. Here is some of his wisdom:

• **External frame packs** hold the pack a short distance from your body. Because of this, there is air movement between you and the pack, and they are much cooler to wear than internal packs. The frame allows for additional pouches and equipment to be tied on. They're usually slightly cheaper than internal frames, but they aren't as adjustable. Because they are held away from the body, they wobble a bit on uneven ground. They're also not as comfortable, as there is no padding between the metal frame and your body.

• **Internal frame packs** hug your body and are more comfortable. They are more stable when hiking on uneven ground, as they don't wobble and your center of gravity will be closer to normal. They are a lot hotter, though.

They usually have more adjustments for fit than external frame packs, and therefore are better choices for women and small men. Packs are generally sized for average to tall men. Short women can have a real problem finding equipment that fits properly. Don't try buying a pack from a catalog or website. It's best to have the pack fitted to your body at the outfitting store, or it won't ride properly. A correctly fitted pack will transfer nearly all the weight on your waist, hips, and legs, not to your back.

Being Physically Fit

Your body needs to train for a backpacking trip. Even if you can hike for several miles, doing it carrying another 30 to 60 pounds is an entirely different situation. Your fully loaded pack will weigh about one-fourth of your body weight. Don't exceed one-third. If your pack doesn't fit properly and the weight is riding on your back instead of being distributed between your hips and shoulders, you can hurt yourself.

Before starting out on a backpacking trip, fully load your pack and have a knowledgeable friend check the fit—you can even go back to the outfitters and ask someone knowledgeable there to check the fit. Then, try carrying the weight for some distance, preferably on a short hike. That will usually point out problem areas.

The most common mistake beginners make, Gautam says, is bringing more than they need or can carry. They typically bring twice the amount of food they can eat, and load too much weight for their physical preparation. If you're not physically prepared to carry much more than your own weight, you're not ready to backpack. As a result, one place to find brand new gear is on the Appalachian Trail, a few miles from any access point.

Gautam strongly recommends you go with a knowledgeable person. Backpacking by yourself is dangerous. If you get hurt, what are you going to do? And a pack of beginners hitting the trail without a more experienced person along is a recipe for disaster.

Other Gear

Another beginner's mistake is to be unprepared for contingencies. If you're relying on matches to light your stove, what if they get wet? Gautam always brings two lighters and two boxes of matches, all protected in a plastic bag.

For shelter, backpackers have the option of either a lightweight tent or a **bivvy sack**. Bivvy sacks offer no privacy for changing, and a claustrophobic person like me would be climbing the walls, if there were any. Gautam calls them a poor man's tent.

Even if you're backpacking, you don't have to do without the comfort of a sleeping pad. Some specialty sleeping bags and pads are made to zip together. The bag is actually missing the bottom, so weight is saved.

When you get away from civilization and light pollution, it can be so dark on a moonless night you can't see your hand in front of your face. Gautam brings two small penlights when he backpacks. It doesn't take a lot of light to see your way to your tent at midnight when there's no "light pollution" from electric lights, and batteries for large flashlights are heavy. As he puts it, "You're not trying to signal the space shuttle."

Don't plan on an extended trip for your first backpacking trip. Plan on spending just one or two nights out, with no more than 5–10 miles hiked per day.

FOOD AND COOKING STOVES

There's nothing wrong with the cook taking a vacation. I've camped with a friend who wanted to eat nothing but granola bars and sandwiches, with nothing to clean up. But I prefer camping with friends who feel that food is a big part of the trip. As a result, we've prepared elaborate meals at least as good as anything we had at home. Sitting around a campfire telling lies after a good and satisfying meal is wonderful fun. Besides, food just plain tastes better when you're camping. Whether you decide on granola bars, macaroni and cheese, or complicated feasts, just make sure everyone in your party agrees on the strategy for the trip before you go.

THE BACKPACKER'S MENU

Backpackers now have incredibly good options in freeze-dried foods that are lightweight and delicious. Unfortunately, they're also very expensive and are usually high in sodium. I don't know anyone who exclusively eats these expensive meals, but it's amazing the variety that is available. There's even freeze-dried ice cream. If you can't have the real thing because you left your freezer at home, it's a nice treat to bring along, even if you're not backpacking.

Cheaper options for backpackers and other campers are easily found in your grocery store. For good "starters" for your dinner, check out the ethnic food section for boil-in-bag Indian entrees and curry sauces. The pasta aisle has rice and rice mixes, packaged ramen noodles, and various noodle and sauce combinations. The soup aisle contains instant soups, instant flavored "baked" potatoes, and sauce mixes. The cereal aisle has granola and breakfast bars. Dried fruit such as raisins, peaches, apricots, and prunes add flavor and fiber.

Don't forget something hot to drink, flavorings to add to your water (especially if you're treating it with chemicals), other beverages, and snacks. Liquids are heavy, but those little boxes of juice and "nuked" milk are great for adding variety and flavor to your meals. If you buy the ones packaged in waxed cardboard, the containers make good fire starters. Anything you don't burn completely needs to be packed out, so keep that in mind if a snack or drink comes packaged in foil or plastic. If you do burn it, you should pick up and pack out the foil remains.

Planning

Before that trip to the grocery store, take a few minutes and plan each meal. The biggest problem you'll likely run into is boredom with the menu, so plan on plenty of variety.

A hot mug of coffee, tea, or cocoa is wonderful in the morning. If you drink it at home, you're going to miss it when you're camping. It's also just a great way to start the day, as you sit looking out over the view you picked the day before, warming your hands and watching the steam rise in the early morning chill. Even my granola bar friend requires coffee in the morning.

• *Breakfast:* Instant hot cereals like oatmeal or grits are a good breakfast option if you're backpacking. Add cut-up dried fruit and sunflower seeds or other nuts before pouring in the boiling water, and you'll have a more satisfying, chewy meal. A friend of mine eats beef jerky for breakfast, but I don't particularly care for it even at a more reasonable hour. The trick is to pick things you like that can be cooked in one pot, using a minimum of fuel, and requiring little clean up. Granola and breakfast bars are an option if you don't want to cook, but at least drink some juice or flavor your water with a drink mix.

• *Lunch:* For lunch, most of us don't want to stop what we're doing long enough to cook a meal. Most people prefer to eat easily prepared food at lunchtime and spend the other time hiking and exploring, which is why they're camping in the first place. Sandwiches are a good option, but you'll probably want to use pita bread or bagels instead of loaf bread, which squishes in your pack. Good fillings are peanut and other nut butters, tuna, bean mixtures, and those gift cheeses and meats from the cheese shop that can withstand nuclear blasts without refrigeration. Some people go the heavy hors d'oeuvres route, and snack on beef jerky, crackers, cheese, trail mix, and dried fruit.

One friend of mine eats cereal for lunch. After breakfast, she boils water and pours it over a mixture of slow cooking oatmeal and dried fruit. She wraps the sealed bowl well, puts it in the center of her pack, and, by lunchtime, the cereal is cooked and still pretty warm.

• *Dinner:* Dinner is where I want to create something really good. The trick is, you're working on a single burner, have only one pan to cook with, need to eat it all with no leftovers, and don't want to create a cleaning nightmare. Ideally, you should be able to clean the pot by boiling water in it, as even biodegradable soap takes a while to break down and can pollute the groundwater. The ingredients of your dinner need to require no refrigeration (except on the first day), and provide decent nutrition. The packaging should be such that you can reduce it in size and reuse it on your next trip, or burn it completely. Otherwise it goes in your trash bag to be packed out.

I like dinners that contain a starch, vegetables, a protein source, and sauce or seasonings to liven it up. The starch can be noodles, pasta, or rice. The vegetables can be fresh, frozen (the first day), dried, or canned. For protein, I use beans, meat, cheese, or seeds. The sauces depend on the type of meal being fixed.

Sometimes I'll start with a box of macaroni and cheese, which provides the starch, protein, and sauce. Since there is plenty of cheese sauce in one of these, I can add dried vegetables while the water is boiling, and end up with something even a kid will eat.

I also add rice, vegetables, and meat or beans to boiling water, then spice it up with instant soup or curry mix. Mix the soup and sauces in very well or you'll end up with some pretty disgusting clumps in your food. If you've ever had sour cream and onion dip that wasn't properly mixed, you know what I mean.

Most dried beans take hours of soaking and cooking time that might not be worth it when you're backpacking. Unless you have a pressure cooker to bring along, don't plan on using kidney, red, navy, or most other beans on your trip. Lentils and split peas would be a better choice as they cook fairly quickly. While I eat brown rice at home, it takes too long to cook when I'm camping, so I take along white rice and rice mixes. My lunchtime cereal friend soaks dry beans all day while she hikes, then replaces the water and cooks them at night. I don't think it's worth the time and fuel to cook them, but that's up to you.

• *Snacks:* The last item you'll want to plan and pack is a full complement of snacks. Snack foods are anything you can eat while walking, stopping for a break, as an addition to a meal, as a quick lunch, etc. Bring some that are salty, some that are sweet, some that are a combination, and some that are none of the above.

The traditional hiker's snack is trail mix, otherwise known as GORP. GORP stands for Good Ole Raisins and Peanuts. Over the years, GORP has morphed into a much tastier but definitely not healthier snack. Most trail mix you buy today contains M&Ms or other candies. One mix I made contained one-third really good granola, one-third mixed M&Ms and dried fruits, and one-third mixed nuts, including Brazil nuts, cashews, peanuts, filberts, and almonds. It certainly provided the calories and fat I needed for the hiking on that trip, and was so good I still remember it nearly two decades later. You can spend a lot of money on GORP, or you can make your own for much less (see recipe). I frequently substitute other dried fruits for the raisins. The great thing about making your own trail mix is that it is completely versatile and can be suited to your tastes.

Good Ol' Raisins & Peanuts (GORP)

You can spend a lot of money on GORP, or you can make your own for much less *and* tailor it to your own tastes.

GORP

6 cups granola, plain or flavored
2 cups cocktail peanuts
2 cup raw sunflower kernels
2 cups chopped dried fruit (typically raisins, but you can use any dried fruit, such as pineapple, peaches, or apples)
2 cups M&Ms

Mix well and divide into small Ziploc bags. Keep one handy for when your appetite strikes.

This basic GORP recipe can be modified by using unsalted dry roasted peanuts, varying the dried fruit or nuts, using Cheez-Its, Goldfish, or Chex cereals instead of some or all of the granola, using Reese's Pieces instead of M&Ms, or changing the proportions. Unless you're camping in the winter, don't use non-coated chocolate candy as it'll melt and make a real mess in the bag. You can still eat it, but you'll spend as much time licking your fingers clean as hiking.

Besides GORP, other snack foods to bring include crackers, jerky, other non-refrigerated meats and cheeses, soy and other nuts, fruit, and your own specialties. You might also have fun making your own version of Chex mix. Just remember to have the snacks within reach as you're driving to your destination, as well, and not in the trunk. I usually have some travelling to do before getting to a campground, and make lots of stops to check out interesting places on the way. If your passengers get restless, pull out the GORP.

Other Backpacking Tips

You can always bring frozen items for the first day or two of your trip. Gautam freezes meat, seals it in a Ziploc bag, then wraps it in the most insulating thing he carries, his sleeping bag. By the end of the first day, he has a defrosted steak to cook over a fire or the backpacker's grill he takes along. He brings a liberal amount of fresh foods for the first day or two as well.

If you do much backpacking, you might want to try dehydrating your own food. You'll save a lot of money and sodium over the dehydrated items you can buy. You can get a cheap dehydrator at a discount store for less than $15, or pick up a good one at a garage sale for even less. Dehydrated foods are much lighter than canned, and there's no waste to pack out.

If you're planning on a long hike, be sure to consume meals with higher carbohydrate content and less grease. You'll also want to eat more of the high sodium dehydrated foods, as you lose a lot of salt when you sweat. Gautam prepares high carbohydrate instant meals by packing one-half cup of instant rice with one-quarter cup soup mix, and in 15 minutes cooking time has a complete meal. He either brings paper plates he'll burn whenever he has the opportunity, or eats out of the pot. By using a variety of seasonings, backpackers can cook standard fare with minimal preparation and cleanup.

Always carry some emergency food and fuel, just in case you get lost and are stuck out on the trail an extra day or so.

I don't fish, but my friends who do always try to catch some during a trip. Gautam recommends against counting on catching fish on a backpacking or camping trip, or you'll jinx it and go without a meal or two. Always bring enough food for the trip. Then, if you do catch any, you can always pack back out some of what you brought.

Keep in mind that backpacking doesn't have to mean total deprivation. Is there a category of food that you need to eat at least every other day in order to feel good? For me, it's something raw. If I don't eat any raw fruit or vegetables for a couple of days, my stomach is just slightly queasy. I know people who can be gone four days and live off beef jerky and coffee, but I wouldn't enjoy that. I always take apples, oranges, and baby carrots, as they don't bruise or spoil as quickly as softer fruits and vegetables. Just remember that raw fruits and vegetables are mostly water, and so are heavy. Your feel-good food might be bread or sweets. Whatever it is, incorporate some of it into your meal plan.

And one last thing: Be sure to try out all recipes before hitting the trail. If a recipe bombs at home, you can always pitch it out and order a pizza. But Pizza Hut doesn't deliver off the beaten trail. Once you've decided on tried and true recipes, lay out all of the food for a trip before you leave, and pack single meal quantities in paper cups and Ziploc bags, adding the appropriate seasonings. That way, you don't have anything to measure or repackage while on the trail.

THE CAR CAMPER'S MENU

If you're car, truck, or van camping, you have the added luxury of an ice chest, and you probably have at least one more burner than if you're backpacking. Washing dishes and disposing of trash is much less of a problem, also, which opens up many other possibilities for meals.

It always surprises me when my neighbors at a campground ask me if I know where the nearest grocery store is located. It's not the end of the world if you run out of food and have to find a store on a camping trip. But it sure isn't the way I want to spend a vacation of less than four or five days, especially when it's so easy to prevent this from happening. Figure out how many breakfasts, lunches and dinners you're going to need, times how many people are on the trip, and draw up your plan from there. Add in a liberal component of snacks. I usually do a lot of hiking on camping trips, and always carry snacks on the trail.

My friends and I usually divide the chore of cooking by splitting the meals between us. We usually take half the dinners each and then either lunches or breakfasts, which builds in variety as we each try to outdo the other. We each bring a full complement of snacks, too. Don't forget the GORP (see recipe)! It's handy, delicious, and can be varied to suit any requirement, from salty to sweet, and anything in between.

• *Breakfast:* I may eat the same cold cereal every day at home, but when I'm camping, I want hot cereal, Potatoes Wonderful (see recipe), French toast, pancakes, and whatever else my friends and I can dream up. If you'd like to make pancakes while you're camping, you can pick up a mix that requires nothing more than water to be added. But when I'm car camping, I bring along eggs, milk, oil, and other fresh ingredients. Just be sure to make a list of everything you'll need beforehand.

• *Lunch:* Lunches are easier when you have the convenience of a cooler and the ability to keep bread from being destroyed in your pack. A friend of mine always has fresh fruit salad and bagels for lunch. You can cook a hot meal, but I'm not usually around the campground at lunchtime, so I normally have a sandwich.

• *Dinner:* For dinner, we pull out all the stops. You can get a camp oven that is basically a metal box that sits on a burner, or you can bake in a Dutch oven on your stove. I've made bread while camping that had all our neighbors stopping by to say hello. Dinners can be grilled steak or chicken with stir-fried vegetables and some sort of rice or pasta dish, or a skillet creation with a Chinese, Italian, or Indian sauce, or whatever your personal tastes dictate. With a two-burner stove and optionally a grill over a barbecue or fire, the possibilities seem endless after the limitations of backpacking.

If your camping trip is for more than two days, you'll probably need to pick up additional ice for the cooler. I usually start out my trip with a lot of frozen foods. They help to keep the cooler cold, and defrost before I need to cook with them.

THE RVer's MENU

The choices get even more limitless in an RV. With the added convenience of a freezer, refrigerator, oven, microwave, and another burner or two, you can literally cook any meal you could at home. If you're not a full-time RVer but rather a vacation camper, though, I recommend developing some special, well-loved favorite recipes that are only prepared while on the road, like Potatoes Wonderful. Keep some favorites reserved for your trips and they'll stay very special treats.

Potatoes Wonderful

My friend Betty Baker developed the following recipe for Potatoes Wonderful. She says, "This is the 'fat and cholesterol be damned' version. You can use BacoBits, Pam, nonfat cheese, and Egg Beaters, but I like it better this way." So do I.

2 medium potatoes
1/2 C cheddar cheese
6 strips bacon
1 small onion
1 green pepper
6 eggs
4 sourdough English muffins

Bake the potatoes at home and keep them chilled; you can also cook the potatoes by wrapping them in foil and putting them in your fire pit with hot coals, but at home in the oven is a lot easier. Next, fry the bacon in a large frying pan, then remove it from pan and crumble, leaving the bacon grease in the pan. Grate the cheese; if you don't have a grater, cut up the cheese in slivers. Chop the onions and green pepper; if you're feeding "picky eaters" who don't like one of these ingredients, make your bits big enough to be "picked out."

Chop the potatoes, leaving the skin on. Put the onions and the green pepper into the bacon grease and fry until the onions start to get clear. Add the potatoes to the skillet and fry until they're heated through. Next, scramble six eggs and stir into the skillet; if all the grease has been absorbed, leaving none to cook with, add some butter to the skillet so the eggs don't stick to the pan. As eggs begin to cook, stir in the cheese. When the cheese has melted and the eggs have cooked, stir in the crumbled bacon. Split some sourdough English muffins and lay them "nook and cranny" side down on top of the mixture, then put the lid on and remove from the heat.

This should feed four hungry campers.

EXTRA CAMPING FOODS TO BRING

Besides the GORP and Potatoes Wonderful mentioned above, there are some foods that I always take when camping.
- Instant hot cocoa and hot cider
- Marshmallows, for cocoa and for toasting for s'mores
- Graham crackers and chocolate bars for s'mores
- Herb teas for cold nights
- Peanut butter for fill-in lunches
- Instant oatmeal and grits for breakfasts when you can't face anything harder than boiling water
- Cookies
- Granola bars
- Crackers and cheese
- Wine (hey, I'm on vacation)

COOKING AT CAMP

Camp stoves have improved a lot since that temperamental Kenmore stove my mother had to struggle with when our family camped. Today, backpackers can choose from stoves that burn white gas, propane, butane, wood, or pellets. Car campers have some of the same options in larger models.

Campfires: A Word of Precaution

One mistake Gautam frequently sees beginners make is to plan to cook over a fire. In this region, fires are frequently prohibited because of drought conditions. Even if the fire is not illegal, gathering wood may be, or there may not be any dry wood available. Even if there is plenty of downed wood, don't take more than you need, as downed wood provides protection and homes for wildlife.

There may also be no safe place to build a fire. Fires should be built on rock or gravel, not on open ground. A ring of rocks helps contain it above ground, but the real danger lies below ground, in the peat that is so common in this region. Fire can spread through the peat layer and come up many yards away. You need to dig

---

Keep It Wild Tip 3: Campfires

- Fire use can scar the backcountry so take extreme precaution when preparing to build and maintain a fire.
- Where fires are permitted, use existing fire rings. If a fire ring isn't available, use a lightweight stove for cooking.
- For fuel, gather sticks from the ground that are no thicker than the diameter of your wrist. Don't break branches off live, dead, or downed trees; this could cause personal injury and also scar the natural setting.
- When leaving, put out the fire completely, pack out all trash from the fire ring, and scatter the ashes away from the site. Forest fires *can* be started by campfires not properly dismantled.

---

down to an inert layer to ensure your fire won't spread, then put it out completely *before* you go to bed.

Another mistake Gautam says beginners make is to underestimate the difficulty of starting a fire, and to bring matches or a lighter but no other tools. Some of his friends make their own fire starter pellets by mixing melted wax with dryer lint, but he prefers to buy the fire starter sticks that are readily available in the camping department of discount stores. They're light, cheap, and foolproof.

Gautam has many times come upon a vacated campsite with embers still glowing in the pit. This is very dangerous and is why fires are prohibited even in wet years in some areas.

Stoves

A backpacking stove solves the problem of how you're going to cook your meal when you're unable to build a fire. It's also a lot easier to adjust the flame on a stove, making it easier to keep the temperature constant.

white gas stove

Gautam prefers **white gas stoves** for his backpacking needs because he can measure out and take with him just what he needs, saving on weight, and there are no fuel cartridges to dispose of. His knowledge of how much fuel to take for a trip has been gleaned from years of experience, though. If you're a beginner, take a full container of fuel, keep track of how many meals you cooked, and measure what you have left when you get back. That will give you a rough idea of how much fuel you need for future trips. Bear in mind that higher elevations require more fuel, as would certain meals such as cooking beans or brown rice. Since most meals require some cooking, plan to bring more than you expect to use until you're very comfortable with estimating. GORP is great as a snack, but you won't want it for dinner if your fuel runs out.

Propane and butane stoves that use disposable cartridges are a bit trickier, because you can't tell precisely how much fuel you have in a cartridge, so you may end up carrying an extra one that is not used. If you're hiking with friends, though, the weight of the stove and fuel should be shared amongst you, so that is not a big drawback. On the plus side, you don't need to prime the stove before lighting it, so they're a heck of a lot easier to use.

I'm fascinated with the stoves that burn wood, leaves and pinecones. They can also burn pellets you can bring along for times when no fuel can be found. That would certainly cut down on the weight factor. For sheer ease of use, though, I still recommend the cartridge stoves.

BOB RACE (4)

butane stove

multi-fuel stove

For car camping, it would be difficult to improve on the standard Coleman camp stove. It uses propane cartridges, so you may need to carry an extra tank on a trip, but if you've got a vehicle, you should be able to tuck an extra in. These stoves are easy to light and work much the same as the one at home, a big plus. I don't mind cooking when I camp, but I don't want to make it hard. I am, after all, on vacation.

If you're going to be staying at a developed campground, throw in a few **fire logs** while you're packing. They're made of compressed peat, sawdust, and wax, and can be lit with just a match or two. Fire logs can either provide a fire if no wood is available, or are great fire starters when placed under firewood. Even if you aren't cooking over a fire, you'll want to roast marshmallows after dinner for s'mores. Granola bars just can't compete!

WATER

Unless you're backpacking, finding safe water to drink shouldn't be much of a problem. Most campgrounds have drinking water available (see the individual listings for that information), and even gas stations sell bottled water these days. Always plan on having a few bottles of water on hand regardless in case you decide the water at your campground may be safe, but you still don't want to drink it. Besides, you'll need a few bottles to throw in your daypack when out hiking.

stove with heat exchanger

You haven't lived until you've camped where the "clean" water has a yellowish cast and smells of sulfur. RVers may want to add a water filter to their rig to improve the taste of the local supply, as well as add a measure of safety. When I'm car camping, I bring along a two and one-half gallon jug of water, just in case. It's cheap, doesn't take up too much room, and stays out on the picnic table at my campsite for ready access for cooking and filling water bottles. If the local supply turns out to be fine, I use that when I run out of the jug. Otherwise, I find a grocery store and buy more. You can also find collapsible gallon water jugs in the camping section of most discount stores. Fill that up before you leave with the water from home, and you'll have enough to get by until you can buy more if needed. The jugs are convenient for ferrying water to your site from a group spigot at the campground, and fold up for storage.

If you're backpacking, you have a different problem. Water is heavy. At roughly eight and one-third pounds per gallon, you cannot carry all of your drinking, cooking and bathing water with you. You should assume that all water you encounter while hiking is contaminated with bacteria, fertilizer run-off, industrial pollutants, or all of the above. Even in the mountains, the water supply is not pure.

Deer, fish, bears, and other animals drink, swim, walk, and leave droppings in water, even in "pure" mountain streams.

If you can't drink the water and can't carry enough with you, what can you do? You must treat the water you find, by boiling, using chemicals, or filtering.

Boiling water

Boiling untreated water will kill the bugs that can make you sick. It won't remove particulate matter, and won't render harmless industrial pollutants or fertilizer run-off, but depending on where you hike, those might not be a problem. In this region, unless you're near the top of a mountain, you need to assume farm chemicals are in your water. Airborne pollutants can contaminate even a spring at the top of a mountain. A rolling boil of five minutes or so (depending on elevation) is required to kill giardia (the most likely bug you'll encounter), cryptosporidia and other protozoa, and bacteria.

Chemical treatment

Chemical treatment will kill the bacteria and protozoa, but again won't remove dirt suspended in the water or deal with the chemical pollution. Plus, it just plain tastes bad. Still, it's a good idea to have iodine tablets or other chemical treatment available as a backup to other methods. Verify that the bottle says it is effective against giardia, cryptosporidia, and bacteria, and that it will also kill the eggs and larvae, then follow the instructions *exactly* as to the quantity to use and the length of time required. If you plan to use chemicals like chlorine or iodine, do yourself a favor and pack along some instant drink mixes to improve the taste.

Filters

The last and best option is a water filter. They vary widely in price and in effectiveness. Like most specialized camping gear, buying a water filter requires a conversation with a knowledgeable salesperson at a good camping supply store

---

Keep It Wild Tip 4: Sanitation

- If there are refuse facilities available, use them to help concentrate impact.
- If no restroom is available, deposit human waste in a "cat hole" dug six to eight inches deep and at least 75 paces (200 feet) from any water source or campsite. Fill the cat hole with soil when finished.
- Use toilet paper sparingly. When finished, either *carefully* burn it in a *controlled* fire or, better yet, pack it out.
- To wash dishes or your body, carry water at least 200 feet away from the source and use small amounts of phosphate-free biodegradable soap. After washing, strain water using a cloth (to remove food particles) and scatter away from site.
- Scour your campsite for even the tiniest piece of trash and any other evidence of your stay. Pack out all waste, even if it's not yours.
- Never litter.

If you don't treat your water properly, you run the risk of ingesting a microscopic protozoan called *Giardia lamblia*. Though the disease is not life-threatening, *giardiasis*, or giardia for short, is sure to make you feel like dying with waves of cramps, vomiting, and diarrhea. Giardia usually clears up on its own, with lots of liquids and nutritious foods. However, a doctor can prescribe something to get you back on your feet in about a week.

The symptoms of giardia exposure can take several days to start. You'll usually be home from your trip before experiencing any trouble.

Make sure your water purifier can filter this and other microorganisms. And keep in mind that iodine tablets do not kill all forms of giardia, particularly giardia cysts.

BOB RACE (2)

(see Resources for recommended outfitters). Unless you know what you want, don't try to buy this mail order or in the camping department of the local discount store. You want a filter that is easy to use, easy to clean, has a good pump volume, and removes the bugs mentioned above. If the filter also removes viruses, so much the better. Most filtration units have replaceable cartridges and must be cleaned periodically. You can extend the life of a cartridge if it has a pre-filter for larger particles that would quickly clog the main filter.

Filters come in different sizes and weights, from what amounts to a straw that filters as you drink, to models that use a small hand pump to produce more output. It is important to check whether the design of the filter separates the inflow of contaminated water from the outflow of purified water. It does no good to use a filter if it's impossible to keep the outflow lines clean.

CLOTHING AND WEATHER PROTECTION

It was a warm, sunny day, and Betty and I were wearing t-shirts and jeans on our hike up Blood Mountain. The trail is strenuous and we were hot, sweaty, and tired when we got to the top. Our cotton clothes absorbed the moisture as we hiked and helped to keep us cool and comfortable. Once at the top, though, the wind picked up, the temperature dropped, our bodies cooled off, and our wet, clammy

Hiking Preparedness

It is amazing to me that so many of the people you see at the wonderful state and national parks in our country never venture farther from their car than the visitor center. Strike off on a trail for just a short distance in even a heavily visited park, and you are soon far from the madding crowd. And as the sounds of civilization are left behind you, the sounds of nature are suddenly all that you hear.

Getting into nature and away from our hectic lives is a big reason many of us camp. So it's not surprising that many campers also hike.

I don't do anything halfway. My first hike was nearly six miles, far too long for a beginner, especially when all I carried was a bowl of water for my dog.

So if you're new to hiking, take my word for it when I say you'll enjoy it a whole lot more if you're a bit more prepared than I was my first time out. The pointers below should get you started on a great wilderness adventure:

Review trail maps. Before setting out on any hike, at least look at a map of the trail. Most state parks in the region will have maps at the visitor center. At any staffed park, a ranger can give you a good idea of the length and difficulty of the trail. For longer trails, there may be periodic maps posted under Plexiglas along the way. At the least, know whether it is a loop or you will be doubling back on the same trail, and if it is blazed or how it is marked. Blazes are splashes of paint, usually on trees, but they may also be painted on bare rock. Many times connecting trails use different color blazes, so know what color you're looking for, and if a different color is used for the opposite direction. If you're a beginner, don't even consider striking off into the wilderness areas unless you're with a knowledgeable hiker who is carrying a topographic map and a compass.

Wear proper shoes. Next, make sure you have adequate footwear. You might be able to get by with a pair of sturdy jogging shoes for a short stroll of two miles or less—if you're wearing good socks—but anything less will be torture on your feet. The purpose of your hiking boots is to prevent blisters on your feet, provide stability for your ankles, and cushion you from the rocks on the trail. Well-fitted boots are so comfortable you'll forget you have them on. Ill-fitting boots will have you muttering under your breath within 20 minutes. For more information on purchasing and breaking-in boots, see Footwear in Clothing and Weather Protection.

Don't skimp on socks. Socks are as essential as well-fitting boots in preventing blisters. I feel the best protection for your feet comes with a combination of two pairs of socks. The thin inner sock should be of some sort of wicking material, such as polypropylene, that will keep your feet dry. The outer sock should be of a thick cushioning fabric. I like wool, even in the summer. It's cushy and keeps my feet cool and comfortable. Wearing two pairs of socks means that any rubbing that occurs will be between the socks, not between your sock or shoe and your foot.

Strap on a day pack. Carrying your gear is easy if you use a day pack. These are readily available both as backpack-style packs and hip or fanny packs.

If you plan to be gone more than an hour, a day pack provides the room for water, a snack, a small first aid kit, a rain poncho, and whatever else you choose to take, such as rock, tree, bird, or wildflower identification books.

The key to making any of these work for you is in the pocket configuration. I like a large main compartment for snacks, lunch, a poncho, a first aid kit, and field guides, a smaller compartment for little items that would get lost in the bigger pocket, such as a compass, Swiss Army knife, and keys, and a separate area for water. My favorite day pack has a long, sizeable pocket on the bottom, which holds a two-liter bottle of water, a water bowl for the dogs, and plastic grocery sacks for picking up their trash on the trail.

Carry water at all times. Bottled water comes in a variety of sizes, and the small half-liter bottles can even be slipped in your pocket. I now refuse to hike with anyone who appears to not be carrying enough water, because otherwise I know they'll be into my supply before the day is over. I've seen people start a six-mile hike with less than a liter of water, which is totally inadequate. Plan to drink plenty of water. In this region of the country, the temperature in the summer is frequently over 100 degrees, and you can become dehydrated while sitting in a lawn chair in the backyard. When you add in the additional water you'll need when you're exerting yourself, it's easy to become dehydrated.

What else you choose to carry depends on your situation and how long you'll be out. These are the items that are always in my daypack. When I get ready to go camping or hiking, I throw in water and treats for myself and the dogs, and we're ready to go.

- Cloth hiking hat for protection from the sun and bugs. When it's desperately hot, a cloth hat can also be soaked in a stream to cool you off.
- Bug spray
- Cheap rain poncho from the discount store
- First-aid kit, which you can buy already assembled, or you can create your own. See Health and Safety for a list of first-aid necessities
- Small flashlight, which will help you find your way back to camp or the car if you misjudge the daylight on a long hike like I did once. It gets dark earlier in the mountains, and in this region a lot of us hike in the fall when the temperature is more pleasant but the days are becoming shorter.
- Swiss army knife
- Windbreaker that stuffs into its own pocket
- Space blanket

Whether you're returning to your campsite at night, or taking your campsite with you on your back, you're going to see a part of our country while hiking that most people never do. Not all waterfalls and scenic views have roads leading up to them. Nothing compares with getting out in nature and enjoying it on foot.

clothes offered no protection from the cold. If we hadn't had windbreakers in our packs, we would have been in trouble. As it was, we were just uncomfortable.

Hypothermia is a serious condition where your body temperature falls to about 95 degrees or below. If untreated, your body starts shutting off blood flow to various organs, leading to kidney, lung, and heart failure, and ultimately death. The key to prevention is wearing the proper clothing, and reacting promptly when problems arise. You'll need to learn to dress in layers and to make sure those layers are made from suitable fabrics. (See Staying Healthy for information on treating hypothermia.)

GET DRESSED

I attended one of Gautam's Sierra Club backpacking seminars several years ago. The second day, it rained all day, and his point about fabric choices hit home. Most of us were dressed in jeans. After towels, what's the slowest thing to dry when you're doing your laundry? This might have been a good thing if the temperature had been 30 degrees warmer, but as it was, with cloudy skies, a little wind, and the temperature hovering around 50 degrees, most of us were miserable, even with jackets.

The Art of Layering

Gautam says the key to being comfortable is layering with the proper fabrics. He recommends three layers. Next to your skin, you want a light, wicking layer that will move moisture away from your body. There are wonderful synthetic fabrics like polypropylene that pull moisture off your skin and help keep it dry. Some people prefer silk for the first layer, but never use cotton unless the temperature is guaranteed to stay above 75 degrees.

The second layer is for insulation, and should trap heat and air to keep you warm. This can be wool or one of the synthetic fibers such as Polartec.

Gautam says the final layer is for protection from the elements, and should be wind- and water-resistant. A windbreaker works well.

Rain Gear

Do you remember the old *Saturday Night Live* commercial for the product that was both a floor wax and a dessert topping? The **cheap plastic rain poncho** you get at the local discount store is similarly versatile. It's a rain poncho. It's a ground cloth. It's a windproof layer when you left your sweater in the car. Heck, if you get lost and stuck out overnight, you can rig one up as a temporary shelter. When it gets yucky or the snaps rip out, it can be replaced quickly and inexpensively for your next outing. You'll never get it back in the plastic sleeve it comes in, but it compresses down to a flat packet for stuffing in your pack.

My day pack is never without one. It's not the best rain protection available, but it's so useful and quick to pop on that I always have one with me. It doesn't weigh much, and if you're in any of the mountainous parts of the region, it's good insurance against an unexpected shower. If I'm actually expecting rain, though, I'll bring other more serious rainwear as well.

If you do a lot of hiking, you might want to invest in the serious rain protection of a breathable **rain jacket and pants**. It rains a lot in the mountains. When rain is anticipated, you could always choose another activity for your day, but unanticipated, brief showers won't slow you down if you're able to stay comfortable. The key is a breathable layer that also keeps you dry. A top of the line rain jacket, unlike a poncho, is a multi-purpose shell, as it both insulates and is a vapor barrier. It's also vented, to allow moisture to escape. Some people get by with coated nylon, but I prefer three-ply Gore Tex.

Waterproof: impervious to water. Though rain won't penetrate this material, if you're at all mobile you'll soon find yourself wet from perspiration that can't evaporate. **Water-resistant: resistant but not impervious to water.** You'll stay dry using this material only if it isn't pouring.

Another option for rain protection is a **quality rain poncho**, never to be confused with the cheap plastic model from the discount store mentioned earlier. The cheap models are a lot like wearing a plastic bag. They are adequate in the short run, but if you are forced to wear one very long or to keep moving while wearing one, you'll soon find you're sweating under the unbreathable layer, and nearly as wet inside as out. Good rain ponchos are breathable, and long enough to provide coverage at least to your knees. Like quality rain jackets and pants, they require a surprising investment of cash, but will keep you much more comfortable during a shower. I suggest you make do with the plastic rain poncho until the annoyance factor makes it worthwhile to go the more expensive route.

I prefer ponchos since they can be pulled on rather quickly when the rain starts, as opposed to donning pants and a jacket. Also, I am usually with my dogs, and they're just not happy about hiking in the rain. With a poncho, I can snap up the sides and squat down, offering rain protection to my dogs as well. I can also pop one on to wear while I put on the rain pants and jacket I'll want if it looks like the rain will last a while.

In wind and driving rain, though, a poncho is nearly useless as it attempts to become airborne. In that situation, nothing beats a good rain jacket and rain pants. Keep in mind you'll need a pack cover if you aren't using a poncho, or your gear will be soaked.

Since the weather is so unpredictable in this region, always bring your **rain fly** and put it on when tent camping. In a trailer or RV, you'll want the awning up to keep the area dry and less muddy. Most RVs today have the awning built-in so it can be extended at any time. When Betty and I camped in her pop-up years ago, it had to be lowered to put the awning on, a major nuisance when we forgot to slide it on before cranking the rig up.

Wind Protection

I always carry a windbreaker in my day pack. It's a lightweight jacket that stuffs into its own pocket and was free when I sent in a few granola bar box tops. You can't tell when you leave your car at the trailhead what the conditions are going to feel like a few miles down the trail. It can be many degrees cooler at the top of the mountain you're climbing than it is at the trailhead.

With the proper clothing and rain gear, your trip won't be ruined if the temperature drops, the wind picks up, or rain clouds gather. Enjoy and stay dry.

FOOTWEAR

Most folks can get away with wearing jogging shoes around the campsite. But if you're going to venture beyond the grounds, make sure you have adequate footwear. With a good pair of socks, those jogging shoes will suffice for a short stroll of two miles or less, but any further distance will be torture on your feet. The purpose of your hiking boots is to prevent blisters on your feet, provide stability for your ankles, and cushion you from the rocks on the trail. Well-fitted boots are so comfortable you'll forget you have them on. Ill-fitting boots will have you muttering under your breath within 20 minutes.

• *Selecting boots:* Boots should be purchased from a salesperson who knows how to fit them and be sized to account for the extra space needed when your feet have swelled during the course of the day. Wear your hiking socks when trying on the boots. A lot of the outdoor gear catalogs I get sell boots, often at a discount. Don't even be tempted, unless you are replacing a worn and well-loved pair with the exact same model. You need a knowledgeable salesperson who'll take the time necessary to fit you properly.

• *Waterproofing:* Once you've purchased your boots, you need to waterproof them. Buy a good waterproofing spray or seam sealer at the outdoors store, and seal the boots before wearing them.

• *Breaking them in:* You'll also need to break them in before heading out on an all-day hike. We all remember the blisters we got in September when we started school with new shoes. As bad as that was, it's nothing compared with the blisters from new boots. Why, you ask? Because there are a lot more places for you to get blisters from boots, and because once you get them, you're usually miles from the car. At least at school, you were sitting down most of the day.

You break boots in the same way you break in any other pair of shoes, by wearing them for short periods of time and working up to longer lengths of time and distance walked.

Socks

Socks are as essential as well-fitting boots in preventing blisters. I feel the best protection for your feet comes with a combination of two pairs of socks. The thin inner sock should be of some sort of wicking material, such as polypropylene, to keep your feet dry. The outer sock should be of a thick cushioning fabric. I like wool, even in the summer. It keeps my feet cool and comfortable.

I wear two pairs of socks so if any sliding or rubbing goes on inside my boot, it is between the two socks, and not between my foot and a sock. If you're backpacking, be sure to bring plenty of pairs, as dirty socks compress and are nearly useless in preventing blisters.

• *Treating blisters:* Even if you've broken in your well-fitting boots and have on the proper socks, you can still end up with a blister. That's where moleskin comes in. Moleskin is a thick, soft, cushiony material that comes on a roll. Cut a piece larger than the blister, then cut out a doughnut hole so it won't be pressing on the sore. Cover the whole thing with a bandage. The moleskin keeps your sock from contact with the blister and increases your comfort tremendously.

OTHER APPAREL

You lose a surprising amount of heat through your head. I've always got my hiking hat in my day pack, but I also carry a wool watch cap from late fall through early spring. It's warm by itself, and stretchy enough to pull on over my hiking hat when necessary. Watch caps are great to bring along when camping. If the temperature drops, they're soft and comfortable to sleep in, and covering your head will keep you several degrees warmer.

HEALTH AND SAFETY

I always carry a first aid kit in my daypack when I'm hiking or camping. I was never a Girl Scout, but I do believe in being prepared. It is doubly important to have basic supplies if you're backpacking, since you can't easily get to the nearest emergency room.

The most common problems you're going to encounter when visiting the woods include blisters, sprained ankles, bee stings, poison ivy, snake bites, skinned knees and other abrasions, sunburn, dehydration, hypoglycemia, and hypothermia. The odds are that you will have few to none of these problems, but it doesn't hurt to have a well-stocked first aid kit for emergencies.

You can buy a first-aid kit just about anywhere these days. I don't like pre-packaged first aid kits because they invariably contain items I don't think I need, and are missing items experience has taught me I don't want to be without. So I put together my own (see First-Aid Kit Checklist).

INSECT BITES

If you live, camp, or hike in the South, you know that insects are a problem. Heck, insects are a problem everywhere. While vacationing in Alaska, I found the mosquitoes there were so large they are sometimes called the state bird. Canadians refer to fly swatters as "fly bats." They must have a problem with the insects if they've developed a sport of killing them.

The difference is, when you're at home and your barbecue is in danger of being ruined by bugs, everyone can simply traipse inside. When you're camping or hiking, you've got to deal with the problem more directly.

Minimizing bugs at your campsite starts with site selection. Scout the area before setting up camp and verify there are no fire ant mounds, stagnant water sources, hornet's nests, or other obvious problem signs. If the hungry hordes descend once you've set up your camp, your choices are to either live with it or use some form of chemical repellent on yourself or around your site.

Repellents

Several of my friends are sold on the effectiveness of **citronella candles**. I've never been too impressed with them. On one camping trip over the Fourth of July, the June Bugs were so thick a friend accidentally drank one in her rum and Coke. I set out candles at three-foot intervals to create a bug-free zone, and the next morning I found at least four dead June Bugs in every candle jar. I suppose it's possible the bugs flew overhead and were overcome by the fumes, but if the stuff repels them, what were they doing flying overhead? Yet I continue to bring the candles on camping trips because I feel every little bit helps. To be fair, they are more effective against mosquitoes than June Bugs.

As for **chemical protection**, there are products containing DEET, and products containing anything else. I've found DEET is the most effective in repelling flying and crawling critters. Unfortunately, there have been a lot of reports that the stuff causes cancer and is generally bad news. Apparently the chemical gets in your system and stays there, building up over the years and wreaking havoc. This is pretty dismaying for people like me who have relied on it over a long period of time.

And, as I said, it is more effective than anything else I've tried. Some people swear by Avon's Skin So Soft lotion, but I haven't found it does much against the mosquitoes, gnats, and biting flies I've encountered in this region. Skintastic, available in grocery and discount stores, seems to work better, but it actually contains a low level of DEET.

If you don't want to apply poison to your bare skin, you can spray or dab it on your clothing along your collar, cuffs, and the hem of your pants. This obviously only works if you have on long sleeves and long pants. A friend of mine wears a ponytail scrunchie on each wrist, and sprays it on her "bracelets," but somehow I can't picture any of my male friends doing that.

I don't apply bug spray unless and until I need it. If I'm hiking and am besieged by flying gnats, or enjoying the evening at my campsite and find I'm the main course for some bug buffet, I'll apply repellent by dabbing it on sparingly as needed. You can always apply more. Flying insects seem to be somewhat repelled by a smoky fire, but frankly, so am I! I would use this as a last resort, because not only you, your clothes, and your tent or rig will end up smelling like smoke, but your neighbors won't be too thrilled with you, either.

Some people just seem to attract mosquitoes more than other people do. If you're one of them, you may be doing something to make the problem worse. Don't wear perfume or after-shave in the woods, and use unscented deodorant and lotions. I've heard that eating bananas causes your skin to give off an odor attractive to bugs. Try not eating bananas for several days before your next camping trip, and see if that helps. I've also heard that eating garlic will repel bugs. I'm pretty skeptical about this because I've heard the same was true for dogs and fleas, and that hasn't worked for mine.

Ticks

No discussion of insects would be complete without a mention of ticks. If you've brought your pet along, be sure to check him or her thoroughly at the end of the day and periodically during hikes. Also provide head checks on your human companions, and have them return the favor. I've found enough ticks during head checks that I don't hike without what my sister Tricia uncharitably calls my "woodswoman" hat. Ticks are generally reputed to hang out in tall grass and jump on unwary people and pets as they pass by. I'm convinced they can climb trees. In this region, they are frequently found in Spanish moss. Wearing a hat gives you a chance to pick them off before they get their teeth in you.

Most of the information you'll find on ticks will give you elaborate instructions for removing the little beasties without leaving behind their mouthparts under your skin. All of these instructions mention using tweezers to remove them, pulling straight out. Unfortunately, when you find one of the little buggers has its clamps on you, you want it out immediately, and tweezers may not be close at hand.

The trick with ticks is to find them before they've started to feed. At that point, they are small members of the spider family, with flat round bodies, about the size of the tip of a round eraser on the end of a pencil. They move slowly so are easy to catch, but they have very hard, strong exoskeletons. I find the easiest way to kill them is to roll them between two fingernails. Until you hear the crunch, they will live to come after some other hiker or camper.

After they have burrowed in and started to feed, the body balloons out grotesquely until they seem to be a member of the grape family. Removing them now is trickier, as part of the tick is actually under your skin. If it breaks off while being removed and part stays inside you or your pet, it can cause infection. The tweezers method is the most approved way to remove them, but if you don't have your tweezers on you, use a tissue and do the best you can. Flush the wound thoroughly with water, apply an ointment such as Neosporin, and hope for the best.

This region of the country has a lot of ticks. I once hiked in a particularly infested park and removed over one hundred ticks from my two dogs at the end. My hiking buddy and I checked each other out as thoroughly as possible, but I still found a tick in my bed the next morning.

The dab-on liquid monthly flea and tick repellents such as Frontline are effective protection for your pet. The similar products from the discount store are just not in the same league as the ones you can get from the vet. They are a fraction of the cost, but you get what you pay for. If a dog shares your home, tent, or camper, I recommend these products highly.

A different kind of tick and a different threat altogether is the **deer tick**, which is much, much smaller than the common tick. The deer tick looks like a brown speck on your arm and can carry **Lyme disease**. The longer a tick stays on you feeding, the more likely it is that you will contract the disease, so vigilance is important. The most common first symptom of Lyme disease is a red rash in the shape of a bulls-eye, with unbroken skin in the middle. If you miss that, you may develop flu-like symptoms such as headache, fever, nausea, or body aches. Lyme disease is serious but treatable with antibiotics in the early stages. There is a vaccine for both you and your pet, so you may want to consider it if you spend a lot of time in the woods as I do.

SNAKES

If you do much hiking, particularly around water, you are likely to encounter a snake or two. Especially in dry years, I see snakes frequently near lakes. Another favorite resting spot seems to be in the trail under a fallen log. Watch where you put your feet, look before stepping over a log, and you'll probably be fine.

Note there is no snake bite kit on my first-aid list. Although there are three types of poisonous snakes—**rattlesnakes, cottonmouths** (or water moccasins), and **copperheads**—in this part of the country, and numerous non-poisonous ones, the odds of getting bitten are pretty slim. Most snakebites are dry, meaning that no venom is injected. Even if venom is injected and the snake is poisonous, experts now recommend against the traditional slash and suck out the venom approach as too dangerous.

© ARTTODAY.COM (2)

Tourniquets are also dangerous in the hands of amateurs. If you feel you must apply a tourniquet, it goes between the bite wound and the victim's heart, and should be snug but not so tight you can't slip a finger between the band and the skin. If the area swells, move the tourniquet so it is above the swelling. You can use your belt, extra bootlaces, a tee shirt, or a bandana. Remember to remove any jewelry or constricting clothing near the bite. If the area swells, these natural tourniquets could cut off circulation.

In the unlikely event you are bitten by a snake, take a good look at the varmint and seek medical attention if you suspect it is poisonous. See "Plants and Other Wildlife" for more information on snakebites.

POISON IVY

Besides wildflowers and kudzu, the one plant you are practically guaranteed to spot on every hike and in every park in this region is poison ivy. I don't remember visiting any park that wasn't crawling with the stuff. All parts of the plant are poisonous. Even in the winter, when the plant dies back and seems dormant, you can have a reaction from handling the vines. Poison ivy is the second reason I don't wear shorts in the woods (ticks are the first). If you wear long pants, your legs are protected.

If you aren't familiar with poison ivy, just remember the saying, "Leaves of three, let it be."

Not everyone is allergic to the resin from the plant. If you aren't, consider yourself fortunate but not entirely out of the woods. Some people become sensitive to the plant over time with repeated exposure. I've seen other people have reactions to it that were so bad they needed antibiotics from the resultant infections.

The neighbor of a friend pulled up all the poison ivy in his yard one winter and burned it. As he breathed in the fumes, the resins affected his respiratory system.

Dogs don't seem to have a reaction to the stuff, but they pick up the resin on their fur and then pass it on to your arms and legs, another reason to wear long pants. If you do touch the plant or pet a dog that rolled in it, the best thing to do is quickly wash the resin off. If you're home, you can run in and wash your arm or leg with soap and water. On the trail, waterless cleansers will remove the resin. I rinse with water, use a waterless hand cleaner, apply a little calamine lotion, and hope for the best.

If you start getting the telltale itchy, oozing rash, cover it with calamine lotion and take Benadryl, an antihistamine. Both of these are always in my first aid kit in my pack because poison ivy is everywhere I go. Though the Benadryl makes me sleepy, it also interrupts the itchy cycle and helps give the bumps time to heal without my scratching at them. Scratching the bumps causes more oozing, which just spreads the rash and prolongs your agony.

SUN EXPOSURE

Without the proper precautions, prolonged exposure in the sun can mean three things: sunburn, heat exhaustion, and/or heat stroke. When camping, the last thing you want hindering the experience is having to deal with any of these health concerns. So, limit exercise in the hottest part of the day. Wear a hat. Take breaks in the shade. Wear lightweight, light-colored clothing that reflects sunlight. And, drink plenty of liquids.

Don't underestimate the value of shade when camping in this region! The individual campground listings indicate whether campsites get any shade.

Sunburns are preventable with a little extra planning. First, liberally apply a sunscreen lotion with a blocking rating of at least 15. Be sure to reapply the lotion every two hours, but especially after swimming or heavy sweating. Wearing a hat and sunglasses can also help protect your skin and eyes. And, don't be fooled by overcast skies; the sun's rays can penetrate these clouds, leaving you with red or even blistered skin when you least expected it.

Heat exhaustion comes on when your personal cooling system starts to shut down, usually after prolonged activity in hot, humid weather. Skin may become cold, pale, and clammy. The victim may become weak and may even vomit. The person's body temperature will be normal or slightly elevated. At these signs, lie down in the shade. Remove any restrictive clothing and raise legs above the victim's head to encourage blood flow. Drink salted water.

Heatstroke, also called sunstroke, is really dangerous. Usually, the skin is hot

Frostbite

Frostbite is the very dangerous condition where the skin and tissues freeze. In most cases, the person is simply not dressed warmly enough. Frostbite usually begins with the hands and feet. At first, the skin will become red and painful. Later, it will become white and numb as feeling in that area is lost. If untreated, the skin will die and turn black. Preventing frostbite is as easy as dressing properly and preparing for cold weather. Bring gloves, hat, and extra socks, and always use a sleeping pad under your bag when camping in the winter. If an extremity suffers mild frostbite, slowly rewarm it against another part of your body. Do not rub the area or use direct heat (campfire, lamp, etc.) to rewarm. The key to reducing the extent of tissue damage to is to rewarm slowly.

Although frostbite may seem a remote possibility in this region, the temperatures at night can dip well below freezing and even below zero in the winter. It's a lot easier to prevent frostbite than to treat it.

and dry. The victim will not sweat, and the internal body temperature may be 106 degrees or higher. Dizziness, vomiting, diarrhea, and confusion are also symptoms. If any of these symptoms occur, call 911 or go to a hospital without delay. If you are in the backcountry (or on the way to the hospital), remove the victim's clothing. Lower the body temperature with cool water or sponges, fans, or air conditioners. Do NOT give the sufferer any liquids.

COLD-WEATHER EXPOSURE

One problem you might encounter while camping is **hypothermia**. Hypothermia is the condition where your body temperature falls to about 95 degrees or below. If untreated, it can lead to kidney, lung, and heart failure, and ultimately death. The initial symptoms are chills and shivering, and if untreated may include apathy, withdrawal, impaired judgement, slurred speech, dizziness, nausea, dilated pupils, and pale skin. If untreated, the shivering stops, breathing and heartbeat slow, and eventually coma results. The key to prevention is wearing the proper clothing and reacting promptly when problems arise.

Most people get hypothermia when they get wet and have no way to get dry. You don't have to fall in an ice-cold creek to get hypothermia. Your body temperature starts to drop when wet, and if there's any wind, your temperature will fall faster and lower. If it's hot out, that's not an issue, but if it's cloudy, damp, windy, and 60 degrees or below, you can get chilled.

How serious the chill gets depends on what you do next. The best thing to do is change into something dry and bundle up. If that's not possible, then donning a windbreaker or one of those cheap plastic ponchos will help a lot, as it prevents the wind from chilling you to the bone. If you're still cold, add another layer or two under the windbreaker. And put on a hat. You lose a lot of heat through your head, which is why it always feels cooler when you take your hat off.

The worst fabric to wear when you're chilled is cotton. It holds water well (think about drying your towels and jeans), clings to your body, and provides no insulation when wet. The best is wool, because it insulates even when wet. The synthetic downs also insulate when wet.

The key to preventing hypothermia is to not ignore shivering. After a certain point, your mind stops working logically, and I've heard stories of people who took

---

First-Aid Kit Checklist

You can pick up a first-aid kit at an outdoors store or even the camping department of a discount store, but I prefer to create my own so I don't carry items I don't use. I have two kits. One stays in my daypack at all times so I have it with me every time I hit a trail. The other, heavier one stays at camp.

For day hikes, I bought a pouch and stocked it with the following supplies. Since I carry this in my daypack at all times, I've pared down to what I consider the essentials:

• **suntan lotion** which you'll apply every two hours as needed. SPF 15 is probably sufficient. When you select a suntan lotion, look for zinc oxide, titanium dioxide, or avobenzone in the ingredients. PABA used to be the active ingredient in many lotions, but it only protects from UVB rays. It's the UVA rays that cause skin cancer, so avoid the lotions that rely on PABA for ultraviolet protection.
• **Band-Aid bandages**
• **gauze**
• **Swiss army knife** that includes tiny scissors to cut gauze and other bandaging supplies
• **bandage tape**
• **antiseptic ointment**
• **Benadryl** for relieving allergy, sinus, and cold symptoms. You or someone you're hiking with may have an unexpected reaction to one of the little beasties you encounter in the woods, so don't leave home without it. Benadryl is also good to reduce the itchiness of poison ivy.
• **aspirin, baby aspirin, acetaminophen,** and **ibuprofen tablets,** each for a different purpose: Aspirin seems to work better than other pain relievers for the heat of sunburn. My dogs get baby aspirin when necessary. I carry acetaminophen for the children traveling with me. For headaches, I prefer ibuprofen. Keep in mind you're not trying to replace the local drugstore in your daypack. I carry a dose or two of each of these with me while hiking, and then have more in the first aid kit I leave at camp. I use either clear plastic film cans or snack-size Ziploc plastic bags, and write the drug and expiration date on a piece of masking tape on the outside.
• **Tums tablets** for indigestion
• **moleskin** for blisters. Moleskin is a thick, cushiony product that comes on a roll. Cut to the size you need, cut out a doughnut in the middle for the blister, and press on. Cover the whole thing with a Band-Aid and you can probably keep going.

- **tweezers** for removing splinters and ticks
- **eye wash drops** to effectively wash out your eye if you get something in it, such as DEET from your bug repellent, or tiny bits of grit the wind blew in
- **vet wrap,** a stretchy, self-adhesive material that clings to itself but not to your skin or hair, so it doesn't hurt when it's removed. It comes on a roll in lots of fun colors, and works for people and pets to hold on a bandage when you don't want to use tape.
- **extra bootlaces** because what would you do if a bootlace broke several miles from the car? On some trails, it wouldn't be the end of the world. On any in the mountainous areas, it could be a very big deal. I've carried this pair of extra bootlaces for over 20 years, and never needed them. Also, although all experts agree that amateurs should never use tourniquets, it just feels like I should have something that could be used if necessary. Besides, they don't weigh much or take up space.
- **Lifesavers candies** to treat low blood sugar
- **Safety pins**
- **Waterless cleaner,** to remove poison ivy resins from skin if you're exposed

Optional Items
- **Space blanket,** a wafer-thin aluminum sheet that weighs practically nothing but does a decent job of reflecting back your body heat—useful if you get chilled or may be developing hypothermia
- **Ace bandage** for those with weak ankles

For camping trips, I also pack another first aid kit that stays in the tent or the car, with the following:
- **sun block** for those times you didn't use enough suntan lotion the day before and want to prevent further skin damage.
- **sunburn ointment**
- **hydrogen peroxide**
- **calamine lotion** for reducing the itchiness cause by insect bites as well as poison ivy
- **aspirin, baby aspirin, acetaminophen,** and **ibuprofen tablets.** These are refills for the one or two doses I carry in my daypack.
- **laxative**
- **needle and thread**
- **cough drops**
- **vitamin E capsules**
- **prescription drugs** and other personal medications you need

Though not technically a first aid item, don't underestimate the value of water. I always carry more than I plan to drink. Extra water can be used to wash off your skin when you've been exposed to poison ivy, rinse off a wound, or lower your body temperature by soaking a bandana you wear around your neck or over your head.

Just about the only time I open my first aid kit is when I'm getting ready for a hike or a camping trip. Then I check the expiration dates for all medicines and usually end up tossing them out and replacing them from my medicine chest. You may never need to use your supplies, either, but it's better to be prepared.

off their clothing in arctic conditions because they believed they were too warm. Once you lose the ability to think clearly, you'd better hope others in your group still have their wits about them.

DEHYDRATION AND HYPOGLYCEMIA

Dehydration and hypoglycemia are the worst problems I've seen while hiking. I always carry water and snacks on a hike, but on one hike, neither of my friends were carrying snacks, and one didn't have enough water. The problem got worse when we got lost and ended up being out several hours longer than we'd planned. Unfortunately, the only snacks I had with me were pretzels, and the salt compounded the water shortage. Now I always carry extra snacks and water in case I'm out longer than expected or my companions are ill-prepared, and some of my snacks are the pure sugar of Lifesavers candies.

Hypoglycemia occurs when your blood sugar drops below normal. Initially, your body reacts by making you hungry. If you don't eat some easily digested carbohydrates and the hypoglycemia continues, you may become light-headed, grouchy, dizzy, quiet, or disoriented.

Hypoglycemia is easy to prevent and treat. Always carry snacks when hiking, and carry some that are salty, some that are sweet, and some that are easily digested. I like pretzels for my salty snack, GORP for my salty/sweet combination, and Lifesavers candies for quickly digested sugar.

You might not realize your blood sugar is getting low, but your companions might. I get uncharacteristically quiet, as talking becomes too much of an effort. If you're hiking or expending more energy than is normal for you, eat snacks and drink fluids to keep your blood sugar level high enough.

Dehydration doesn't just mean that your body is in need of water. It also means that you're in danger of a rising body temperature, nausea, and in hot weather, suffering from heat-related illness. The solution? Replace your body fluids by drinking lots of water, 8–10 cups per day, and up to a gallon (16 cups) if the weather is warm or if you're really active.

If you're feeling thirsty, you are mildly dehydrated. But if you're experiencing headaches and dry mouth—and your urine output is under two cups over 24 hours—chances are your case is serious. Replace electrolytes (salt, potassium, and bicarbonate) by drinking fruit juice or an energy drink such as Gatorade. If these drinks or purified water are not available, drink whatever liquid is at hand. That's right, even if the water may be contaminated, avoiding or treating serious cases is worth the risk.

Although physicians once recommended that hikers take salt pills, they now believe that regular diets, including dehydrated foods that campers often consume, provide enough salt without supplements.

Other Issues

Use the same sense when you go camping that you do at home. Don't camp or hike alone in isolated areas, and be aware of what is going on around you.

PLANTS AND WILDLIFE

One of the benefits of camping and hiking in our region is the variety of wildlife we have a chance to experience. I don't see a lot of animals when I'm hiking since I usually have a dog or two attached to the tie that binds. That's why I so enjoy them when I do have an opportunity to see them. The plants, though, can't get away from me, even if I'd like some of them to, like poison ivy! Until I started looking for wildflowers along the trail, or whistle pigs along the road, though, I never saw them. Now I see them on nearly every hiking and camping trip. Become aware of the natural world around you and you may enjoy your outings even more.

© ARTTODAY.COM (6)

WILDFLOWERS

I first met my good friend Betty Baker when we worked together as programmers. Her family frequently hiked on the weekends. On Monday mornings over coffee, she would tell me about the wild-

flowers they had spotted along the trail. When she invited me to come along with them, they introduced me to a world of beauty I had been passing by unnoticed.

Not all wildflowers are worthy of special notice, at least to me. Some fall into that category of plants I'd normally call weeds. But pay attention to the plants blooming on the trail as you hike, and you'll likely see wild violets, showy orchis, pink and yellow lady-slipper orchids, trillium, cardinal flowers, fire pinks, wild geranium, and spring beauty, any of which is lovely enough to rival what you get from the florist.

Though you might find something blooming just about year round, springtime has the greatest quantity and variety of wildflowers. Every park and hiking trail you visit is going to have something blooming in the spring. For that matter, you'll find them blooming along the road on the way there. It's incredible to me that orchids can grow wild, and not

only grow but bloom and thrive. If you've been oblivious to the flowers you've been hiking by for years, at least take a look as you spot color at your feet.

If you're as new to wildflowers as I was, I recommend that you find Betty and convince her to go hiking with you. Barring that, pick up a field guide to wildflowers, available at most bookstores. Like field guides on other subjects, you may need to look through several to find one that has the plants organized in a manner that makes sense to you, so you can find something easily while hiking. I prefer them organized by color, and I like the ones with photos rather than drawings.

Where To View Wildflowers
Though you'll find wildflowers on virtually every hike, you might want to check out a few places where the show is truly spectacular. Cloudland Canyon State Park in northwest Georgia is thick with blooming rhododendron and mountain laurel in May. Sosebee Cove, near Vogel State Park in northwest Georgia, has a spectacular variety of wildflowers for such a tiny spot. Nearly every wildflower native to Georgia can be found here, including many varieties of trillium, showy orchis, rhododendron, bloodroot, and asters. The show begins in mid-April and continues through September. Two sources of information on native wildflowers are the Georgia Native Plant Society, 770/343-6000, www.gnps.org, and the Alabama Wildflower Society, 334/745-2494, www.auburn.edu/~deancar.

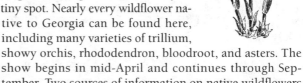

BOB RACE

If you don't mind traveling a bit farther, the annual Wildflower Pilgrimage is held in the Smokies the last week of April. There are guided hikes on spiders, amphibians, and photography, in addition to the wildflowers. The convention center in downtown Gatlinburg, Tennessee also contains an exhibit during the Pilgrimage of many of the native wildflowers, so if you don't see one on a hike, you can see it here. Plus, they're not labeled out in the woods, but they are at the exhibit.

BEARS
When my friends Martin and Gayle got married, they honeymooned by camping their way up from Georgia to Virginia and back. Avid outdoorspeople, they had a wonderful trip, until the night they heard bears ravaging their campsite.

They were at a seldom-used wildlife management area, and there were no other campers nearby. They had left bagged trash and their cooler out on the picnic table.

Shivering with fear in their tent, they listened to incredible growls and roars as the animals tore through the trash bag, dumped over the cooler, and raided their pantry. Martin had brought along a pistol, but it was thankfully locked in the car.

The bears wrought havoc for hours before the approaching dawn drove them away. When they felt it was safe to look out, the newlyweds found their campsite completely destroyed. The cooler's lid had been torn off, and trash bits were strewn over a 10 square-yard area. Footprints of the marauders were everywhere, but they were raccoon prints, not those of bears. I'm sure they'll never forget that night!

My friend Veronica had a much closer bear experience. She went backpacking on the Appalachian Trail one summer with her husband and two other couples. The first day out, they saw a mother bear with two cubs as they hiked. The bears initially ignored them, but one of her friends got closer than he probably should have to take pictures. When he returned to the group, the bears followed.

They camped near one of the shelters on the trail that night and had to chase the bears off several times to keep them from getting too close. When they got up the next morning, the bears were gone, so they set out for the next shelter. When they reached it, the bears were already there, waiting for them. Again they drove off the bears and finally went to sleep when it appeared they had left.

It was a warm night, and Veronica had opened all the windows of her tent so she could watch the stars. Her husband was fast sleep when she heard rustling nearby. Turning her head, she saw the two cubs pawing at something on the ground next to her, just outside the tent.

She wasn't initially afraid. She could see the two other tents a short distance away, and the cubs were adorable, so she was charmed to have an opportunity to be so close to the wild creatures. Then she heard the mother coming.

As the mother walked towards her babies, she tripped over one of the tent guy wires and fell into the tent onto Veronica's lap. With all the doors and windows unzipped, the tent was little more than a mosquito net on poles. The only thing separating the two of them was a layer of mosquito netting.

Veronica lay perfectly still as the mother struggled to her feet. Then the bear did an odd thing: she looked around, first one way and then the other, as if checking to see if anyone had seen her trip. When she was satisfied there was no one watching, she grunted at her cubs, and they bounded off after her into the darkness.

Veronica was lucky. Although black bears are not the notoriously deadly animals grizzlies are, they are very strong and potentially very dangerous, very wild animals. They live throughout this region but are seldom seen. When humans and bears meet, the end result is generally tragic for either the bear or the people involved. Periodically, bears wander down the Chattahoochee River and end up in metropolitan Atlanta where I live. They can usually be rounded up and removed back to north Georgia. Sometimes they must be destroyed.

Bears, like most wild animals, are supposed to be more afraid of you than you are of them. What I've found is that they will seemingly ignore you until you cross an invisible line and they feel threatened, and then they'll not hesitate to defend themselves. It's possible that, had her friend not stalked the animals to get photos,

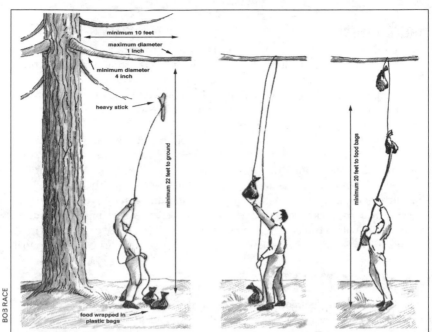

*In an area frequented by bears, a good **bear-proof food hang** is a must. Food should be stored in a plastic bag 10 feet from the trunk of the tree and at least 20 feet from the ground.*

they wouldn't have seen them again. It's also possible that the bears had learned that humans mean food will be around, either in their packs or in the trash they leave behind, and so stayed close by.

Bearproof Your Campsite

Most campgrounds in this region will have bear-proof trash containers, and I advise you to use them. Letting bears raid trash bags and non-secured cans only encourages them to hang around people, which can have deadly consequences, usually for the bear. Don't leave food or your cooler out on the picnic table. In areas where bears are a problem, you shouldn't have food in your tent, either, or you could have a close encounter like Veronica did.

If you're backpacking, Gautam recommends storing your food in your pack and hanging it in a tree. Select a strong branch that extends several feet from the tree. Tie the pack to a rope and throw the other end over the branch, hoisting the pack at least 10 feet off the ground before tying off the end.

In some areas, raccoons can be nearly as troublesome as bears. On Cumberland Island, Georgia, campsites have food cages that are locked against the varmints. Coolers have to be tied shut and tied to an immovable object, like a picnic table, or they are dragged off during the night.

OTHER BEASTIES

You are much more likely to encounter **raccoons** or **skunks** at your campsite than bears. The recommendations for these animals are the same as those for their larger buddies. Keep your food and trash out of reach and don't approach them. I have frequently seen skunks raiding trash bags placed by the road as I returned to a campground at night, and you don't want to experience one of these critters coming to your tent looking for more.

Other wildlife you may see on your trip include **deer**, **woodchucks** (called whistle pigs because of their distinctive call), **wild pigs** and **boars**, **squirrels**, various **birds**, and **opossums**. It's a thrill for me to see all of these except for the wild boars. They have the same pleasant personalities as grizzly bears and are quick to anger and attack. If you see one of those, climb a tree or get out of there.

One of the most exciting parts of the camping experience is seeing wildlife. Enjoy the experience but keep in mind these are wild animals. Any animal can be dangerous, particularly during breeding season or if they perceive you are a threat to their young.

FAMILY FUN

When I was a kid, my family camped several times near Branson, Missouri, at Table Rock Dam. Each day we'd head out on the lake and fish. We kids weren't allowed to talk (scared the fish), move (rocked the boat), or do anything kid-like for hours on end. When we'd return to the shore, there were no bathrooms other than spider-infested, stinky, poorly maintained outhouses. Somehow, bugs always managed to get into the tent. At night, all our air mattresses had slow leaks, and going to bed was a race to fall asleep before the air mattress went flat.

Did I mention it rained? A lot? My parents told us not to touch the sides and roof of the canvas tent, which was all the encouragement three kids needed, so enough water soaked in during a typical night's rain that our beds and clothes stayed wet the whole week we were there.

Years later, after we'd moved to Florida, we took a trip to the Florida Keys and camped in a pop-up instead of a tent. This was a definite step up in comfort, plus there was always a place to get in away from the bugs. We bought a campground directory and would read ahead while Dad drove, picking out our campground for the evening. I remember we drove two hours out of our way to get to one campground because the book said it had a swimming pool. Once there, we discovered

---

Keep It Wild Tip 6: Plan Ahead and Prepare

- Find out about any regulations or environmental issues concerning the area you plan to visit ahead of time.
- Obtain necessary permits.
- Pack food in reusable containers to reduce waste.
- Avoid heavy-use areas, which puts strain on the land and its resources.

we were the only campers under the age of 90. The "pool" turned out to be carved out of rock, was green and slimy with algae, and contained small fish.

It was nearly 10 years before I went camping again. Some friends were heading up to the Coopers Creek Wildlife Management Area in north Georgia, and I reluctantly went along. What I discovered on that trip was that camping could be a lot of fun.

There were still spiders and other bugs, my air mattress still went flat, and the WMA didn't even have an outhouse, so we had to dig holes and bury our waste. So what made the difference for me? During the day, I did things I truly loved, such as hiking and exploring the mountains.

My friend Vickie's early family camping trips were nearly identical to mine. Her family camped along the waterfront of Michigan's thumb, slept on leaky air mattresses, fought off spider and other bug infestations, and did without decent bathroom facilities for a week. She grew up loving camping, though. The difference was, during the day, she and her siblings had fun playing along the shore of the lake while her parents fished.

CAMPING WITH CHILDREN

After talking to my friends about their experiences as kids, and talking to kids camping with their parents, the verdict is clear. Know your kids and what they enjoy, then make sure they have some fun. Otherwise, even ordinarily perfect kids like me turn into whiney brats for your entire vacation. (Just ask my parents.)

When Betty's daughter Starr was young, she'd invite a friend to come along and the four of us camped all over the South. We also drove out to the Grand Canyon and many of the parks in the area for three weeks one summer. The girls might have occasionally tired of the adults constantly stopping to take pictures of every mountain, butte, and wildflower we passed, but they also had a lot of fun. Even on the three-week trip, we did something fun every day. We did a lot of hiking during the day, plus checked out every Anasazi ruin between Georgia and Arizona, and the girls enjoyed it all.

• *Kid-friendly campsites:* Today, it's not hard to find campgrounds with restrooms complete with flush toilets and hot showers. Many campgrounds have actual swimming pools, and some even have game rooms, paddleboats, horseback riding, and miniature golf. You can eliminate some of the potential problems with your kids by choosing campgrounds that have fun activities like these. Also, stay at campgrounds that are kid-friendly (look for a playground in the listing), and avoid those primarily frequented by retirees.

• *Family decision-making:* Next, involve your kids in some of the decisions of the trip. Even when she was seven, Starr had a say in what we were going to have for dinner, and how we were going to spend our day. Everyone wants to feel their opinion matters.

On the trip out to the Grand Canyon, the girls read books about where we were going, plus looked through the guidebooks at the route we were taking for things to do along the way. Everyone had a say in what fun thing we'd stop and do that day. If you're a kid, a whole day of driving is an eternity, and having something to look forward to within a few hours helps a lot.

• *Allow kids to be loud—when appropriate:* Whenever possible, we always stopped at campgrounds that had pools, so the kids could splash and make lots of noise after we'd stopped for the night. If kids don't have an appropriate opportunity to make noise, they're going to do it at inappropriate times.

• *Gifts and games:* A lot of the camping trips I took with Betty and Starr involved driving a long distance. During the drive, we would play games, sing songs, listen to music (bless whoever invented the portable cassette players), and read about where we were going and what we were going to see. One of our favorite games was "I Am Thinking of a Thing," our version of 20 Questions.

Betty started something with Starr that another friend, Don, also did with his kids. Before the trips, they bought small, inexpensive gifts, then each kid got one each morning of the trip. It was not only something to occupy their time for a few hours in the back seat, but it was also something to look forward to. Plus, kids aren't going to be too good at packing enough diversionary games and toys for a trip, and this gives them a variety of things to play with, plus the excitement of something new each day.

• *Structured activities:* The length of time you do any activity should be geared to the child's age and abilities. When Starr was younger, we'd go on lots of short, easy hikes, with plenty of time spent playing and splashing in streams and creeks we crossed. As she got older, the length of our hikes was able to increase. If you want to go fishing, keep in mind that an hour is a long time to sit still when you're a kid. If going to museums is what you like to do on vacation, choose ones that have some age-appropriate areas for your kids, or make them short visits.

As soon as they were old enough, the kids received journals on each trip. After dinner, while Betty and I cleaned up, they would write in their journals about what we'd done and seen that day. Betty and I would jog their memories when they left out something.

• *Chores:* One last thing that started when I was camping with Betty and has continued with other friends is taking turns being "The Mom." Each day, one of us will take on the responsibility, while the other adult can just relax and have fun. Mom has to make sure there's milk for tomorrow's breakfast, food for sandwiches the next day, something fun for everybody to do that day, and either cooks or divvies up the chores. It is, after all, everyone's vacation, and everybody should get a break from the daily responsibilities.

Not every family is ready for the enforced closeness of sharing a single-room tent for a week. Before you head out for a long trip, try it for a weekend first. That'll give you an indication of what an extended trip will be like. If things go well during the day but you find yourselves bickering during the evening and night, try renting an RV. The kids might be a lot easier to get along with if they get to watch a couple of hours of TV at night.

I feel so fortunate that I have had friends along the way who have helped me learn just how wonderful getting into the outdoors can be. As I said, I started out disliking camping intensely. The initial experience was so bad, I would have never believed I could look forward to and enjoy a camping vacation. It doesn't have to be that way. Infect your kids with your love of the outdoors. Starr has been out of college for years and still talks about wonderful trips we took together.

And, if you do take the whole family out all day fishing on a lake, let the kids talk. The fish will get over it.

CAMPING WITH PETS

My dogs like to hike and camp as much as I do, and I love having them with me. But I've found that more and more campgrounds are either starting to hesitate when I ask if pets are allowed or are prohibiting certain breeds.

You and I are the ones who benefit by having our pets with us, and we're also the ones responsible for ensuring we can continue to do so. If you want to be welcomed back, follow the rules of "petiquette":

• Don't leave your dog tied up outside your tent or camper. Even if you're just gone for a quick trip to the comfort station, your pet may become protective if someone walks by and start barking. If you have to leave him for a few minutes, put him inside the camper or your car.

• Always pick up after your pet. After barking, stepping in a mess is the most frequently cited complaint campground owners get about pets. You can buy special pooper scooper contraptions, or just bring plastic grocery bags (I use two) and dispose of any droppings.

• Don't let your pet wander out of your site. Not all areas have leash laws, but you should have your dog under voice control if not on a leash. And if she's not really trustworthy off leash, use one even if it's not required.

I always bring water from home when I'm camping in case the water available isn't what I want to drink. That goes for my dogs as well. Some dogs are sensitive to changes in water. Don't let yours drink from the stream in the campground or he could end up with a nasty case of doggie diarrhea.

Remember to bring snacks along on your hikes for your dogs as well as yourself. They'll expend a lot of energy and can use the extra calories.

Camping Gear Checklist

Sleeping Gear
• Tent (including poles, rain fly, guy lines, stakes, seam sealer, and repair kit)
• Hammer for driving in stakes
• Ground cloth
• Sleeping bag (and liner, for extended season camping)
• Sleeping pad (including repair kit)
• Pillow
• Extra blankets

Cooking Gear
• Stove and fuel
• Matches and lighter stored in waterproof container
• Ziploc bags in various sizes
• Aluminum foil

- Food (separated out in single meal servings in Ziploc bags if backpacking)
- Coffee, tea, and instant hot cocoa and cider
- Marshmallows (small for cocoa, large for toasting)
- Graham crackers and chocolate bars for s'mores
- Instant drink mixes, especially if backpacking and treating water chemically
- Cookies
- Peanut butter
- Instant oatmeal and grits
- Crackers
- Condiments for planned meals, such as ketchup, mustard, steak sauce, and marinade
- Salt, pepper, and other spices
- Pots and skillet
- Tea kettle
- Pot holders and mitts
- Spatulas, cooking spoons, skewers
- Can opener
- Knives, forks, and spoons, including a sharp knife for chopping vegetables
- Plates, bowls, and cups
- Water (just in case)
- Snacks
- Cooler and ice
- Charcoal and grill
- Large trash bags

Clothing and Hiking Items
- Hiking boots (properly broken in)
- Hiking and liner socks
- Camp shoes, especially if you'll be doing a lot of hiking
- Long pants and shirts
- Rain poncho
- Optional heavy duty rain gear or nylon•coated rain pants and jacket
- Hiking hat for sun protection
- Wool knit watch cap for cold weather or higher elevations
- Swimsuit
- Shorts
- Windbreaker
- Jacket or parka, depending on season
- Gloves for cold weather or higher elevations
- Large trash bag for dirty clothes

Personal Care Items
- Towels
- Shower supplies, including soap, shampoo, creme rinse, and wash cloth
- Toiletries
- Flip•flops for the shower, an essential at public restrooms

- Sunglasses
- Lip balm

Miscellaneous
- Small flashlight for each person in your party, two if you're backpacking
- Lantern
- Duct tape
- Swiss army knife
- Citronella candles
- Bug spray
- Hand soap
- Waterless hand cleaner
- First·aid kit (see First Aid section)
- Fanny packs or daypacks
- Folding chairs
- Folding table
- Fire logs
- Small hatchet (if planning on having a fire)
- Fire starter cubes, sticks, or candles
- Broom
- Clothes pins
- Paper towels
- Dish soap
- Dish pan
- Sponge
- Dish towel
- Stove cleaner
- Laundry detergent and dryer sheets for extended trips
- Medicines and special needs
- Camera and film
- Field guides (wildflowers, birds, trees, etc.)
- Journal
- Car games for kids and adults
- Deck of cards
- Books and magazines
- Rope
- Small trowel if you're backpacking, camping, or hiking in an area without restrooms

Pre·Trip Checklist
- Check first·aid kit and replace out of date medicines
- Stop newspaper and mail, or arrange for a neighbor to pick them up
- Turn thermostat to vacation setting
- Turn water heater to vacation setting
- Pay bills and mail
- Water plants

GEORGIA
NORTHWEST MOUNTAINS

NORTHWEST GEORGIA MOUNTAINS

GEORGIA REGIONS

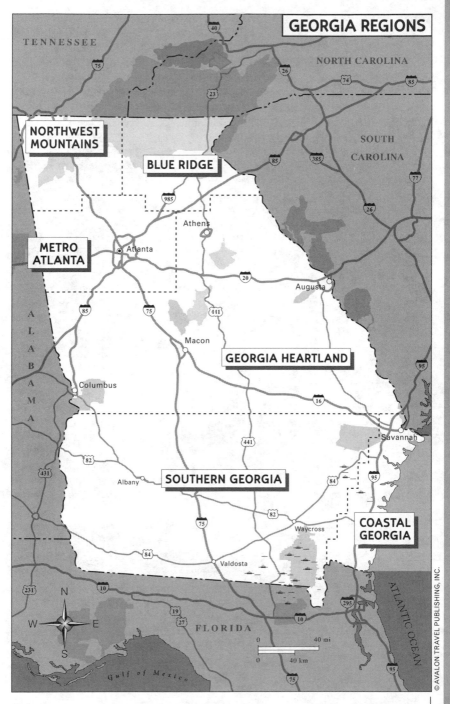

GEORGIA REGIONS

TENNESSEE

NORTH CAROLINA

SOUTH
CAROLINA

NORTHWEST
MOUNTAINS

BLUE RIDGE

Athens

METRO
ATLANTA

Atlanta

Augusta

A
L
A
B
A
M
A

Macon

GEORGIA HEARTLAND

Columbus

Savannah

SOUTHERN GEORGIA

Albany

Waycross

COASTAL
GEORGIA

Valdosta

N

W   E

S

FLORIDA

0   40 mi

0   40 km

Gulf of Mexico

ATLANTIC OCEAN

© AVALON TRAVEL PUBLISHING, INC.

NORTHWEST MOUNTAINS

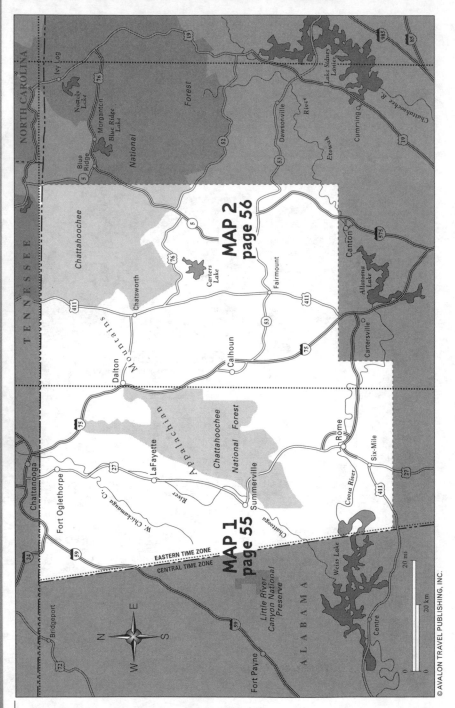

© AVALON TRAVEL PUBLISHING, INC.

MAP 1

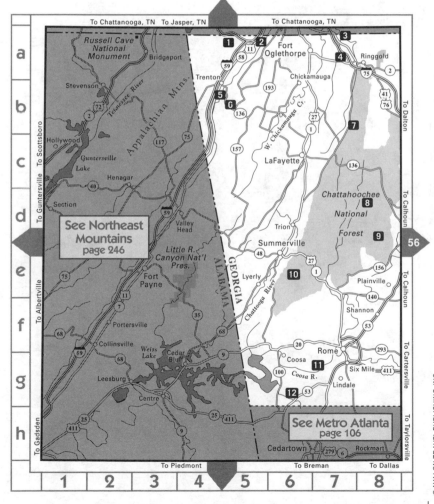

MAP 2

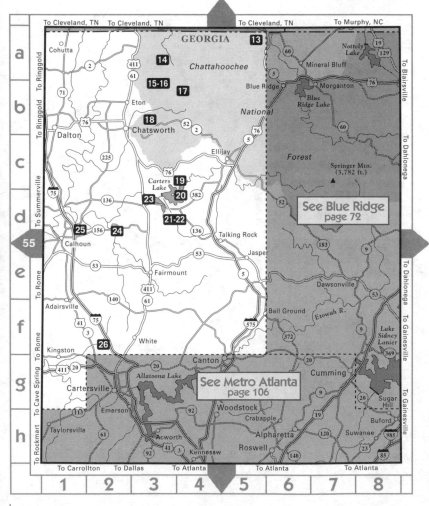

See Blue Ridge
page 72

See Metro Atlanta
page 106

To Cleveland, TN   To Cleveland, TN   To Cleveland, TN   To Murphy, NC

GEORGIA 13

Cohutta

Chattahoochee

14

Mineral Bluff

Nottely Lake

15-16 17

Blue Ridge   Morganton

Blue Ridge Lake

National

18
Chatsworth

Dalton

Eton

Ellijay

Forest

Springer Mtn. (3,782 ft.)

Carters Lake 19

23   20

21-22

Talking Rock

Calhoun   24

25   156

136

Jasper

Fairmount

Dawsonville

Adairsville

Ball Ground   Etowah R.

Lake Sidney Lanier

Kingston   White

26

Canton

Cumming

Cartersville

Allatoona Lake

Sugar Hill

Emerson

Woodstock

Buford

Taylorsville

Crabapple

Acworth

Alpharetta

Suwanee

Kennesaw

Roswell

To Carrollton   To Dallas   To Atlanta   To Atlanta   To Atlanta

To Cleveland, TN

To Ringgold

To Ringgold

To Summerville

To Rome

To Rome

To Cave Spring

To Rockmart

To Blairsville

To Dahlonega

To Dahlonega

To Gainesville

To Gainesville

© AVALON TRAVEL PUBLISHING, INC.

NORTHWEST MOUNTAINS

◼ Lookout Mountain/ Chattanooga West KOA

Location: Trenton, map 1, grid A5.

Campsites, facilities: There are 13 tent sites at this campground. In a separate section, there are 96 RV sites, 38 with full hookups and the rest with water and electric hookups. Pull-through sites are available. All sites have shade. Some campsites have picnic tables, fire rings, and cooking grills. There are also 14 cabins. RV storage is available, and a sanitary disposal station is provided. Restrooms have hot showers and flush toilets. A coin laundry, swimming pool, playground, and recreation room are provided. Ice, LP gas, supplies, groceries, and firewood are available at the campground store. Pets are permitted.

Reservations, fees: Reservations are accepted. The deposit of one night's fee is refundable if the reservation is cancelled at least one day in advance for a campsite or three days for a cabin. Tent sites are $18 per night. RV sites are $22–25 per night. One-room cabins are $38, two-room cabins are $50, and cottages are $110 per night. AAA and KOA discounts apply.

Open: Year-round.

Directions: From Interstate 24, take exit 167/Interstate 59 south and proceed two miles to the Slygo Road exit and turn right. It is 2.6 miles to the campground.

Contact: Lookout Mountain/Chattanooga West KOA, P.O. Box 490, Trenton, GA 30752; 706/657-6815.

Trip notes: The campground is close to Cloudland Canyon (see Cloudland Canyon State Park), and to the Chattanooga and Lookout Mountain attractions. There's fishing and hiking nearby.

◼ The Landing Hang Gliding RV Park and Cabins

Location: Wildwood, map 1, grid A5.

Campsites, facilities: There are 20 tent sites and, in a separate section, 16 pull-through RV sites. There are also 10 cabins for rent. Restrooms have hot showers and flush toilets. Satellite TV is available. The campground has a coin laundry, clubroom, and sanitary disposal station, and ice and LP gas are available. The buildings are wheelchair accessible. Pets are permitted.

Reservations, fees: Reservations are accepted at 800/803-7788, and no deposit is required. Sites with full hookups are $15. Cabins are $44–69.

Open: Year-round.

Directions: From Interstate 75, take Interstate 24 west to Highway 299, and turn right. Turn right onto US 11/Highway 58. Go 4.9 miles and turn left on Sarah Chapel Road, then one mile to Creek Road, and turn right. The campground is 1.5 miles down on the left.

Contact: The Landing Hang Gliding RV Park and Cabins, 1916 Creek Rd., Wildwood, GA 30757; 706/657-8282.

Trip notes: The campground is 15 minutes from Chattanooga and its attractions, and near Raccoon Mountain, Sunset Rock, and Point Park. It is also near the hiking trails at Cloudland Canyon (see Cloudland Canyon State Park). The campground is located in the landing field of a hang gliding school. Daily solo lessons are offered, as well as flying lessons. It is within 30 minutes of a variety of restaurants and sites that offer golfing, horseback riding, rock climbing, mountain biking, caving, and bungee jumping.

❸ Best Holiday Trav-L-Park

Location: Chattanooga, map 1, grid A7.

Campsites, facilities: There are 30 tent sites, some with water and electric hookups. There are also 140 RV sites, all with water and electric hookups. Sites with sewer hookups are available, as are pull-through sites. Both 30- and 50-amp hookups are available. Fire rings are provided, and there are three cabins. Restrooms have hot showers and flush toilets. A playground, swimming pool, and game room are provided. Cable TV hookups are available. Supplies and groceries are available at the campground. The buildings are wheelchair accessible. Leashed pets are permitted, and you *must* clean up after your pet.

Reservations, fees: Reservations are accepted at 800/693-2877. The deposit of one night's fee is refundable with notice. Tent sites without hookups cost $17 per night, and those with water and electric hookups cost $21 per night. RV sites cost $23 per night. There is an additional charge for 50-amp service and for cable TV hookups, each $2. The cabins rent for $36 per night.

Open: Year-round.

Directions: Heading north on Interstate 75, take exit 1B/Ringgold Road in Tennessee. Turn right (west) off the looped exit, then left onto Mack Smith Road and go about two-thirds of a mile. The campground straddles the state line.

Contact: Best Holiday Trav-L-Park, 1709 Mack Smith Rd., Chattanooga, TN 37412; 706/891-9766.

Trip notes: This campground is on the site of a Civil War battlefield, and historic markers provide information. You can view a Civil War video provided by the National Park Service in the lobby. The campground is near the Chattanooga attractions. Modem connections are available.

❹ Chattanooga South KOA Kampground

Location: Ringgold, map 1, grid A7.

Campsites, facilities: There are 30 tent sites at the campground, all with shade. Twenty-three have water and electric hookups, and seven have no hookups. In a separate section for RVs only, half of the 120 sites are pull-through sites with full hookups, and some have just water and electric. All have picnic tables, and some sites have fire rings and cooking grills. Cable TV is available. There are also seven cabins available, as well as group sites. Sites with patios are available for monthly guests. Restrooms have hot showers and flush toilets. The campground store sells ice, groceries, firewood, and LP gas. A coin laundry, playground, swimming pool, clubroom, fitness room, and sanitary disposal station are provided. Pets are permitted.

Reservations, fees: Reservations are accepted, and deposits are refundable if cancelled two days prior to your scheduled arrival time. The rate for tent sites is $15.95–20.95 per night. RV sites are $21.95–$27.95 per night. The one-room cabins are $37 per night, and the two-room cabins are $49.

Open: Year-round.

Directions: Take exit 350 off Interstate 75 and turn west. The campground is on the right, 300 yards from the interstate.

Contact: Chattanooga South KOA

Kampground, 199 KOA Blvd., Ringgold, GA 30736; 706/937-4166, fax 706/937-4165.

Trip notes: The campground is close to Chattanooga and its attractions, and near Raccoon Mountain, Sunset Rock, and Point Park. It is also near the hiking trails at Cloudland Canyon (see Cloudland Canyon State Park).

5 Lookout Lake Campground

Location: Trenton, map 1, grid B4.

Campsites, Facilities: There are 15 RV sites at the campground, all with water and electric hookups. Some sites have picnic tables. Primitive tent camping is also available. Restrooms have hot showers and flush toilets. A boat ramp is provided. Leashed pets are permitted.

Reservations, fees: Reservations are accepted at 706/657-4533. The deposit of one night's fee is not refundable. Primitive tent sites are $10 per night, and sites with water and electricity cost $15.

Open: The campground is open from early spring to late fall, depending on the weather.

Directions: From LaFayette, take Highway 136 northwest to Trenton. Turn left at the caution light in Trenton onto Scenic Highway, and travel about a block to the campground.

Contact: Lookout Lake, P. O. Box 338, Trenton, GA 30752; 706/657-4533, or 706/398-1970.

Trip notes: Fish in Lookout Lake includes bass, blue channel catfish, shell cracker, and blue gill. There are hiking trails around the lake and through the woods. Swimming is not recommended in the lake. The campground is about a mile from Cloudland Canyon State Park.

6 Cloudland Canyon State Park

Location: Trenton, map 1, grid B5.

Campsites, facilities: There are 73 tent or RV sites, all with electric and water hookups. Pull-through sites are available. There are 30 additional tent-only sites in a separate area. Primitive camping is available in the Bear Creek Backcountry area. The park also offers four group sites and 16 cabins. Picnic tables, cooking grills, and fire rings are provided. There are nine restrooms with showers and flush toilets. The backcountry area has pit toilets only. Two sanitary disposal stations, a coin laundry, tennis courts, swimming pool, and playground are on the premises. The camp store sells ice and gifts, and firewood is available. Three of the cottages and two of the campsites, along with the office and day-use restroom, are wheelchair accessible. Pets are allowed on a six-foot maximum length leash. Dogs are not allowed in the cabins. You cannot tie your dog's leash to any state property, including trees.

Reservations, fees: Reservations are accepted at 800/864-7275, for a two-night minimum stay. Holiday weekends require a stay of at least three nights. Nightly camping fees for the primitive sites range from $9 for single sites to $25 for a group site; tent sites are $15, and RVs are $17 with hookups. The rates for the cabins vary from $75–110 per night, depending on size and season. Like all of Georgia's state parks, there is a $2 per day parking fee, or you can purchase an annual Georgia ParkPass for $25. Campers pay for one daily pass for their entire stay.

Open: Year-round.

Directions: From LaFayette, take Highway 136 northwest towards Trenton. The park is 18 miles west of LaFayette and eight miles east of Trenton.

Contact: Cloudland Canyon State Park, 122 Cloudland Canyon Park Dr., Rising Fawn, GA 30738; 706/657-4050; email: cloudcan@bellsouth.net; website: www.gastateparks.org.

Trip notes: Cloudland Canyon is most spectacular in May when the mountain laurel and rhododendron are blooming along the trails. At other times of the year, you'll see honeysuckle, dogwood trees, and other wildflowers blooming. Hiking is very popular along the 4.7-mile West Rim Loop Trail, with side excursions to two waterfalls. One waterfall loop is 1.6 miles roundtrip and the other is 0.6 miles roundtrip. The waterfall trails are short; they are very steep and have built-in stairs. Although there are several benches along the way, you will definitely appreciate any hours spent on the Stairmaster on the way back up! The 7.1-mile Bear Creek Backcountry trail allows primitive camping by permit only, available at the visitor center. Wild turkeys, deer, foxes, and raccoons can be found at various times of the year. Although I've hiked the trails extensively, I've only seen deer from the swimming pool area at dusk. The view from the pool area is spectacular at sunset, as well as from the picnic area throughout the day. Fishing for catfish is available year-round one mile away at Lookout Lake (on Highway 136 towards LaFayette). The park is near Chattanooga and its attractions.

◼ Houston Valley ORV Area

Location: LaFayette, map 1, grid B7.
Campsites, facilities: There are no designated sites at this park, but you can camp anywhere except the parking area or the off-road vehicle trails. Restrooms have vault toilets. No drinking water is available. Pets are permitted.

Reservations, fees: Reservations are not accepted. There is no fee for camping, but there is a $5 per vehicle day-use fee.

Open: The campground is open from April through December, and closed in the winter.

Directions: From Interstate 75, take exit 348 and turn west onto Highway 151 south. At Wood Station, turn left onto Nickajack Gap Road. After you cross Taylors Ridge, turn right onto Capehart Road, which runs into the ORV area after about a half-mile.

Contact: Houston Valley ORV Area, US Forest Service, P.O. Box 465, LaFayette, GA 30728; 706/695-6736.

Trip notes: If you're looking for a peaceful, quiet, woods experience, you've come to the wrong place! The 26 miles of trails are designated for motorcycles and three- or four-wheelers only. No four-wheel drive vehicles are permitted. Although you can hike the trails, believe me, you wouldn't want to, as this is heavily used for off-road vehicles.

◼ The Pocket

Location: LaFayette, map 1, grid D8.
Campsites, facilities: There are 27 tent or small camper sites at this campground, all with shade. Picnic tables, fire rings, cooking grills, and piped water are provided. Firewood is usually available. Restrooms have flush toilets but no showers. The restrooms are wide enough for wheelchairs and generally accessible, but there is no ramp. Leashed pets are permitted.

Reservations, fees: Reservations are not accepted. The rate is $8 per night plus a $2 parking fee.

Open: The campground is generally open from the first of April through November. If your planned stay is in those months, call first to verify the date.

Directions: From Interstate 75, take exit 320 and turn west on Highway 136. Stay on Highway 136 when, after seven miles, it makes a 90-degree turn to the right. Seven miles after the turn, turn left onto Pocket County Road at the Forest Service sign. The campground is seven miles from Highway 136.

Contact: The Pocket, US Forest Service, P.O. Box 365, LaFayette, GA 30728; 706/695-6736; website: www.fs.fed.us/conf.

Trip notes: Though this is very much a no-frills campground, kids in particular love cooling off in the creek, which is about knee-high for an adult. There is a 2.5-mile loop trail through the deep woods. Common but seldom seen wildlife include deer, wild turkeys, and snakes. Fishing is available at nearby Lake Marvin, along with canoe rentals. On the way to the campground on Pocket County Road, you'll pass Keown Falls and the Johns Mountain Overlook. This is a somewhat isolated campground, and probably not the best choice for camping alone.

9 Hidden Creek

Location: LaFayette, map 1, grid D8.

Campsites, facilities: There are 16 tent sites at this horse camp, all with a picnic table, fire ring, tent pad, and parking spur. Pit toilets and piped water are available. Leashed pets are permitted.

Reservations, fees: Reservations are not accepted. There are no fees for this campground.

Open: Year-round.

Directions: From Interstate 75, take Highway 156 at exit 315 southwest 7.5 miles to Everett Springs Road, and turn right. After

two miles, turn right on Rock Creek Road. After three miles, turn right on Forest Service Road 955, which goes into the campground.

Contact: Hidden Creek, US Forest Service, P.O. Box 465, LaFayette, GA 30728; 706/695-6736.

Trip notes: Though there are no trails as such, there are miles and miles of unused Forest Service roads through this area for hiking. If you're looking for a quiet, peaceful woods experience, you've found it. Because of the somewhat remote location and the small number of campers here, though, I wouldn't recommend camping alone at this campground.

10 James H. (Sloppy) Floyd State Park

Location: Summerville, map 1, grid E6.

Campsites, facilities: There are a total of 25 campsites suitable for tents or RVs. All of the sites have water and electric hookups, and seven are pull-through. Most have shade. Picnic tables, fire rings, and cooking grills are provided. There are also two pioneer areas for groups, which have camping areas as well as Adirondack (three-sided) buildings. The pioneer sites have pit toilets. The developed campground has restrooms with hot showers and flush toilets. A coin laundry, tennis courts, playground, boat ramp, and sanitary disposal station are provided. Buildings are wheelchair accessible. Pets are permitted on a six-foot maximum length leash.

Reservations, fees: Reservations are accepted at 800/864-7275. In the Atlanta area, call 770/389-7275. The deposit of one night's fee is not refundable, but can be moved once to another date. The fee for tent sites is $13, and $15 for campers and RVs. Like all of Georgia's state parks, there is a $2 per day parking fee, or you can purchase an annual Georgia ParkPass for $25. Campers pay for just one daily pass for their entire stay.

Open: Year-round.

Directions: From Interstate 75, take Highway 140 west. At Highway 27, turn north. After you cross Taylors Ridge, turn left at the sign for the park.

Contact: James H. Floyd State Park, 2800 Sloppy Floyd Lake Rd., Summerville, GA 30747; 706/857-0826; website: www.ga stateparks.org.

Trip notes: Sloppy Floyd State Park has two lakes but no swimming areas. Fishing is available year-round for bass, bream, and catfish. Johnboats and paddleboats are available for rent. Hiking is plentiful. The Lake Trail is three miles long. The Taylors Ridge Trail is one mile one-way to an old marble mine, and two miles to the Pinhoti Trail, which stretches for 120 miles in Alabama and 100 miles in Georgia. (For more information on the Pinhoti Trail, see Resources.) Raccoons can be a problem with trash, so use the varmint-proof garbage containers provided.

⓫ Coosa River Trading Post and Campground

Location: Rome, map 1, grid G7.

Campsites, facilities: Seven of the 31 RV sites at this campground have full hookups, and six are pull-through sites. Most have shade. Picnic tables, fire rings, and cooking grills are provided, and RV storage is available. There is one group site for organizations. Restrooms have hot showers and flush toilets. Ice, LP gas, firewood, and some groceries are available at the campground. The nearest supply store is five miles away.

A coin laundry, boat ramp, dock, clubroom, playground, and sanitary disposal station are on the premises. The buildings are wheelchair accessible. Leashed pets are permitted but can't be tied up outside your camper.

Reservations, fees: Reservations are accepted. The deposit of one night's fee is refundable with three day's notice. Rates are $16–20 per night.

Open: Year-round.

Directions: From Interstate 75 take the Rome/Canton exit, and turn west onto Highway 20. Stay on Highway 20 when it joins up with US 411, then take US 411 when they split. Turn right on Walker Mountain Road, then turn right again after three miles at the sign for Lock and Dam Park.

Contact: Coosa River Trading Post and Campground, 181 Lock and Dam Rd., Rome, GA 30161; 706/234-5001.

Trip notes: Rome is a delightful place to visit. The Coosa River provides fishing opportunities for crappie, striped and white bass, and catfish. The walking/biking paths along the rivers are shady and pleasant, and take you between several parks. Rome is near Cloudland Canyon (see Cloudland Canyon State Park), Allatoona Lake, and Atlanta. Wildlife in the area includes deer and wild turkeys. The campground is near the Pinhoti Trail, an approach trail to the Appalachian Trail (see Resources).

⓬ Cedar Creek Park and Campground

Location: Cave Springs, map 1, grid G6.

Campsites, facilities: There are 38 RV sites. All of the RV sites have full hookups, and one-third of them are pull-through sites. Some sites offer shade. Picnic tables and cooking grills are provided. Three group sites with pavilions are available. RV storage is available. Restrooms have hot showers and flush toilets. A driving range and a sanitary disposal station are provided. Firewood is furnished, and ice and some groceries are available. The buildings are wheelchair accessible. Leashed, well-behaved pets are permitted.

Reservations, fees: Reservations are accepted. Deposits are only required for holidays and are refundable if you cancel your reservation at least five days before your scheduled arrival. Rates are $13.50 per night.

Open: Year-round.

Directions: From Rome, take US 411/27 west. When they fork, stay on US 411. It is eight miles more to the campground, which will be on your right.

Contact: Cedar Creek Park and Campground, 6770 Cave Springs Rd., Cave Springs, GA 30124; 706/777-3030.

Trip notes: Fishing for catfish and bream are available at the creek year-round. You can rent canoes at the campground. A gravel sandbar is used as a beach in the swimming area. The campground is about 60 miles from Birmingham, Atlanta, and Chattanooga, and close enough for day trips to Cloudland Canyon (see Cloudland Canyon State Park), Keown Falls, and Rome.

13 Allegheny Retreat

Location: Blue Ridge, map 2, grid A5.

Campsites, Facilities: The campground has 10 tent sites and 6 RV sites. Three of the RV sites have water and electric hookups, and some have shade. RVs must be less than 32 feet in length. Picnic tables and fire rings are provided, and some cooking grills are available. There is one cabin for rent. A sanitary disposal station is provided. Wood and ice are available at the campground. Restrooms have hot showers and flush toilets.

Reservations, fees: Reservations are accepted at 706/492-2665. The deposit of one night's fee is only required for stays of a week or more, and is refundable if cancellation is at least 48 hours in advance. Tent campers pay $8 per person. If using a pop-up, the fee is $16 for two persons, plus $4 for hookups if needed. The fee for RVs is $24 per night. The cabin rents for $70.

Open: The cabin is available year-round. The campground is open from April 1-November 15.

Directions: From Atlanta, take Interstate 575 north to Highway 515, and continue north. Turn left in Blue Ridge onto Highway 5 north, and travel 11 miles to McCaysville. Turn left at the light in McCaysville onto West Tennessee Avenue, which becomes Mobile Road. After 1.5 miles, turn left onto Old Mobile Road. Travel 0.4 miles and turn left onto Fightingtown Creek Road. At the bottom of the hill, turn left onto Country Lane. The campground will be on the right.

Contact: Allegheny Retreat, 227 Country Lane, McCaysville, GA 30555; 706/492-2665.

Trip notes: This lovely campground is on Fightingtown Creek, and fishing is good for trout and bass. There is a swimming area in the creek, and tubes are for rent. The Division of Recreational Services of Georgia State University did a study at the campground, and identified 101 different wildflowers that bloom there in the spring. There is a short nature trail by a mountain stream that leads through mountain laurel and rhododendron, but no other hiking in walking distance. Horseback riding is available within two miles. Bike trails and white-water river rafting are available on the Ocoee River, about 20 minutes from the campground. Blue Ridge, 11 miles away, has many antique shops, and the Blue Ridge Scenic Railway, a three-hour rail trip that goes up along the Toccoa River to McCaysville and back. There are also antique shops in McCaysville. Coffee, tea, hot chocolate, and cappuccino are served every morning on the deck over the creek, and the camp host brings fresh cookies to the campers each afternoon. A wake-up call is provided for campers needing an early rise for the raft trips.

14 Hickey Gap Campground

Location: Chatsworth, map 2, grid A3.
Campsites, facilities: There are five primitive tent sites. Tent pads, picnic tables, fire rings, and pit toilets are provided. There is no drinking water. Pets are permitted.
Reservations, fees: No reservations are accepted. Sites are $5 per night.
Open: Year-round.
Directions: From Interstate 75, take US 411 north through Chatsworth. In Crandall, turn right on Grassy Street. After the railroad crossing, turn right on the first road (unmarked). After 0.25 miles, turn left at the Forest Service sign. The pavement will end, and it will be dirt and gravel for the rest of the way to the campground.
Contact: Lake Conasauga Recreation Area, 401 Maddox Parkway, Chatsworth, GA 30705; 706/695-6736.
Trip notes: The campground is along Mill Creek and is near the trail to Mill Creek Falls, which are particularly nice in the spring when the rhododendron and mountain laurel are

blooming. Due to the somewhat isolated location, use caution if you're camping alone.

15 Lake Conasauga Recreation Area

Location: Chatsworth, map 2, grid B3.
Campsites, facilities: There are 35 tent sites, most with shade. Picnic tables and fire rings are provided. The group site can accommodate many tents, but it has no picnic tables or water. Restrooms in the main area have flush toilets but no showers, and vault toilets are at the group site. A boat ramp is provided. Boat motors must be electric only. Pets are permitted.
Reservations, fees: No reservations are accepted. Campsites are $8 per night.
Open: The campground is closed in winter. Opening and closing dates vary, but the campground is generally open mid-April–October. Call for the exact dates.
Directions: From Interstate 75, take US 411 north through Chatsworth. In Eton, turn right on Old CCC Camp Road. After five miles, the pavement ends and the road becomes a Forest Service road. Continue on the gravel road for 15 more miles, following the signs, and taking all left forks to the campground.
Contact: Lake Conasauga Recreation Area, 401 Maddox Parkway, Chatsworth, GA 30705; 706/695-6736.
Trip notes: Fishing for trout is available year-round in the lake. There are several trails, including the 1.5-mile Lake Trail, the two-mile Tower Trail, and the Songbird Management Trail, which continues for one mile off the Tower Trail. You'll also pass a sign for the trail to Panther Creek Falls and Emery Creek Falls on your way to the campground. This

trail is fairly difficult because of water crossings, but the falls are worth it after periods of rain. Swimming is available in the lake. Black bears, deer, and wild hogs are common in the area. There are two camping areas. Loop A has six sites right on the lake, and fills up first. Loop B campsites have a long walk to the lake. The 15 miles of gravel road can take a toll on your car, but vehicles with high clearance will have an easier time.

16 Lake Conasauga Recreation Area Overflow Campground

Location: Chatsworth, map 2, grid B3.
Campsites, facilities: There are five primitive campsites with vault toilets and no piped water. Picnic tables are provided. Pets are permitted.
Reservations, fees: No reservations are accepted. The camping fee is $5 per night.
Open: This area is only open when the Lake Conasauga Recreation Area Campground (see above) is full.
Directions: From Interstate 75, take US 411 north through Chatsworth. In Eton, turn right on Old CCC Camp Road. After five miles, the pavement ends and the road becomes a Forest Service road. Continue on the gravel road for 15 more miles, following the signs and taking all left forks past the main campground to the overflow area.
Contact: Lake Conasauga Recreation Area, 401 Maddox Parkway, Chatsworth, GA 30705; 706/695-6736.
Trip notes: See Lake Conasauga Recreation Area Campground for information.

17 Jacks River Field

Location: Chatsworth, map 2, grid B4.
Campsites, facilities: There are five primitive sites. Picnic tables and fire rings are provided. Restrooms have vault toilets. No drinking water is available. Pets are permitted.
Reservations, fees: No reservations are accepted. Sites are $5 per night.
Open: Year-round.
Directions: From Interstate 75, take US 411 north through Chatsworth. In Eton, turn right on Old CCC Camp Road. After five miles, the pavement ends and the road becomes a Forest Service road. Continue on the gravel road, following the signs for Lake Conasauga until you come to Potato Patch Mountain and a T-junction. The sign for Lake Conasauga points to the left. Turn right, away from Lake Conasauga, and continue for six miles. The campground will be on the right.
Contact: Lake Conasauga Recreation Area, 401 Maddox Parkway, Chatsworth, GA 30705; 706/695-6736.
Trip notes: The 2.6-mile South Fork Trail leads off from the campground to Jacks River Falls, which is a beautiful waterfall after a period of rain. The trail is not strenuous but is quite rocky, and you will have to cross a creek on steppingstones to get to the falls. You'll want sturdy high-top hiking boots to avoid getting your feet wet. This campground is in a somewhat isolated location, so it's not recommended if you're camping alone.

18 Fort Mountain State Park

Location: Chatsworth, map 2, grid B3.

Campsites, facilities: The campground has 70 sites for tents or RVs, all with water, electric, and cable TV hookups. About half are pull-through sites. Picnic tables and fire rings are provided. There are also 15 cabins. Restrooms have hot showers and flush toilets. A coin laundry and sanitary disposal station are provided. Buildings are wheelchair accessible. Horses are not allowed in the campground or cabin areas, but stables are available. Leashed pets are permitted in the campground, but not in the cabin area. You must clean up after your pet.

Reservations, fees: Reservations are accepted at 800/864-7275. In the Atlanta area, call 770/389-7275. The deposit is non-refundable, but the date can be moved once. The rate for tent sites is $16, $18 for RVs. Cabins are $75–110. There is a two-night minimum on cabins except during the summer and the month of October, when the minimum is five nights. Like all of Georgia's state parks, there is a $2 per day parking fee, or you can purchase an annual Georgia ParkPass for $25. Campers pay for one daily pass for their entire stay.

Open: Year-round.

Directions: From Interstate 75, take the Chatsworth/US 411 exit and turn east. Turn right on Highway 52. The park is eight miles from US 411, on the left.

Contact: Fort Mountain State Park, Rt. 7, Box 7008, Chatsworth, GA 30705; 706/695-2621; website: www.gastateparks.org.

Trip notes: This park has always been a popular camping destination, and since its renovation in 1999, it's even more so. Make sure you make reservations for your trip. The 17-acre lake has a sand beach for swimming and allows no motorized boats; johnboats and paddleboats are available for rent. Fishing is available. In addition to miniature golf, there are 30 miles of mountain biking trails, 37 miles of horse trails, and 14 miles of hiking trails.

19 Woodring Branch Campground

Location: Carters Lake, map 2, grid C4.

Campsites, facilities: There are 11 tent sites and 31 sites for either tents or RVs, some with electric and water hookups. Both 30-amp and 50-amp hookups are available. Picnic tables, fire rings, and cooking grills are provided. Restrooms have hot showers and flush toilets. A coin laundry, boat ramp, playground, and sanitary disposal station are provided. Pets are permitted.

Reservations, fees: Reservations are accepted at 877/444-6777. The fee for sites without hookups is $12. For sites with water and 30-amp service, the fee is $16. Sites with 50-amp service are $18.

Open: The campground is open from April through October. Call and verify the date if you plan to visit near the beginning or the end of the season, as the exact dates vary yearly.

Directions: From Interstate 575, take Highway 282 west to the north side of Carters Lake and follow the signs.

Contact: Woodring Branch Campground, US Army Corps of Engineers, P.O. Box 96, Oakman, GA 30732; 706/334-2248; website: www.sam.usace.army.mil/op/rec/carters/.

Trip notes: Fishing is available year-round for bass, crappie, and catfish. There are hiking trails through the area, and swimming is available in the lake.

20 Ridgeway Campground

Location: Carters Lake, map 2, grid D3.
Campsites, facilities: The campground has 12 primitive campsites. Pit toilets, piped water, and boat ramps are provided. Pets are permitted.
Reservations, fees: Reservations are not accepted. Sites are $6 a night.
Open: Year-round.
Directions: From Interstate 575, take Highway 282/US 76 west to the lake, and follow the signs. To get to this campground, you must travel on gravel roads that are not always well maintained.
Contact: Ridgeway Campground, US Army Corps of Engineers, P.O. Box 96, Oakman, GA 30732; 706/334-2248; website: www.sam.usace.army.mil/op/rec/carters/.
Trip notes: This primitive campground has both mountain bike and hiking trails. Fishing is available year-round for bass, crappie, and catfish, and swimming is available in the lake.

21 Doll Mountain

Location: Carters Lake, map 2, grid D3.
Campsites, facilities: There are 26 tent sites and 39 sites for either tents or RVs at this campground, the latter having electric and water hookups. Picnic tables, fire rings, and cooking grills are provided. Restrooms have hot showers and flush toilets. A coin laundry, boat ramp with dock, playground, and sanitary disposal station are provided. Pets are permitted.
Reservations, fees: Reservations are accepted at 877/444-6777, and no deposit is required. Tent sites are $12 per night. Sites with 30-amp service and water are $16, or $18 for 50-amp service.
Open: The campground is open from May through mid-September. Call and verify the date if you plan to visit near the beginning or the end of the season, as the exact dates vary yearly.
Directions: From Interstate 575, take Highway 382 to the south side of Carters Lake and follow the signs.
Contact: Doll Mountain, US Army Corps of Engineers, P.O. Box 96, Oakman, GA 30732; 706/334-2248, or 706/276-4413; website: www.sam.usace.army.mil/op/rec/carters/.
Trip notes: This is the nicest of the Carters Lake campgrounds. Fishing is available year-round for bass, crappie, and catfish. There are hiking trails through the area, and swimming is available in the lake.

22 Harris Branch

Location: Carters Lake, map 2, grid D3.
Campsites, facilities: There are 16 primitive campsites and two group sites. Restrooms have showers and flush toilets. A coin laundry, playground, and sanitary disposal station are provided. Pets are permitted.
Reservations, fees: Reservations are accepted at 706/276-4545. The tent sites are $12 per night. The group sites are $30.
Open: The campground is closed in

the winter. It generally opens early May and closes mid-September, but call to confirm the dates if your planned visit is near those times.

Directions: From Interstate 575, take Highway 382 west to the lake and follow the signs.

Contact: Harris Branch, US Army Corps of Engineers, P.O. Box 96, Oakman, GA 30732; 706/334-2248; website: www.sam.usace.army.mil/op/rec/carters/.

Trip notes: This campground on the south side of Carters Lake has a beach in the swimming area. Fishing is available year-round for bass, crappie, and catfish.

23 Talking Rock Creek

Location: Chatsworth, map 2, grid D3.

Campsites, facilities: There are nine RV campsites, all with full hookups. Most sites have shade. Picnic tables are provided. There are also two cabins available. RV storage is available. Restrooms have hot showers and flush toilets. A swimming pool, playground, and fitness room are provided. The facilities are wheelchair accessible. Pets are permitted.

Reservations, fees: Reservations are accepted, and no deposit is required. Campsites are $12 per night, and cabins are $65.

Open: Year-round.

Directions: From Chatsworth, take US 411 south to Highway 136 and turn left. The campground will be on the right about 1.5 miles from US 411.

Contact: Talking Rock Creek, 222 Talking Rock Creek Dr., Chatsworth, GA 30705; 706/334-2519.

Trip notes: Hiking trails lead through and from the campground, which is close to Carters Lake.

24 Salacoa Creek Park

Location: Calhoun, map 2, grid D2.

Campsites, facilities: The campground has 35 tent or RV sites, all with water and electric hookups, including two pull-through sites. Most have shade. Picnic tables, fire rings, and cooking grills are provided. Restrooms have hot showers and flush toilets, and a sanitary disposal station is provided. Ice and firewood are available. A boat ramp, dock, and playground are provided. Boat motors must be 10 horsepower or less. Leashed pets are permitted.

Reservations, fees: Reservations are accepted. The required deposit of one night's fee is not refundable on cancellation. Sites cost $15 per night.

Open: The campground is closed in the winter, from approximately the first of October to the first of March. Dates vary as the campground usually opens on a Friday, so if you plan to camp around these dates, call first.

Directions: From Interstate 75, take Highway 156/Red Bud Road at exit 315 and turn east. Stay on Highway 156 for 10 miles, then turn right at the sign for the park.

Contact: Salacoa Creek Park, 388 Park Dr. NE, Ranger, GA 30734; 706/629-3490.

Trip notes: The campground is on a 136-acre lake. Some campsites are on the lake, and some a short walk away. Fishing is available year-round for bass, crappie, bream, catfish, and carp. Johnboats are available for rent. Though there are no hiking trails per se, the path to the dam and spillway is five miles round-trip. There is a sand beach at the swimming area. Wild turkeys and deer are plentiful in the area.

25 Calhoun KOA

Location: Calhoun, map 2, grid D1.

Campsites, facilities: There are 10 tent sites at this campground, all with water and electric hookups. There are also 80 RV sites in a separate section, most with water and electric, and some with full hookups. Both 30- and 50-amp hookups are available. Most are pull-through sites, and most have some shade. Picnic tables, fire rings, and cooking grills are provided. There are also four cabins. Restrooms have hot showers and flush toilets. A coin laundry, swimming pool, playground, game room, and sanitary disposal station are provided. Cable TV hookups are available. Ice, LP gas, and some groceries are available at the campground. The buildings are wheelchair accessible. Leashed pets are permitted, but cannot be left outside at night.

Reservations, fees: Reservations are accepted. They require a credit card to hold a reservation. Tent sites are $17 per night, and RV sites are $20–25, depending on hookups.

Open: Year-round.

Directions: From Interstate 75, take Highway 156/Red Bud Road at exit 315 and turn east. The campground is 1.5 miles from the interstate.

Contact: Calhoun KOA, 2523 Red Bud Road NE, Calhoun, GA 30701; 706/629-7511.

Trip notes: The campground is convenient to the interstate.

26 Cartersville KOA

Location: Cartersville, map 2, grid F2.

Campsites, facilities: There are 17 tent sites with water and electric hookups, all with some shade. There are also 101 RV sites, half with water and electric, and half with full hookups. All RV sites are pull-through, and some have shade. Sites with full hookups have cable TV available. Phone hookups are available for monthly guests. There is one group site. Picnic tables are provided, and RV storage is available. Restrooms have hot showers and flush toilets. A coin laundry, swimming pool, playground, game room, and sanitary disposal station are provided. The campground store sells ice, LP gas, some groceries, and gifts. The buildings are wheelchair accessible. Leashed pets are permitted.

Reservations, fees: Reservations are accepted, and no deposit is required. Sites with electricity and water are $18, and sites with full hookups are $20 per night. KOA card discounts are available.

Open: Year-round.

Directions: From Interstate 75, take exit 296 onto Cassville-White Road and turn west. The campground is on the left near the interstate.

Contact: Cartersville KOA, 800 Cassville-White Road NW, Cartersville, GA 30121; 770/382-7330.

Trip notes: The campground is 11 miles to Allatoona Lake and offers more amenities than the US Army Corps of Engineers campgrounds located there. (See listings for Metro Atlanta.)

BLUE RIDGE

Tallulah Gorge State Park

BLUE RIDGE

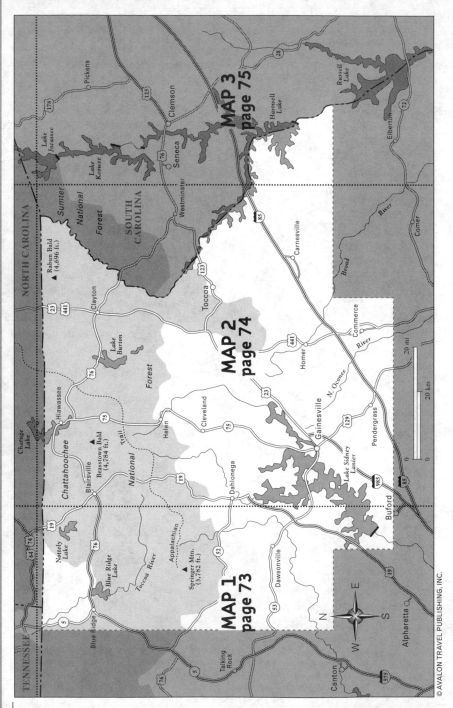

© AVALON TRAVEL PUBLISHING, INC.

MAP 1

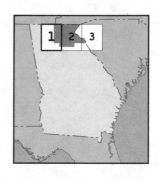

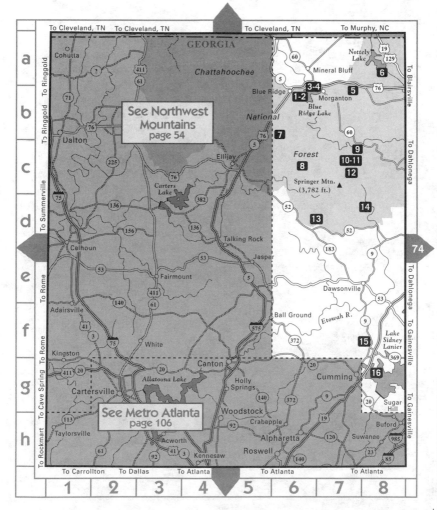

To Cleveland, TN   To Cleveland, TN   To Cleveland, TN   To Murphy, NC

GEORGIA

Chattahoochee

Cohutta

To Ringgold

To Ringgold

Nottely Lake

Mineral Bluff

Blue Ridge

See Northwest Mountains page 54

Dalton

National

Morganton

Blue Ridge Lake

To Blairsville

To Dahlonega

Ellijay

Forest

Carters Lake

Springer Mtn. (3,782 ft.)

To Summerville

Calhoun

Talking Rock

Jasper

To Rome

Fairmount

Dawsonville

Adairsville

Ball Ground

Etowah R.

To Rome

To Cave Spring

Kingston

White

Canton

Lake Sidney Lanier

See Metro Atlanta page 106

Cartersville

Allatoona Lake

Holly Springs

Cumming

Sugar Hill

To Rockmart

Taylorsville

Woodstock

Crabapple

Buford

Suwanee

Alpharetta

Roswell

To Carrollton   To Dallas   To Atlanta   To Atlanta   To Atlanta

Acworth

Kennesaw

To Dahlonega

To Gainesville

To Gainesville

74

© AVALON TRAVEL PUBLISHING, INC.

MAP2

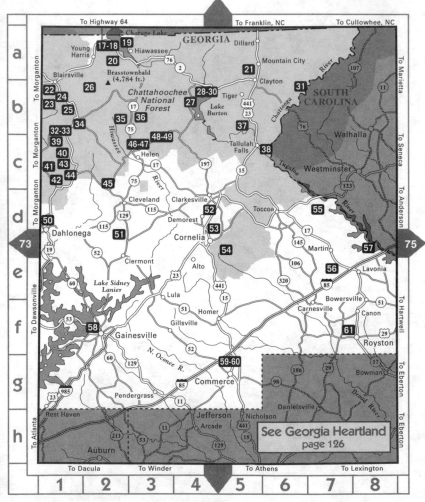

To Highway 64   To Franklin, NC   To Cullowhee, NC

GEORGIA

Chatuge Lake

Young Harris   **17-18**   **19**   Hiawassee   Dillard

20   76   Mountain City

Brasstownbald (4,784 ft.) ▲   2   **21**   Clayton

Blairsville

22   **24**   **26**   *Chattahoochee National Forest*   **28-30**   **31**   **SOUTH CAROLINA**

23   **25**   **27**   Lake Burton   Tiger   441   23

34   **35**   **36**   **37**   Walhalla

32-33   17   75   **48-49**   76

39   **46-47**   Tallulah Falls   **38**   Westminster

40   Helen   197   Tugaloo   123

41   **43**   17   15

42   **44**   **45**   75   Cleveland   Clarkesville   **52**   Toccoa   **55**

50   115   129   115   Demorest   **53**   17   Martin   **57**

Dahlonega   **51**   Cornelia   145

19   52   Clermont   **54**   106   **56**   Lavonia

Alto   320   85

Lake Sidney Lanier   60   23   441   Bowersville   51

Lula   15   Carnesville   Canon

53   51   Homer   **61**

58   Gillsville   29   Royston

Gainesville   52   *N. Oconee R.*   **59-60**

60   129   17

985   85   Commerce   106   29   Bowman

23   Pendergrass   98   *Broad River*

Rest Haven   11   Danielsville

Jefferson   Nicholson   **See Georgia Heartland**
11   Arcade   441   **page 126**
211   53   15

Auburn   129

To Dacula   To Winder   To Athens   To Lexington

To Morganton / To Dawsonville / To Atlanta

To Marietta / To Seneca / To Anderson / To Hartwell / To Eberton

73   **75**

1   2   3   4   5   6   7   8

a b c d e f g h

MAP3

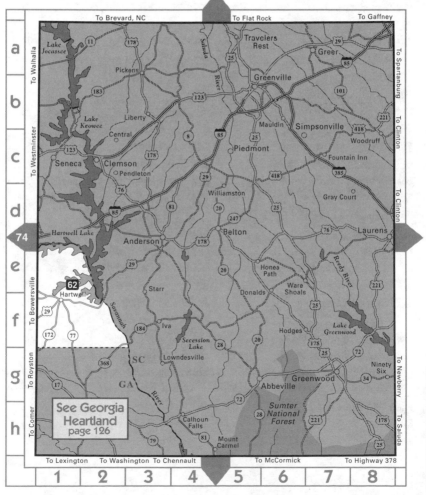

a

Lake Jocassee
11
178
Saluda River
Travelers Rest
29
Greer
85
To Spartanburg

To Walhalla

Pickens

25

Greenville

b

183
123
101
221
To Clinton

Lake Keowee
Liberty
Mauldin
Simpsonville
418
Woodruff

To Westminster

Central
8
85
25
Piedmont
Fountain Inn

c

123
178
Seneca
Clemson
Pendleton
29
418
385
To Clinton

76

Williamston

Gray Court

d

85
81
20
247
25
76
Laurens

Hartwell Lake
Anderson
178
Belton

74

e

29
20
Honea Path
Ware Shoals
Reedy River
221
To Bowersville

62
Hartwell
Starr
Donalds
25

f

29
184
Iva
Secession Lake
20
Hodges
Lake Greenwood
178
25
72

172
77
Savannah River

g

368
SC
Lowndesville
28
25
Greenwood
34
Ninety Six
To Newberry

17
GA
River
72
Abbeville

To Comer

See Georgia Heartland page 126
Calhoun Falls
28
Sumter National Forest
221
178
To Saluda

h

79
81
Mount Carmel
25

1   2   3   4   5   6   7   8

To Royston

© AVALON TRAVEL PUBLISHING, INC.

BLUE RIDGE

1 Rolling Thunder River Company

Location: Blue Ridge, map 1, grid B6.

Campsites, Facilities: The camping area consists of two one-acre areas complete with fire rings and cooking grills. A bunkhouse contains 33 beds for indoor camping. Restrooms have hot showers and flush toilets. A pavilion, horseshoes, and beach volleyball are provided. Pets are permitted.

Reservations, fees: Reservations are recommended at 800/408-7328. No deposit is required. The fee for camping is $5 per person. Bunkhouse camping costs $8 per person.

Open: The campground is generally open from April 1–October 31. The dates vary somewhat due to weather conditions.

Directions: From Atlanta, take Interstate 75 north to Interstate 575, and go north. Go north on Highway 515 from Interstate 575. At Blue Ridge, turn left onto Highway 5. Travel 10 miles to McCaysville, and turn right onto Highway 60. The campground is half a mile down on the left.

Contact: Rolling Thunder River Company, 20 Hughes Street, McCaysville, GA 30555; 706/492-5752; website www.rollingthunderriverco.com.

Trip notes: The Toccoa River changes names at the Tennessee border and becomes the Ocoee. Rolling Thunder offers canoeing and tubing on the Toccoa River, and guided raft trips on the Ocoee River. Tubes rent for $5, canoes for $30, and 3-hour raft trips cost $36-45 per person. Longer raft trips are offered on Saturdays for $85 per person. Fishing is available for trout in the Toccoa. Hiking is available within 10 miles at the Ocoee Whitewater Center and in the Cohutta Wilderness.

2 Toccoa Valley Campground

Location: Blue Ridge, map 1, grid B6.

Campsites, Facilities: There are 21 tent sites at the campground. Electric hookups are available. There are also seven RV sites, all with full hookups. Pull-through sites are available. Some sites have shade. Picnic tables and fire rings are provided. Restrooms have hot showers and flush toilets. A boat ramp is provided. Ice, wood, and bait are available at the campground. Leashed pets are permitted. You must clean up after your pet.

Reservations, fees: Reservations are accepted at 706/838-4317. The deposit of one night's fee is non-refundable. Tent sites cost $10 per night, and RV sites cost $20. Fees are for up to three people per site. Additional guests at a site cost $2 per night.

Open: The campground is generally open from April 1–October 1. The dates vary somewhat due to weather conditions.

Directions: From Atlanta, take Interstate 75 north to Interstate 575, and go north. Go north on Highway 515 from Interstate 575. At Blue Ridge, turn right onto Windy Ridge, then left onto Old Highway 76 at the three-way stop. Turn immediately right onto Aska Road. The campground is 13 miles down on the left.

Contact: Toccoa Valley Campground, 11481 Aska Road, Blue Ridge, GA 30513; 706/939-4317.

Trip notes: Fishing is available in both the Toccoa River and in Big Creek, a trout stream that cuts through the campground. Tubes and canoes can be rented at the campground. Tubes cost $6, and canoes $25, which includes the shuttle service from the take out point, six miles down the Toccoa River.

3 Lake Blue Ridge Campground

Location: Blue Ridge, map 1, grid B7.

Campsites, Facilities: There are 58 campsites for tents or small RVs. Picnic tables and cooking grills are provided. Restrooms have cold showers and flush toilets. Drinking water is available. A boat ramp is provided. Leashed pets are permitted.

Reservations, fees: Reservations are not accepted. The fee is $10 per night for waterfront sites, $8 for other sites.

Open: The campground is open from April through Labor Day weekend.

Directions: From Blue Ridge, take old US 76 east for 1.5 miles, and turn right onto Dry Branch Road. The campground is three miles from the highway.

Contact: Lake Blue Ridge Campground, Toccoa Ranger District, 990 East Main St., Suite 1, Blue Ridge, GA 30513; 706/632-3031.

Trip notes: Fishing is available for bass, bream, catfish, perch, and crappie. There is a one-mile hiking trail along the lake. Access to the Appalachian Trail is a 30-minute drive from the campground.

4 Morganton Point Campground

Location: Blue Ridge, map 1, grid B7.

Campsites, Facilities: There are 43 campsites suitable for tents or small RVs. Picnic tables and cooking rings are provided. Restrooms have hot showers and flush toilets. A boat ramp is provided. Drinking water is available. Some campsites and one restroom are wheelchair accessible. Leashed pets are permitted.

Reservations, fees: Reservations are not accepted. Campsites on the water are $10 per night, and sites off-water are $8.

Open: The campground is open from April through Labor Day weekend.

Directions: From Blue Ridge, take Highway 515 east to Highway 60 and turn right. Turn right on County Road 616, and follow the signs.

Contact: Morganton Point Campground, Toccoa Ranger District; 990 East Main St., Suite 1, Blue Ridge, GA 30513; 706/632-3031.

Trip notes: Lake Blue Ridge offers fishing for bass, bream, catfish, perch, and crappie.

5 Whispering Pines Campground

Location: Blue Ridge, map 1, grid B7.

Campsites, facilities: The nine tent sites offer water and electrical hookups. Of the 18 RV sites, 15 have full hookups, and the rest have water and electric hookups only. Pull-through sites are available. Both 30- and 50-amp service are available. Most RV sites are restricted to 32 feet, but a few sites can accommodate rigs up to 40 feet. RV storage is available. There is one rental cabin that sleeps up to five people. Picnic tables and fire rings are provided. Restrooms have hot showers and flush toilets. Ice and LP gas are available at the campground, and the nearest supply store is eight miles away. The campground provides a coin laundry, playground, swimming pool, and sanitary disposal station. Some of the facilities are wheelchair accessible. Pets are permitted in the campground, but not in the cabin. They must be kept on leash and cleaned up after.

Reservations, fees: Reservations are accepted. Of the $15 deposit, $10 is refundable if the reservation is cancelled 10 or more days before your scheduled arrival. Sites are $15 per night, $90 per week, or $270 per month for two people. There is an extra charge of $2.50 nightly, $10 weekly, or $30 monthly for each additional person. The cabin rents for $80 per night for two, plus $5 for each additional person.

Open: Year-round.

Directions: From Blairsville, take US 76 west. After entering Fannin County, the first mile marker is 17. Just after mile marker 14, turn left on Whispering Pines Road.

Contact: Whispering Pines Campground, 290 Whispering Pines Rd., Morganton, GA 30560; 706/374-6494.

Trip notes: The campground is located near Lake Blue Ridge and most sites are on Hemptown Creek. The creek offers fishing, mainly for trout and catfish. Swimming is available at Lake Blue Ridge, and there are many hiking and biking trails in the national forest areas. It is nine miles from the quaint antique shops in Blue Ridge, 30 miles from Brasstown Bald, the highest point in Georgia, and 20 miles from the Ocoee River, a popular whitewater river for rafters and kayakers.

6 Canal Lake Campground, Inc.

Location: Lake Nottely, map 1, grid A8.

Campsites, facilities: There are 10 sites suitable for tents or RVs, all with water and electric hookups. Some shade is available. Picnic tables and fire rings are provided. Restrooms have hot showers and flush toilets. A sanitary disposal station, coin laundry, and boat dock are provided. Leashed pets are permitted.

Reservations, fees: Reservations are accepted, and no deposit is required. Site fees are $20 per night.

Open: The campground is open from April through November.

Directions: From Blairsville, take US 19/129 north two miles and turn left onto Pat Coldwell Road. After one mile, turn right onto Canal Lake Road.

Contact: Canal Lake Campground, Inc., 1035 Canal Lake Rd., Blairsville, GA 30512; 706/745-1501.

Trip notes: The campground is on Lake Nottely, which is stocked with bass, crappie, bream, and catfish. It is 10 miles from the Appalachian Trail, but there is no hiking trail from here directly to the AT.

7 Camp Cherry Log

Location: Cherry Log, map 1, grid B6.

Campsites, facilities: There are 44 campsites at this campground suitable for tents or RVs. Ten of the sites have no hookups, two have water and electric only, and the remainder have full hookups. There are also two cabins and an RV available for rent. Picnic tables and fire rings are provided at some sites. RV storage is available. Restrooms have hot showers and flush toilets. A coin laundry, swimming pool, recreation room, and library are provided. Pets are permitted.

Reservations, fees: Reservations are accepted. The deposit is not refundable. The fee for tents is $10, pop-up campers cost $15, and RVs cost $20. The cabins rent for $35, and the RV for $40 per night.

Open: The campground is open from March 15 through November.

Directions: The campground is located between Blue Ridge and Ellijay off Highway 515. From Blue Ridge, go south on Highway 515. Near mile marker 18 turn left onto County Road 257. At Rock Creek Road turn left and after about a mile, turn right onto unpaved Little Rock Creek Road to the campground.

Contact: Camp Cherry Log,

P.O. Box 147, Cherry Log, GA 30522; 706/635-5006.

Trip notes: Although tent camping is permitted, this is primarily an RV park. There are short walking trails at the campground. It is within 30 minutes of Blue Ridge Lake and Carters Lake, both of which offer fishing and additional hiking trails.

8 Diamond Lure Campground

Location: Ellijay, map 1, grid C6.

Campsites, Facilities: Tents can be set up on any of the 75 RV sites if vacant. About half of the sites have full hookups. Pull-through sites and shade are available. Picnic tables and fire rings are provided. Restrooms have hot showers and flush toilets. Ice is available at the campground. A coin laundry and clubhouse are provided. Leashed pets are permitted.

Reservations, fees: Reservations are accepted at 706/273-3075. Deposits are not required. The site charge for tents is $10, pop-ups $12, and RVs $15–18, depending on length. An additional $2 each is charged for more than two guests per site.

Open: The campground allows overnighters only from April 1–December 31. Long-term guests stay year-round.

Directions: From Atlanta, take Interstate 75 north to Interstate 575, and go north. Go north on Highway 5/515 from Interstate 575. At Ellijay, turn right at onto Highway 52 east. Nine miles past Ellijay, turn right onto Clear Creek Road. Turn left onto Diamond Lure Road, 1000 feet from the highway.

Contact: Diamond Lure Campground, 514 Diamond Lure Road, Ellijay, GA 30540; 706/273-3076.

Trip notes: The small lake at the campground is stocked with bass, bream, and bluegill. There is a swimming area in the lake as well.

The campground is about 12 miles from Amicalola State Park. About half of the guests here are overnighters, with the rest staying for a season or longer.

9 Deep Hole

Location: Dahlonega, map 1, grid C7.

Campsites, facilities: There are eight tent sites. Picnic tables, fire rings, and cooking grills are provided. Vault toilets and piped water are provided. Leashed pets are permitted.

Reservations, fees: Reservations are not accepted. The fee is $10 per night for waterfront sites, $8 for other sites.

Open: Year-round.

Directions: From Dahlonega, take US 19 north to Stone Pile Gap and go north onto Highway 60. Watch for the Forest Service sign for Deep Hole. An unmarked Forest Service road goes to the campground.

Contact: Deep Hole, Dockery Lake, Brasstown Bald Ranger District, 400 Walmart Way, Dahlonega, GA 30533; 706/864-6173.

Trip notes: The campground provides access to the Mill Shoals Trail, the Yellow Mountain Trail, and the Eyes on the Wildlife Trail. Wildlife is plentiful in the area. I have seen deer, bears, and skunks near this campground. The forest service campgrounds are no-frills, but if you enjoy getting away from it all and immersing yourself in the woods and mountains, this campground is hard to beat.

10 Mulky Campground

Location: Dahlonega, map 1, grid C7.

Campsites, facilities: There are 11 tent sites at this campground. Picnic tables, fire rings, and cooking grills are provided. Vault toilets are provided. Leashed pets are permitted.

Reservations, fees: No reservations are accepted. The fee is $10 per night for waterfront sites, $8 for other sites.

Open: The campground is open from March through October.

Directions: From Dahlonega, take US 19 north to Stone Pile Gap and turn onto Highway 60. After 17.7 miles, turn onto Forest Service Road 4 at the sign for Coopers Creek. The campground is 4.9 miles from the highway.

Contact: Mulky Campground, Dockery Lake, Brasstown Bald Ranger District, 400 Walmart Way, Dahlonega, GA 30533; 706/864-6173.

Trip notes: The campground provides access to the Mill Shoals Trail, the Yellow Mountain Trail, and the Eyes on the Wildlife Trail. Wildlife is plentiful in the area. I have seen deer, bears, and skunks near this campground. The Forest Service campgrounds are no-frills, but if you enjoy getting away from it all and immersing yourself in the woods and mountains, they are hard to beat.

11 Coopers Creek

Location: Dahlonega, map 1, grid C7.

Campsites, facilities: There are 17 campsites for tents or small campers. Picnic tables, fire rings, and cooking grills are provided. Vault toilets and piped water are provided. Leashed pets are permitted.

Reservations, fees: No reservations are accepted. The fee is $8 for sites away from the water, $10 for creekside sites.

Open: The campground is open from April through October.

Directions: From Dahlonega, take US 19 north to Stone Pile Gap and turn onto Highway 60. After 17.7 miles, turn onto Forest Service Road 4 at the sign for Coopers Creek. Pass the Mulky Campground after 4.9 miles and continue 0.8 miles to Coopers Creek.

Contact: Coopers Creek, Dockery Lake, Brasstown Bald Ranger District, 400 Walmart Way, Dahlonega, GA 30533; 706/864-6173.

Trip notes: Trout fishing is available in the creek. The campground provides access to the Mill Shoals Trail, the Yellow Mountain Trail, and the Eyes on the Wildlife Trail. Wildlife is plentiful in the area. I have seen deer, bears, and skunks in and near this campground. My first camping experiences in Georgia were at Coopers Creek, and it remains one of my favorite campgrounds.

12 Frank Gross Campground

Location: Dahlonega, map 1, grid C7.

Campsites, facilities: There are nine tent sites at this campground. Picnic tables, fire rings, and cooking grills are provided. Vault toilets are provided. There is no drinking water. Leashed pets are permitted.

Reservations, fees: No reservations are accepted. Campsites are $10 per night for waterfront sites, $8 for other sites.

Open: The campground is open from March through October.

Directions: From Dahlonega, take US 19 north to Stone Pile Gap and turn onto Highway 60. After 17.7 miles, turn left onto Forest Service Road 69. Go past the fish hatchery to the campground.

Contact: Frank Gross Campground, Dockery Lake, Brasstown Bald Ranger District, 400 Walmart Way, Dahlonega, GA 30533; 706/864-6173.

Trip notes: The campground is on Rock Creek, which offers fishing for trout. There are miles of hiking trails leading from the campground. Wildlife is plentiful in the area. I have seen deer, bears, and skunks near this campground. This Forest

Service campground offers no frills, but if you enjoy getting away from it all and immersing yourself in the woods and mountains, it's hard to beat.

13 Amicalola Falls State Park

Location: Dawsonville, map 1, grid D6.

Campsites, facilities: There are 20 campsites at the campground, all with full hookups and shade. Two are pull-through sites. Trailers over 17 feet in length are prohibited. There are also 14 cabins and one primitive campsite. Fire rings are provided. Restrooms have hot showers and flush toilets. A coin laundry, cable TV, and playground are provided. Ice, firewood and some gifts are available at the campground store. The buildings are wheelchair accessible. Leashed pets are permitted in the campground, but not in the cabins.

Reservations, fees: Reservations are accepted at 800/864-7275. Within the Atlanta area, call 770/389-7275. The deposit of the first nights' fee is not refundable, but your reservation date can be moved once. The rate is $13 for tents, $15 for RVs, and $25 for pioneer camping. Like all of Georgia's state parks, there is a $2 per day parking fee, or you can purchase an annual Georgia Park-Pass for $25. Campers pay for just one daily pass for their entire stay.

Open: Year-round.

Directions: From Dahlonega, take Highway 52 west to the park and follow the signs.

Contact: Amicalola Falls State Park, 418 Amicalola Falls Lodge Rd., Dawsonville, GA 30534; 706/265-8888.

Trip notes: Amicalola Falls, at 729 feet, is the highest waterfall east of the Mississippi River. It is beautiful at any time of year and spectacular in late spring or after a rain. It's also worth a visit in the winter when it ices over. The trail to the falls is paved and,

though steep, can be navigated by most. Wildlife in the area includes deer, black bears, bobcats, snakes, and raccoons. The park is near the entrance to the Appalachian Trail. It is centrally located for many of the attractions in north Georgia, including the Dahlonega Gold Museum (20 miles), the Bill Elliott Museum (10 miles), and the huge North Georgia Premium Outlet Mall (25 miles).

14 Nimblewill Creek Campground

Location: Dahlonega, map 1, grid D8.

Campsites, Facilities: Wilderness camping is available anywhere off the road where not posted. No drinking water or facilities are available. Leashed pets are permitted.

Reservations, fees: Reservations are not accepted. Camping is free, but the $2 day-use fee applies.

Open: The campground is available from April through October.

Contact: Nimblewill Creek Campground, Dockery Lake Forest Service, 400 Walmart Way, Dahlonega, GA 30533; 706/864-6173.

Directions: From Dahlonega, take Highway 52 west. Continue 2.8 miles past the Etowah River, and turn right onto Nimblewill Church Road. Continue straight onto Forest Service Road 83 when Nimblewill Church Road forks off to the left. The camping area is 4.6 miles from Highway 52. There are no developed campsites, but camping is allowed anywhere not posted otherwise. The pavement ends at the signs for the campground, and the road is not maintained for passenger cars.

Trip notes: Trout fishing is available. Hiking is available throughout the area, including at nearby Amicalola State Park. Wildlife includes deer, bears, and skunks. This forest service campground is strictly no-frills, but if you enjoy getting away from it all and immersing yourself in the woods and mountains, this one is hard to beat. The falls are quite pretty, and provide a natural water slide.

15 Mitchell's Campground

Location: Lake Lanier, map 1, grid F8.
Campsites, facilities: There are 30 RV sites with full hookups. RVs must be 36 feet or less in length. Picnic tables are provided. Restrooms have hot showers and flush toilets. A coin laundry is provided. The facilities are wheelchair accessible.
Reservations, fees: Reservations are not accepted. The minimum stay is one week for $25.
Open: Year-round.
Directions: From Atlanta, take Highway 400 north to Highway 369, and turn north. After one mile, turn right on Shady Grove Road.
Contact: Mitchell's Campground, 5620 Shady Grove Rd., Cumming, GA 30041; 770/887-8906.
Trip notes: The campground is one mile from Lake Lanier.

16 Shady Grove Campground

Location: Lake Lanier, map 2, grid G8.
Campsites, facilities: There are 115 campsites suitable for tents or RVs. Half the sites have water and electric hookups; the rest have none. There are also eight walk-in sites. Picnic tables, fire rings, and cooking grills are provided. Restrooms have hot showers and flush toilets. A coin laundry, boat ramp, and playground are provided. Pets are permitted.
Reservations, fees: Reservations are

accepted through the National Recreation Reservation Service (NRRS) at 877/444-6777; www.reserveusa.com. The full amount is payable in advance. Walk-in sites are $12, sites with no hookups are $14, and sites with water and electric hookups are $20.
Open: The campground is open from April through mid-September.
Directions: Take Highway 400 north to exit 17/Highway 306, and turn right. Turn right onto Highway 369. After 1.25 miles, turn right on Shady Grove Road. Turn left into the park at the dead end.
Contact: Shady Grove Campground, P.O. Box 567, 1050 Buford Dam Rd., Buford, GA 30515; 770/887-2067 or 770/945-9531.
Trip notes: Bass, crappie, and catfish are available in the lake. There are no marked trails in the area, but you can hike and mountain bike throughout the area. There is a sand beach in the swimming area. No alcohol is allowed in the park.

17 Bald Mountain Park

Location: Hiawassee, map 2, grid A2.
Campsites, facilities: There are 350 campsites. Of these, one third have water and electric hookups and can be used for either tents or RVs. The others have full hookups, including cable TV, and are reserved for RVs. Picnic tables are provided. There are two cabins. RV storage is available. Restrooms have hot showers and flush toilets. A coin laundry, sanitary disposal station, swimming pool, playground, miniature golf, and clubroom are provided. The restrooms, some sites, and the clubroom are wheelchair accessible. Leashed pets are permitted.
Reservations, fees: Reservations are accepted and

held with a credit card. There is a $20 non-refundable deposit. Sites with water and electric hookups are $17, and sites with full hookups are $21.

Open: The campground is open from April through October.

Directions: Take Highway 17/75 north through Helen, up and over Unicoi Gap. Turn left onto US 76, then left onto Highway 288 and follow the signs.

Contact: Bald Mountain Park, 3540 Fodder Creek Rd., Hiawassee, GA 30546; 706/896-2274.

Trip notes: The campground has a 3-acre lake stocked with catfish, bream, bass, and trout. Fodder Creek also runs through the property, and contains trout. Bring your own pan to try for gold in the creek, or you can go to one of the commercial establishments in Helen or Dahlonega and use their equipment. Paddleboats are permitted in the lake. Hiking is available both in the Chattahoochee National Forest and on the Appalachian Trail. White water rafting is available nearby on the Chattooga River, and tubing is available in Helen. The campground is 23 miles from Helen and Clayton, and 20 miles from Blairsville.

18 Lake Chatuge Campground

Location: Hiawassee, map 2, grid A2.

Campsites, Facilities: There are 30 campsites for tents or small campers. Picnic tables and cooking grills are provided. Restrooms have vault toilets and cold showers. A boat ramp is provided. Leashed pets are permitted.

Reservations, fees: No reservations are accepted. The fee is $8 for all sites.

Open: The campground is open from late April through late October.

Directions: From Hiawassee, take US 76 northwest two miles, and turn left on Highway 288. The campground is about a mile from US 76 on the left.

Contact: Lake Chatuge Campground, Chattahoochee-Oconee National Forest, 1755 Cleveland Highway, Gainesville, GA 30501; 706/745-6928.

Trip notes: The lake offers fishing for bass, bream, and catfish. There is a short hiking trail by the lake. The town of Hiawassee hosts several mountain festivals and fairs, especially in the fall.

19 Georgia Mountain Campground

Location: Hiawassee, map 2, grid A2.

Campsites, facilities: There are 92 tent sites and 189 RV sites in separate sections. There are 96 RV sites with full hookups, two of which are pull-through sites. About one-third of the campsites have some shade. Picnic tables are provided, and group sites are available. Restrooms have hot showers and flush toilets. Tennis courts, a boat ramp, playground, and cable TV hookups are available. A sanitary disposal station is provided. Ice is available, and additional supplies are one-half mile away. Leashed pets are permitted.

Reservations, fees: Reservations are accepted. A deposit is required, but it's refundable if you cancel at least 48 hours before your scheduled arrival, less one day's charge. Tent sites are $13 per night, and RV sites are $15–22, depending on hookups.

Open: Year-round.

Directions: From Hiawassee, take US 76 west for one mile. The campground will be on the right.

Contact: Georgia Mountain Campground, P.O. Box 444, Hiawassee, GA 30546; 706/896-

4191; email: gamtfair@alltel.net; website: www.georgia-mountain-fair.com.

Trip notes: The campground is within walking distance of the Georgia Mountain Fair, which is held each August, and the Music Hall, which hosts country music concerts and festivals throughout the year. Most campsites are on Lake Chatuge, and boating, fishing for bass and bream, water skiing, and other lake activities are popular. Hiking, kayaking, and rafting are available nearby. Wildlife in the area includes deer and black bears.

20 Longridge Campground

Location: Hiawassee, map 2, grid A2.

Campsites, facilities: There are 15 RV sites with full hookups, and a large area for primitive camping. Some sites have picnic tables. RV storage is available. Restrooms have hot showers and flush toilets. Bait is available at the campground. Leashed pets are permitted.

Reservations, fees: Reservations are accepted. The deposit is refundable with a two-week notice. All sites are $20 per night.

Open: Year-round.

Directions: From Blairsville, take US 76 east to Highway 288 and turn right. After 2.5 miles, turn right onto Longridge Road.

Contact: Longridge Campground, 1390 Longridge Rd., Hiawassee, GA 30546; 706/896-3453.

Trip notes: The campground has a catch-and-release pond stocked with bass, catfish, bream, trout, and crappie. It is 10 miles from Unicoi State Park, and the Appalachian Trail. Hiawassee is the home of the Georgia Mountain Fair, which is held in August. Although primitive tent camping is permitted, this is primarily an RV park.

21 Black Rock Mountain State Park

Location: Clayton, map 2, grid A5.

Campsites, facilities: There are 48 tent or RV sites, most with shade, and all with water, electric, and cable TV hookups. RVs may be a maximum of 40 feet in length. There are also 12 walk-in sites and 10 cabins. Each site has a picnic table, fire ring, and cooking grill. Restrooms have hot showers and flush toilets. In addition, backpackers can hike to one of four group backcountry sites that have fire rings and no other facilities. Each of these sites requires a moderate (0.9- to 4-mile) hike over moderate-to-difficult terrain. The trading post sells ice, firewood, snacks, and gifts. A coin laundry, playground, and sanitary disposal station are in the campground. The buildings are wheelchair accessible. Pets are permitted in the campground but are prohibited from the cabin area. Pets must be on a six-foot maximum length leash.

Reservations, fees: Reservations are a must; call 800/864-7275, or from the Atlanta area, call 770/389-7275. This popular park fills up early in the year, especially for holiday weekends. The deposit is non-refundable, but the date can be moved once. Walk-in tent sites have no hookups and are $10 per night. Tent sites with hookups are $15 per night. The fee for RVs and campers is $17 per night. The cabins are $70–115 per night, depending on number of bedrooms and the view. Like all of Georgia's state parks, there is a $2 per day parking fee, or you can purchase an annual Georgia ParkPass for $25. Campers pay for just one daily pass for their entire stay.

Open: Year-round.

Directions: The park is three miles north of Clayton on US 23/ 441.

Contact: Black Rock Mountain State Park, P.O. Drawer A, Mountain City, GA 30562; 706/746-2141.

Trip notes: This part of Georgia has wonderful hiking trails, many leading to waterfalls. From the Tennessee Rock Trail overlook, you can see Tennessee and North Carolina. There is an abundance of wildlife in the area and the campground, including black bears, ruffed grouse, chipmunks, bobcats, raccoons, songbirds, hawks, and owls. Bears are a common problem in the campground. Never take your food into your tent. While most campers lock it in their cars, a friend had her car opened like a sardine can by an industrious bear. Fishing in the area streams and rivers is popular, as they are stocked with trout, bass, bream, and catfish. The park offers spectacular views of the Blue Ridge Mountains. In the spring, wildflowers such as the pink ladyslipper orchid, rhododendron, and mountain laurel bloom in the park and along the trails. The park is about 15 miles from both the Chattooga and Ocoee Rivers, where those willing to brave the frigid water can go kayaking and rafting.

22 Lake Nottely RV Park

Location: Lake Nottely, map 2, grid B1.

Campsites, facilities: Of the 80 RV sites at this campground, 25 have full hookups, and the rest have water and electric hookups. One pull-through site is available. All but 10 have shade. RVs may be no longer than 40 feet. A coin laundry, boat ramp, and dock are provided. Ice is available at the campground. The buildings are wheelchair accessible. Leashed pets are permitted.

Reservations, fees: Reservations are accepted. The fee is $18 per night.

Open: The campground is open from April through November.

Directions: The campground is 2.2 miles west of Blairsville off Kiutuestia Creek Road.

Contact: Lake Nottely RV Park, 350 Haley Circle, Blairsville, GA 30512; 706/745-4523, fax 706/745-8806.

Trip notes: With Brasstown Bald and the Appalachian Trail nearby, there are plenty of hiking trails in the area. Fishing is available on the lake.

23 Mountain Oak Cabins and Campground

Location: Tifton, map 2, grid B1.

Campsites, Facilities: The campground has a total of 47 campsites suitable for tents or RVs. Eighteen of the sites have water and electric hookups, and the rest have full hookups. Both 30- and 50-amp hookups are available. Cable TV hookups are provided. The sites with full hookups have picnic tables, and some grills are available. There are also five cabins. Restrooms have hot showers and flush toilets. A coin laundry, playground, volleyball court, basketball court, horseshoes area, and pavilion are provided. Wood is available. There are two supply stores within half a mile of the campground. Pets are permitted in the campground, but not in the cabins.

Reservations, fees: Reservations are accepted at 888/781-6867, and are held with a credit card. Sites with power and water hookups are $14, full hookup sites with 30-amp service are $17, and those with 50-amp service are $20 per night. The cabins rent for $79–99 per night.

Open: Year-round.

Directions: From Atlanta, take Interstate 75 north to Interstate 575, and turn north. Continue onto Highway 515 about 36 miles after

Interstate 575 ends. Turn right on Kiutuestia Creek Road. After 1.3 miles, turn right on Blue Ridge Highway. Follow Blue Ridge Highway when it turns to the left, then turn right on Mulkey Gap Road. The campground is about a mile down on the left, and is approximately two miles from Highway 515.

Contact: Mountain Oaks Cabin and Campground, 2388 Mulkey Gap Road, Blairsville, GA 30512; 706/781-6867.

Trip notes: The campground is two miles from Lake Nottley, and about five miles from the trout fishing and hiking in the Coopers Creek area. They are 13 miles from the Blood Mountain approach to the Appalachian Trail. Horseback riding stables are just three miles away, and Vogel State Park is about 10 miles from the campground.

24 Nottely River Campground, Cabins, and Tubing

Location: Blairsville, map 2, grid B1.

Campsites, Facilities: There are 46 sites suitable for either tents or RVs, all with water and electricity. All sites have shade. Six have full hookups. RVs are restricted to 32 feet or less. There are also three cabins, two fully furnished and one more rustic. Group sites are available. Picnic tables and fire rings are provided. Restrooms have hot showers and flush toilets. Ice and firewood are available, with the nearest supply store less than two miles away. A sanitary disposal station and a recreation field are provided. Pets are permitted in the campground but not in the cabins.

Reservations, fees: Reservations are accepted. Campsites are $16–20 per night, and cabins are $50–80.

Open: April through November.

Directions: The campground is 4.5 miles south of Blairsville on US 19/129.

Contact: Nottely River Campground, Cabins, and Tubing, 3695 Nottely River Campground Rd., Blairsville, GA 30512; 706/745-6711.

Trip notes: Fishing, tubing, kayaking, rafting, swimming, and canoeing are available on the Nottely River, which flows by the campground. Tubes are available for rent. The campground is in a beautiful wooded area and is a convenient place to camp for trips to Blairsville, Helen, Dahlonega, and Vogel State Park. Wildflowers bloom abundantly in the spring and summer, and wildlife is plentiful all year.

25 Cedar Mountain Campground

Location: Blairsville, map 2, grid B1.

Campsites, facilities: There are 70 campsites, 22 of which have full hookups and are reserved for RVs. The rest have water and electric hookups and can be used by tents or RVs. Picnic tables are provided. Restrooms have hot showers and flush toilets. Leashed pets are permitted.

Reservations, fees: Reservations are accepted. The deposit is refundable with cancellation at least 24 hours in advance of your scheduled arrival. Sites are $12 per night for tents and popup campers, $18 for RVs.

Open: The campground is open from April through October.

Directions: From Blairsville, go eight miles south on US 129, and follow the signs.

Contact: Cedar Mountain Campground, 6550 Cedar Mountain Trout Farm Rd., Blairsville, GA 30512; 706/745-5853.

Trip notes: Fishing is available in the two trout ponds at the campground. It is six miles from the Appalachian Trail.

26 Trackrock Campground and Cabins

Location: Blairsville, map 2, grid B2.

Campsites, facilities: The campground has 22 tent sites and 90 RV sites. Sixty-seven of the RV sites have full hookups. RVs must be less than 35 feet in length. Group sites are available, as are five cabins. RV storage is available. Restrooms have hot showers and flush toilets. A coin laundry, playground, pavilion, and sanitary disposal station are provided, as are picnic tables and fire rings. Ice, LP gas, and firewood are available at the campground store. Leashed pets are permitted in the campground, but not in the cabins.

Reservations, fees: Reservations are accepted, and a deposit of half of the full fee is required. Refunds are only given if you cancel at least 30 days in advance of your arrival. Fees are $16 for sites with water and electric hookups, $18 for full hookups. The seventh night is free when you stay for a week. Use of air conditioners and electric heaters costs $1 extra per day. Monthly rates are $240–280. The cabins are $89–99 per night, depending on whether or not you're on the lake.

Open: Year-round.

Directions: From Blairsville, take Highway 515/US 76 east about four miles, turn right on Trackrock Gap Road, and follow the signs.

Contact: Trackrock Campground and Cabins, 4887 Trackrock Camp Rd., Blairsville, GA 30512; 706/745-2420, fax 706/745-0741; email: trackrock@alltel.net; website: www.trackrock.com.

Trip notes: Fishing for catfish, bass, and bream is available year-round at the lake, and there is a sand beach at the swimming area. The campground is worth a visit just to see the prehistoric petroglyphs. It is 45 minutes from both Helen and Dahlonega, and near to rafting, tubing, and quaint shopping.

27 Moccasin Creek State Park

Location: Lake Burton, map 2, grid B4.

Campsites, facilities: There are 54 sites suitable for either tents or RVs. All have shade, and all have water and electric hookups. Of these, 15 are pull-through sites. All have picnic tables, fire rings, and cooking grills. The two restrooms have hot showers and flush toilets. Ice, firewood, and gifts are available at the camp store. A boat ramp, coin laundry, playground, and sanitary disposal station are provided. The buildings are wheelchair accessible. Leashed pets are permitted. The leash may be a maximum of six feet in length.

Reservations, fees: Reservations are accepted at 800/864-7275. Within the Atlanta area, call 770/389-7275. The deposit is nonrefundable, but the date can be moved once. From March through November, regular sites are $16 for tents or $18 for campers, and waterview premium sites are $18 for tents or $20 for campers. From December through February, rates for regular sites are $12 for tents or $14 for RVs, and waterview premium sites cost $14 for tents and $16 for campers.

Open: Year-round.

Directions: The park is located on Lake Burton. From US 76/Highway 2, take Highway 197 south three miles. The campground will be on the right.

Contact: Moccasin Creek State Park, Rt. 1, Box 1634, Clarkesville, GA 30523; 706/947-3194.

Trip notes: This beautiful park is 25 miles from Tallulah Gorge and the Chattooga River, a popular rafting/canoeing/kayaking spot, and 20 miles from Black Rock Mountain State Park and the Alpine town of Helen. Lake Burton offers abundant fishing for bass, catfish, bluegill, and crappie. The Nature Trail is 1.25 miles long, and the Hemlock Falls Trail is five miles long. Burton Beach offers a sand beach in the swimming area. Wildflowers bloom in the spring.

28 Tate Branch Campground

Location: Clayton, map 2, grid B4.
Campsites, facilities: There are 19 campsites suitable for tents or small RVs. Picnic tables and cooking grills are provided. Restrooms have vault toilets. Drinking water is available. Leashed pets are permitted.
Reservations, fees: Reservations are not accepted. The fee is $12 per night.
Open: Year-round.
Directions: From Clayton, take US 76 west for eight miles, turn right at the Forest Service sign, and follow the signs.
Contact: Tate Branch Campground, Tallulah Ranger District, P.O. Box 438, Clayton, GA 30525; 706/782-3320.
Trip notes: The river offers good trout fishing. There is a one-mile marked trail along the river, and numerous unmarked trails through the area.

29 Sandy Bottom Campground

Location: Clayton, map 2, grid B4.
Campsites, facilities: There are 12 campsites suitable for tents or small RVs. Picnic tables, fire rings, and cooking grills are provided. Restrooms have vault toilets. Leashed pets are permitted.
Reservations, fees: Reservations are not accepted. The fee is $10 per night.

Open: The campground is open from late March through October.
Directions: From Clayton, take US 76 west eight miles, turn right at the Forest Service sign, and follow the signs.
Contact: Sandy Bottom Campground, Tallulah Ranger District, P.O. Box 438, Clayton, GA 30525; 706/782-3320.
Trip notes: The Tallulah River offers good trout fishing. The Coleman River Trail follows along the river for about a mile, and numerous other unmarked trails wind through the area.

30 Tallulah River Campground

Location: Clayton, map 2, grid B4.
Campsites, facilities: There are 17 campsites at this campground, all suitable for either tents or small RVs. Picnic tables and cooking grills are provided. The restroom has vault toilets and no showers. Drinking water is available. The restroom is wheelchair accessible. Leashed pets are permitted.
Reservations, fees: Reservations are not accepted. The fee is $12 per night.
Open: The campground is open from late March through October.
Directions: From Clayton, take US 76 west for eight miles, and follow the signs.
Contact: Tallulah River Campground, Tallulah Ranger District, P.O. Box 438, Clayton, GA 30525; 706/782-3320.
Trip notes: Trout fishing is available in the river. There are several hiking trails through the area, including the one-mile long Coleman River Trail.

31 Willis Knob Campground

Location: Clayton, map 2, grid B6.
Campsites, Facilities: The

campground has a total of eight sites suitable for tents or RVs in two group areas. Individual sites may be rented during the week, but group camping only is permitted on the weekends. Vault toilets and drinking water are provided. Bring rope to secure your horse. Leashed pets are permitted.

Reservations, fees: Reservations are required at 706/782-3320. The deposit of one night's fee is required to hold a reservation, with the full fee payable at least two weeks in advance. The campsites are divided into two group sites, with three campsites in one and five in the other. You must rent a group site on the weekends. Individual sites may be rented on Sunday through Thursday nights. The smaller group site is $36 per night, and the larger is $60. Individual sites may be rented for $12 per night.

Open: Year-round.

Directions: From Gainesville, take US 23/441 north to Clayton, and turn right onto Rickman Road. Turn right on Warwoman Road, then right on Willis Knob Road. The horse camp is two miles down on the left.

Contact: Willis Knob Campground, US Forest Service, 809 Highway 441 South, Clayton, GA 30525; 706/782-3320; website www.fs.fed.us/conf/rec/rogs/camping/wlsnb cmp.htm.

Trip notes: This is a horse camp, and is not recommended for fishing or hiking. The 17-mile horse trail intersects with other trails leading into South Carolina. Although it runs along the Chattooga River, the fishing is much better in the headwaters area.

32 Vogel State Park

Location: Blairsville, map 2, grid B1.

Campsites, facilities: The campground has a total of 85 campsites which are available for either tents or RVs. Pull-through sites and shade are available. Picnic tables, fire rings, and cooking grills are provided. There are also 18 primitive sites and 35 cabins. Restrooms have hot showers and flush toilets. The camp store sells ice, firewood, and some groceries. Other amenities include a coin laundry and playground. The visitor's center, cabins, and restrooms are wheelchair accessible. Leashed pets are permitted. Pets may not be left alone at a campsite, and the leash may be a maximum of six feet.

Reservations, fees: Reservations are accepted at 800/864-7275, or in the Atlanta area, call 770/389-7275. The deposit is non-refundable, but the date can be moved once. Fees are $10 for primitive walk-in sites, $16 for tent sites with water and electric hookups, and $18 for campers and RVs. Like all of Georgia's state parks, there is a $2 per day parking fee, or you can purchase an annual Georgia ParkPass for $25. Campers pay for just one daily pass for their entire stay.

Open: Year-round.

Directions: From Highway 400, go north on US 19 at Dahlonega. Turn north on US 129 and proceed about 12 miles. Turn left on Vogel State Park Road into the park and follow the signs to the campground.

Contact: Vogel State Park, 7485 Vogel State Park Rd., Blairsville, GA 30512; 706/745-2628; email: vogel@alltel.net; website: www.ga stateparks.org/dnr/parks/park_ex/vogel.

Trip notes: Built by the Civilian Conservation Corps (CCC) in the 1930s, the park is located in a mountain cove surrounded by the Chattahoochee National Forest, and is very popular with families escaping the heat of Atlanta in the summer. Vogel is such a lovely place that many campers never leave the park during their visit. If you want to venture out for a day trip, Alpine Helen is 25 miles away, and Brasstown Bald, the highest point in Georgia, is just 15 miles. There are several hiking trails in the area, including the Appalachian Trail just three miles away from the campground, the Bear Hair Gap trail is about four miles away, and the Coosa Backcountry Trail is about 13 miles away. The lake contains an abundance of bass, bream, trout, and catfish, along with a large population of ducks. Although feeding wildlife is normally prohibited at parks, duck food can be purchased at the camp store. They are also very fond of oyster crackers and leftover bread. Bring an extra loaf on any trip here.

33 Lake Winfield Scott

Location: Dahlonega, map 2, grid B1.
Campsites, facilities: There are 33 campsites for tents or small campers. Picnic tables and cooking grills are provided. Restrooms have hot showers and flush toilets. A boat ramp is provided. No gas motors are allowed on the lake. The restrooms are wheelchair accessible. Leashed pets are permitted.
Reservations, fees: No reservations are accepted. The fee is $10 per night.
Open: The campground is open from May through October.
Directions: From Dahlonega, take US 19 north to US 129, and follow the signs. The campground is 18.3 miles from Dahlonega.
Contact: Lake Winfield Scott, Dockery Lake, Brasstown Bald Ranger District, 400 Walmart Way, Dahlonega, GA 30533; 706/864-6173.
Trip notes: The lake is stocked with game fish. There is a short trail around the lake. Several hiking trails lead from the campground to the Appalachian Trail. There is a swimming area in the lake.

34 Goose Creek Cabins and Campground

Location: Blairsville, map 2, grid B1.
Campsites, Facilities: The campground has 24 sites suitable for tents or RVs, all with water and electric hookups. All sites have good shade. Picnic tables and fire rings are provided. There are also 20 cabins. Restrooms have hot showers and flush toilets. Ice, wood, and snacks are available at the campground. A playground, lodge, and game room with billiards and videos are provided. The restrooms are wheelchair accessible. Pets are permitted in both the campground and the cabins.
Reservations, fees: Reservations are accepted at 706/745-5111. The deposit of one night's rent is refundable with seven days notice. Campsites cost $15–21 per night, and cabins cost $50–169 per night.
Open: The campground is open May 1–October 31. The cabins are open year-round.
Directions: From Atlanta, take Highway 400 north to Dahlonega and turn onto US 19 north. After approximately 25 miles, pass Vogel State Park. The campground is about half a mile north of Vogel State Park on the right, about 10 miles south of Blairsville.
Contact: Goose Creek Cabins and Campground, 7061 Highway 19/129 South, Blairsville, GA 30512; 706/745-5111.
Trip notes: Eight of the sites are on Goose Creek, which is deep enough for children to play in but not swim. There are two trout ponds at the campground, where for a fee per pound you can rent poles, bait, and have the fish cleaned and iced. The campground is near to Vogel State Park, Lake Winfield Scott, Wolf Creek, and Coopers Creek, which offer fishing, hiking, and swimming. Wildlife com-

monly seen at the campground include deer, black bear, and wild turkeys.

35 Chattahoochee River Campground

Location: Helen, map 2, grid B2.

Campsites, facilities: There are 34 campsites suitable for tents or small RVs. Picnic tables and fire rings are provided. Vault toilets are provided. Drinking water is available from a hand pump. Leashed pets are permitted.

Reservations, fees: Reservations are not accepted. Sites are $10 per night.

Open: The campground is open from late March through mid-December.

Directions: From Helen, take Highway 75 north eight miles. Turn left just past mile marker 15 onto Chattahoochee River Road, and follow it for five miles to the campground.

Contact: Chattahoochee River Campground, Chattooga Ranger District, P.O. Box 1960, Clarkesville, GA 30523; 706/754-6221.

Trip notes: This campground is mainly used for fishing trips. There is hiking nearby, but a better choice would be Andrews Cove. A large rig or heavy vehicle would have a difficult time negotiating the roads leading up and through this campground. It is near Helen and its attractions.

36 Andrews Cove

Location: Helen, map 2, grid B3.

Campsites, Facilities: There are 10 campsites for tents or small campers. Picnic tables and cooking grills are provided. Restrooms have vault toilets. Drinking water is available by hand pump. Leashed pets are permitted.

Reservations, fees: No reservations are accepted. Sites are $10 per night.

Open: The campground is open from May through mid-November.

Directions: From Helen, go north on Highway 75 for approximately 5.5 miles. Watch for signs to the campground.

Contact: Andrews Cove, Chattahoochee-Oconee National Forest, 1755 Cleveland Highway, Gainesville, GA 30501; 706/754-6221.

Trip notes: This campground is one of my favorites. Fishing for trout is available in Andrews Creek, and the two-mile one-way Andrews Cove Trail provides access to the Appalachian Trail. The campground is six miles from the High Shoals Scenic Area.

37 Rabun Beach Campground

Location: Clayton, map 2, grid B5.

Campsites, facilities: There are 80 campsites suitable for tents or small RVs, 20 with water and electric hookups. Picnic tables, fire rings, and cooking grills are provided. Restrooms have hot showers and flush toilets. A boat ramp is provided. Leashed pets are permitted.

Reservations, fees: Reservations are not required. Campsites without hookups are $12 per night, and sites with water and electric are $18.

Open: The campground is open from mid-May through mid-November.

Directions: From Clayton, take US 441/23 south for seven miles, turn right at the Forest Service sign, and follow the signs.

Contact: Rabun Beach Campground, Tallulah Ranger District, P.O. Box 438, Clayton, GA 30525; 706/782-3320.

Trip notes: Fishing for bass, bream, perch, trout, and catfish is available in the lake. The 1.3-mile Rabun Beach Trail leads to a waterfall. There is a sand beach in the swimming area.

Tallulah Gorge State Park

Location: Tallulah Falls, map 2, grid C6.

Campsites, Facilities: There are 50 campsites suitable for tents or RVs, all with water and electric hookups. Pull-through sites are available. Picnic tables and fire rings are provided. Primitive camping is available. Restrooms have hot showers and flush toilets. Ice is available at the campground. A sanitary disposal station, tennis courts, and boat ramp are available. The facilities are wheelchair accessible. Leashed pets are permitted.

Reservations, fees: Reservations are accepted at 800/864-7275 or 706/754-7979; within the Atlanta area, call 770/389-7275. The deposit of one night's fee is non-refundable, but your reservation can be moved once to another date. Site fees are $12–14. Like all of Georgia's state parks, there is a $2 per day parking fee, or you can purchase an annual Georgia ParkPass for $25. Campers pay for just one daily pass for their entire stay.

Open: Year-round.

Directions: From Tallulah Falls, go north on US 441 to the park and campground.

Contact: Tallulah Gorge State Park, P.O. Box 248, Tallulah Falls, GA 30573; 706/754-7970.

Trip notes: Tallulah Gorge is two miles long and 1,000 feet deep; it's an impressive site at any time of year. Fishing is available in the lake and the river, and there is a sand beach in the swimming area. Whitewater canoeing and kayaking are dependent on planned extra releases of water, which take place only on the first two weekends of April, the first three weekends of November, and certain other days in the fall that vary each year. There are 20 miles of hiking and biking trails in the gorge, including the handicapped access trail that is part of the Rails-to-Trails Project.

DeSoto Falls

Location: Dahlonega, map 2, grid C1.

Campsites, facilities: There are 24 campsites for tents or small campers. Picnic tables, fire rings, and cooking grills are provided. Restrooms have hot showers and flush toilets. The restrooms are wheelchair accessible. Leashed pets are permitted.

Reservations, fees: Reservations are not accepted. The fee is $8 per night.

Open: The campground is open from May through October.

Directions: From Dahlonega, take US 19 north to Turners Corner, and bear left onto US 19/129. The campground is 16.2 miles from Dahlonega on the left side.

Contact: DeSoto Falls, Dockery Lake, Brasstown Bald Ranger District, 400 Walmart Way, Dahlonega, GA 30533; 706/864-6173.

Trip notes: Trout fishing is available along Frogtown Creek. Two trails lead from the campground to the two falls, totaling about two miles round trip. Bears are frequently seen in this campground. Use the bear-proof trash cans provided. This Forest Service campground has more amenities than most, and still provides an intimate woods and mountain experience.

Boggs Creek

Location: Dahlonega, map 2, grid C1.

Campsites, facilities: There are 12 campsites for tents or small campers. Vault toilets are provided. Leashed pets are permitted.

Reservations, fees: No reservations are accepted. The fee is $6 per night.

Open: Year-round.

Directions: From Dahlonega, take US 19 north. Turn left at Turners Corner and stay on US 19/129 to the sign for the campground. It is 13.5 miles from Dahlonega.

Contact: Boggs Creek, Dockery Lake, Brasstown Bald Ranger District, 400 Walmart Way, Dahlonega, GA 30533; 706/864-6173.

Trip notes: Fishing for trout is available in Boggs Creek. There are hiking trails in the area.

41 Dockery Lake

Location: Dahlonega, map 2, grid C1.

Campsites, facilities: There are 11 campsites for tents or small campers. Picnic tables, fire rings, and cooking grills are provided. Wilderness camping is available anywhere off the hiking trails as well. Vault toilets and piped water are provided for the developed sites. The fishing deck is wheelchair accessible. Leashed pets are permitted.

Reservations, fees: No reservations are accepted. The fee is $8 per night.

Open: The campground is open from mid-April through October.

Directions: From Dahlonega, take US 19 north, and bear left at Stone Pile Gap onto Highway 60. After about 20 miles, turn right onto Forest Service Road 654 and follow the signs about one mile from the highway.

Contact: Dockery Lake, Dockery Lake Forest Service, 400 Walmart Way, Dahlonega, GA 30533; 706/864-6173.

Trip notes: Fishing is available for trout in the 3-acre lake. There is a 0.5-mile hiking trail

around the lake, and a six-mile round-trip trail up to Millers Gap on the Appalachian Trail.

42 Dicks Creek Campground

Location: Dahlonega, map 2, grid C1.

Campsites, Facilities: There are 4 tent sites with pads, and wilderness camping is available anywhere off the hiking trail as well. No drinking water is available. Vault toilets are provided in the campground. Leashed pets are permitted.

Reservations, fees: Reservations are not accepted. Camping is free, but the $2 day-use fee applies.

Open: The campground is available from April through October.

Contact: Dicks Creek Campground, Dockery Lake Forest Service, 400 Walmart Way, Dahlonega, GA 30533; 706/864-6173.

Directions: From Dahlonega, take US 19 north for 11.7 miles and turn left onto Forest Service Road 34 at the sign for Waters and Dick Creeks. Go past the Waters Creek Campground. The pavement ends 2.1 miles from US 19, and the gravel road is not maintained for passenger cars. Don't attempt this campground if your car has low clearance, or after heavy rains. At 2.3 miles, you'll have to ford the creek to continue. The pit toilets and sites with tent pads are on the right after fording the creek. The creek varies in depth depending on rainfall, but is generally about two to three inches during the season.

Trip notes: Trout fishing is available. Hiking is available throughout the national forest, including spur trails up to the Appalachian Trail. Wildlife is plentiful, including deer, bears, and skunks. This forest service campground is strictly no-frills, but if you enjoy getting away from it all and immersing yourself in the woods and mountains, this one is hard to beat. The low falls are quite pretty, and provide a natural water slide. The Forest Service does not recommend playing in or around the falls, however, as several people have been killed or severely injured.

43 Waters Creek

Location: Dahlonega, map 2, grid C1.
Campsites, facilities: There are eight campsites suitable for tents or small campers. Picnic tables, fire rings, and cooking grills are provided. Wilderness camping is available anywhere off the hiking trail as well. No drinking water is available. Vault toilets are provided in the campground. Leashed pets are permitted.
Reservations, fees: No reservations are accepted. The fee is $6 per night.
Open: The campground is available from April through October.
Directions: From Dahlonega, take US 19 north for 11.7 miles and turn left onto Forest Service Road 34. The campground is about 1.5 miles from the highway.
Contact: Waters Creek, Dockery Lake Brasstown Bald Ranger District, 400 Walmart Way, Dahlonega, GA 30533; 706/864-6173.
Trip notes: Trout fishing is available. The five-mile one-way trail from the campground is a spur trail up to Neels Gap on the Appalachian Trail. Wildlife is plentiful in the area. Wildlife sightings near the campground include deer, bears, and skunks. This Forest Service campground is strictly no-frills, but if you enjoy getting away from it all and immersing yourself in the woods and mountains, this one is hard to beat.

44 Turner Campsites

Location: Cleveland, map 2, grid C1.
Campsites, facilities: The campground has 130 RV sites, 123 with full hookups and all but 10 with shade. Pull-through sites and RV storage are available. Picnic tables are provided, and half the sites have fire rings. Restrooms have hot showers and flush toilets. Ice, groceries, firewood, and LP gas are available at the campground. The nearest supply store is 10 miles away. A coin laundry and playground are on the premises, and cable TV hookups are available. While the campground states that pets are permitted, they may not be walked in the campground.
Reservations, fees: Reservations are accepted. The deposit of one night's fee is refundable with a 10-day cancellation notice. Daily site fees are $18–22. Weekly rates are available, with the seventh night free.
Open: The campground is open year-round, but the majority of the sites are closed during freezing weather.
Directions: From Dahlonega, go north 13 miles on US 19 to the intersection with US 129. The campsite is located at the junction of US 19 and US 129.
Contact: Turner Campsites, 142 Turner Campsite Rd., Cleveland, GA 30528; 706/865-4757.
Trip notes: The campground is centrally located to many of the communities in north Georgia. Dahlonega, with its gold museum and shops, is just 13 miles away. Cleveland, home of Babyland General Hospital, where Cabbage Patch dolls can be adopted, is 10 miles away. The Alpine village of Helen, home of a boisterous Oktoberfest celebration, is 18 miles away. Fishing for trout is available at the campground from April through October. Hiking is available nearby on

the Appalachian Trail. The campground is also just 20 miles from Anna Ruby Falls, and 25 miles from Brasstown Bald, the highest point in Georgia.

45 Jenny's Creek Family Campground

Location: Cleveland, map 2, grid C2.

Campsites, facilities: There are 20 camp-sites for tents or small campers, all with water and electric hookups, and another 25 without hookups. There are also 20 RV sites with full hookups. Picnic tables and fire rings are provided. Restrooms have hot showers and flush toilets. A coin laundry is provided. Firewood, ice, and groceries are available at the campground. Leashed pets are permitted, but you can't leave your pet unattended. You must clean up after your pet.

Reservations, fees: Reservations are accepted. Deposits are only required for holiday weekends and are refundable if the cancellation is made at least seven days in advance. Site fees are $14–18, depending on hookups. The seventh night of your trip is free.

Open: Year-round.

Directions: The campground is five miles north of Cleveland on US 129.

Contact: Jenny's Creek Family Campground, 4542 Highway 129N, Cleveland, GA 30528; 706/865-6955.

Trip notes: The campground has a 0.75-acre fishing pond stocked with bream, bass, and catfish. It is five miles from hiking trails. There is a creek along the back of the property where you can wade in to cool off, or try your luck panning for gold. The campground is five miles from Babyland General Hospital, home of Cabbage Patch dolls, and nine to Alpine Helen.

46 Cherokee Campground of White County

Location: Helen, map 2, grid C3.

Campsites, facilities: This campground has 25 tent sites, all with good shade, and 48 RV sites in a separate section, all with hookups. Pull-through sites are available. All camp-sites have picnic tables, and most have fire rings. Group sites and RV storage are available. Restrooms have hot showers and flush toilets. Some sites have patios. The campground store carries ice and firewood. Phone lines and cable TV are available. A sanitary disposal station and coin laundry are provided. Buildings are wheelchair accessible. Pets are permitted if kept on leash and not left unattended. You must clean up after your pet.

Reservations, fees: Reservations are accepted at 888/878-2268, and the deposit for your first night is refundable with a 48-hour notice. Tent and RV fees are $18–$22. There are additional fees of $2 each for cable TV and extra tents at a site.

Open: Year-round.

Directions: From Helen, take Highway 356 north to Bethel Road at mile marker five.

Contact: Cherokee Campground, 45 Bethel Rd., Sautee, GA 30571; 706/878-2267.

Trip notes: Alpine Helen is just five miles away and offers shopping and dining. Helen is a bustling tourist town year-round but is busiest from September through November during the Oktoberfest season, when bands from Germany as well as local musicians play at restaurants and bars. Nearby Cleveland has Babyland General Hospital, where Cabbage Patch dolls may be adopted. The campground is also close to Brasstown Bald, the highest point in Georgia, and to many hiking trails and waterfalls. The Appalachian Trail is two miles away. Nearby rivers offer fishing, tubing, kayaking, and rafting. Wildlife common in the area includes black bears, coyotes, rabbits, opossum, deer, and raccoons.

47 Unicoi State Park

Location: Helen, map 2, grid C3.

Campsites, Facilities: There are 84 campsites suitable for tents or RVs, all with water and electric hookups. Picnic tables and fire rings are provided. Cabins are available. Restrooms have hot showers and flush toilets. Ice, groceries, and locally-made crafts are available at the campground. A sanitary disposal station, tennis courts, and playground are provided. The buildings are wheelchair accessible. Leashed pets are permitted.

Reservations, fees: Reservations are accepted at 800/864-7275, 800/573-9659, or 770/389-7275 (within the Atlanta area). The deposit of one night's fee is non-refundable, but your reservation can be moved once to another date. Site fees are $14–20 per night. Like all of Georgia's state parks, there is a $2 per day parking fee, or you can purchase an annual Georgia ParkPass for $25. Campers pay for just one daily pass for their entire stay.

Open: Year-round.

Directions: From Helen, go northeast about two miles on Highway 356 to the park and campground.

Contact: Unicoi State Park, P.O. Box 997, Helen, GA 30545; 706/878-3982.

Trip notes: Fishing is available in a trout stream and a lake. Canoes and paddleboats

are available for rent. There is a sand beach in the swimming area. Unicoi has 12 miles of hiking trails and an 8-mile mountain biking trail. The park hosts special wildflower programs in the spring. Call the program department at 706/878-3983 for dates and times.

48 Creekwood Campground

Location: Helen, map 2, grid C3.

Campsites, facilities: There are 18 RV sites with full hookups. Picnic tables are provided, and some sites have fire rings. Primitive campsites are also available, as are three cabins. Some shade is available. Restrooms have hot showers and flush toilets. Pets are permitted in the campground but not in the cabins.

Reservations, fees: Reservations are accepted at 800/856-7941. The deposit of one night's fee is not refundable. The fee for tents is $12, $25 for RVs.

Open: Year-round.

Directions: From Helen, take Highway 75 north to Highway 356 and turn right. The campground is about six miles down on the right.

Contact: Creekwood Campground, 5730 Highway 356, Sautee, GA 30571; 706/878-2164.

Trip notes: The campground is about seven miles from Alpine Helen.

49 Sleepy Hollow Campground

Location: Sautee, map 2, grid C3.

Campsites, facilities: There are 20 sites for tents or campers, all with water and electric hookups. There are an additional 34 RV-only sites with full hookups. Picnic tables and fire rings are provided. Restrooms have hot showers and flush toilets. A sanitary disposal station, sports field, and playground are provided. Pets are permitted.

Reservations, fees: The campground does not publish its rates.

Open: Year-round.

Directions: From Cleveland, take Highway 75 north to Highway 356 and turn right. After passing Unicoi State Park, turn right on Sky Lake Road. One-half mile farther, turn left onto Sleepy Hollow Road.

Contact: Sleepy Hollow Campground, 307 Sleepy Hollow Rd., Sautee, GA 30571; 706/878-2618.

Trip notes: The campground has a fishing pond stocked with trout, and borders the Chattahoochee National Forest, which provides hiking trails. Sautee Creek flows through the campground. It is 2.5 miles from Unicoi State Park, which offers more hiking trails and fishing.

50 Etowah River Campground

Location: Dahlonega, map 2, grid D1.

Campsites, facilities: The campground has 22 tent sites and 62 pull-through RV sites. The RV sites all have full hookups, offering 30- or 50-amp service. Some shade is available. Picnic tables and fire rings are provided. Restrooms have hot showers and flush toilets. The nearest supply store is two miles away, but ice and firewood are available at the campground. A playground is provided. The facilities are wheelchair accessible. Leashed pets are permitted, and you must clean up after your pet.

Reservations, fees: Reservations are accepted without a deposit. Fees for tents, primitive sites, and vans are $12. Pop-up campers and RVs cost $20 per night.

Open: Year-round.

Directions: From the square in Dahlonega, go west on Highway 52 about four miles, turn right on Siloam Road, and follow the signs.

Contact: Etowah River Campground, 437 Rider Mill Rd., Dahlonega, GA 30533; 706/864-9035, email: elowahrivercamp @alltel.net.

Trip notes: The campground is located near a trout stream for fishing, and the Appalachian Trail for hiking. The Etowah River is popular for rafting and kayaking. The town of Dahlonega is six miles from the campground, and offers the Gold Museum State Historic Park and old town square with quaint shops. The Coopers Creek Wildlife Management Area offers other hiking opportunities and more rugged camping experiences. Commonly seen wildlife in the area includes deer, black bears, and groundhogs or "whistle pigs."

51 Leisure Acres Campground & RV Park

Location: Cleveland, map 2, grid D2.

Campsites, facilities: There are 15 tent sites and 92 RV sites, all with full hookups. Pull-through sites are available. Both 30- and 50-amp hookups are available. RVs may be no longer than 42 feet. Some shade is available. Picnic tables and fire rings are provided. Cabins are also available. RV storage is available. Restrooms have hot showers and flush toilets. A sanitary disposal station, coin laundry, swimming pool, playground, and clubroom are provided. The restrooms are wheelchair accessible. Leashed pets are permitted.

Reservations, fees: Reservations are accepted, and no deposit is required. The fee

for tents is $15. RV sites are $17.75–21.65.
Open: Year-round.
Directions: The campground is two miles south of Cleveland on US 129. Coming from Cleveland, turn right onto Westmoreland Road about 0.5 miles to the campground.
Contact: Leisure Acres Campground & RV Park, 3840 Westmoreland Rd., Cleveland, GA 30528; 706/865-6466.
Trip notes: Leisure Acres has a private lake stocked with catfish, crappie, and bream. Paddleboats are available for rent. There is a walking trail around and through the campground. Wildlife in the area includes deer, wild turkeys, and bears. The campground is two miles from Babyland General Hospital in Cleveland, the birthplace of Cabbage Patch dolls, and from a public golf course. It is seven miles to Lake Lanier, and 12 to Alpine Helen.

52 Mr. Bud's Campground

Location: Clarksville, map 2, grid D4.
Campsites, Facilities: There are 117 campsites suitable for tents or RVs, all with full hookups. Picnic tables and fire rings are provided. RV storage is available. Restrooms have hot showers and flush toilets. A coin laundry and large pavilion are provided. The buildings are wheelchair accessible. Leashed pets are permitted.
Reservations, fees: Reservations are accepted at 706/947-3420. The deposit of one night's fee is refundable if cancellation is made at least 24 hours in advance. Sites rent for $18 for tent campers, and $20 for pop-ups and RVs.
Open: The campground is open from March 15 through November 15.
Directions: From Gainesville, take Highway 365 north. Continue straight onto US 441

when it merges in. Turn left onto Highway 197 north. Fifteen miles from US 441, go through a 3-way stop. The campground is about six miles from the 3-way stop on Highway 197.
Contact: Mr. Bud's Campground, 7796 Highway 197, Clarksville, GA 30523; 706/947-3420.
Trip notes: Fishing is available at Lake Burton and at Moccasin Creek State Park, both within five miles. There are hiking trails and swimming at the state park, and an ATV trail within a quarter mile. The area has a great deal of deer and black bears, which occasionally wander through the campground.

53 Hazel Creek RV Park

Location: Mt. Airy, map 2, grid D4.
Campsites, Facilities: There are 14 RV sites at this campground, all with full hookups. Ten of the sites are pull-through, and some shade is available. A few picnic tables are provided. Small dogs of 10 pounds or less are permitted. Dogs must be leashed, and you must pick up after your pet.
Reservations, fees: Reservations are accepted at 706/754-1551. No deposit is required. Sites cost $15 per night, or $80 per week. There are additional charges for more than two persons per site.
Open: Year-round.
Directions: From Gainesville, take Highway 365 north. About two miles north of the Highway 197 overpass, turn left at mile marker 51 onto Cody Road. Turn left at the second driveway to the campground.
Contact: Hazel Creek Campground, 230 RV Park Circle, Mt. Airy, GA 30563; 706/754-1551.
Trip notes: The campground is on Hazel Creek, which supports an abundance of wildlife including migratory birds, muskrats, beavers, turtles, and deer. Fishing is available at Lake

Russell, just two miles away. The city of Cornelia has a public swimming pool that is about five miles from the campground.

54 Lake Russell Campground

Location: Cornelia, map 2, grid E5.

Campsites, Facilities: There are 42 campsites suitable for tents or small RVs, none with hookups. Picnic tables and cooking grills are provided. Group sites are available. Restrooms have hot showers and flush toilets. A sanitary disposal station is provided. Leashed pets are permitted.

Reservations, fees: No reservations are permitted. The camping fee is $10 per night.

Open: The campground is open from Memorial Day weekend through October.

Directions: From Gainesville, take Highway 365/US 23 north to Highway 197. Turn right on Highway 197, then right at the dead end onto Dicks Hill Parkway, and follow the signs.

Contact: Lake Russell Campground, Chattahoochee-Oconee National Forests, 1755 Cleveland Highway, Gainesville, GA 30501; 706/754-6221.

Trip notes: The 100-acre lake offers fishing for bass, bream, perch, and catfish. There are three hiking trails. Access to the Appalachian Trail is a 30-minute drive from the campground.

55 Toccoa RV Park and Campground

Location: Toccoa, map 2, grid D7.

Campsites, facilities: There are two tent sites with water and electric hookups, and 28 RV sites in a separate section. All but one of the RV sites have full hookups. Twenty are pull-through sites, and eight have shade. RV storage is available. Picnic tables and cooking grills are provided. Restrooms have hot showers and flush toilets. Phone hookups are available. A coin laundry and pavilion are provided, and there are three sanitary disposal stations. Some facilities are wheelchair accessible. Pets must be leashed.

Reservations, fees: Reservations are accepted. All sites are $12 per night, or $70 a week.

Open: Year-round.

Directions: From Interstate 85, take Highway 17 north for 10 miles. Turn right on Oak Valley Road.

Contact: Toccoa RV Park and Campground, Box 2136, Oak Valley Rd., Toccoa, GA 30577; 706/886-2654.

Trip notes: The campground is near fishing, hiking, golf, kayaking, and rafting. It is 18 miles from Tallulah Falls (in Tallulah Gorge), 12 miles from Currahee Mountain, seven from Toccoa Falls, six from Henderson Falls Park, two from Lake Hartwell, and two from Traveler's Rest State Historic Site.

56 Sunset Campground

Location: Lake Hartwell, map 2, grid E7.

Campsites, facilities: There are six tent sites with access to piped water, and 31 RV sites with full hookups. Pull-through sites are available. Picnic tables are provided. Restrooms have hot showers and flush toilets. A coin laundry and clubroom are provided. Ice and snacks are available at the campground store. Pets are permitted.

Reservations, fees: Reservations are accepted, and no deposit is required. The fee for tents is $12, and $18 for RVs. Good Sam, AAA, and AARP discounts apply.

Open: Year-round.

Directions: From Atlanta, head north on Interstate 85 to exit 173/Highway 17, and turn left. The campground is 3.1 miles down on the left.
Contact: Sunset Campground, 17139 State Road 17, Martin, GA 30557; 706/356-8932.
Trip notes: The campground is four miles from Lake Hartwell, and four miles from Tugaloo State Park.

57 Tugaloo State Park

Location: Lake Hartwell, map 2, grid E8.
Campsites, facilities: The 117 campsites are available for either RVs or tents. Pull-through sites and shade are available. There are no hookups. In addition, there are six primitive sites and 20 cabins available. The developed campsites have picnic tables, fire rings, and cooking grills. Restrooms have hot showers and flush toilets. A coin laundry, playground, and boat ramp are at the park, along with minimal supplies such as ice and firewood. The nearest grocery store is six miles away. Swimming is available at the manmade beach. Buildings are wheelchair accessible. Pets are permitted in the campground, but not in the cabin area. Dogs must be kept on a six-foot leash.
Reservations, fees: Reservations are accepted at 800/864-7275. Within the Atlanta area, call 770/389-7275. The deposit is non-refundable, but the date can be moved once. The fee for tents is $12 nightly, and for RVs is $14. There is an additional $2 fee for either if on the water. Like all of Georgia's state parks, there is a $2 per day parking fee, or you can purchase an annual Georgia ParkPass for $25. Campers pay for just one daily pass for their entire stay.
Open: Year-round.

Directions: The campground is located off Highway 328 on Tugaloo State Park Road.
Contact: Tugaloo State Park, 1763 Tugaloo State Park Rd., Lavonia, GA 30553; 706/356-4362; email: tugaloosp@hartcom.net.
Trip notes: Tugaloo is located where the Chattooga River spills into Lake Hartwell, and has abundant fishing. Bass, crappie, catfish, and perch are plentiful. Other wildlife in the area includes deer, fox, raccoons, and skunks. The park is in the northeast corner of the state and so is near Tallulah Gorge (30 miles), Alpine Helen (45 miles), and Traveler's Rest Historic Site (20 miles).

58 Lake Lanier Lodges

Location: Lake Lanier, map 2, grid F2.
Campsites, facilities: There are 14 RV sites, all with full hookups. Shade is available. There are also 10 cabins available. Picnic tables and cooking grills are provided. Restrooms have hot showers and flush toilets. Ice, LP gas, and some groceries are available at the campground. A boat ramp, dock, and playground are provided. Cable TV hookups are available. The buildings are wheelchair accessible. Pets are permitted in the campground, but not in the cabins.
Reservations, fees: Reservations are accepted. The deposit is not refundable. Campsites are $20 per night or $375 monthly.
Open: Year-round.
Directions: From Atlanta, take Interstate 85 north to Interstate 985. Turn left onto Friendship Road at exit 8. At the third light, turn right onto McEver Road. After four miles, turn left onto Lights Ferry Road. The campground is just over one mile down on the right.
Contact: Lake Lanier Lodges,

6598 Lights Ferry Rd., Flowery Branch, GA 30542; 770/967-1804.

Trip notes: The lake is stocked with bass, bream, crappie, and catfish. There is a swimming area and walking trails at the lake.

59 The Pottery Campground

Location: Commerce, map 2, grid G5.

Campsites, facilities: There are 52 RV sites, all with full hookups. Pull-through sites and shade are available. Picnic tables and some cooking grills are provided. Restrooms have hot showers and flush toilets. Leashed pets are permitted.

Reservations, fees: Reservations are accepted, and the deposit is refundable with a 24-hour advance cancellation. The fee is $20 per night. Good Sam discounts apply.

Open: Year-round.

Directions: From Atlanta, take Interstate 85 north to exit 149/US 441, and turn right. Turn right again onto Pottery Road one-quarter mile from the interstate.

Contact: The Pottery Campground, 100 Pottery Rd., Commerce, GA 30529; 800/223-0667 or 706/335-3120

Trip notes: The campground is next to outlet shopping, and two miles from the Atlanta International Dragway.

60 Commerce/Athens KOA Kampground

Location: Commerce, map 2, grid G5.

Campsites, facilities: There are 20 tent sites at this campground, 73 RV sites, and one cabin. Thirty of the RV sites have full hookups, and the rest have water and electric. Pull-through sites are available. There is some shade. Picnic tables are provided. Restrooms have hot showers and flush toi-

lets. A sanitary disposal station, coin laundry, swimming pool, and playground are provided. Ice, LP gas, groceries, and supplies are available at the campground. Leashed pets are permitted. Do not leave your pet unattended.

Reservations, fees: Reservations are accepted at 800/KOA-3408 (800/562-3408). A credit card will hold your reservation, and you will be charged one night's fee if you do not cancel your reservation in advance. Tent sites are $16.50, sites with water and electric hookups are $21.50, and sites with full hookups are $23.

Open: Year-round.

Directions: From Interstate 85, turn south on US 441 at exit 149. After 1.5 miles, turn onto County Road 466 and follow the signs.

Contact: Commerce/Athens KOA Kampground, 5473 Mt. Olive Rd., Commerce, GA 30529; 706/335-5535.

Trip notes: The campground is one mile from an outlet mall, and two miles from a public golf course.

61 Victoria Bryant State Park

Location: Royston, map 2, grid F7.

Campsites, Facilities: There are 25 campsites suitable for tents or RVs, all with water and electric hookups. Picnic tables and fire rings are provided. Pull-through sites are available. Primitive camping is available. Restrooms have hot showers and flush toilets and are wheelchair accessible. Ice is available at the campground. A sanitary disposal station, swimming pool, and playground are provided. Golf is available at the park. Leashed pets are permitted.

Reservations, fees: Reservations are accepted at 800/864-7275 or 770/389-7275 in the Atlanta area. The deposit of one night's fee is non-refundable, but your reservation can be moved once to another date. Site fees are $13–15 per night. Like all of Georgia's state parks, there is a $2 per day parking fee, or you can purchase an annual Georgia Park-Pass for $25. Campers pay for just one daily pass for their entire stay.

Open: Year-round.

Directions: From Franklin Springs, go north on Highway 327 two miles to the park and campground.

Contact: Victoria Bryant State Park, 1105 Bryant Park Rd., Royston, GA 30662; 706/245-6270.

Trip notes: There are two ponds stocked with bream, bass, and crappie, and a stream that flows through the park. The park has five miles of hiking and biking trails and a 9-hole golf course.

62 Hart State Park

Location: Lake Hartwell, map 3, grid E1.

Campsites, facilities: The tent section of the campground has 25 sites. The separate RV section has 53 sites. Half of these are pull-through sites, and five have full hookups. All sites have shade. There are also two cabins for rent. Picnic tables, fire rings, and cooking grills are provided. The restrooms have hot showers and flush toilets. A coin laundry, sanitary dump station, playground, and camp store are provided. Boat ramps and docks are available. The buildings are wheelchair accessible. Pets are permitted in the campground but not in the cabins, and must be kept on a six-foot leash.

Reservations, fees: Reservations are accepted at 800/864-7275, or at 770/389-7275 in the Atlanta area. The deposit is non-refundable, but the date can be moved once. Campsite fees are $11–15 per night. The cabins are $70–80 per night from Labor Day through March, and 80—90 per night during the summer. Like all of Georgia's state parks, there is a $2 per day parking fee, or you can purchase an annual Georgia ParkPass for $25. Campers pay for just one daily pass for their entire stay.

Open: Year-round.

Directions: From Interstate 85, take Highway 17 south to Bowersville and turn east on Highway 51. The park is four miles north of downtown Hartwell.

Contact: Hart State Park, 330 Hart State Park Rd., Hartwell, GA 30643; 706/376-8756.

Trip notes: Fishing is available in the lake for bass, crappie, catfish, and perch. Paddleboats are available for rent, and there is a beach in the swimming area. There are two nature trails of about a mile each at the park. The campground is within 15 miles of two golf courses and is near to Hartwell Dam. It is just south of Tugaloo State Park.

METRO ATLANTA

LAKE ALLATOONA

METRO ATLANTA

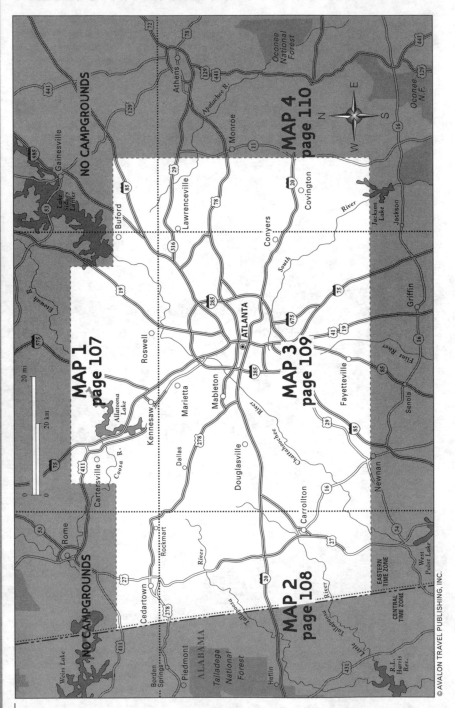

© AVALON TRAVEL PUBLISHING, INC.

MAP 1

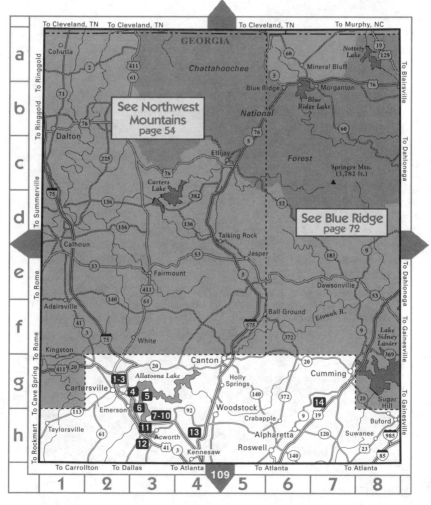

© AVALON TRAVEL PUBLISHING, INC.

MAP 2

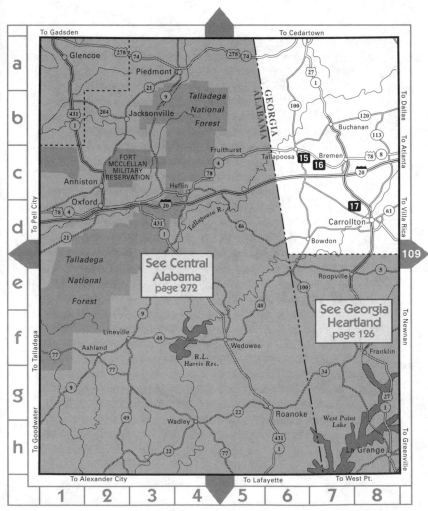

To Gadsden • To Cedartown

Glencoe • (278) (74) • (278) (74)

GEORGIA / ALABAMA

Piedmont • (27) • (1)

(21) • Talladega National Forest • (100)

(9) • Buchanan • (120)

(431) (204) • Jacksonville • (113) • To Dallas / To Atlanta

(1) • (78) (8)

FORT McCLELLAN MILITARY RESERVATION • Fruithurst • (4) • Tallapoosa • **15** • Bremen • (20)

16

Anniston • Heflin • (78)

Oxford • (78) (4) • (20) • **17** • (61) • To Villa Rica

(21) • (431) • Tallapoosa R. • Carrollton

(1) • (46) • Bowdon

109

Talladega National Forest • **See Central Alabama page 272**

Roopville • (5)

(100) • **See Georgia Heartland page 126** • To Newnan

(9) • (48)

Lineville • (48) • Wedowee • Franklin

Ashland • (77) • R.L. Harris Res. • (34)

(77) • (27)

(9) • West Point Lake • (1) • To Greenville

(49) • (22) • Roanoke

Wadley • (431) • La Grange

(22) • (77) • (1)

To Pell City

To Talladega

To Goodwater

To Alexander City • To Lafayette • To West Pt.

1 2 3 4 5 6 7 8

a b c d e f g h

MAP 3

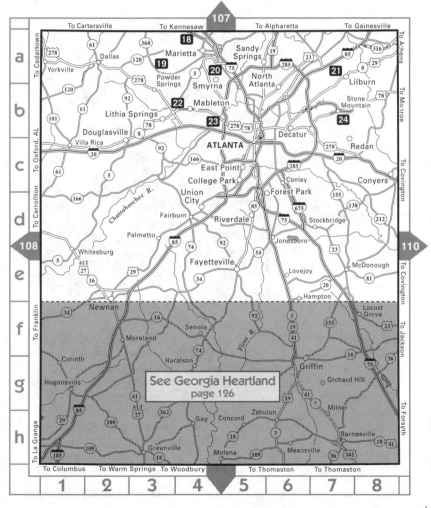

To Cartersville   To Kennesaw   To Alpharetta   To Gainesville

108

110

To Cedartown
To Oxford, AL
To Carrollton
To Franklin
To La Grange

To Athens
To Monroe
To Covington
To Covington
To Jackson
To Forsyth

a

61
360
278
Dallas
120
120
Yorkville
120
278
19
Marietta
18
5
20
75
Sandy Springs
19
285
North Atlanta
23
85
316
8
29
21
Lilburn
78

b

92
61
22
Mableton
23
278
78
Decatur
Stone Mountain
78
24
Powder Springs
Smyrna
Lithia Springs
101
278
Douglasville
8
78
Villa Rica
20
ATLANTA
278
20
Redan

c

61
5
92
166
East Point
College Park
285
Conley
Forest Park
155
138
Conyers
166

d

Chattahoochee R.
Fairburn
Union City
85
675
75
Stockbridge
23
212
Palmetto
85
74
92
Riverdale
Jonesboro

e

5
Whitesburg
ALT 27
16
29
34
Fayetteville
54
Lovejoy
20
81
McDonough
Hampton

f

34
Newnan
16
Senoia
92
Flint R.
3
19
41
155
Locust Grove
23
Moreland
74
Haralson
41
16
75
36
Griffin

g

Corinth
Hogansville
41
ALT 27
362
See Georgia Heartland
page 126
Zebulon
19
41
7
Milner
Orchard Hill

h

85
29
100
Gay
Concord
18
3
Meansville
341
18
41
Barnesville
Greenville
18
Molena
109
36
185
109

To Columbus   To Warm Springs   To Woodbury   To Thomaston   To Thomaston

1   2   3   4   5   6   7   8

MAP 4

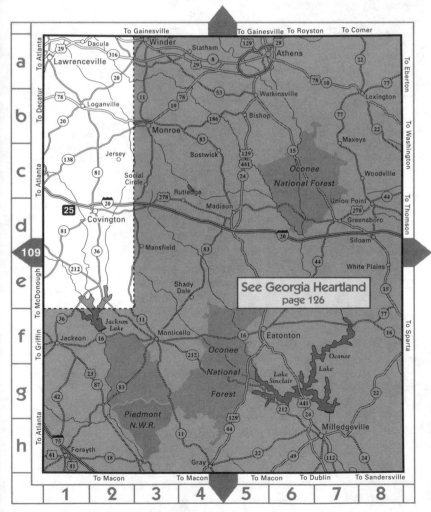

See Georgia Heartland
page 126

To Gainesville · To Gainesville · To Royston · To Comer
To Atlanta · To Decatur · To Atlanta · To McDonough · To Griffin · To Atlanta
To Eberton · To Washington · To Thomson · To Sparta

Dacula · Winder · Statham · Athens
Lawrenceville
Loganville · Watkinsville · Lexington
Monroe · Bishop · Maxeys
Jersey · Bostwick · Oconee · Woodville
Social Circle · Rutledge · National Forest
Covington · Madison · Union Point
Greensboro
Mansfield · Siloam
White Plains
Shady Dale
Jackson Lake · Monticello · Eatonton
Jackson · Oconee · Lake Sinclair · Oconee Lake
National
Piedmont N.W.R. · Forest · Milledgeville
Forsyth · Gray

To Macon · To Macon · To Macon · To Dublin · To Sandersville

109

METRO ATLANTA

1 Sweetwater Campground

Location: Allatoona Lake, map 1, grid G3.

Campsites, facilities: There are 52 tent sites, and 99 sites suitable for tents or RVs. Pull-through sites are available. RVs are restricted to 40 feet or less. All of the sites have shade. Two have full hookups, and the rest offer water and electric only. There are nine group sites. All campsites have picnic tables, fire rings, and cooking grills. Restrooms have hot showers and flush toilets. Boat ramps and docks are provided, along with a sanitary disposal station, swimming area, and coin laundry. The restrooms are wheelchair accessible. Up to two leashed pets per site are permitted. No livestock is permitted in the campground, including horses and miniature pigs.

Reservations, fees: Reservations are accepted through Reserve America, 877/444-6777. Full payment is required at time of reservation, and there is a $10 cancellation fee. Reservations must be made at least five days in advance. The nightly fee is $14 with no hookups, $18 with water and electric, and $20 with full hookups.

Open: The campground is closed in the winter. The actual dates vary yearly, but the campground is generally open from April through Labor Day.

Directions: From Interstate 75, take Highway 20 east two miles and turn right at the sign for the Sweetwater Campground.

Contact: Sweetwater Campground, P.O. Box 487, Cartersville, GA 30120; 770/382-4700; website: www.sam.usace.army.mil/op/rec/allatoon.

Trip notes: Fishing for bass and crappie is available at the lake. Other wildlife you may see includes deer, bobcats, foxes, groundhogs, and wild turkeys. There is a sand beach in the swimming area.

2 Upper Stamp Creek Campground

Location: Allatoona Lake, map 1, grid G3.

Campsites, facilities: There are 18 sites for tents or RVs, and two restricted to tents. Sites with water and electric hookups are available. All but one have shade, and all sites have picnic tables, fire rings, and cooking grills. Some sites have patios. RVs must be 40 feet or less. Restrooms have hot showers and flush toilets. There are boat ramps at the campground, along with a sanitary disposal station. The nearest supply store is two miles away. The restrooms are wheelchair accessible. Up to two leashed pets per site are permitted. No livestock is permitted in the campground, including horses and miniature pigs.

Reservations, fees: Reservations are accepted through Reserve America, 877/444-6777. Full payment is required at time of reservation, and there is a $10 cancellation fee. Reservations must be made at least five days in advance. The nightly fee is $14 with no hookups, and $18 with water and electric.

Open: The campground is closed in the winter. The actual dates vary yearly, but the campground is generally open from April through Labor Day.

Directions: From Interstate 75, take Highway 20 east. Turn right at the sign for the Upper Stamp Creek Campground.

Contact: Upper Stamp Creek Campground, P.O. Box 487, Cartersville, GA 30120; 770/382-4700; website: www.sam.usace.army.mil/op/rec/allatoon.

Trip notes: Fishing for bass and crappie is available at the lake. Other wildlife you may see includes deer, bobcats, foxes, groundhogs, and wild turkeys. There is a sand beach at the swimming area. Wildflowers can be found along the 1.5-mile Laurel Ridge Trail, eight miles from the campground.

3 McKaskey Creek Campground

Location: Allatoona Lake, map 1, grid G3.

Campsites, facilities: There are 19 tent-only sites, and 32 sites for tents or RVs. Most sites have shade. Pull-through sites are available. RVs are restricted to 40 feet or less. Most sites have water and electric hookups. All campsites have picnic tables, fire rings, and cooking grills. Restrooms have hot showers and flush toilets. Boat ramps are on the premises, along with a sanitary disposal station and coin laundry. Supplies are available one mile away. The restrooms are wheelchair accessible. Up to two leashed pets per site are permitted. No livestock is permitted in the campground, including horses and miniature pigs.

Reservations, fees: Reservations are accepted through Reserve America, 877/444-6777. Full payment is required at time of reservation, and there is a $10 cancellation fee. Reservations must be made at least five days in advance. The fee is $14 per night with no hookups, and $18 with water and electric hookups.

Open: The campground is closed in the winter. The actual dates vary yearly, but the campground is generally open from April through Labor Day.

Directions: From Interstate 75, take Highway 20 east one mile and turn right onto the Highway 20 Spur. Turn left at the sign for the campground.

Contact: McKaskey Campground, P.O. Box 487, Cartersville, GA 30120; 770/382-4700; website: www.sam.usace.army.mil/op/rec/allatoon.

Trip notes: Fishing for bass and crappie is available at the lake. Wildlife you may see

includes deer, bobcats, foxes, groundhogs, and wild turkeys. The campground has a sand beach in the swimming area. Wildflowers can be found along the 1.5-mile Laurel Ridge Trail, which is three miles from the campground.

4 Macedonia Campground

Location: Allatoona Lake, map 1, grid G3.

Campsites, facilities: There are 24 primitive campsites. Pit toilets are provided. Leashed pets are permitted.

Reservations, fees: No reservations are accepted. There are no fees for this campground.

Open: Year-round.

Directions: Take Highway 20 east from Interstate 75. After about six miles, just after you cross Stamp Creek, turn right at the sign for Macedonia Campground. You will travel approximately five miles on the access road before reaching the campsite.

Contact: Macedonia Campground, c/o Mobile District, US Army Corps of Engineers, P.O. Box 487, Cartersville, GA 30120; 770/382-4700, fax 770/386-6758.

Trip notes: This is a no-frills campground, but the price is certainly right. Because of the somewhat remote location and lack of monitored campsites, I don't recommend camping alone here, but if you're after a quiet fishing spot, this is it.

5 Red Top Mountain Lodge and Campground

Location: Red Top Mountain, map 1, grid G3.

Campsites, facilities: There are 29 tent sites with water and electric hookups, and 24 primitive tent sites. All of the 38 RV sites have water and electric hookups and 12 are pull-through sites. All campsites have some shade. RVs must be 40 feet or less in length. There are also 18 rental cabins available. Picnic tables, fire rings, and cooking grills are provided. Restrooms have hot showers and flush toilets. Ice, firewood, and cable TV hookups are available. Tennis courts and a sanitary disposal station are at the campground, and a playground, boat ramp, and dock are in the park. One campsite is wheelchair accessible. Leashed pets are permitted.

Reservations, fees: Reservations are accepted up to one year in advance at 800/864-7275. In the Atlanta area, call 770/389-7275. The deposit is non-refundable, but the date can be moved once. Site fees are $12–14 for tent sites, and $16–18 for RV sites. The cabins are $89–119 per night. Like all of Georgia's state parks, there is a $2 per day parking fee, or you can purchase an annual Georgia ParkPass for $25. Campers pay for just one daily pass for their entire stay.

Open: Year-round, except for the primitive sites, which are generally open from April through Halloween. Call for the exact dates if your visit is around those dates.

Directions: From Atlanta, go north on Interstate 75. Exit east on Red Top Mountain Road, and travel 1.5 miles to the campground.

Contact: Red Top Mountain Lodge, 50 Lodge Rd., Cartersville, GA 30121; 770/975-0055.

Trip notes: Fishing is available at the lake in the park. There are five hiking trails, ranging from 0.75 miles to 5.5 miles in length. Bicycles are prohibited on the trails. There is a sand beach at the park's swimming area. Deer are so plentiful at this park that you are nearly guaranteed to see them on your visit, both on the trails and along the road. Even with my dogs with me, we see them on every hike. The park is just 30 minutes north of Atlanta, and so is a convenient place to stay and see the sites in the city.

6 Allatoona Landing Marine Resort

Location: Allatoona Lake, map 1, grid H3.

Campsites, facilities: There are 16 tent sites, plus 126 sites for RVs up to 40 feet. Sixteen of the RV sites have full hook-ups, and all have water and electric. Pull-through sites are available. Some sites have cable TV. Fully furnished trailers are also available to rent. Picnic tables, fire grills, barbecues, coin laundry, swimming pool, playground, boat ramp, boat docks, and a sanitary disposal station are provided. Restrooms have hot showers and flush toilets. Groceries, gifts, ice, food, LP gas, and firewood are available at the campground. Leashed pets are permitted.

Reservations, fees: Reservations are recommended at 800/346-7305. Site fees range are $16–26. There is a $25 non-refundable fee for pets in the rental trailers.

Open: Year-round.

Directions: From Atlanta, take Interstate 75 north to the Emerson-Allatoona exit (exit 283) and turn right. The camp is two miles down on the left.

Contact: Allatoona Landing Marine Resort, 24 Allatoona Landing Rd., Cartersville, GA 30121; 770/974-6089.

Trip notes: Most visitors are interested in relaxing on the sand beach or fishing in the lake. Bass, crappie, trout, and catfish are plentiful. The lake supports a healthy population of waterfowl, along with an equally healthy but less visible population of snakes. Hiking is available nearby at Red Top Mountain State Park on trails that range from one to 5.5 miles in length. The Etowah Indian Mounds at Cartersville are nearby and definitely worth a visit.

☑ Payne Campground

Location: Allatoona Lake, map 1, grid H3.

Campsites, facilities: There are 11 tent-only sites at this campground, 10 of them shaded, and 49 sites for tents or RVs up to 40 feet in length. Two sites have full hookups. Pull-through sites are available. Most sites have shade. All sites have picnic tables, fire rings, and cooking grills. Restrooms have flush toilets and hot showers. A coin laundry, playground, and sanitary disposal station are on the premises, plus a boat ramp and docks. The buildings are wheelchair accessible. Up to two leashed pets per site are permitted. No livestock is permitted in the campground, including horses and miniature pigs.

Reservations, fees: Reservations are accepted through Reserve America, 877/444-6777. Full payment is required at time of reservation, and there is a $10 cancellation fee. Reservations must be made at least five days in advance. Site fees are $14–20, depending on hookups.

Open: The campground is generally open from April through Labor Day, but the exact open and close dates vary. The campground is closed in the winter.

Directions: From Interstate 75, take exit 277/Highway 92 and turn right. Go one mile, then turn left onto Kellogg Creek Road and follow the signs. You will travel down Kellogg Creek Road for about three miles. The campsite will be on the right, before you cross the lake.

Contact: Payne Campground, P.O. Box 487, Cartersville, GA 30101; 770/382-4700.

Trip notes: Fishing for bass and crappie is available at the lake. Other wildlife you may see includes deer, opossum, squirrels, and wild turkeys. There is a beach area for swimming.

☑ Clark Creek South Campground

Location: Allatoona Lake, map 1, grid H3.

Campsites, facilities: There are 17 tent-only sites, most of which have shade. There are 23 sites for either tents or RVs, all with shade. Water and electric hookups are available, as are pull-through sites. RVs are restricted to 40 feet or less. All campsites have picnic tables, fire rings, and cooking grills. Restrooms have hot showers and flush toilets. A boat ramp, dock, sanitary disposal station, and coin laundry are available. The buildings are wheelchair accessible. Up to two leashed pets per site are permitted. No livestock is permitted in the campground, including horses and miniature pigs.

Reservations, fees: Reservations are accepted through Reserve America, 877/444-6777. Full payment is required at time of reservation, and there is a $10 cancellation fee. Reservations must be made at least five days in advance. Campsite fees are $14–18, depending on hookups.

Open: The campground is closed in the winter. The actual dates vary yearly, but the campground is generally open from April through Labor Day. Call for the exact dates.

Directions: The campground is two miles east of Interstate 75 at exit 278.

Contact: Clark Creek South Campground, P.O. Box 487, Cartersville, GA 30120; 770/3824700; website: www.sam.usace.army.mil/op/rec/allatoona.

Trip notes: Fishing for bass and crappie is available at the lake. Other wildlife you may see includes deer, bobcats, foxes, groundhogs, and wild turkeys. There is a beach area for swimming.

⑨ McKinney Campground

Location: Allatoona Lake, map 1, grid H3.

Campsites, facilities: There are 150 tent or RV sites, 140 of them with shade. Ten of them are pull-through sites. Most sites have water and electric hookups. RVs are restricted to 40 feet or less. All campsites have picnic tables, fire rings, and cooking grills. Restrooms have hot showers and flush toilets. A boat ramp, dock, sanitary disposal station, and coin laundry are available. The buildings are wheelchair accessible. Up to two leashed pets per site are permitted. No livestock is permitted in the campground, including horses and miniature pigs.

Reservations, fees: Reservations are accepted through Reserve America, 877/444-6777. Full payment is required at time of reservation, and there is a $10 cancellation fee. Reservations must be made at least five days in advance. The fee is $18 per night.

Open: Year-round.

Directions: The campground is three miles east of Interstate 75 at exit 278.

Contact: McKinney Campground, P.O. Box 487, Cartersville, GA 30120; 770/382-4700; website: www.sam.usace.army.mil/op/rec/allatoon.

Trip notes: Fishing for bass and crappie is available at the lake. Other wildlife you may see includes deer, bobcat, fox, ground-hogs, and wild turkeys. There is a beach area for swimming.

⑩ Clark Creek North Campground

Location: Allatoona Lake, map 1, grid H3.

Campsites, facilities: There are 24 tent or RV sites, some with water and electric hookups. Some pull-through sites are available and most sites have shade. RVs are restricted to 40 feet or less. All campsites have picnic tables, fire rings, and cooking grills. Restrooms have hot showers and flush toilets. Boat ramps and docks are one-quarter mile away at the Clark Creek South Campground. The campground has a sanitary disposal station and coin laundry. Up to two leashed pets per site are permitted. No livestock is permitted in the campground, including horses and miniature pigs.

Reservations, fees: Reservations are accepted through Reserve America, 877/444-6777. Full payment is required at time of reservation, and there is a $10 cancellation fee. Reservations must be made at least five days in advance. The fee for a campsite with water and electric hookups is $18.

Open: The campground is generally open from April through Labor Day, but the actual open and close dates vary. The campground is closed in the winter.

Directions: The campground is two miles east of Interstate 75 at exit 278.

Contact: Clark Creek North Campground, P.O. Box 487, Cartersville, GA 30120; 770/382-4700; website: www.sam.usace.army.mil/op/rec/allatoon.

Trip notes: Fishing for bass and crappie is available at the lake. Other wildlife you may see includes deer, bobcats, foxes, ground-hogs, and wild turkeys. There is a beach area for swimming nearby at the Clark Creek South Campground.

⑪ Old Highway 41 #3 Campground

Location: Allatoona Lake, map 1, grid H3.

Campsites, facilities: There are 50 campsites for either tents or RVs up to 40 feet.

Four of them are pull-through sites, and most have water and electric hookups. Some sites have full hookups. Cable TV is available. Most of the sites have shade, and all have picnic tables, fire rings, and cooking grills. Restrooms have hot showers and flush toilets. There is a sanitary disposal station, coin laundry, playground, fitness room, and boat ramp at the campground. Up to two leashed pets per site are permitted. No livestock is permitted in the campground, including horses and miniature pigs.

Reservations, fees: Reservations are accepted through Reserve America, 877/444-6777. Full payment is required at time of reservation, and there is a $10 cancellation fee. Reservations must be made at least five days in advance. Site fees are $18–20, depending on hookups.

Open: The campground is generally open from April through Labor Day, but the exact open and close date varies. The campground is closed in the winter.

Directions: From Atlanta, take Interstate 75 north to exit 278/Glade Road and turn left. At the intersection with Highway 92, exit on the right and turn left onto Highway 293/Acworth Road. The campground is on the left, about a mile from Highway 92.

Contact: Old Highway 41 #3, P.O. Box 487, Cartersville, GA 30120; 770/382-4700; website: www.sam.usace.army.mil/op/rec/allatoon.

Trip notes: This is one of several US Army Corps of Engineers campgrounds on Allatoona Lake. A sand beach and swimming area are nearby, and fishing is available at the campground for bass and crappie. Wildlife in the area includes a large deer population, bobcats, foxes, groundhogs, and wild turkeys.

12 Lakemont Campground

Location: Allatoona Lake, map 1, grid H3.

Campsites, facilities: There are 150 RV sites at this campground. All but 10 have full hookups, and most are pull-through sites. All have some shade. Picnic tables are provided. Restrooms have hot showers and flush toilets. A coin laundry, boat dock, swimming pool, and playground are provided. Most leashed pets are permitted, but certain breeds are restricted, including Dobermans, pit bulls, and Rottweilers.

Reservations, fees: Reservations are not accepted. Campsites are $13–18 per night.

Open: Year-round.

Directions: From Atlanta, take Interstate 75 north to exit 278 and turn west. Turn right onto Highway 92 at the second light. At the dead end, turn right onto US 41. The campground is on the left at the lake.

Contact: Lakemont Campground, 5134 N. Shores Rd., Acworth, GA 30101; 770/966-0302.

Trip notes: Bass, trout, catfish, and crappie are available in the lake. The campground borders COE property but there are no marked trails in the area.

13 Victoria Campground

Location: Allatoona Lake, map 1, grid H4.

Campsites, facilities: There are 74 tent or RV sites. Most have shade, and pull-through sites are available. All have water and electric hookups and two have full hookups. RVs are restricted to 40 feet or less. All campsites have picnic tables, fire rings, and cooking grills. Restrooms have showers and flush toilets. A sanitary disposal station is on the premises, along with a coin laundry. Buildings are wheelchair accessible. The campground is approximately one-quarter mile to boat ramps and docks on the lake. Up to two leashed pets per site are permitted. No livestock is permitted in the campground, including horses and miniature pigs.

Reservations, fees: Reservations are accepted through Reserve America, 877/444-6777. Full payment is required at time of reservation, and there is a $10 cancellation fee. Reservations must be made at least five days in advance. The fee for a campsite with water and electric hookups is $18, and $20 for full hookups.

Open: The campground is generally open from April through Labor Day, but the exact open and close dates vary. The campground is closed in the winter.

Directions: From Interstate 575, take the Bells Ferry Road exit east for 2.5 miles and follow the signs.

Contact: Victoria Campground, P.O. Box 487, Cartersville, GA 30120; 770/382-4700; website: www.sam.usace.army.mil/op/rec/allatoon.

Trip notes: Fishing for bass and crappie is available at the lake. Other wildlife you may see includes deer, bobcats, foxes, groundhogs, and wild turkeys. There is a beach area for swimming.

🔢 Twin Lakes RV Park

Location: Lake Lanier, map 1, grid G7.

Campsites, facilities: There are 90 RV sites at this campground. Seven are pull-through sites, and 72 have full hookups. Six of the sites have some shade. Group sites are available. LP gas and cable TV are available. Leashed pets are permitted. You must clean up after your pet. Pets may be left unattended

in your camper as long as they don't disturb other campers.

Reservations, fees: Reservations are not accepted. The rate is $15 per night.

Open: Year-round.

Directions: From Atlanta, take Highway 400 north to exit 13/Highway 141, and turn left. Turn left onto Highway 9 south. The campground is one mile from Highway 141, on the right.

Contact: Twin Lakes RV Park, 3300 Shore Dr., Cumming, GA 30040; 770/887-4400.

Trip notes: Fishing for bass, bream, crappie, and catfish is available at the two private lakes in the campground. Lake Lanier is seven miles away. The majority of campers here rent monthly.

🔢 Big Oak RV Park

Location: Tallapoosa, map 2, grid C6.

Campsites, facilities: The campground has three sites reserved for tents and 43 sites for RVs. Of the RV sites, 29 have full hookups, and half are pull-through sites. RVs are restricted to 40 feet or less. Both 30- and 50-amp hookups are available. Picnic tables are provided. Restrooms have hot showers and flush toilets. LP gas is available, and a grocery store is next to the campground. A coin laundry, playground, and sanitary disposal station are available. Facilities are wheelchair accessible. Leashed pets are permitted. They must sleep inside your camper or tent, and you must clean up after your pet.

Reservations, fees: Reservations are accepted. Site fees are $14–16, depending on hookups.

Open: Year-round.

Directions: From Interstate 20, take exit 5 and turn north on Highway 100.

Contact: Big Oak RV Park, 1179 Highway 10D, P.O. Box 531, Tallapoosa, GA 30176; 770/574-5522.

Trip notes: This campground is mainly a quiet, wooded overnight rest stop along Interstate 20, and most of the campers are older and retired. This might not be the best choice for families with small children because of a lack of amenities for kids, although there is a small playground. There is a short walking trail, and some wildflowers in the spring.

16 Tally Valley Park, Inc.

Location: Tallapoosa, map 2, grid C7.
Campsites, facilities: There are 40 campsites suitable for tents or RVs. Three have full hookups, and the rest have water and electric only. About half are pull-through sites. Most sites have shade. Fire rings and firewood are provided. Restrooms have hot showers and flush toilets. A sanitary disposal station, clubroom, and swimming pool are provided. Leashed pets are permitted.
Reservations, fees: All sites are $16.
Open: The campground is open from mid-March through November.
Directions: From Atlanta, take Interstate 20 west to the US 27 exit and turn north. Turn west on US 78, and travel 6.5 miles to the campground.
Contact: Tally Valley Park, Inc., P.O. Box 424, Tallapoosa, GA 30176; 770/574-2076.
Trip notes: The campground is about an hour from Atlanta.

17 John Tanner State Park

Location: Carrollton, map 2, grid D8.
Campsites, facilities: All of the 32 RV sites at this campground have full hookups and shade. Eight are pull-through sites. RVs are restricted to 40 feet or less. Picnic tables and cooking grills are provided. There are also six cabins and a lodge. Restrooms have showers and flush toilets. The nearest grocery store is about one mile away, but ice, snacks, and some gifts are available at the campground. Cable TV hookups are available. A coin laundry, playground, boat ramp, and sanitary disposal station are provided. The buildings are wheelchair accessible. Pets are permitted on a six-foot or shorter leash.
Reservations, fees: Reservations are accepted at 800/864-7275 or 770/389-7275 within the Atlanta area. The deposit is non-refundable, but the date can be moved once. Fees are $14 for tents, $16 for RVs and trailers. Like all of Georgia's state parks, there is a $2 per day parking fee, or you can purchase an annual Georgia ParkPass for $25. Campers pay for just one daily pass for their entire stay.
Open: Year-round.
Directions: From Interstate 20, take exit 11/US 27/Highway 1 south 1.5 miles to Bowdon Junction Road and turn right. After three miles, turn left onto Mt. Zion Road, then right onto Tanner Beach Road.
Contact: John Tanner State Park, 354 Tanner Beach Rd., Carrollton, GA 30117; 770/830-2222.
Trip notes: The two lakes offer fishing for bass, bream, and catfish, and a swimming area with the largest sand beach in the state park system. Fishing boats, paddleboats, and canoes can be rented. Motorized boats are allowed only during daylight hours. Miniature golf is available at the park year-round. There are two hiking trails. There's a one-mile trail around the upper lake and a short nature trail near the northwest end of the park. Other amenities at the park include horseshoe pits and volleyball. Nearby

attractions include the Sweetwater Creek State Conservation Park and Pickett's Mill Battlefield State Historic Site, both of which have much more extensive hiking trails. The park is located an hour from Atlanta.

18 Atlanta North KOA

Location: Atlanta, map 3, grid A4.

Campsites, facilities: There are 18 tent sites with water and electric hookups, and 214 RV sites in a separate section. Most RV sites have full hookups, and the rest have water and electric only. Picnic tables are provided. There are also rental cabins, a tent, and tepees. RV storage is available. Restrooms have hot showers and flush toilets. A sanitary disposal station, coin laundry, swimming pool, playground, and clubroom are provided. Ice, LP gas, supplies, and groceries are available at the campground. The buildings are wheelchair accessible. Pets are permitted.

Reservations, fees: Reservations are accepted at 800/562-4194, and no deposit is required. Tent sites are $20, and RV sites are $28. The tent rents for $28 per night, tepees for $30, and cabins are $34–40.

Open: Year-round.

Directions: From Interstate 75, take the Barrett Parkway exit and turn west. Cross over US 41 and turn right on Old US 41. The campground will be on the right.

Contact: Atlanta North KOA, 2000 Old US Highway 41, Kennesaw, GA 30152; 770/427-2406.

Trip notes: The campground is 15 minutes from Allatoona Lake, and less than one mile from Kennesaw Mountain National Battlefield Park, which has miles of hiking and horseback riding trails. The campground is 10 minutes from a water park, and 45 from the Six Flags Over Georgia amusement park.

19 Arbor Mill Mobile Home Park

Location: Marietta, map 3, grid A3.

Campsites, facilities: This is primarily a mobile home park, but there are up to six RV sites available, all with full hookups. There are no restrooms. Pets must be 45 pounds or less and must be kept inside.

Reservations, fees: Reservations are not accepted. The fee is $20 per night, or $100 per week.

Open: Year-round.

Directions: The campground is located at the intersection of West Cobb Loop and Turner Road, and must be entered off the West Cobb Loop. From Powder Springs Road, go one mile on Macland Road and turn right onto the West Cobb Loop.

Contact: Arbor Mill Mobile Home Park, 2600 Turner Road SW, Suite 106, Marietta, GA 30064; 770/427-7998.

Trip notes: There are two small lakes on the property, with bass, bream, catfish, and crappie. No swimming or boating is allowed in the lakes, which have a large turtle population. The campground is within 20 minutes of the Six Flags Over Georgia theme park, Allatoona Lake, White Water water park, Kennesaw Mountain National Battlefield Park, and Sweetwater Creek State Park.

20 Brookwood RV Resort Park

Location: Atlanta, map 3, grid A4.

Campsites, facilities: This RV-only campground has 60 sites, all with full hookups. Some shade is available. Some sites have picnic tables, and all have patios. Restrooms have hot showers and flush toilets. A coin laundry and swimming pool are provided. Ice and LP gas are available at the campground.

The restrooms are wheelchair accessible. Well-behaved pets are permitted.

Reservations, fees: Reservations are accepted, and no deposit is required. Sites are $39.95 per night.

Open: Year-round.

Directions: From Atlanta, take Interstate 75 north to exit 261/Highway 280/Delk Road and take the west exit. At the second exit off of Highway 280, turn right on US 41 north, and travel one-third mile to Wylie Road. Turn right on Wylie Road. The campground is at the top of the hill.

Contact: Brookwood RV Resort Park, 1031 Wylie Rd., Marietta, GA 30067; 770/427-6853.

Trip notes: The campground is six miles from Kennesaw Mountain National Battlefield Park, two miles from a White Water water park, and two miles from the antique shops on the square in Marietta.

21 Jones RV Park

Location: Atlanta, map 3, grid A7.

Campsites, facilities: The campground has 160 RV sites, all with full hookups. Pull-through sites are available. About half of the sites have shade. Restrooms have hot showers and flush toilets. Gravel pads are provided, and cable TV hookups are available. A coin laundry and small playground are on the premises, and some limited supplies are available at the office. Leashed pets are permitted.

Reservations, fees: Reservations are accepted and recommended. Rates are $20 per night.

Open: Year-round.

Directions: From Atlanta, take Interstate 85 north to the Indian Trail exit and turn right. At the first light, turn right onto Goshen Springs Road, which goes into the campground.

Contact: Jones RV Park, 5200 Goshen Springs Rd., Norcross, GA 30093; 770/923-0911, fax 770/381-2142.

Trip notes: Although technically the campground allows tents, it is primarily an extended-stay RV and mobile home park. A large percentage of campers here are construction workers and their families who have long-term contracts in the area. Because there is always so much building going on in the Atlanta area, and very few RV parks, there is usually a lengthy waiting list. Vacationers would have better luck finding a site at one of the state park campgrounds, or at Stone Mountain Park. The campground is near all that Atlanta has to offer: museums, sports, and theater, as well as proximity to the mountains. It is near Lake Lanier and Stone Mountain Park, which offer swimming, boating, and hiking.

22 Atlanta West Campground

Location: Atlanta, map 3, grid B4.

Campsites, facilities: There are 100 tent sites, all with water and electric hookups, and 100 RV sites. Half of the RV sites have full hookups, and the rest have water and electric only. Pull-through sites are available. Most campsites have picnic tables. Restrooms have hot showers and flush toilets. A sanitary disposal station, coin laundry, and swimming pool are provided. The facilities are wheelchair accessible. Leashed pets are permitted.

Reservations, fees: Reservations are accepted, and no deposit is required. The fee for tents is $14.50 per night, and $20.50 for RVs.

Open: Year-round.

Directions: From Atlanta, take Interstate 20 west and

exit onto Thornton Road. Go north to Maxham Road and turn right, then left onto Old Alabama Road.

Contact: Atlanta West Campground, 2420 Old Alabama Rd., Austell, GA 30168; 770/941-7185.

Trip notes: There is a small creek running through the campground that has some game fish. The campground is three miles from the Six Flags Over Georgia theme park.

23 Arrowhead Campground

Location: Atlanta, map 3, grid B4.

Campsites, facilities: Half of the 10 tent sites at the campground have shade. Of the 130 RV sites, all have full hookups, most are pull-through sites and about half have shade. Limited RV storage is available. Some sites have picnic tables, and the pavilion offers a cooking grill. Restrooms have hot showers and flush toilets. Limited groceries, ice, LP gas, and gifts are available at the campground store. Other amenities include a playground, swimming pool, clubroom, and coin laundry, and a sanitary disposal station is on the premises. There is some wheelchair access. Pets are permitted with a $5 additional fee.

Reservations, fees: All sites are $25 per night.

Open: Year-round.

Directions: From Atlanta, take Interstate 20 to exit 13, and go north one-half mile on Six Flags Drive.

Contact: Arrowhead Campground, 7400 Six Flags Dr. SW, Austell, GA 30168; 770/732-1130, or 800/631-8956.

Trip notes: The campground is one-quarter mile from the Six Flags Over Georgia theme park, and 10 miles to all of Atlanta's downtown attractions. It is a thirty-minute drive to Kennesaw Mountain National Battlefield Park, which has miles of hiking and horseback trails, and to a large water park.

24 Stone Mountain Family Campground

Location: Stone Mountain Park, map 3, grid B7.

Campsites, Facilities: This large campground has 149 RV sites with full hook-ups, 220 campsites for tents and pop-ups with water and electricity, and 54 primitive walk-in sites. Three sanitary disposal stations and nine comfort stations with flush toilets and hot showers are available. Note that the water pressure at the campground is very high (80–112 psi), so a regulator or gauge is needed. Picnic tables, fire rings, and barbecue grills are available at most sites. Three coin laundries provide convenience. A pavilion is available for rent. The camp store, which has a game room, sells fresh produce in addition to regular camping staples, ice, firewood, and LP gas. Two RV service centers are within 10 miles of the park. A water taxi transports visitors from the campground to the park. Boat motors on the lake are restricted to 10 horsepower and 10 miles per hour at all times. A playground and sports field are provided. All facilities are wheelchair accessible. Leashed pets are permitted, but you must clean up after your pet.

Reservations, fees: Reservations are accepted from 90 days up to one weeks before arrival. Half of the campsites may be reserved; the rest are available on a first come, first served basis. The maximum stay is two weeks except from November 1st through March 31st, when monthly stays are allowed.

Rates are $22–32 per night, depending on hookups, and include admission to the laser show during the summer.

Open: Year-round.

Directions: From Atlanta, take the Stone Mountain Freeway (US 78) east 16 miles to the park.

Contact: Stone Mountain Family Campground, P.O. Box 778, Stone Mountain, GA 30086; 770/498-5710, reservations 800/385-9807; website: www.stonemountainpark.com.

Trip notes: Stone Mountain Park used to be part of the state park system but has been privatized. The park includes 3,200 acres of lakes and woodlands, with a beach, fishing area (particularly for crappie, bass, and catfish), a paddlewheel riverboat, a scenic railroad, an antebellum plantation, a wildlife preserve and petting zoo, an antique car museum, several nature trails, a marina, a championship golf course and miniature golf, tennis courts, bike, paddleboat and water bike rentals, a large playground, and cable cars to the top of the mountain.

Stone Mountain is the largest expanse of exposed granite in the world. The granite has huge relief carvings of three Confederate war heroes astride their horses and is the site of spectacular laser shows throughout the summer. The park hosts numerous special events throughout the year, including the Yellow Daisy Festival, named for the plant which grows nowhere else in the world. The campground is 15 miles from Turner Field, 12 miles to Zoo Atlanta and the Cyclorama, and 20 miles to Underground Atlanta, the World of Coca-Cola, and the Jimmy Carter Library. This campground is an excellent first destination for new campers from the Atlanta area to test their equipment. For tent and pop-up campers, the full-service facility has available nearly anything you might forget

on a first camping trip. There are two RV service centers within 10 miles. The time to find out that your new tent didn't come with a rain fly or tent stakes, or your RV's awning doesn't extend, is not when you're tucked away in a remote area, far from supplies and help.

25 Riverside Estates RV and Mobile Home Park

Location: Atlanta, map 4, grid D1.

Campsites, facilities: There are 172 RV sites, all with full hookups. Pull-through sites and some shade are available. Picnic tables are provided. RV storage is available. Restrooms have hot showers and flush toilets. A coin laundry, swimming pool, and playground are provided. Ice, LP gas, and snacks are available at the campground. Cable TV hookups are available. The buildings are wheelchair accessible. Pets must be inside or on a leash at all times.

Reservations, fees: Reservations are not accepted. The fee is $18 per night, or $77 per week. Good Sam, Woodalls, Wheelers, and AAA discounts apply.

Open: Year-round.

Directions: From Atlanta, go east on Interstate 20 32 miles and turn right onto Almon Road at exit 88. Turn left onto the access road. The campground is 100 yards down the access road.

Contact: Riverside Estates RV and Mobile Home Park, 1891 Access Rd., Covington, GA 30014; 770/787-3707.

Trip notes: The campground is seven miles from the Georgia International Horse Park, site of some of the events of the 1996 Olympics. It is 20 miles to Stone Mountain.

GEORGIA HEARTLAND

FDR State Park

GEORGIA HEARTLAND

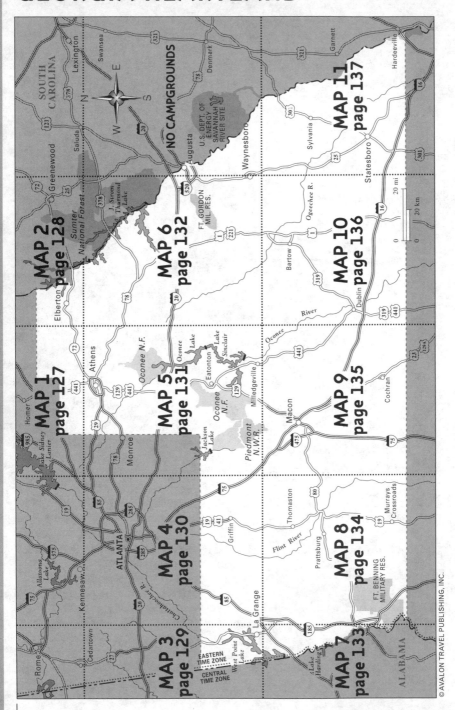

MAP 1

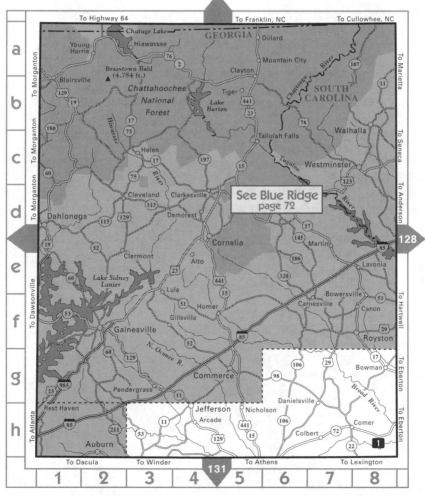

To Highway 64   To Franklin, NC   To Cullowhee, NC

Chatuge Lake   GEORGIA   Dillard

Young Harris   Hiawassee   Mountain City

Brasstown Bald ▲ (4,784 ft.)   Clayton

Blairsville

Chattahoochee National Forest   Tiger   Lake Burton

SOUTH CAROLINA

Tallulah Falls   Walhalla

Helen   Tugaloo   Westminster

Cleveland   Clarkesville

See Blue Ridge page 72

Dahlonega   Demorest   Martin

Clermont   Cornelia   Lavonia

Alto

Lake Sidney Lanier   Lula   Bowersville   Canon

Homer   Carnesville

Gillsville

Gainesville   Royston

N. Oconee R.

Bowman

Commerce   Broad River

Pendergrass   Danielsville

Rest Haven   Jefferson   Nicholson

Arcade   Colbert   Comer

Auburn

To Dacula   To Winder   To Athens   To Lexington

To Morganton   To Dawsonville   To Atlanta

To Marietta   To Seneca   To Anderson   To Hartwell   To Eberton

MAP 2

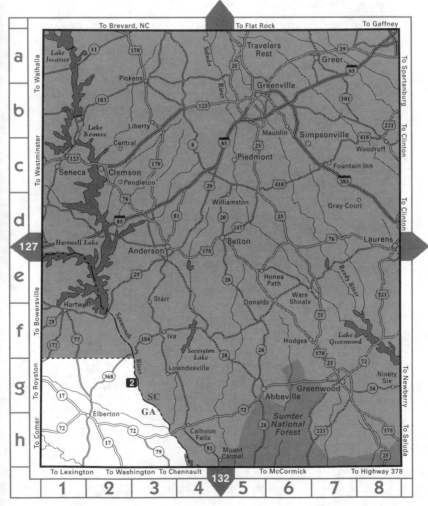

To Brevard, NC — To Flat Rock — To Gaffney

MAP 3

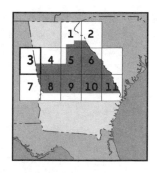

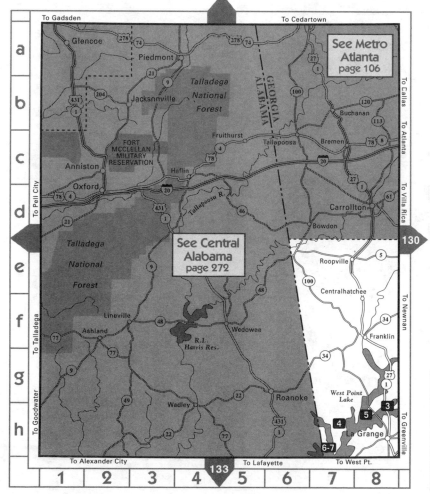

To Gadsden

To Cedartown

Glencoe

Piedmont

See Metro
Atlanta
page 106

Talladega
National
Forest

Jacksonville

GEORGIA
ALABAMA

Buchanan

FORT
MCCLELLAN
MILITARY
RESERVATION

Fruithurst

Tallapoosa

Bremen

Anniston

Heflin

Oxford

Carrollton

Tallapoosa R.

Bowdon

See Central
Alabama
page 272

Talladega

Roopville

National

Centralhatchee

Forest

Lineville

Franklin

Ashland

R.L.
Harris Res.

Wedowee

West Point
Lake

Wadley

Roanoke

La Grange

To Alexander City

To Lafayette

To West Pt.

To Talladega

To Goodwater

To Pell City

To Villa Rica

To Newnan

To Greenville

To Callas

To Atlanta

© AVALON TRAVEL PUBLISHING, INC.

MAP 4

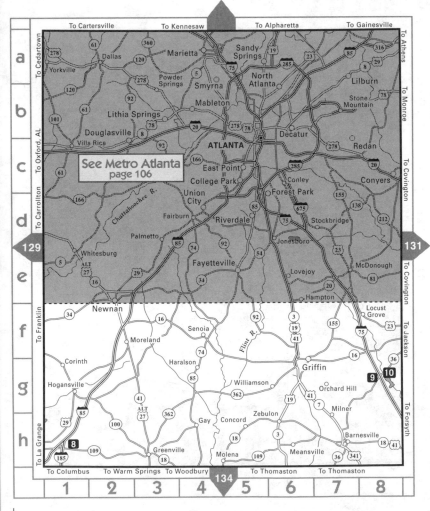

To Cartersville   To Kennesaw   To Alpharetta   To Gainesville

a
To Cedartown
278 — 61 — 360 — Marietta — Sandy Springs — 19 — 316
Dallas — 120 — 75 — 285 — 23 — 85
Yorkville — 278 — Powder Springs — 5 — North Atlanta — 8 — 29 — To Athens
120 — 92 — Smyrna — Lilburn — 78

b
To Oxford, AL
61 — Mableton — Stone Mountain — To Monroe
101 — Lithia Springs — 78 — 20 — 278 — 78
Douglasville — 8 — 78 — **ATLANTA** — Decatur
Villa Rica — 92 — 278 — Redan

c
To Carrollton
61 — **See Metro Atlanta page 106** — 166 — East Point — 285 — 20 — To Covington
166 — College Park — Conley — Conyers
Chattahoochee R. — Union City — Forest Park — 155 — 138
Fairburn — 85 — 675 — Stockbridge — 212

d
129
Palmetto — 85 — 74 — 92 — Riverdale — 75 — Jonesboro
Whitesburg — 23 — McDonough — 131
5 — ALT 27 — 29 — Fayetteville — 54 — 81 — To Covington

e
16 — 34 — Lovejoy — 20 — Hampton

f
To Franklin
34 — Newnan — 16 — Senoia — 92 — 3 — 155 — Locust Grove — To Jackson
Moreland — 19 — 75 — 23
41

g
Corinth — Haralson — 74 — Griffin — 16 — 36
Hogansville — 85 — Williamson — Orchard Hill — **9** **10**
41 — ALT 27 — 362 — 19 — 41 — Milner — To Forsyth
100 — 362 — Gay — Concord — Zebulon — 7

h
To La Grange
85 — Barnesville
29 — **8** — 109 — Greenville — 18 — Molena — 109 — Meansville — 18 — 41
185 — 18 — 3 — 36 — 341

To Columbus   To Warm Springs   To Woodbury   **134**   To Thomaston   To Thomaston

1   2   3   4   5   6   7   8

© AVALON TRAVEL PUBLISHING, INC.

130 Georgia

MAP 5

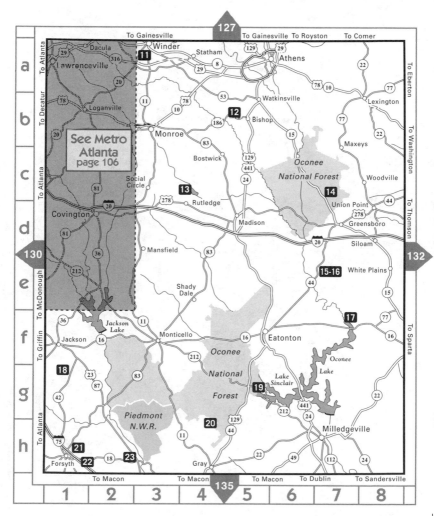

MAP 6

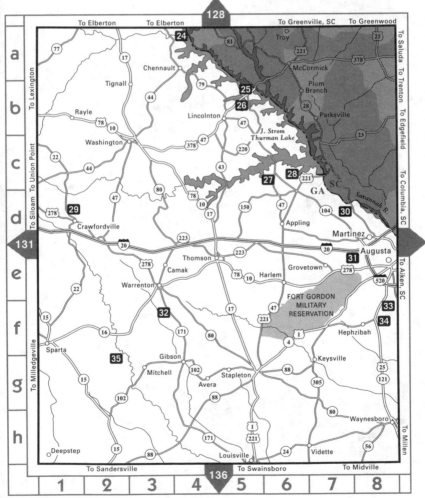

MAP 7

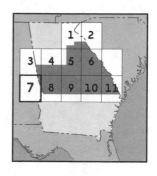

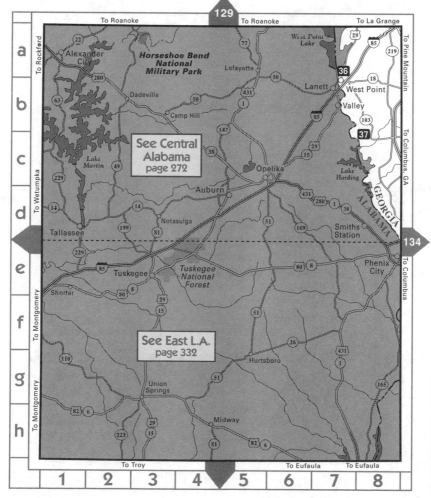

MAP 8

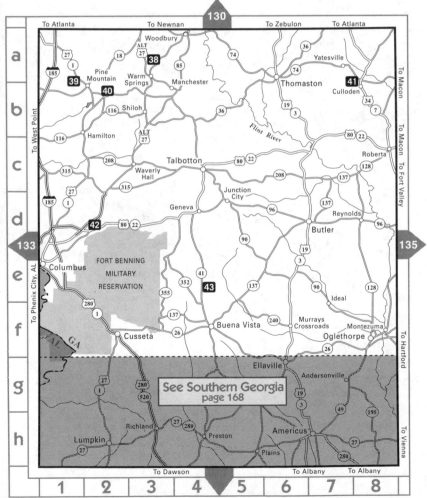

© AVALON TRAVEL PUBLISHING, INC.

MAP 9

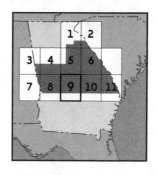

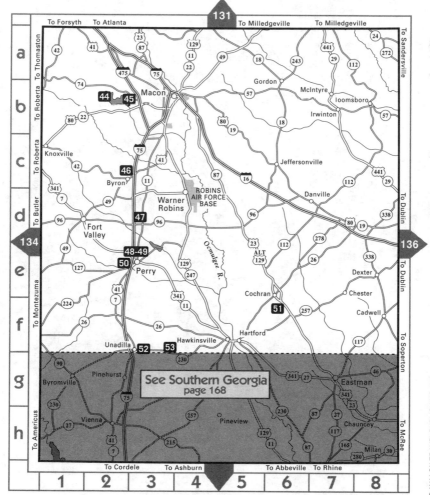

To Forsyth   To Atlanta   131   To Milledgeville   To Milledgeville

a To Thomaston · To Roberta   42   41   23   87   129   11   22   49   18   243   29   112   441   24   272   To Sandersville

475   75   Gordon   57   McIntyre   Ioomsboro

b To Roberta   44   45   Macon   80   22   80   19   18   Irwinton   57

c To Roberta · To Butler   Knoxville   42   341   46   Byron   11   41   87   16   Jeffersonville   112   441   29   To Dublin

d 134   7   49   ROBINS AIR FORCE BASE   Warner Robins   47   96   96   Danville   80   338   19   136

e To Montezuma   96   Fort Valley   48-49   50   Perry   129   247   Ocmulgee R.   23   ALT 129   112   278   26   338   Dexter   To Dublin

f 224   41   7   341   11   26   Cochran   Chester   257   Cadwell   51   Hartford   117   To Soperton

26   Unadilla   52   53   Hawkinsville   230

g To Americus   90   Byromville   Pinehurst   **See Southern Georgia page 168**   341   27   Eastman   46   341   23   To McRae

75

h 230   27   Vienna   257   Pineview   230   87   27   Chauncey   To McRae
41   7   215   129   11   87   117   165   Milan   280   30

To Cordele   To Ashburn   To Abbeville   To Rhine

1   2   3   4   5   6   7   8

© AVALON TRAVEL PUBLISHING, INC.

MAP 10

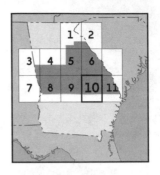

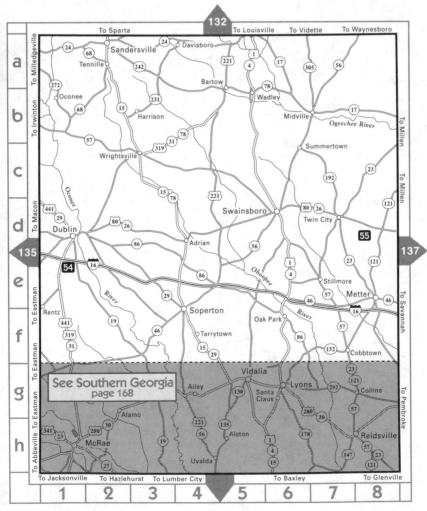

To Sparta · To Louisville · To Vidette · To Waynesboro

132

To Milledgeville

a
To Sparta
24
68
Sandersville
24
Davisboro
Tennille
221
1
242
4
17
305
56
Bartow
78

b
To Irwinton
272
Oconee
231
Wadley
17
68
15
Harrison
Midville
Ogeechee River
57
78
31
Summertown

c
Wrightsville
319
15
78
221
192
23
Swainsboro
121

d
To Macon
441
Oconee
29
80
26
80
26
Twin City
55
Dublin
86
Adrian
56
23
121

e
54
16
River
86
Ohoopee
1
4
Stillmore
23
121
29
46
57
Metter
To Savannah

f
To Eastman
Rentz
441
19
Soperton
River
16
319
46
Oak Park
57
31
Tarrytown
15
29
86
152
Cobbtown

g
To Eastman
To Eastman
See Southern Georgia
page 168
Ailey
Vidalia
23
121
Lyons
292
Collins
130
Santa
Claus
280
57
To Pembroke

h
To Abbeville
341
23
280
Alamo
19
221
135
Alston
178
Reidsville
30
30
McRae
56
1
57
23
27
Uvalda
4
147
121
15

To Jacksonville · To Hazlehurst · To Lumber City · To Baxley · To Glenville

1 2 3 4 5 6 7 8

135 ◄

137 ►

MAP 11

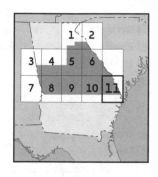

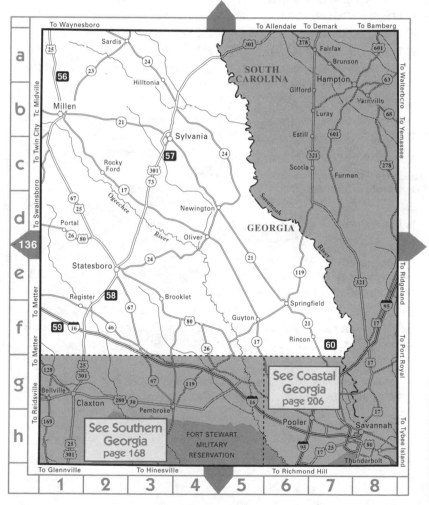

A HEARTLAND

1 Watson Mill Bridge State Park

Location: Comer, map 1, grid H8.

Campsites, Facilities: There are 21 campsites suitable for tents or RVs, all with water and electric hookups. Picnic tables and fire rings are provided. Pull-through sites are available. Primitive camping is available. Restrooms have hot showers and flush toilets. Ice is available at the campground. A sanitary disposal station is provided. Restrooms are wheelchair accessible. Leashed pets are permitted.

Reservations, fees: Reservations are accepted at 800/864-7275 or 770/389-7275 (within the Atlanta area). The deposit of one night's fee is non-refundable, but your reservation can be moved once to another date. Fees range from $13–15. Like all of Georgia's state parks, there is a $2 per day parking fee, or you can purchase an annual Georgia Park-Pass for $25. Campers pay for just one daily pass for their entire stay.

Open: Year-round.

Directions: From Atlanta, take Highway 316 northeast to Athens. Take the Loop 10 bypass around the city, and exit onto US 29 north towards Danielsville. Stay on US 29 for about two miles, and turn right onto Highway 72 towards Comer. Turn right at Comer's one traffic light onto Highway 22. After three miles, turn left onto Watson Mill Road. It is three more miles to the park and campground.

Contact: Watson Mill Bridge State Park, 650 Watson Mill Rd., Comer, GA 30629; 706/783-5349.

Trip notes: Watson Mill Bridge is the longest covered bridge in Georgia and is over 100 years old. Fishing is available for catfish, bass, and bream. Canoes and paddle boats are available for rent. There are 20 miles of hiking, biking, and horseback riding trails through the heavily-wooded area.

2 Richard B. Russell State Park

Location: Russell Lake, map 2, grid G3.

Campsites, facilities: There are 28 campsites suitable for tents or RVs, all with water and electric hookups. Pull-through sites are available. Picnic tables and fire rings are provided. Rental cabins are available. Restrooms have hot showers and flush toilets, and are wheelchair accessible. Cable TV hookups are available. A sanitary disposal station, boat ramp, and dock are provided. Leashed pets are permitted.

Reservations, fees: Reservations are accepted at 800/864-7275 or 770/389-7275 within the Atlanta area. The deposit of one night's fee is non-refundable, but your reservation can be moved once to another date. Fees range from $14–17. Like all of Georgia's state parks, there is a $2 per day parking fee, or you can purchase an annual Georgia ParkPass for $25. Campers pay for just one daily pass for their entire stay.

Open: Year-round.

Directions: From Atlanta, take Interstate 85 north to Highway 17 and turn south. At Elberton, turn north on Highway 77, then right on Ruckersville Road. Follow Ruckersville Road to the lake and the park.

Contact: Richard B. Russell State Park, 2650 Russell State Park Rd., Elberton, GA 30635; 706/213-2045.

Trip notes: Fishing is available in the lake. Canoes and paddleboats are available for rent. There is a sand beach in the swimming area. There are six miles of hiking trails, including one with handicapped access, and a disc golf course.

❸ Ringer Campground

Location: West Point Lake, map 3, grid H8.

Campsites, facilities: There are 37 sites that can be used for either tents or RVs, but no hookups are provided. Three sites are pull-through. Some sites will not accommodate RVs more than 30 feet long. RV storage is available nearby. Picnic tables and fire rings are provided. Restrooms have vault toilets. No drinking water is available. A boat ramp and dock are available. The restrooms are wheelchair accessible. Leashed pets are permitted.

Reservations, fees: Reservations are not accepted. There are no fees for this campground.

Open: Year-round.

Directions: From LaGrange, go north on US 27, and follow the signs.

Contact: Ringer Campground, 500 Resource Management Dr., West Point, GA 31833; 706/645-2937.

Trip notes: Fishing for bass, bream, catfish, and crappie is available in 26,000-acre West Point Lake. There is a sand beach in the swimming area. The campground is located within 20 miles of Callaway Gardens, which hosts an Azalea Festival each spring, FDR State Park and FDR's Little White House State Historic Site.

❹ Holiday Campground

Location: West Point Lake, map 3, grid H7.

Campsites, facilities: There are 127 campsites suitable for either tents or RVs. Of these, 92 have full hookups. Some sites won't accommodate RVs more than 40 feet long. There are also 45 primitive sites for tents only. Picnic tables, fire rings, and cooking grills are provided. RV storage is available nearby. Restrooms have hot showers and flush toilets. A coin laundry, tennis court, boat ramp, dock, playground, and sanitary disposal station are provided. The buildings are wheelchair accessible. Pets are permitted and must be leashed while in the campground. You must clean up after your pet.

Reservations, fees: Reservations are accepted through the National Recreation Reservation Service (NRRS) at 877/444-6777; website: www.reserveusa.com. The full amount is payable in advance. Site fees are $14–36 per night, depending on hookups and location.

Open: Year-round.

Directions: From LaGrange, take Highway 109 west eight miles and follow the signs. The campground is just past Whitetail Ridge Campground.

Contact: Holiday Campground, 954 Abbottsford Rd., LaGrange, GA 30240; 706/884-6818.

Trip notes: Fishing for bass, bream, catfish, and crappie is available in 26,000-acre West Point Lake. There is a sand beach in the swimming area. It is within 20 miles to such sites as Callaway Gardens, home of the spring Azalea Festival, and to both FDR State Park and his Little White House State Historic Site.

❺ Three Creeks Campground

Location: LaGrange, map 3, grid H8.

Campsites, facilities: The campground has 35 RV sites, all with full hookups, and three sites suitable for tents or small campers. Most of the sites offer shade. Pull-through sites are available. Picnic tables are provided at most of the sites. RV storage is available. Restrooms have hot showers and flush toilets. Ice and firewood are available at the campground. A coin laundry, swimming pool, water slide, skating rink, batting cage, playground, and clubroom are provided. The restrooms are wheelchair accessible. Leashed pets are permitted.

Reservations, fees: Reservations are accepted. Non-refundable deposits are required for holiday weekends. Rates are $18–22 per night, $120–132 per week, and $300–325 per month.

Open: Year-round.

Directions: From Interstate 85, take exit 18 and turn west on Highway 109. About eight miles past LaGrange, turn right onto Vernon Ferry Road. The campground is one mile down on the left.

Contact: Three Creeks Campground, 305 Old Roanoke Rd., LaGrange, GA 30240; 706/884-0899.

Trip notes: The campground has a private pond stocked with catfish. It is located on West Point Lake, which has a sand beach in the swimming area and boat ramps. It is 20 miles from Callaway Gardens, a beautiful spot at any time of the year, but incredibly so in the spring when the azalea gardens are in full bloom. Wildlife in the area includes deer, wild turkeys, squirrels, and beavers.

6 Stateline Campground

Location: West Point Lake, map 3, grid H7.

Campsites, facilities: There are 61 tent sites, 55 with shade. In a separate section, there are 61 RV sites, 54 with full hookups and most with shade. Some sites cannot accommodate RVs longer than 35 feet. RV storage is available nearby. Picnic tables, fire rings, and cooking grills are provided. Restrooms have showers and flush toilets. A coin laundry, boat ramp, dock, playground and sanitary disposal station are available. Buildings are wheelchair accessible. Leashed pets are per-

mitted. You must clean up after your pet.

Reservations, fees: Reservations are accepted through the National Recreation Reservation Service (NRRS) at 877/444-6777; website: www.reserveusa.com. The full amount is payable in advance. Site fees are $12–18 per night.

Open: The campground is open from April 1 until Labor Day.

Directions: From LaGrange, go west on Highway 109 for 10 miles. After you cross the lake, turn left on Old Stateline Road/County Road 288. The road dead-ends into the park.

Contact: Stateline Campground, 1000 County Road 288, Five Points, AL 36855; 706/882-5439.

Trip notes: West Point Lake is a 26,000-acre lake straddling the state line of Georgia and Alabama and offering fishing for bass, bream, catfish, and crappie. The park straddles the border as well, with the campground located about 20 miles from Callaway Gardens. The gardens host an Azalea Festival each spring, FDR State Park, and FDR's Little White House State Historic Site.

7 Whitetail Ridge Campground

Location: West Point Lake, map 3, grid H7.

Campsites, facilities: There are 58 sites that can accommodate either tents or RVs, all of which have water and electric hookups. Pull-through sites are available. Most sites have shade. Some sites are too short for RVs greater than 35 feet in length. Group sites are available. RV storage is available nearby. Picnic tables, fire rings, and cooking grills are provided. Restrooms have hot showers and flush toilets. A coin laundry, boat ramp, dock, playground, and sanitary disposal station are provided. The restrooms are wheelchair accessible. Leashed pets are permitted, but you must clean up after your pet.

Reservations, fees: Reservations are accepted through the National Recreation Reservation Service (NRRS) at 877/444-6777; website: www.reserveusa.com. The full amount is payable in advance. Single sites are $20, and double sites, with room for two tent pads or RV spots, are $40. Primitive sites are $14.

Open: Year-round.

Directions: From LaGrange, go west eight miles on Highway 109. After crossing the Wade Milam Bridge, turn left onto Thompson Road. After one mile, bear left onto Abbottsford Road. The campground is 0.75 miles down on the left.

Contact: Whitetail Ridge Campground, 565 Abbottsford Rd., LaGrange, GA 30240; 706/884-8972.

Trip notes: West Point Lake offers fishing for bass, bream, crappie, and catfish. The campground is located within 20 miles of Callaway Gardens, which hosts an Azalea Festival each spring, FDR State Park and FDR's Little White House State Historic Site.

8 Pyne Road Park

Location: West Point Lake, map 4, grid H1.

Campsites, facilities: There are 10 primitive tent sites at this campground and 24 RV sites. The RV sites all have water and electric hookups. Picnic tables, fire rings, and cooking grills are provided. Restrooms have hot showers and flush toilets. A sanitary disposal station, boat ramp, dock, and horse corral are provided. Leashed pets are permitted.

Reservations, fees: Reservations are not accepted. Primitive tent sites are $10 per night, and RV sites are $15. Discounts for seniors and the disabled apply.

Open: The campground is open from the end of February through October.

Directions: From LaGrange, take Interstate 85 north and turn right on Highway 109 West. Follow Highway 109 five miles to the Troup County Park on the left.

Contact: Pyne Road Park, 4481 Roanoke Road Highway 109 West, La Grange, GA 30241; 706/884-1414.

Trip notes: Fishing is available in the lake for bass, crappie, catfish, and bream. There are hiking and horseback riding trails throughout the park. There is a sand beach in the swimming area. The park has a large amount of wildlife, including deer, wild turkeys, and red foxes. There is usually a deer in an observation pen. The nearby marina rents pontoon boats and paddleboats. The campground is near a skating rink and swimming pool, and about 20 miles from Callaway Gardens.

9 High Falls Campground

Location: Barnesville, map 4, grid G8.

Campsites, facilities: There are 51 tent sites, most with water and electric hookups, and 69 RV sites, all with full hookups. Most sites have picnic tables and fire rings. Restrooms have hot showers and flush toilets. A sanitary disposal station, coin laundry, swimming pool, playground, and clubroom are provided. Ice, LP gas, and groceries are available at the campground. Pets are permitted.

Reservations, fees: Reservations are accepted at 800/428-0132. The deposit of one night's fee is refundable with a two-day notice. All campsites are $16 per night.

Open: Year-round.

Directions: From Atlanta, take Interstate 75 south to exit 198/High Falls Road. Cross over the interstate to the campground.

Contact: High Falls Campground, 1046 High Falls Park Rd., Barnesville, GA 30204; 770/358-2205.

Trip notes: The campground is two miles from the state park, which offers fishing, paddleboats for rent, and hiking trails.

10 High Falls State Park

Location: Jackson, map 4, grid G8.

Campsites, facilities: There are 112 campsites suitable for tents or RVs, all with water and electric hookups. Pull-through sites are available. Primitive camping is also available. Restrooms have hot showers and flush toilets. A sanitary disposal station, boat ramp, dock, miniature golf, and swimming pool are provided. The restrooms are wheelchair accessible. Leashed pets are permitted.

Reservations, fees: Reservations are accepted at 800/864-7275 or 770/389-7275 (within the Atlanta area). The deposit of one night's fee is non-refundable, but your reservation can be moved once to another date. Fees range from $15–20. Like all of Georgia's state parks, there is a $2 per day parking fee, or you can purchase an annual Georgia Park-Pass for $25. Campers pay for just one daily pass for their entire stay.

Open: Year-round.

Directions: From Interstate 75, take exit 198/High Falls Road east 1.8 miles to the park and campground.

Contact: High Falls State Park, 76 High Falls Park Dr., Jackson, GA 30233; 478/993-3053.

Trip notes: Fishing is available in the lake for bass, crappie, and bream. Pontoon boats, canoes, and paddleboats are available for rent. There are three hiking trails, waterfalls, and the ruins of an old grist mill.

11 Fort Yargo State Park

Location: Winder, map 5, grid A3.

Campsites, facilities: There are 40 RV sites and 35 tent sites, all with water and electric hookups. Pull-through sites are available. The RV sites all have shade. There are also seven primitive campsites and three cabins. Picnic tables, fire pits, and cooking grills are provided. Restrooms have hot showers and flush toilets. A sanitary disposal station is provided, along with tennis courts, a playground, boat ramp, and dock. The maximum motor size for boats is 10 horsepower. Facilities are wheelchair accessible. Dogs are permitted on a maximum six-foot leash. Pets are not allowed on the beach or in the cabins.

Reservations, fees: Reservations are accepted at 800/864-7275 or 770/389-7275 (within the Atlanta area). The deposit of one night's fee is non-refundable, but your reservation can be moved once to another date. Fees range from $0–17. Like all of Georgia's state parks, there is a $2 per day parking fee, or you can purchase an annual Georgia Park-Pass for $25. Campers pay for just one daily pass for their entire stay.

Open: Year-round.

Directions: From Atlanta, go North on Interstate 85 and turn east on Highway 316 towards Lawrenceville. Just after entering Barrow County, turn left at the light onto Highway 81. The park is about four miles north of Highway 316, on the right.

Contact: Fort Yargo State Park, P.O. Box 764, Winder, GA 30680; 770/867-3489; email: ft_yargo@innerx.net; website: www.gastate parks.org.

Trip notes: Fort Yargo is gorgeous in the springtime. Wild violets are plentiful near the fort, a small structure built to protect settlers from the Indians. Swimming is popular along the beach area of the 260-acre lake. Deer, rabbits and raccoons are said to be plentiful, but I've never spotted any on my visits here, probably because I've always had a dog or two in tow.

12 Pine Lake Campground

Location: Athens, map 5, grid B5.

Campsites, facilities: There are seven tent sites with water and electric hookups. In a separate section, there are 30 RV sites with full hookups. All sites have shade. Pull-through sites are available. Picnic tables, fire rings, and cooking grills are available. The restrooms have hot showers and flush toilets. A coin laundry, playground, and clubroom are available. Ice and firewood are available at the campground. Buildings are wheelchair accessible. Leashed pets are permitted.

Reservations, fees: Reservations are accepted. The deposit is refundable if cancellation is given 48 hours before your scheduled arrival. The rate is $19.50 per night, or $400 per month.

Open: Year-round.

Directions: From Athens, take US 129/ 441 south 12 miles to the junction of Highway 186. Go west on Highway 186 1.4 miles to the campground.

Contact: Pine Lake Campground, 5540 High Shoals Rd., Bishop, GA 30621; 706/769-5486, email: pinelakerv@aol.com.

Trip notes: The campground has a lake stocked with catfish, bass, and bream, and a one-mile nature trail. It is 12 miles from Athens and the State Botanical Gardens.

13 Hard Labor Creek State Park

Location: Rutledge, map 5, grid C4.

Campsites, facilities: There are 51 campsites suitable for either tents or RVs, all with water and electric hookups. Pull-through sites are available. Picnic tables and fire rings are provided. Cabins are available. Restrooms have hot showers and flush toilets. Ice, supplies, and groceries are available at the campground. A sanitary disposal station, boat ramp, and dock are provided. The restrooms are wheelchair accessible. Leashed pets are permitted.

Reservations, fees: Reservations are accepted at 800/864-7275 or 770/389-7275 (within the Atlanta area). The deposit of the first night's fee is non-refundable, but your reservation date can be moved once. Fees range from $12–17. Like all of Georgia's state parks, there is a $2 per day parking fee, or you can purchase an annual Georgia ParkPass for $25. Campers pay for just one daily pass for their entire stay.

Open: Year-round.

Directions: From Atlanta, take Interstate 20 east to exit 105, and go north through Rutledge. The park and campground will be on your right on Fairplay Road.

Contact: Hard Labor Creek State Park, P.O. Box 247, Rutledge, GA 30663; 706/557-3001.

Trip notes: Fishing is available in two lakes and the creek. Paddleboats, canoes, and pontoon boats are available for rent. There are 2.5 miles of hiking trails and over 20 miles of trails for horseback riding. The park has a public golf course. There is a sand beach in the swimming area at the lake.

14 Oconee River Campground

Location: Greensboro, map 5, grid C7.

Campsites, facilities: There are six campsites at this campground, all suitable for tents or small RVs. Picnic tables and cooking grills are provided. Pit toilets are provided. Drinking water is available at a hand pump. A boat ramp is provided. Leashed pets are permitted.

Reservations, fees: Reservations are not accepted. The fee is $5 per night.

Open: Year-round.

Directions: From Greensboro, take Highway 15 northwest for 12 miles to the campground.

Contact: Oconee River Campground, Oconee Ranger District, 7110. 1199 Madison Rd., Eatonton, GA 31024; 706/485-7110, or 706/485-1776.

Trip notes: Fishing is available in the river for bass, crappie, bream, and catfish. There is a 1-mile hiking trail to the Scull Shoals area.

15 Parks Ferry Campground

Location: Lake Oconee, map 5, grid E7.

Campsites, facilities: The campground has 51 tent sites with access to drinking water. There are also 53 sites suitable for tents or RVs, all with water and electric hookups. Picnic tables and cooking grills are provided. Restrooms have hot showers and flush toilets. A sanitary disposal station, coin laundry, boat ramp, and playground are provided. The buildings are wheelchair accessible. Leashed pets are permitted.

Reservations, fees: Reservations are accepted at 888/GPC-LAKE (888/472-5253). The deposit of $10 is not refundable, but applies toward your camping fee. The fee for tents is $12, and $14 for RVs.

Open: The campground is open from May through August.

Directions: From Atlanta, take Interstate 20 east. Exit south on Highway 44 and follow the signs.

Contact: Parks Ferry Campground, 125 Wallace Dam Rd. NE, Eatonton, GA 31024; 706/485-8704.

Trip notes: Fishing is available for bass, crappie, bream, and catfish. There is a hiking trail from the campground that totals about 1.5 miles. There is a sand beach in the swimming area.

16 Old Salem Recreation Area

Location: Lake Oconee, map 5, grid E7.

Campsites, facilities: The campground has 35 tent sites with access to drinking water. There are also 99 sites suitable for tents or RVs, all with water and electric hookups. Picnic tables and cooking grills are provided. Restrooms have hot showers and flush toilets. A sanitary disposal station, coin laundry, boat ramp, and playground are provided. The buildings are wheelchair accessible. Leashed pets are permitted.

Reservations, fees: Reservations are accepted at 888/GPC-LAKE (888/472-5253). The deposit of $10 is not refundable, but applies toward your camping fee. The fee for tents is $12, and $14 for RVs.

Open: The campground is open from March through October.

Directions: From Atlanta, take Interstate 20 east. Exit south on Highway 44 and follow the signs.

Contact: Old Salem Recreation Area, 125 Wallace Dam Rd. NE, Eatonton, GA 31024; 706/467-2850, or 706/485-8704.

Trip notes: Fishing is available for bass, crappie, bream, and catfish. There is a hiking trail from the campground that totals about 2.5 miles. There is a sand beach in the swimming area.

17 Lawrence Shoals Campground

Location: Lake Oconee, map 5, grid F7.

Campsites, facilities: The campground has 39 tent sites with access to drinking water. There are also 53 sites suitable for tents or RVs, all with water and electric hookups. Picnic tables and cooking grills are provided. Restrooms have hot showers and flush toilets. A sanitary disposal station, coin laundry, boat ramp, and playground are provided. The buildings are wheelchair accessible. Leashed pets are permitted.

Reservations, fees: Reservations are accepted at 888/GPC-LAKE (888/472-5253). The deposit of $10 is not refundable, but applies toward your camping fee. The fee for tents is $12, and $14 for RVs.

Open: The campground is open from February through November.

Directions: Take Interstate 75 south from Atlanta and exit east on Highway 16. Follow the signs to Wallace Dam and the campground, about 13 miles east of Eatonton.

Contact: Lawrence Shoals Campground, 125 Wallace Dam Road NE, Eatonton, GA 31024; 706/485-5494, or 706/485-8704.

Trip notes: Fishing is available for bass, crappie, bream, and catfish. There is a hiking trail from the campground that totals about one mile. There is a sand beach in the swimming area.

18 Indian Springs State Park

Location: Jackson, map 5, grid G1.

Campsites, facilities: There are 88 campsites suitable for tents or RVs, all with water and electric hookups. Picnic tables and fire rings are provided. Primitive camping is also available. Restrooms have hot showers and flush toilets. Ice is available at the campground. A sanitary disposal station, miniature golf, boat ramp, and dock are provided. The restrooms are wheelchair accessible. Leashed pets are permitted.

Reservations, fees: Reservations are accepted at 800/864-7275 or 770/389-7275 (within the Atlanta area). The deposit of one night's fee is non-refundable, but your reservation can be moved once to another date. Fees range from $13–15. Like all of Georgia's state parks, there is a $2 per day parking fee, or you can purchase an annual Georgia Park-Pass for $25. Campers pay for just one daily pass for their entire stay.

Open: Year-round.

Directions: From Atlanta, take Interstate 75 south to exit 205/Highway 16 and turn east. After about eight miles, turn right on Highway 42 and continue five more miles to the park and campground.

Contact: Indian Springs State Park, 678 Lake Clark Rd., Flovilla, GA 30216; 770/504-2277.

Trip notes: Fishing is available in the lake for bass, bream, catfish, and crappie. Pontoon boats and paddleboats are available to rent. There is a sand beach in the swimming area. This is one of the oldest state parks in the United States. Some of the buildings were built during the Depression. There is a short, 0.75-mile nature trail.

19 Lake Sinclair Beach Campground

Location: Eatonton, map 5, grid G5.

Campsites, Facilities: There are 44 campsites suitable for tents or small RVs. Picnic tables and cooking grills are provided. Restrooms have hot showers and flush toilets. Drinking water is available. A sanitary disposal station and boat ramp are provided. Leashed pets are permitted.

Reservations, fees: Reservations are not accepted. The fee is $7 per night.

Open: The campground is open from mid-April through mid-December.

Directions: From Eatonton, take US 129 south for 10 miles and turn left onto Highway 212. After one mile, turn left on Twin Bridges Road and follow the signs.

Contact: Lake Sinclair Beach Campground, Oconee Ranger District, 1199 Madison Rd., Eatonton, GA 31024; 706/485-7110 or 706/485-1776.

Trip notes: Fishing is available in the lake for bass, crappie, bream, and catfish. The 1.8-mile Twin Bridges Trail leads from the campground, and there are 144 miles of shore line. There is a beach in the swimming area.

20 Hillsboro Lake Campground

Location: Hillsboro, map 5, grid H4.

Campsites, Facilities: This small campground has five campsites for tents or small RVs. Picnic tables and cooking grills are provided. Pit toilets are provided. Drinking water is available at a hand pump. Leashed pets are permitted.

Reservations, fees: Reservations are not accepted. This is a no-fee campground.

Open: Year-round.

Directions: From Interstate 75, take US 129 northeast to Gray and turn left onto Highway 11. At Hillsboro, turn southeast onto Hillsboro Lake Road for three miles to the campground.

Contact: Hillsboro Lake Campground, Oconee Ranger District, 1199 Madison Rd., Eatonton, GA 31024; 706/485-7110 or 706/485-1776.

Trip notes: The small lake is stocked with bass, bream, and catfish.

21 Forsyth KOA

Location: Forsyth, map 5, grid H1.

Campsites, facilities: All of the 10 tent sites at this campground have shade. There are 102 RV sites in a separate section, a few with shade. There are 85 sites with full hookups. Pull-through sites are available. Each of the sites has a picnic table. There are also nine cabins. Restrooms have hot showers and flush toilets. The campground store sells groceries, ice, LP gas, and gifts. The campground provides a coin laundry, swimming pool, playground, and sanitary disposal station. Cable TV hookups are available. The buildings are wheelchair accessible. Leashed pets are permitted.

Reservations, fees: Reservations are accepted with a credit card guarantee at 800/562-8614. Site fees are $17 for tents, and $21–24 for RV sites. Cabins are $26.

Open: Year-round.

Directions: The campground is located between exits 186 and 187 off Interstate 75. From exit 186, turn right onto Juliette Road, then left onto Frontage Road.

Contact: Forsyth KOA, 414 S. Frontage Rd., Forsyth, GA 31029; 478/994-2019.

Trip notes: Fishing for bream, bass, and catfish is available at the private lake at the campground. Paddleboats are available to rent. Fishing and boating are also available at Lake Juliette, Lake Tobesofkee, High Falls Lake, Jackson Lake, and the Ocmulgee River, a favorite of canoers. The campground is well situated for trips to Macon, Warm Springs, and Callaway Gardens.

22 L & D RV Park

Location: Forsyth, map 5, grid H1.

Campsites, facilities: There are 28 RV sites at this campground. Most sites have full hookups, and the rest have water and electric only. Pull-through sites are available. Primitive tent sites are also available in a separate section. Picnic tables are provided for the developed campsites. RV storage is available. Restrooms have hot showers and flush toilets. A sanitary disposal station and coin laundry are provided. The facilities are wheelchair accessible. Leashed pets are permitted.

Reservations, fees: Reservations are not necessary. Tent sites are $12 per night, and RV sites are $18–20. Good Sam discounts apply.

Open: Year-round.

Directions: From Interstate 75, turn east at exit 185 onto Highway 18/Dames Ferry Road. The campground will be on the right, about two miles from the interstate.

Contact: L & D RV Park, 1655 Dames Ferry Rd., Forsyth, GA 31029; 478/994-5401.

Trip notes: Fishing is available at Lake Juliette, eight miles from the campground. There are hiking trails nearby at Rum Creek. The campground is 13 miles from Gerald Plantation, a pre-Civil War plantation open for tours. The town of Forsyth has an interesting museum of Native American and Civil War artifacts.

23 Lake Juliette - Dames Ferry Public Access Area

Location: Lake Juliette, map 5, grid H2.

Campsites, Facilities: There are 34 sites useable for both tents and RVs, all with water and electric hookups. Picnic tables and cooking grills are provided. Rest rooms have hot showers and flush toilets. Ice is available at the campground. A sanitary disposal station and boat ramps are provided. Leashed pets are permitted.

Reservations, fees: Reservations are accepted at 478/994-7945. The deposit of one night's fee is non-refundable. Site fees are $12 per night for tents, and $14 for RVs.

Open: The campground is open from April through September.

Contact: Lake Jackson Land Management Office, 180 Dam Road, Jackson, GA 30233; 478/994-7945.

Directions: At Macon, go north on Interstate 75 and turn east on Highway 87/Riverside Drive at exit 171. The campground is on the left, 12 miles from the interstate.

Trip notes: The 3600-acre lake is owned by Georgia Power, and maintained in cooperation with the Georgia Department of Natural Resources. Boat engines greater than 25 horsepower are prohibited, along with water skiing and jet skis. The lake is stocked with fish, including bass, catfish, and bream.

24 Bobby Brown State Park

Location: Elberton, map 6, grid A4.

Campsites, facilities: There are 61 sites for use by tents or RVs, all with water and electric hookups. Of these, 8 are pull-through sites and 55 have shade. RVs are restricted to 30 feet or less. Picnic tables and cooking grills are provided. RV storage is available nearby. Restrooms have hot showers and flush toilets. The nearest grocery store is three miles away, and RV supplies are available eight miles from the campground. A coin laundry, ice, firewood, and some gifts are available at the grocery store. The park offers a clubroom, swimming pool, playground, boat dock, and ramp. There are two sanitary disposal stations on the premises. The buildings are wheelchair accessible. Pets are permitted, but must be on a six-foot maximum length leash at all times.

Reservations, fees: Reservations are accepted at 800/864-7275 or 770/389-7275 within the Atlanta area. The deposit is non-refundable, but the date can be moved once. Rates are $12 for tent sites off the water and $14 for waterfront sites; for RVs, the fees are $14 for off-water sites and $16 for premium waterfront sites. Like all of Georgia's state parks, there is a $2 per day parking fee, or you can purchase an annual Georgia Park-Pass for $25. Campers pay for just one daily pass for their entire stay.

Open: Year-round.

Directions: From Interstate 85 near the South Carolina border, take Highway 17 south to Elberton. At Elberton, turn left onto Highway 72 east and follow the signs to the park.

Contact: Bobby Brown State Park, 2509 Bobby Brown State Park Rd., Elberton, GA 30635; 706/213-2046.

Trip notes: The park is located where the old town of Petersburg once stood. Located where the Broad and Savannah Rivers flow into the Clarks Hill Reservoir, foundations from the old town are visible when water levels are low. The 70,000-acre lake is the largest manmade lake east of the Mississippi. Fishing is popular at the lake, and catfish, striped and large mouth bass, crappie, perch, and trout are plentiful. The park's hiking trail is 1.9 miles long. Wildflowers at the park include jonquils, wild azaleas, dogwoods, red buds, and wisteria. Deer, wild turkeys, squirrels, raccoons, opossums, foxes, chipmunks, great blue herons, and various snakes are plentiful. Paddleboats can be rented at the campground, and kayaking is popular on the Savannah River. There are several historic sites in the area, including some above water, such as the Robert Toombs house site and pioneer Nancy Hart's cabin.

25 Elijah Clark State Park

Location: Clark Hill Lake/Lake Strom Thurmond, map 6, grid B5.

Campsites, facilities: There are 165 campsites suitable for tents or RVs, all with water, electric, and cable TV hookups. Picnic tables and fire rings are provided. There are also rental cabins. Restrooms have hot showers and flush toilets. A sanitary disposal station, coin laundry, miniature golf, boat ramp, dock, and playground are provided. The restrooms are wheelchair accessible. Leashed pets are permitted.

Reservations, fees: Reservations are accepted at 800/864-7275 or 770/389-7275 (within the Atlanta area). The deposit of one night's fee is not refundable, but the reservation can be moved once to another date. The fee for tents is $16, for trailers it's $18. Senior citizens and disabled veterans discounts apply. Like all of Georgia's state parks, there is a $2 per day parking fee, or you can purchase an annual Georgia Park-Pass for $25. Campers pay for just one daily pass for their entire stay.

Open: Year-round.

Directions: From Atlanta, take Interstate 20 east to exit 172/Thomson, and turn left onto Highway 17. After three miles, turn right onto Highway 43, which joins with US 378, and head towards Lincolnton. Stay on US 378 to the campground, which is about seven miles outside Lincolnton.

Contact: Elijah Clark State Park, 2959 Mc-Cormick Highway, Lincolnton, GA 30817; 706/359-3458.

Trip notes: Fishing is available for bass, crappie, and catfish. There are two trails, totaling just under four miles. The campground is 25 miles from the historic Robert Toombs house and museum in Washington.

26 Soap Creek Marina

Location: Lake Strom Thurmond, map 6, grid B5.

Campsites, Facilities: The campground has 35 RV sites, 20 with full hookups. The remaining 15 sites have water and electric hookups. Pull-through sites are available. Both 30- and 50-amp hookups are available. Picnic tables are provided. RV storage is available. Restrooms have hot showers and flush toilets. A sanitary dump station, boat ramp, and dock are provided. Ice and some groceries are available at the campground. The restrooms are wheelchair accessible. Leashed pets are permitted.

Reservations, fees: Reservations are not accepted. Campsites are $15 per night, plus $3 extra for an electric hookup.

Open: Year-round.

Directions: Take the Thomson exit off Interstate 20 and go north on Highway 17. Turn right onto Highway 43 to Lincolnton, then right on Highway 378 to the campground.

Contact: Soap Creek Marina, 3000 Soap Creek Lodge Rd., Lincolnton, GA 30817; 706/359-3124.

Trip notes: Fishing for bass, crappie, catfish, and bream is available in the lake.

Pontoon boats are available to rent. There is a sand beach in the swimming area. A 3-mile trail from the marina leads to the Bartram Trail, a strenuous trail that stretches for nearly 40 miles.

27 Mistletoe State Park

Location: Appling, map 6, grid C6.

Campsites, facilities: There are 91 campsites with full hookups that can be used by either tents or RVs. In addition, there are four primitive sites and 10 cabins. Picnic tables, fire rings, and cooking grills are provided. Restrooms have hot showers and flush toilets. Ice and firewood are available at the campground. A coin laundry, boat ramp, playground, and sanitary disposal station are provided. One cabin is wheelchair accessible. Pets are permitted on a six-foot maximum length leash at the campground, but are not permitted in the cabins.

Reservations, fees: Reservations are accepted at 800/864-7275 or 770/389-7275 (within the Atlanta area). The deposit is non-refundable, but the date can be moved once. Sites are $13–15. Like all of Georgia's state parks, there is a $2 per day parking fee, or you can purchase an annual Georgia ParkPass for $25. Campers pay for just one daily pass for their entire stay.

Open: Year-round.

Directions: Take exit 175/Highway150 and head north on Highway 150. Follow the signs to Mistletoe Road and the park.

Contact: Mistletoe State Park, 3723 Mistletoe Rd., Appling, GA 30802; 706/541-0321.

Trip notes: Fishing is available at the campground. There are 15 miles of hiking/biking trails at the park. Canoes and johnboats rentals are available. Wildlife in the area includes deer, wild turkeys, foxes, and squirrels.

28 Wildwood Park

Location: Augusta, map 6, grid C6.
Campsites, Facilities: The campground has 10 tent sites and 49 RV sites. All have water and electric hookups, and some have shade. Pull-through sites are available. Picnic tables, fire rings, and cooking grills are provided. A sanitary disposal station and a boat ramp are provided. Wood is available at the campground. Restrooms have hot showers and flush toilets. Most of the restrooms are wheelchair accessible. Leashed pets are permitted.
Reservations, fees: Reservations are accepted at 706/541-0586. The deposit of one night's rent is refundable with ten days notice. Campsites cost $16 per night. Senior citizens are discounted $3.
Open: Year-round.
Directions: From Atlanta, take Interstate 20 east to the Harlem/Appling exit, and turn left onto US 221. Travel four miles to the 4-way stop in Appling, and turn left onto Highway 104. The campground is one mile down on the right.
Contact: Wildwood Park, 6212 Holloway Road, Appling, GA 30802; 706/541-0586.
Trip notes: The campground is on Clark Hill Lake, also known as Strom Thurmond Lake, where fishing is good for bass, bream, catfish, and perch. Hiking is available on a 7-mile portion of the Bartram Trail, and mountain biking on a 6-mile trail. Wildlife commonly seen in the area includes deer, wild turkeys, and fox.

29 A. H. Stephens State Historic Park

Location: Crawfordville, map 6, grid D1.
Campsites, facilities: The 25 sites are suitable for both tents and RVs. All have water and electric hookups and shade, and nine are pull-through sites. The campsites have picnic tables, fire rings, and cooking grills. Cabins are also available. Restrooms have hot showers and flush toilets. The campground store sells ice and firewood. There is a swimming pool and playground, as well as a sanitary disposal station. The boat ramp can be used to launch non-electric boats only. The buildings are wheelchair accessible. Pets are permitted in the campground but not in the cabins.
Reservations, fees: Reservations are accepted at 800/864-7275. In the Atlanta area, call 770/389-7275. Deposits are refundable for the cabins (with a penalty), but not on campsites. Fees range from $13 for tents to $15 for trailers. The large group camp is $500 per night with a capacity of 150.
Open: The campsites are open all year.
Directions: From Atlanta, take Interstate 20 east. Turn north on Highway 22, then east on US 278, and follow the signs.
Contact: A. H. Stephens State Historic Park, P.O. Box 310, Crawfordville, GA 30631; 706/456-2602; email: ahssp@g-net.net.
Trip notes: The campground is within an hour's drive of Augusta, antebellum Madison, Athens, and Millegeville. The lake is stocked with bass, catfish and crappie. The hiking trails may also be used for horseback riding. Deer, squirrels and fox are plentiful. The group camp area has a sand beach, and paddleboats are available at the lake.

30 Ridge Road Campground

Location: Strom Thurmond Lake, map 6, grid D7.

Campsites, facilities: There are 69 campsites suitable for tents or RVs, all with water and electric hookups. Pull-through sites are available. Most sites have shade. Picnic tables, fire rings, and cooking grills are provided. Restrooms have hot showers and flush toilets. A sanitary disposal station, boat ramp, dock, and playground are provided. Pets are permitted.

Reservations, fees: Reservations are accepted through the National Recreation Reservation Service (NRRS) at 877/444-6777; website: www.reserveusa.com. The full amount is payable in advance. Campsites range from $14–18 per night, depending on location.

Open: The campground is open from April through September.

Directions: From Augusta, go north on Highway 104/Washington Road, and turn right onto Ridge Road.

Contact: Ridge Road Campground, 5886 Ridge Rd., Appling, GA 30802; 706/541-0282.

Trip notes: The lake offers fishing for bass, catfish, bream, and crappie.

31 Heritage Mobile Home Community, Inc.

Location: Augusta, map 6, grid E8.

Campsites, Facilities: There are 25 RV sites at this park, all with full hookups. Some shade is available. Picnic tables are provided, and some sites have cooking grills. There are no restrooms. Pets are allowed, but must be kept inside.

Reservations, fees: Reservations are accepted, and the deposit is refundable if cancellation is made at least one week in advance of your scheduled arrival. Campsites are $15 per night.

Open: Year-round.

Directions: From Atlanta, take Interstate 20 east to Belaire Road and turn right. Turn left onto Wrightsboro Road. The campground is one mile east on Wrightsboro Road.

Contact: Heritage Mobile Home Community, Inc., 3863 Wrightsboro Rd., Augusta, GA 30909; 706/863-3333.

Trip notes: This is primarily a mobile home park, but campsites are available for RVs for overnight stays. The park is less than five miles from a public golf course.

32 Rocky Comfort Plantation, Inc.

Location: Warrenton, map 6, grid F3.

Campsites, facilities: This small campground has 12 RV sites. All are pull-through sites with full hookups and shade. Picnic tables are provided at each site. A sanitary disposal station is on the premises. Pets are permitted if kept leashed.

Reservations, fees: Reservations are accepted. The rate from April through October is $20 per night, and $15 from November through March. Good Sam, Escapees and WIP members receive a 15% discount.

Open: Year-round.

Directions: From Atlanta, take Interstate 20 east. Exit south on US 278, then turn south on Highway 171 at Warrenton. The campground is seven miles south of US 278, and 18 miles south of Interstate 20.

Contact: Rocky Comfort Plantation, Inc., 1136 Johnson Circle SW, Warrenton, GA 30828; 706/465-2424.

Trip notes: The campground caters to retired campers, so it may not be a good choice for families with small children. It is a quiet, peaceful environment. Wildlife in the area includes deer and wild turkeys.

33 Flynn's Inn Camping Village

Location: Augusta, map 6, grid F8.

Campsites, facilities: There are 50 campsites suitable for tents or RVs, all with full hookups. Half are pull-through sites, and some sites have shade. There are also 10 primitive campsites. Restrooms have hot showers and flush toilets. A coin laundry is provided. Pets are permitted.

Reservations, fees: Reservations are accepted, and no deposit is required. The fee for tents is $14 per night. For RVs, 30-amp sites are $14, and 50-amp sites are $20.

Open: Year-round.

Directions: From Interstate 20, take exit 196A and turn south onto Interstate 520. At exit 7, turn right onto US 25 and head south about four miles. The campground will be on the left.

Contact: Flynn's Inn Camping Village, P.O. Box 5842, Augusta, GA 30916; 706/798-6912, or 706/796-8214.

Trip notes: The campground is four miles from a public golf course, and 11 miles from downtown Augusta.

34 Fox Hollow Campground

Location: Augusta, map 6, grid F8.

Campsites, Facilities: There are 21 sites that can be used by tents or RVs. All sites have full hookups, and most have shade. A pull-through site is available. Campsites have picnic tables. Restrooms have hot showers and flush toilets. The nearest groceries and supplies are about two miles from the campground. All sites have telephone connections. The restrooms are wheelchair accessible. Small pets are permitted. No big dogs are allowed. Your pet must be kept indoors except while being walked on leash.

Reservations, fees: Reservations are not accepted. Campsites cost $15 per night, $90 per week, and $125 per month. Monthly guests also pay for electricity. All charges are for two people per site.

Open: Year-round.

Directions: From Augusta, take US 25 south five miles. The campground will be on the left, behind Calamity Jane's Western Wear. The office is in the clothing store.

Contact: Fox Hollow Campground, 4032 Peach Orchard Road, Hephzibah, GA 30815; 706/592-4563.

Trip notes: The campground is about 10 miles from the location of the Masters Golf Tournament, and about five miles from the nearest restaurant.

35 Hamburg State Park

Location: Mitchell, map 6, grid G2.

Campsites, facilities: There are 30 campsites at this park, all suitable for either tents or RVs. All of the sites have water and electrical hookups. Seven are pull-through sites, and half the sites have shade. All have picnic tables, fire rings, and cooking grills. Restrooms have hot showers and flush toilets. The campground sells ice and some gifts, and the nearest supply store is seven miles away. The nearest groceries are 18 miles away. A coin laundry, playground, boat ramp, and sanitary disposal station are provided. While the bathhouses are wheelchair accessible, the sites are not. Pets are permitted on a six-foot leash, and you must clean up after your pet.

Reservations, fees: Reservations are accepted at 800/864-7275 or 770/389-7275 (within the Atlanta area) up to 11 months In advance. The deposit is non-refundable, but the date can be moved once. Rates range from $13 for a tent to $15 for a camper. Seniors get a discount. Like all of Georgia's state parks, there is a $2 per day parking fee, or you can purchase an annual Georgia Park-Pass for $25. Campers pay for just one daily pass for their entire stay.

Open: Year-round.

Directions: From Atlanta, take Interstate 20 east to exit 138 and turn south on Highway 15. About a mile south of Sparta, turn left onto Sparta Shoals Road. At the four-way stop, turn left onto Hamburg State Park Road. The park is three miles south of the four-way stop, and about 45 minutes from Atlanta.

Contact: Hamburg State Park, 6071 Hamburg State Park Rd., Mitchell, GA 30820; 478/552-2393; email: hamburg@accucomm.net; website: www.accucomm.net/~hamburg/.

Trip notes: Fishing is available at the 225-acre lake for largemouth bass, crappie, bream, and catfish. Hiking is available nearby. You can rent canoes, johnboats, and paddleboats at the park. Wildlife in the area includes deer, wild turkeys, Canada geese, raccoons, wood ducks, and armadillos. The area's main claim to fame is the Aaron Burr jail in Warthen, which is open to the public.

36 R. Shaefer Heard Campground

Location: West Point Lake, map 7, grid A7.
Campsites, facilities: All of the 117 camp-

sites can accommodate either tents or RVs, but some sites won't hold an RV longer than 35 feet. All sites have full hookups. Pull-through sites are available. Most of the sites have shade. Picnic tables, fire rings, and cooking grills are provided. RV storage is available nearby. Some restrooms have pit toilets, other have showers and flush toilets. A coin laundry, tennis court, boat ramp, dock, playground, and sanitary disposal station are provided. The nearest supply store is three miles away. The buildings are wheelchair accessible. Leashed pets are permitted, and you must clean up after your pet.

Reservations, fees: Reservations are accepted through the National Recreation Reservation Service (NRRS) at 877/444-6777; website: www.reserveusa.com. The full amount is payable in advance. Rates range from $14 for a primitive site to $20 for a single site and $40 for a double.

Open: Year-round.

Directions: From Interstate 85, take exit 2/Highway 18 and turn north. Turn right at the first light onto Highway 29. After 2.5 miles, turn left at the COE sign, then immediately right onto the campground road.

Contact: R. Shaefer Heard Campground, 101 Shaefer Heard Park Rd., West Point, GA 31833; 706/645-2404.

Trip notes: Fishing for bass, bream, catfish, and crappie is available in 26,000-acre West Point Lake. There is a sand beach in the swimming area. The campground is located within 20 miles of Callaway Gardens (home of the spring Azalea Festival), FDR State Park, and FDR's Little White House State Historic Site.

37 Blanton Creek Park

Location: Lake Harding, map 7, grid B8.
Campsites, facilities: There are 51 camp-

sites suitable for tents or campers, all with water and electric hookups. Some shade is available. Some sites have picnic tables. Restrooms have hot showers and flush toilets. A sanitary disposal station, coin laundry, and boat ramp are provided. Small, leashed pets are permitted.

Reservations, fees: Reservations are accepted, and no deposit is required. The fee for tents is $12, and $14 for campers. Golden Age discounts apply.

Open: The campground is open from April through Labor Day.

Directions: From Columbus, take Interstate 185 north to exit 25/Highway 103. Turn left onto Lick Skillet Road. The campground is at 1001 Lick Skillet Road.

Contact: Blanton Creek Park, 1516 Bartletts Ferry Rd., Fortson, GA 31808; 706/643-7737.

Trip notes: The campground is on Lake Harding, which is stocked with bass, catfish, bream, and crappie. Wildlife in the area includes alligators, wild turkeys, deer, and foxes.

38 Ramsey RV Park

Location: Warm Springs, map 8, grid A3.

Campsites, facilities: There are eight tent sites at this campground, and 18 RV sites in a separate section. All the RV sites have full hookups, and 10 are pull-through sites. About half of the sites have shade. The sites have picnic tables and cooking grills. The restrooms have hot showers and flush toilets. The nearest supply store is just over a mile away. A coin laundry, sanitary disposal station, and swimming pool are provided. Cable TV hookups are available. The buildings are wheelchair accessible. Leashed pets are permitted, but they must be walked in a designated area.

Reservations, fees: Reservations are ac-

cepted, and the deposit is refundable if your reservation is cancelled at least three days before your scheduled arrival. Sites cost $14 per night.

Open: Year-round.

Directions: From Warm Springs, take Alternate Highway 85 1.25 miles north.

Contact: Ramsey RV Park, 5153 Whitehouse Parkway, P.O. Box 160, Warm Springs, GA 31830; 706/655-2480.

Trip notes: The campground is one and one-half miles from former President Roosevelt's Little White House State Historic Site, built in this area because of FDR's belief in the curative powers of the springs. It's also just 15 miles from Callaway Gardens, home of spectacular azalea gardens.

39 Pine Mountain Campground

Location: Pine Mountain, map 8, grid B1.

Campsites, facilities: There are 152 campsites suitable for tents or RVs. One-third of the campsites have full hookups, and the rest have water and electric only. Pull-through sites are available. Picnic tables, fire rings, and some cooking grills are provided. RV storage is available. Restrooms have hot showers and flush toilets. Patios are available. A sanitary disposal station, coin laundry, spa, swimming pool, playground, miniature golf, and clubroom are provided. Ice, LP gas, supplies, groceries, and gifts are available at the campground, along with video and bike rentals. The buildings are wheelchair accessible. Pets are permitted.

Reservations, fees: Reservations are accepted. The deposit is refundable if your reservation is cancelled 10 days in advance. Otherwise, you can change your reservation to another date. Site fees are $18–26 per night.

Open: Year-round.

Directions: From Atlanta, take Interstate 85 to Interstate 185 and head south. Turn left onto US 27 at exit 42. The campground is eight miles from the exit.

Contact: Pine Mountain Campground, 8804 Hamilton Rd., Pine Mountain, GA 31822; 706/663-4329.

Trip notes: The campground has a catch and release pond stocked with bluegill, bream, and catfish, and 14 miles of trails for hiking and biking. It is 2.5 miles from Callaway Gardens, eight miles from FDR's Little White House, and two miles from a wild animal park. The most frequently seen wildlife includes foxes and cows, which wander out of neighboring fields and through the campground.

40 F.D. Roosevelt State Park

Location: Pine Mountain, map 8, grid B2.

Campsites, facilities: There are 140 campsites suitable for either tents or RVs. All have shade, and all have water and electric hookups. Pull-through sites are available. There are also 11 primitive sites on Pine Mountain. Group sites are available. Picnic tables, fire rings, and cooking grills are provided. Restrooms have hot showers and flush toilets. A coin laundry, swimming pool, playground, and sanitary disposal station are provided. Ice, firewood, snacks, and some gifts are available, with the nearest grocery and supply stores five miles away. The buildings are wheelchair accessible. Leashed pets are permitted in the campground.

Reservations, fees: Reservations are accepted at 800/864-7275 or 770/389-7275 (within the Atlanta area). The deposit of one night's stay is non-refundable, but your reservation date can be moved once. Rates are $13 per night for tents, and $15 per night for anything else. Like all of Georgia's state parks, there is a $2 per day parking fee, or you can purchase an annual Georgia Park-Pass for $25. Campers pay for just one daily pass for their entire stay.

Open: Year-round.

Directions: From Pine Mountain, take US 27 east five miles and follow the signs.

Contact: F.D. Roosevelt State Park, Box 2970, Highway 190 East, Pine Mountain, GA 31822; 706/663-4858.

Trip notes: Two lakes in the park offer fishing for bass, catfish, and bream during the spring and fall. There are also several trails, including the 23-mile Pine Mountain Trail and six loop trails for day hikes. Numerous wildflowers bloom throughout the park, including goldenrod, butterfly weed, plumleaf azalea, trumpet vine, and Carolina jasmine. Wildlife in the park includes wild turkeys, red foxes, deer, and coyotes. The campground is four miles from Callaway Gardens and nine miles from the Little White House State Historic Site.

41 Heart of Georgia RV Park

Location: Yatesville, map 8, grid B8.

Campsites, facilities: Of the 32 pull-through sites at this all RV campground, half have full hookups. Picnic tables are provided. The restrooms have hot showers and flush toilets. The nearest supply store, selling ice, groceries, and LP gas, is one-half mile away. Cable TV hookups are free. There is a sanitary disposal station on the premises. Leashed pets are permitted.

Reservations, fees: Reservations are accepted. The campground does not publish its rates.

Open: Year-round.

Directions: This campground is about an hour south of Atlanta. From Atlanta, take Interstate 75 south to exit 201/Highway 36, and turn west. Turn south on US 341, then west on Highway 74. The entrance is on the left.

Contact: Heart of Georgia RV Park, 6722 Highway 74, Yatesville, GA 31097; 706/472-3437.

Trip notes: There are five lakes at the campground, each stocked with catfish, bass, and bream. The swimming area has a sand beach. The campground is near the Little White House State Historic Site, the Andersonville Civil War POW historic site, Plains, home of former President Jimmy Carter, an outlet mall, and rapids on the Flint River.

42 Lake Pines Campground

Location: Columbus, map 8, grid D2.

Campsites, facilities: There are eight shaded tent sites, all with water and electric hookups. In a separate section, 61 of the 69 RV sites have full hookups. Both 30- and 50-amp hookups are available. About half of the RV sites have shade. Pull-through sites are available. There are no length restrictions for RVs. Picnic tables are provided. Restrooms have hot showers and flush toilets. The nearest supply store is two miles away. The park offers a swimming pool, coin laundry, clubroom, and wedding chapel. A sanitary disposal station is provided, and RV storage is available. Pets must be leashed, and you must pick up after your pet.

Reservations, fees: Reservations are not accepted. Fees are $15 for tents and $18 for RVs, plus $1 for 50-amp service.

Open: Year-round.

Directions: Coming from the north, take exit 10 off Interstate 185 and head east towards Macon. After 9.5 miles, turn right on Garrett Road. From the south, take exit 6 off Interstate 185, and turn east onto Spur 22. After eight miles, turn right on Garrett Road.

Contact: Lake Pines Campground, 6404 Garrett Rd., Midland, GA 31820; 706/561-9675.

Trip notes: The campground is located between the Little White House State Historic Site at Warm Springs and Providence Canyon, and offers good access to both, as well as to Callaway Gardens and Plains, home of former President Jimmy Carter. Deer and hawks are plentiful in the area, as well as the occasional fox and coyote. Two short trails of less than a mile each offer some opportunity for hiking, and there are good trails at the attractions listed above.

43 Country Vista Campground

Location: Buena Vista, map 8, grid E4.

Campsites, facilities: There are 44 campsites suitable for tents or RVs, all with full hookups. Pull-through sites and shade are available. Picnic tables, fire rings, and cooking grills are provided. RV storage is available. Restrooms have hot showers and flush toilets. A coin laundry and clubroom are provided. The facilities are wheelchair accessible. Pets are permitted.

Reservations, fees: Reservations are accepted, and no deposit is required. The fee for camping is $16. Senior citizen discounts apply.

Open: Year-round.

Directions: From Interstate 75, go west on US 280/Highway 30. Continue on Highway 30 from Americus to Highway 41, then go north on 41 for six miles.

Contact: Country Vista Campground, Rt. 1, Box 14, Buena Vista, GA 31803; 229/649-2267.

Trip notes: The campground is about 20 miles from Plains, and 25 from the Andersonville Civil War POW historic site and cemetery.

44 Claystone Park

Location: Lake Tobesofkee, map 9, grid B2.

Campsites, Facilities: There are 12 tent sites and 30 RV sites at the campground. All sites have water and electric hookups, and there is good shade. Pull-through sites are available. Picnic tables, fire rings, and grills are provided. Restrooms have hot showers and flush toilets. A sanitary disposal station, coin laundry, playground, boat ramp, and dock are provided. Ice is available, and groceries and supplies are half a mile from the campground. The restrooms and boat ramp are wheelchair accessible. Leashed pets are permitted.

Reservations, fees: Reservations are not accepted. Sites rent for $15 per night.

Open: Year-round.

Directions: In Macon, take Interstate 475 to exit 5 and turn west on Thomaston and Mercer University Drive. Turn left at the second light onto Mosley Dixon Road to the campground.

Contact: Claystone Park, Tobesofkee Recreation Area, 6600 Mosley Dixon Road, Macon, GA 31220; 478/474-8770.

Trip notes: Lake Tobesofkee is popular for fishing (for small and large mouth bass, crappie, bream, and catfish), water-skiing, and jet skiing. There is a short nature trail. There is a sand beach in the swimming area.

45 Arrowhead Park

Location: Lake Tobesofkee, map 9, grid B2.

Campsites, Facilities: There are 76 campsites suitable for tents or RVs, all with water and electric hookups. Pull-through sites are available. The overflow camping area has 10 tent sites with no hookups. Picnic tables, fire rings, and grills are provided. The campground has good shade. Lakefront campsites are available. Restrooms have hot showers and flush toilets. A sanitary disposal station, coin laundry, playground, boat ramp, and dock are provided. Ice is available. The restrooms and boat ramp are wheelchair accessible. Leashed pets are permitted.

Reservations, fees: Reservations are not accepted. Sites rent for $15 per night.

Open: Year-round.

Directions: In Macon, take Interstate 475 to exit 3 and turn west on Eisenhower Parkway. After four miles, turn right onto Tidwell Road. At the dead-end, turn left onto Columbus Road. The campground will be on the right.

Contact: Arrowhead Park, Tobesofkee Recreation Area, 6600 Mosley Dixon Road, Macon, GA 31220; 478/474-8770.

Trip notes: Lake Tobesofkee is popular for fishing (for small and large mouth bass, crappie, bream, and catfish), water-skiing, and jet skiing. There is a sand beach in the swimming area.

46 Interstate Campground

Location: Macon, map 9, grid C3.

Campsites, facilities: There are 105 RV campsites with full hookups. All are pull-through sites. Shade is available. Picnic tables are provided. RV storage is available. Restrooms have hot showers and flush toilets. A coin laundry, swimming pool, and playground are provided. Supplies and some groceries are available at the campground. The facilities are wheelchair accessible. Leashed pets are permitted.

Reservations, fees: Reservations are accepted, and no deposit is required. Campsites are $20 per night.

Open: Year-round.

Directions: From Interstate 75 take exit 149/Highway 49 and turn west. Make a right onto Frontage Road to the campground.

Contact: Interstate Campground, 305 Chapman Rd., Byron, GA 31008; 478/956-5511.

Trip notes: The campground is about 10 miles from Lake Tobesofkee, which offers water-skiing and fishing for bass, crappie, and catfish. About 25% of the guests at this campground are permanent residents.

47 Ponderosa Campground

Location: Perry, map 9, grid D3.

Campsites, facilities: This RV park has 53 sites, all with full hookups. All are pull-through sites, and half have shade. All sites have picnic tables and patios. The restrooms have hot showers and flush toilets. The office sells ice and LP gas. A coin laundry, swimming pool, and playground are provided. The facilities are wheelchair accessible. Leashed pets are permitted.

Reservations, fees: Reservations are accepted, but no deposit is required. Sites rent for $19 per night.

Open: Year-round.

Directions: From Interstate 75, exit east onto Highway 96. The campground is 600 feet east of the interstate and six miles north of Perry.

Contact: Ponderosa Campground, P.O. Box 109, Perry, GA 31069; 478/825-8030.

Trip notes: The campground is 23 miles from the Andersonville Civil War POW site, 12 miles from the Aviation Museum, and 25 miles to historic Macon. It is near two shopping malls.

48 Boland's RV Park

Location: Perry, map 9, grid E3.

Campsites, facilities: There are 65 RV sites at this campground, all with full hookups and all pull-through sites. Of these, 45 have shade. There are no length restrictions. RV storage is available. Restrooms have showers and flush toilets. LP gas and ice are available at the campground, along with a coin laundry, playground, and swimming pool. Cable TV hookups are available. Leashed pets are permitted. You must clean up after your pet, and pets may not be left tied outside your camper.

Reservations, fees: Reservations are accepted. The campground does not publish its rates.

Open: Year-round.

Directions: From Interstate 75, turn east at exit 136. Turn left onto Perimeter Road, which is only about one block from the interstate.

Contact: Boland's RV Park, 800 Perimeter Rd., Perry, GA 31069; 478/987-3371.

Trip notes: The campground is convenient to the interstate.

49 Crossroads Travel Park

Location: Perry, map 9, grid E2.

Campsites, facilities: There are 68 campsites suitable for tents or RVs, most with full hookups. Both 30- and 50-amp hookups are available. Most are pull-through sites. There is some shade available. Picnic tables are provided. RV storage is available. Restrooms have hot showers and flush toilets. Ice, supplies, LP gas, and some groceries are available at the campground. A coin laundry, swimming pool, and playground are provided. The facilities are wheelchair accessible. Pets are permitted. You must clean up after your pet.

Reservations, fees: Reservations are accepted, and no deposit is required. Campsites are $19 for 30-amp service and $21 for 50-amp service, plus $2 for both if you are using an air conditioner. Good Sam, AARP, and AAA discounts apply.

Open: Year-round.

Directions: From Interstate 75, go west on US 341 north at exit 136. The entrance will be on the left.

Contact: Crossroads Travel Park, 1513 Sam Nunn Blvd., Perry, GA 31069; 478/987-3141.

Trip notes: The campground is 1.5 miles from the Georgia Fairgrounds, and 45 minutes from the Andersonville Civil War POW historic site.

50 Fair Harbor RV Park and Campground

Location: Perry, map 9, grid E2.

Campsites, facilities: All of the 33 tent sites at this campground have hookups, and 20 of them have shade. Of the 103 RV sites, all have hookups, and half have shade. Pull-through sites are available. Both 30- and 50-amp hookups are available. Picnic tables, cooking grills, fire rings, and cable TV are provided. Restrooms have hot showers and flush toilets. Ice, LP gas, and firewood are available, and the campground has a sanitary disposal station, clubroom, and coin laundry. Phone service is available. The buildings are wheelchair accessible. Pets are permitted.

Reservations, fees: Reservations are accepted. The daily fee is $22 with full hookups, plus $2 for phone service. The weekly rate is $132.

Open: Year-round.

Directions: Take exit 135 off Interstate 75 and turn west. The campground is 0.2 miles from the interstate.

Contact: Fair Harbor RV Park and Campground, 515 Marshallville Rd., Perry, GA 31069; 877/988-8844, email: fairharbor@yahoo.com; website: www.fairharborrvpark.com.

Trip notes: Fishing is available at the campground. There are two trails of approximately two miles. The campground is about 45 minutes from Andersonville, the site of a Civil War prisoner of war camp and cemetery.

51 Hillside Bluegrass Park

Location: Cochran, map 9, grid F6.

Campsites, Facilities: This large campground has 500 sites suitable for tents or RVs. Sites with full hookups are available, and all sites have water and electric. Pull-through sites are available, and some have shade. Both 30- and 50-amp hookups are available. Primitive tent sites without hookups are also available at the 100-acre campground. Restrooms have hot showers and flush toilets. A sanitary disposal station is provided. Supplies are available less than one mile from the campground, and LP can be delivered to your rig. A covered kitchen pavilion is provided. Leashed pets are permitted.

Reservations, fees: Reservations are accepted at 478/934-6694, and no deposit is required. Primitive tent sites are $3 per night. Sites with water and electricity cost $8, and sites with full hookups are $10.

Open: Year-round.

Directions: From Macon, take Interstate 16 east about six miles to the Cochran/US 23/Highway 87 exit, and turn south. Stay on US 23/Highway 87 when the highway dead-ends just after you pass through Cochran, and drive about half a mile to the campground, which will be on the right. The campground is about 40 miles from the interstate.

Contact: Hillside Bluegrass Park, Rt. 5, Box 41, Cochran, GA 31014; 478/934-6694; email: blugras@bellsouth.net.

Trip notes: Two bluegrass concerts are held here each year, typically in May and September. The campground is adjacent to a golf course.

52 Southern Trails RV Resort

Location: Unadilla, map 9, grid F3.

Campsites, facilities: There are 200 camp-sites suitable for tents or RVs. About one-fourth have water and electric hookups, and the rest have full hookups. Most are pull-through sites, and there is plenty of shade. Most sites have picnic tables. RV storage is available. Restrooms have hot showers and flush toilets. A sanitary disposal station, coin laundry, clubroom, playground, minia-ture golf, and swimming pool are provided. The restrooms are wheelchair accessible. Leashed pets are permitted, and you must clean up after your pet.

Reservations, fees: Reservations are not accepted. The fee is $20 per night. Coast to Coast, RPI, and AOR discounts apply.

Open: Year-round.

Directions: From Interstate 75, take exit 121 and go north on US 41. Turn right on the first paved road (Arena Road), which almost im-mediately turns to the right again. The camp-ground will be on the left.

Contact: Southern Trails RV Resort, 2690 Arena Rd., Unadilla, GA 31091; 478/627-3254.

Trip notes: The campground is convenient to the interstate and is about 40 minutes from Lake Blackshear.

53 South Prong Creek Campground

Location: Unadilla, map 9, grid F3.

Campsites, facilities: There are 40 tent sites, some with water and some with water and electric hookups. There are also 110 RV sites, all with water and electric, and some with sewer hookups as well. Many are pull-through sites. Primitive camping is also available on the 145-acre property, and there are five stationary mobile homes and one cabin for rent. Picnic tables and fire rings are provided on the developed campsites. RV storage is available. Restrooms have hot showers and flush toilets. A coin laundry is provided. Pets are permitted.

Reservations, fees: Reservations are accepted, and no deposit is required. Primi-tive tent camping is $7.50 per night, and other sites are $10–15, depending on hookups. The cabin rents for $200 per month, and the mo-bile homes are $260–360 per month.

Open: Year-round.

Directions: From Interstate 75, take exit 121 and follow the signs for Highway 230 east. The campground is on High-way 230, eight miles from the interstate.

Contact: South Prong Creek Campground, c/o Tall Sycamore Campground, 355 S. County Road 600 East, Lagansport, IN 46947; 478/783-2551.

Trip notes: The fishing pond at the campground is stocked with catfish and there are many trails throughout the property for hiking. The most common wildlife in the area is wild boar. The campground is five miles from a natural springs and swimming area, and near to the Andersonville Civil War POW historic site.

54 Pinetucky Campground

Location: Dublin, map 10, grid E1.

Campsites, facilities: There are 75 sites at the campground, all suitable for tents or RVs. All have shade, and all have electric and water hookups. Full hookups are available, and most are pull-through sites. The maximum length for an RV is 45 feet. Picnic tables, fire rings, and cooking grills are provided. RV storage is available, and a sanitary disposal station is on the premises. Restrooms have showers and flush toilets. The camp store sells LP gas and firewood, and a coin laundry is available. Buildings are wheelchair accessible. Pets are permitted on leash at designated walk areas and in your own campsite.

Reservations, fees: Reservations are accepted. No deposit is required. Sites are $13–20, depending on hookups.

Open: Year-round.

Directions: Dublin is located in the exact center of the state. From Interstate 16, take US 441/ 319 south two miles.

Contact: Pinetucky Campground, 1007 Campground Rd., Dublin, GA 31021; 478/272-6745.

Trip notes: Dublin, as the name suggests, has a large St. Patrick's Day festival each year. The campground is well located for travel throughout the central part of the state. It is five miles from the Oconee River. Pinetucky is situated near country roads popular with runners and bikers, and there are also running and walking trails throughout the campground itself. Common wildlife in the area includes deer, raccoons, squirrels, opossums, wild boars, rabbits, wild turkeys, quail, and doves.

55 George L. Smith II State Park

Location: Twin City, map 10, grid D8.

Campsites, facilities: There are 25 campsites at this campground, all for either tents or RVs, and all with water and electric hookups. Ten of the sites have shade. Pull-through sites are available. Picnic tables, fire rings, and cooking grills are provided. The campground also has four cabins. Restrooms have hot showers and flush toilets. A coin laundry, boat ramp, dock, playground, and sanitary disposal station are at the campground or in the park. Boat motors can be up to 10 horsepower. Buildings are wheelchair accessible. Leashed pets are permitted, but pets are not allowed in the cabins.

Reservations, fees: Reservations are accepted at 800/864-7275 or 770/389-7275 (within the Atlanta area). The deposit of one night's stay is not refundable, but your reservation can be moved once to another date. Rates are $15 for tents and $17 for RVs. Like all of Georgia's state parks, there is a $2 per day parking fee, or you can purchase an annual Georgia ParkPass for $25. Campers pay for just one daily pass for their entire stay.

Open: Year-round.

Directions: From Interstate 16, take exit 104 and go north on Highway 23 towards Twin City, and follow the signs. The park and campground are about 13 miles north of the interstate.

Contact: George L. Smith II State Park, 371 George L. Smith II State Park Rd., Twin City, GA 30471; 478/763-2759.

Trip notes: The lake at this park is stocked with bass, bream, perch, and catfish. Paddleboats and canoes are available to rent. There are three hiking trails, ranging from one-half mile to three miles in length. The park is near Gordonia-Altamaha State Park, which offers a nine-hole golf course, and is also near the freshwater aquarium at Magnolia Springs State Park.

56 Magnolia Springs State Park

Location: South of Augusta, map 11, grid A1.

Campsites, facilities: Three of the sites at this campground are designated for tents and have neither water nor electricity. The other 23 sites have water and electric hookups, and seven are pull-through sites. The campsites have picnic tables, fire rings, and cooking grills. There are six cabins available. The restrooms have hot showers and flush toilets. Firewood, ice, and some gifts are available at the campground store, with groceries and other supplies about four miles away. The swimming pool is open seasonally. The campground also offers a playground, coin laundry, clubroom, boat ramp, and sanitary disposal station. Pets are permitted, but they must be on a six-foot leash at all times.

Reservations, fees: Reservations are accepted at 800/864-7275 or 770/389-7275 (within the Atlanta area). The deposit is non-refundable, but the date can be moved once. Site fees are $13–15 per night. Like all of Georgia's state parks, there is a $2 per day parking fee, or you can purchase an annual Georgia ParkPass for $25. Campers pay for just one daily pass for their entire stay.

Open: Year-round.

Directions: From Augusta, take US 25 south. Stay on US 25 when it makes a hard right just past Waynesboro, and continue another 17 miles to the park. Go past the entrance to the Bo Ginn Aquarium and Aquatic Education Center, and turn left into the park.

Contact: Magnolia Springs State Park, 1053 Magnolia Springs Dr., Millen, GA 30442; 478/982-1660.

Trip notes: The 28-acre lake offers fishing for bass, bream, crappie, bluegill, red breast, and catfish. Boat motors are restricted before 11 A.M. and after 6 P.M. There is a sand beach in the swimming area. In the spring, numerous wildflowers bloom at the park, including lupine, milkweed, and daisies. Wildlife in the area includes deer, wild turkeys, squirrels, raccoons, and beavers. There is a large bird population, including ducks, great blue herons, pileated and red cockaded woodpeckers, wood storks, and songbirds. Hikers and bikers will enjoy the five-mile trail. There are also three nature trails, including the Beaver Nature Trail, which is a little over one mile long.

57 Pinevale Campground

Location: Sylvania, map 11, grid C3.

Campsites, facilities: There are 50 campsites suitable for tents or RVs, all with full hookups. Most are pull-through sites, and some have shade. Some sites have picnic tables. RV storage is available.

Restrooms have hot showers and flush toilets. A coin laundry is provided. Cable TV hookups are available. Pets must be under voice control at all times.

Reservations, fees: Reservations are accepted, and no deposit is required. Campsites cost $12 per night; cable hookups are an extra $2.

Open: Year-round.

Directions: From Interstate 16, go north on US 301 about 35 miles. The campground is one mile south of Sylvania on US 301.

Contact: Pinevale Campground, 1667 Statesboro Highway, Sylvania, GA 30467; 912/863-4347.

Trip notes: Three fishing ponds at the campground are stocked with catfish, bass, and bream. The campground is 60 miles from Savannah and Augusta.

58 Parkwood Motel and RV Park

Location: Statesboro, map 11, grid E2.

Campsites, facilities: The campground has 12 tent sites, eight with hookups. Four of the sites have shade. There are also 37 RV sites, 33 with full hookups. All are pull-through sites. Seven of the RV sites have shade. Group sites are available, and there are 22 cabins. Picnic tables are provided. Restrooms have hot showers and flush toilets. A coin laundry, swimming pool, and cable TV hookups are available. Ice is available, and LP gas may be delivered, or picked up from two miles away. There is a restaurant on the premises. The restaurant is wheelchair accessible. Leashed pets are permitted, but you must clean up after your pet. Pets cannot be left out unattended. Aggressive pets are not tolerated.

Reservations, fees: Reservations are accepted and strongly recommended from March through May, and from September through November. Sites are $15.50–20 per night, depending on width.

Open: Year-round.

Directions: From Interstate 16, take US 301 north approximately nine miles towards Statesboro.

Contact: Parkwood Motel and RV Park, 12188 Highway 301 South, Statesboro, GA 30458; 912/681-3105, email: parkwood@frontiernet.net, website: www.parkwoodrv.com.

Trip notes: The campground is one mile from the Georgia Southern University Wildlife Education Center, and the Lamar Raptor Center also at the University. The Raptor Center includes a self-guided nature walk, habitat displays, raptor demonstrations, and an elevated walkway allowing an unobstructed view of a bald eagle nesting site. Golf is available within three miles.

59 Beaver Run RV Park

Location: Metter, map 11, grid F1.

Campsites, facilities: There are 71 RV sites, half with full hookups and half with water and electric only. A few sites have no hookups. Both 30- and 50-amp hookups are available. Pull-through sites are available. Some sites have picnic tables. RV storage is available. Restrooms have hot showers and flush toilets. A sanitary disposal station and coin laundry are provided. Ice, LP gas, supplies, and snacks are available at the campground. The buildings are wheelchair accessible. Leashed pets are permitted, and you must clean up after your pet.

Reservations, fees: Reservations are accepted, and no deposit is required. Primitive sites are $8 per night and other sites are $19–22, depending on hookups.

Open: Year-round.

Directions: From Interstate 16, take exit 111 and go south on Pulaski Excelsior Road.

Contact: Beaver Run RV Park, Rt. 3, Box 168, Metter, GA 30439; 912/685-2594.

Trip notes: There is a 7.5-acre private lake on the property that is stocked with bass, catfish, bream, and crappie. There are two trails, one of which is five miles in length. Swimming and paddleboats are permitted in the lake. Wildlife in the area includes beavers, deer, and bobcats. The campground is 14 miles from Claxton, home of Claxton Fruitcake, and 18 miles from the Georgia Southern University Lamar Raptor Center and Wildlife Education Center.

60 Greenpeace RV Park

Location: Savannah, map 11, grid F7.

Campsites, facilities: There are 50 RV sites with full hookups. Pull-through sites are available, and shade is plentiful. Fire rings are provided. RV storage is available. There are no restrooms. Pets are permitted.

Reservations, fees: Reservations are not accepted. Campsites are $10 per night.

Open: Year-round.

Directions: From Interstate 95, take exit 109/Highway 21 north five miles to Chimney Road and turn right. After two miles, turn left onto Old Augusta Road. The campground will be on the left within a quarter mile.

Contact: Greenpeace RV Park, 155 Caroni Dr., Rincon, GA 31326; 912/826-5540.

Trip notes: The nearest fishing is in a branch of the Savannah River, less than two miles away. The campground is 18 miles from Savannah. About half of the sites are rented monthly.

SOUTHERN GEORGIA

LAKE OCMULGEE

SOUTHERN GEORGIA

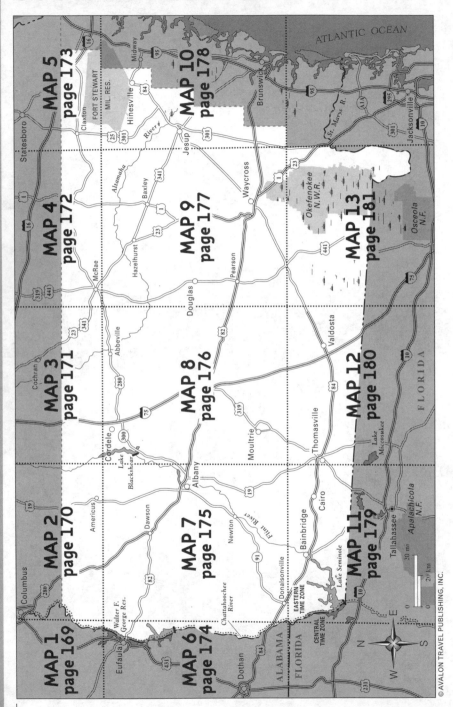

MAP 5 page 173

MAP 10 page 178

MAP 4 page 172

MAP 9 page 177

MAP 13 page 181

MAP 3 page 171

MAP 8 page 176

MAP 12 page 180

MAP 2 page 170

MAP 7 page 175

MAP 11 page 179

MAP 1 page 169

MAP 6 page 174

ATLANTIC OCEAN

FORT STEWART MIL. RES.

Okefenokee N.W.R.

Osceola N.F.

Apalachicola N.F.

FLORIDA

ALABAMA

FLORIDA

EASTERN TIME ZONE

CENTRAL TIME ZONE

Statesboro · Claxton · Midway · Hinesville · Brunswick · Jacksonville · Jesup · Waycross · Altamaha River · Baxley · McRae · Hazelhurst · Pearson · Douglas · Valdosta · Abbeville · Cochran · Cordele · Lake Blackshear · Moultrie · Thomasville · Lake Miccosukee · Americus · Dawson · Albany · Newton · Flint River · Bainbridge · Cairo · Lake Seminole · Tallahassee · Columbus · Walter F. George Res. · Eufaula · Chattahoochee River · Donalsonville · Dothan · St. Marys R.

30 mi

20 km

N E S W

© AVALON TRAVEL PUBLISHING, INC.

MAP 1

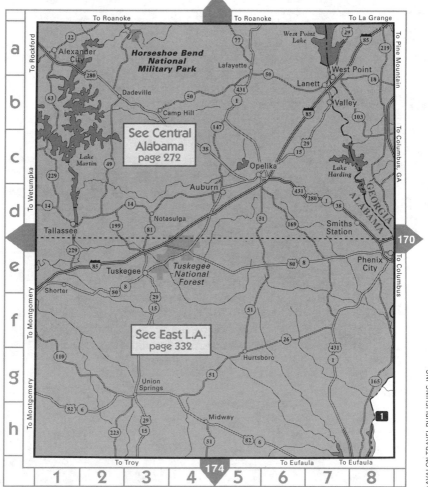

MAP 2

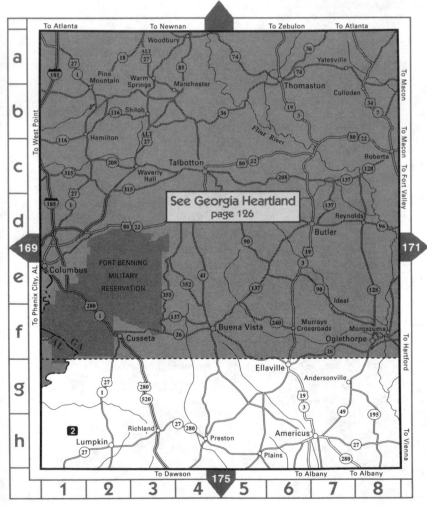

See Georgia Heartland
page 126

© AVALON TRAVEL PUBLISHING, INC.

MAP 3

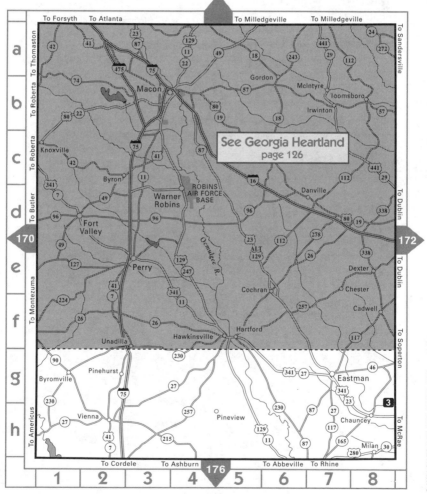

To Forsyth To Atlanta   To Milledgeville   To Milledgeville

a
To Thomaston To Roberta
42 41 23 87 129 11 22 49 18 243 29 112 441 272 24 To Sandersville

b
74 475 75 Macon Gordon 57 McIntyre Toomsboro
80 22 80 19 18 Irwinton 57
To Roberta

c
Knoxville 75 41 87 **See Georgia Heartland page 126** 16 Danville 112 441 29
42 To Roberta To Dublin

d
To Butler
341 7 Byron 11 Warner Robins ROBINS AIR FORCE BASE 96 80 19 338
96 Fort Valley 96 To Dublin
170   **172**

e
49 127 Perry 129 247 Ocmulgee R. 23 ALT 129 112 278 26 338 Dexter Chester
To Montezuma To Dublin

f
224 41 7 341 11 Cochran 257 Cadwell 117
26 26 Hartford To Soperton

Unadilla Hawkinsville

g
90 Pinehurst 341 27 Eastman 46
Byromville 27 341 **3**
230 75 23
To Americus To McRae

h
230 Vienna 257 Pineview 230 87 27 Chauncey
27 41 7 215 129 11 87 117 165 Milan 30
280

To Cordele   To Ashburn **176**   To Abbeville To Rhine

1   2   3   4   5   6   7   8

MAP 4

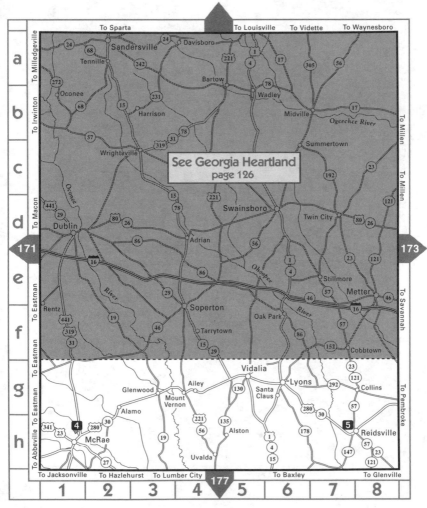

See Georgia Heartland
page 126

To Sparta   To Louisville   To Vidette   To Waynesboro

To Milledgeville

a

Sandersville
Davisboro
Tennille
Bartow
Oconee
Wadley
Harrison
Midville

To Irwinton

b

Ogeechee River

Wrightsville
Summertown

c

Swainsboro

To Macon

d

Dublin
Adrian
Twin City

Metter

To Millen   To Millen

171   173

e

Oconee River
Ohoopee River
Stillmore

To Savannah

f

Rentz
Soperton
Oak Park
River
Tarrytown
Cobbtown

To Eastman

g

Vidalia
Ailey
Lyons
Collins
Glenwood
Santa Claus

Mount
Vernon
Alamo

To Pembroke

h

McRae
Alston
Reidsville
Uvalda

To Abbeville   To Eastman

To Jacksonville   To Hazlehurst   To Lumber City   To Baxley   To Glenville

177

1   2   3   4   5   6   7   8

© AVALON TRAVEL PUBLISHING, INC.

172 Georgia

MAP 5

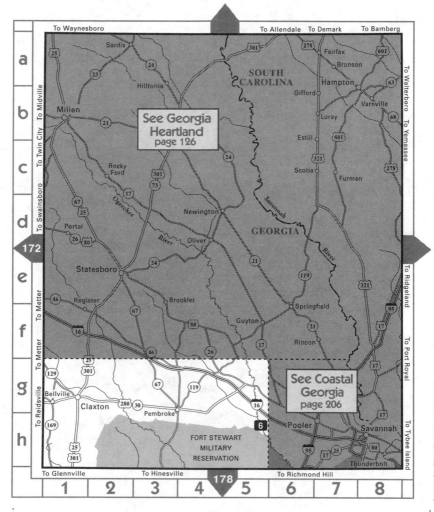

To Waynesboro   To Allendale To Demark   To Bamberg

a

Sardis

SOUTH CAROLINA

Fairfax

Brunson

Hilltonia

Hampton

Gifford

b

Millen

See Georgia Heartland page 126

Luray

Varnville

c

Rocky Ford

Estill

Scotia

Furman

d

Portal

Newington

GEORGIA

Oliver

172

e

Statesboro

f

Register

Brooklet

Springfield

Guyton

Rincon

g

Bellville

Claxton

Pembroke

See Coastal Georgia page 206

Pooler

Savannah

h

FORT STEWART MILITARY RESERVATION

Thunderbolt

To Glennville   To Hinesville   To Richmond Hill

178

MAP 6

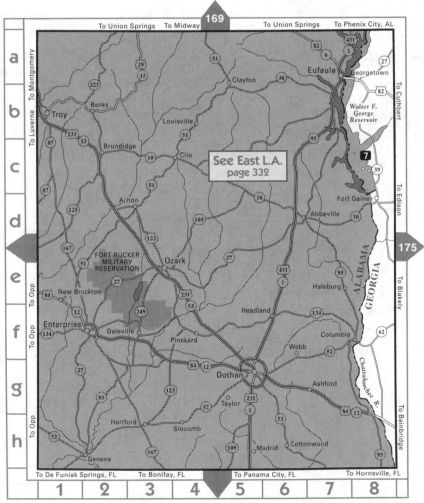

To Union Springs   To Midway   **169**   To Union Springs   To Phenix City, AL

a
To Montgomery
29
15
223
51
Clayton
30
82
6
431
1
Eufaula
Georgetown
27

b
To Luverne
Troy
Banks
231
53
Louisville
51
95
82
To Cuthbert
Walter F. George Reservoir

c
87
Brundidge
10
Clio
51
See East L.A. page 332
7
39
To Edison

d
87
125
Ariton
123
105
10
Abbeville
Fort Gaines
10

e
167
51
FORT RUCKER MILITARY RESERVATION
27
Ozark
27
431
1
Haleburg
95
ALABAMA
GEORGIA
175
To Blakely

f
To Opp
New Brockton
84
12
Enterprise
134
249
231
53
Headland
134
Columbia
62
Chattahoochee R.

g
To Opp
27
Daleville
Pinckard
84
12
Webb
52
Dothan
123
Ashford
84
12
To Bainbridge

h
To Opp
52
85
52
Taylor
231
1
53
Hartford
Slocomb
167
109
Madrid
Cottonwood
95
Geneva

To De Funiak Springs, FL   To Bonifay, FL   To Panama City, FL   To Hornsville, FL

1   2   3   4   5   6   7   8

MAP 7

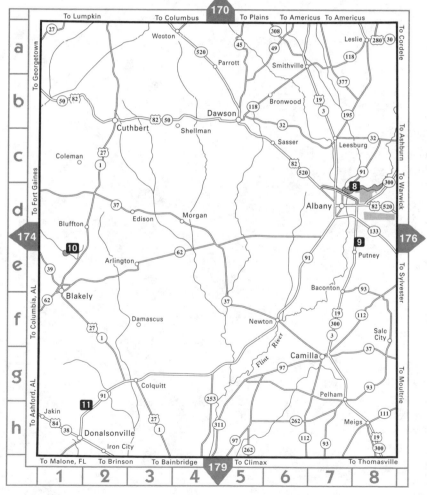

MAP 8

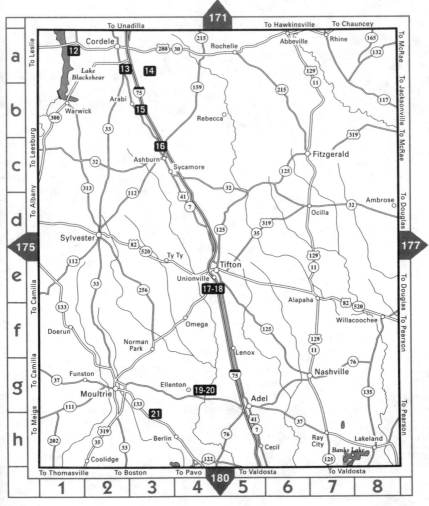

© AVALON TRAVEL PUBLISHING, INC.

MAP 9

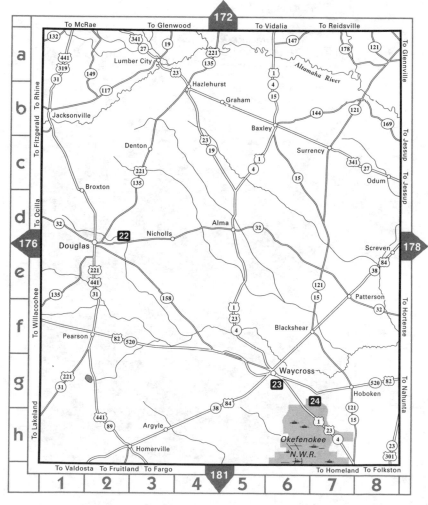

MAP 10

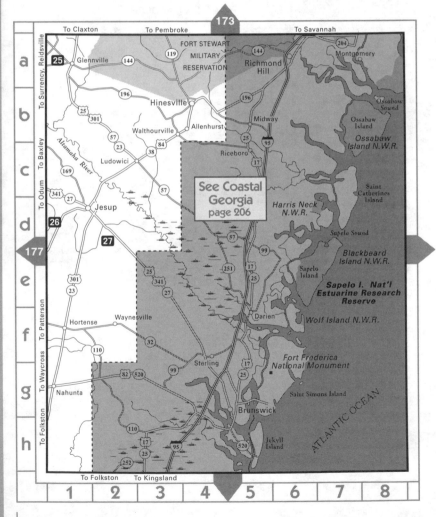

MAP 11

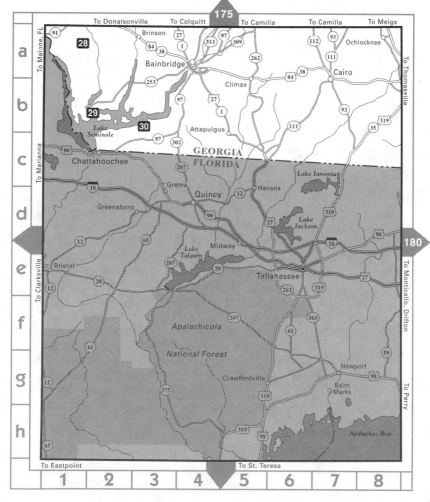

MAP 12

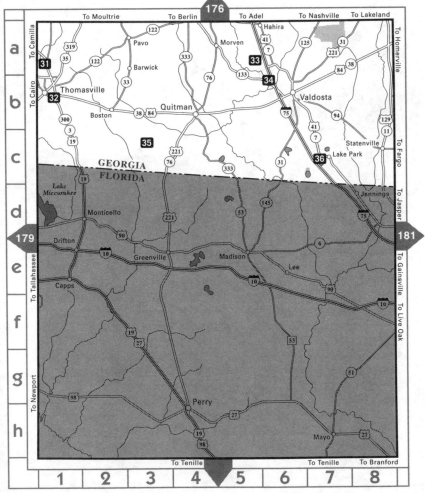

© AVALON TRAVEL PUBLISHING, INC.

MAP 13

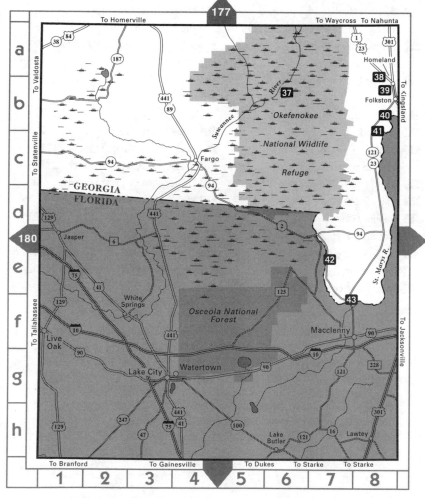

SOUTHERN GEORGIA

◻ Florence Marina State Park

Location: Omaha, map 1, grid H8.

Campsites, facilities: There are 43 sites which can be used by either RVs or tents. All have full hookups, and half are pull-through sites. Forty of the sites have shade. There are also 14 cabins. Picnic tables, fire rings, and cooking grills are provided. Restrooms have hot showers and flush toilets. A coin laundry, tennis courts, boat ramp, dock, swimming pool, playground, and cable TV hookups are available. The buildings are wheelchair accessible. Leashed pets are permitted in the campground, but not in the cabins.

Reservations, fees: Reservations are accepted at 800/864-7275 or 770/389-7275 (within the Atlanta area). Deposits are not refundable, but your reservation date can be moved once. Site fees are $15 for tents, $17 for RVs. Like all of Georgia's state parks, there is a $2 per day parking fee, or you can purchase an annual Georgia ParkPass for $25. Campers pay for just one daily pass for their entire stay.

Open: Year-round.

Directions: Take US 27 south from Interstate 185 to Highway 39 and turn west. The park is at the intersection of Highway 39C and Highway 39.

Contact: Florence Marina State Park, Rt. 1, Box 36, Omaha, GA 31821; 229/838-4244.

Trip notes: The lake offers fishing for crappie, bream, and catfish. Providence Canyon State Park, with beautiful pink rock spires, is just eight miles east of the park. Westville, a recreated 1850s village, is 20 miles away.

◻ Providence Canyon State Park

Location: Lumpkin, map 2, grid H1.

Campsites, Facilities: There are six primitive camping sites along the seven-mile backcountry trail, each suitable for up to ten people. Camping is allowed only in the designated areas. No facilities are provided. Leashed pets are permitted.

Reservations, fees: Reservations are accepted at 800/864-7275. Within the Atlanta area, call 770/389-7275. The deposit of the first night's fee is not refundable, but your reservation date can be moved once. The fee is $3 per person per night. Plan to check-in by 4 P.M. to give you time to hike to your campsite before dark. Like all of Georgia's state parks, there is a $2 per day parking fee, or you can purchase an annual Georgia ParkPass for $25. Campers pay for just one daily pass for their entire stay.

Open: Year-round.

Contact: Providence Canyon State Conservation Park, Route 1, Box 158, Lumpkin, GA 31815; 229/838-6202.

Directions: From Interstate 185 at Columbus, take US 27 south at exit 42 to Lumpkin. Turn right onto Highway 39C. The park is seven miles from Lumpkin on the left.

Trip notes: Providence Canyon can be pretty hot and muggy during the summer. The best time to camp is from mid-October through April. Wildflowers are numerous throughout the backcountry area when rainfall is available. Brochures available at the Visitors Center list the varieties that bloom each month. The main attraction at this state park are the colorful limestone canyons and spires. Hiking the three miles of trails is the best way to experience this park. The seven-mile back-country trail is more strenuous, but much less crowded.

3 Jay Bird Springs Resort

Location: Chauncey, map 3, grid G8.

Campsites, Facilities: The resort has 30 RV sites, most with full hookups. Pull-through sites are available. There are also 25 tent sites with electricity, and another 25 primitive sites. Picnic tables and fire rings are provided. Two cottages and motel rooms are also available. Restrooms have hot showers and flush toilets. Snacks, ice, and wood are available at the campground. A playground, swimming pool, skating rink, miniature golf, game room, and meeting hall are provided. The buildings are wheelchair accessible. Pets are permitted in the campground, but not in the cottages or motel.

Reservations, fees: Reservations are accepted at 229/868-2728. The deposit of the first night's fee is refundable if cancellation is at least one week in advance. Primitive tent sites rent for $8 per night, sites with electricity rent for $12, and full hookup sites rent for $14. The cottages rent for $80–160 per night, and the motel rooms range from $30–60.

Open: Year-round.

Directions: From Macon, take Interstate 16 southeast to the second Dublin exit, and turn right onto US 441. After 25 miles, turn right onto Church Road, which becomes Jay Bird Springs Road. The campground is eight miles from the highway.

Contact: Jay Bird Springs Resort, 1220 Jay Bird Springs Road, Chauncey, GA 31011; 229/868-2728; fax 229/868-6516.

Trip notes: The campground encompasses over 40 acres, and they were in the process of adding hiking trails at press time.

4 Little Ocmulgee State Lodge Park

Location: McRae, map 4, grid H1.

Campsites, facilities: There are a total of 55 campsites which can be used for either tents or RVs. Five of the sites have full hookups, and six are pull-through sites. All have shade. RVs are restricted to 50 feet or less. Picnic tables and fire rings are provided. Restrooms have hot showers and flush toilets. The nearest supply store is two miles away, but ice and firewood are available at the campground. Cable TV hookups are available. Besides the campground, the park has a 30-room lodge and 10 cottages. A coin laundry, tennis courts, boat ramp, dock, miniature golf, and playground are provided. The facilities are wheelchair accessible. Leashed pets are permitted in the campground, but are not allowed in the cabins.

Reservations, fees: Reservations are accepted at 800/864-7275 or 770/389-7275 (within the Atlanta area). The deposit is non-refundable, but the date can be moved once. Rates are $13–15. Like all of Georgia's state parks, there is a $2 per day parking fee, or you can purchase an annual Georgia Park-Pass for $25. Campers pay for just one daily pass for their entire stay.

Open: Year-round.

Directions: The park is located two miles north of McRae on US 441.

Contact: Little Ocmulgee State Lodge Park, P.O. Drawer 149, McRae, GA 31055; 229/868-7474.

Trip notes: Fishing is available at the 265-acre lake at this park. There are two hiking trails, one 1.9 miles and the other 2.6 miles. The lake has a natural sand beach in the swimming area, and paddleboats and canoes can be rented. The park also has an 18-hole golf course.

5 Gordonia-Altamaha State Park

Location: Reidsville, map 4, grid H7.

Campsites, facilities: There are 26 campsites at this park, which can be used for either tents or RVs. Four have full hookups, and the rest have water and electric hookups only. There is one pull-through site. Picnic tables, fire rings, and cooking grills are provided at each site. Restrooms have hot showers and flush toilets. Ice is available. The campground and park offer a coin laundry, tennis courts, a nine-hole golf course, miniature golf, boat docks, swimming pool (in the summer only), playground, and sanitary disposal station. No private boats are allowed, but boats are available for rent. Buildings are wheelchair accessible. Pets are permitted on a six-foot maximum length leash.

Reservations, fees: Reservations are accepted at 800/864-7275 or 770/389-7275 (within the Atlanta area). The deposit is not refundable, but your reservation can be moved to another date once. The fee for tents is $13. Site fees for RVs are $13–17, depending on hookups. Like all of Georgia's state parks, there is a $2 per day parking fee, or you can purchase an annual Georgia ParkPass for $25. Campers pay for just one daily pass for their entire stay.

Open: Year-round.

Directions: From Vidalia, take US 280 towards Reidsville. The park is inside the city limits.

Contact: Gordonia-Altamaha State Park, P.O. Box 1039, Reidsville, GA 30453; 912/557-7744.

Trip notes: Fishing is available at the 12-acre lake. Bass, catfish, and white perch are plentiful. Other wildlife commonly seen in the park includes deer and raccoons. The park is 20 miles from Vidalia, home of the famous sweet onion, and 60 miles from Savannah.

6 Hollow Oak Campground

Location: Savannah, map 5, grid H5.

Campsites, facilities: There are 15 RV sites with full hookups. Picnic tables are provided. Primitive tent camping is also available between two fishponds. The primitive area has vault toilets. There are no other restrooms. Pets are permitted. Due to the number of alligators in the area, pets should be kept inside or on leash at all times and small children should be supervised.

Reservations, fees: Reservations are accepted, and no deposit is required. The primitive campsites cost $10 per night, RV sites are $20.

Open: Year-round.

Directions: From Interstate 16, take the Old River Road exit and turn south. The road dead-ends into the campground.

Contact: Hollow Oak Campground, 2841 Fort Argyle Road Lot 4, Bloomingdale, GA 31302; 912/748-7330.

Trip notes: The ponds are stocked with bass, bream, and catfish, and the campground is on a river that contains bream. Though some people swim, canoe, and tube in the river, there is a healthy alligator population in the river and the fishing ponds, and it is not recommended. The campground is 10 miles from Savannah and a public golf course.

7 Cotton Hill Campground

Location: Walter F. George Lake, map 6, grid C8.

Campsites, facilities: There are 94 campsites suitable for tents or RVs, all with water and electric hookups. There are also 10 primitive tent campsites with access to drinking water. Picnic tables, fire rings, and cooking grills are provided. Restrooms have hot showers and flush toilets. A sanitary disposal station, coin laundry, boat ramp, dock, and playground are provided. Leashed pets are permitted. Because of the alligators in the area, keep a close watch on your pets and small children at all times.

Reservations, fees: Reservations are accepted through the National Recreation Reservation Service (NRRS) at 877/444-6777; website: www.reserveusa.com. The full amount is payable in advance. Primitive tent sites are $14 per night, and sites with water and electric hookups are $16.

Open: Year-round; primitive sites are open only from March through September.

Directions: From Fort Gaines, take Highway 39 north six miles, and turn left at the sign for the campground.

Contact: Cotton Hill Campground, Resource Office, Rt. 1, Box 176, Fort Gaines, GA 31751; 229/768-3061.

Trip notes: Fishing is excellent for bass, catfish, bream, and crappie. There are three hiking trails around and near the lake, and a sand beach in the swimming area. The campground is adjacent to Bagby State Park, which has a public golf course.

8 The Parks at Chehaw

Location: Albany, map 7, grid D7.

Campsites, facilities: There are 14 tent sites and 42 RV sites at this campground. All sites have water and electric hookups. Some shade is available. Restrooms have hot showers and flush toilets. A sanitary disposal station, coin laundry, and playground are provided. The buildings are wheelchair accessible. Leashed pets are permitted.

Reservations, fees: Reservations are not accepted. Tent sites are $8 per night, and RV sites are $14. Senior citizen discounts apply.

Open: Year-round.

Directions: From Tifton, take US 82 west to Highway 91 north. Take the Jefferson Street exit and turn right. The campground is one mile down on the left.

Contact: The Parks at Chehaw, 105 Chehaw Park Rd., Albany, GA 31701; 229/430-5275; website: www.parksatchehaw.org.

Trip notes: Lake Chehaw offers fishing, and the park has trails for hiking and biking, as well as a BMX track.

9 Devencrest Travel Park

Location: Albany, map 7, grid E8.

Campsites, facilities: The 20 tent sites at this campground have shade and no hookups. The 100 RV sites are in a separate section, and all have full hookups. Most of the RV sites are pull-through sites, and about half have some shade. Picnic tables are provided and most sites have patios. RV storage is available. Cable TV hookups are available. A coin laundry, swimming pool, playground, clubroom, and sanitary disposal station are provided. Ice, LP gas, and firewood are available at the campground. Buildings are wheelchair accessible. Pets must remain leashed and under control at all times, and you must clean up after your pet.

Reservations, fees: Reservations are accepted. The deposit is refundable with 24-hour notice. Rates are $65 per week and $220 month for 30-amp electric, water, sewer, and cable TV service. For an additional charge, 50-amp service is available.

Open: Year-round.

Directions: From Albany, take US 19/Highway 300 south six miles.

Contact: Devencrest Travel Park, 1833 Liberty Expressway SE, Albany, GA 31705; 229/432-2641, fax 229/432-0657.

Trip notes: There are catfish and trout in the private fishing ponds in the campground.

10 Kolomoki Mounds State Historic Park

Location: Blakely, map 7, grid E1.

Campsites, Facilities: There are 43 campsites suitable for tents or RVs, all with water and electric hookups. Pull-through sites are available, as are primitive camping sites. Picnic tables and fire rings are provided. Restrooms have hot showers and flush toilets. Ice, supplies, and groceries are available at the campground. A sanitary disposal station, boat ramp, dock, swimming pool, and miniature golf are provided. The facilities are wheelchair accessible. Leashed pets are permitted.

Reservations, fees: Reservations are accepted at 800/864-7275 or 770/389-7275 (within the Atlanta area). The deposit of one night's fee is non-refundable, but your reservation can be moved once to another date. Fees range from $13–15. Like all of Georgia's state parks, there is a $2 per day parking fee, or you can purchase an annual Georgia Park-Pass for $25. Campers pay for just one daily pass for their entire stay.

Open: Year-round.

Directions: From Blakely, go north on Highway 27 six miles.

Contact: Kolomoki Mounds State Historic Park, Rt. 1, Box 114, Blakely, GA 31723; 229/724-2150.

Trip notes: This is one of the most interesting of Georgia's state parks. The park contains seven mounds built between A.D. 1100–1300 by the Native Americans of the Swift Creek and Weeden Island tribes. The museum contains an excavated mound and offers a film and artifacts. Fishing is available in two lakes, and canoes and paddleboats are available for rent. There are five miles of hiking trails.

11 Emerald Lake RV Park and Music Showcase

Location: Colquitt, map 7, grid H2.

Campsites, facilities: There are 20 pull-through RV sites, two with full hookups, and six tent sites. Half of the sites have shade. Picnic tables and cooking grills are available. The group site has a kitchen. Restrooms have hot showers and flush toilets. Ice and firewood are available at the campground, and the nearest supply and grocery store is six miles away. A coin laundry, clubroom, and sanitary disposal station are on the premises. Leashed pets are permitted.

Reservations, fees: Reservations are accepted with no deposit. Sites are $15.

Open: Year-round.

Directions: The campground is on Highway 91, halfway between Colquitt and Donalsonville.

Contact: Emerald Lake RV Park and Music Showcase, 698 Enterprise Rd., Colquitt, GA 31737; 229/758-2929.

Trip notes: The campground is six miles from the site of the Swamp Gravy folk life playground, which draws people from all over the region. Lake Seminole is 15 miles away, and numerous festivals are held in the area. The campground is near the Kolomoki Mounds in Blakely. Fishing is nearby. One of the owners is a professional musician, and guests can bring guitars to pick and sing at the clubhouse in the evening.

12 Georgia Veterans Memorial State Park

Location: Lake Blackshear, map 8, grid A1.

Campsites, facilities: There are 77 campsites suitable for either tents or RVs, all with 30-amp electric, water, and cable TV hookups. Thirty are pull-through sites, and most have some shade. All of the campsites have picnic tables, and either fire rings or cooking grills. Restrooms have hot showers and flush toilets. There are also 10 cabins available. A coin laundry, boat ramps, swimming pool, playground, 18-hole golf course, and sanitary disposal station are provided. Marine gas and supplies are available nearby. One of the sites is wheelchair accessible. Leashed pets are permitted in the campground, but pets are not

permitted in the cabins. You must clean up after your pets, and they must not disturb other campers.

Reservations, fees: Reservations are accepted at 800/864-7275 or 770/389-7275 (within the Atlanta area). The deposit is non-refundable, but the date can be moved once. Rates for waterfront sites are $18 per night, or $15 for a site not on the water. Cabins cost $75–90 per night, depending on the season. Like all of Georgia's state parks, there is a $2 per day parking fee, or you can purchase an annual Georgia ParkPass for $25. Campers pay for just one daily pass for their entire stay.

Open: Year-round.

Directions: From Interstate 75, go west on US 280 for 10 miles.

Contact: Georgia Veterans Memorial State Park, 2459 US 280 West, Unit A, Cordele, GA 31015; 229/276-2371; website: www.sowega.net/~gavets.

Trip notes: This lakefront park offers fishing for crappie, bass, catfish, and bream, particularly in the fall and spring. There is a short (1.5-mile) nature trail in the park, and additional hiking nearby. The 7000-acre lake provides ample recreational activities, including water-skiing, swimming, canoeing, boating and fishing. The park is 35 miles from the Andersonville National Cemetery Historic Site, 35 miles from the Jimmy Carter National Historic Site in Plains, and 45 miles from both the Georgia Agrirama in Tifton, and the Museum of Aviation in Warner Robins.

13 Cordele KOA Kampground

Location: Cordele, map 8, grid A3.

Campsites, facilities: Tents and RVs are in separate sections at this campground. The 20 tent sites all have electric and water hookups. Half of the 50 RV sites have full hookups, and the others have water and electric only. All sites have shade. Cable TV is available. The restrooms have hot showers and flush toilets. There is a playground, swimming pool, and clubroom. The campground store sells ice, LP gas, groceries, and gifts. A sanitary disposal station is provided. The facilities are wheelchair accessible. Pets are permitted at the campsites and must be walked on leash. No pets are allowed in the store, playground, or pool area.

Reservations, fees: Reservations are accepted, and deposits are refundable if the reservation is cancelled 72 hours or more before scheduled arrival. The fee for tents is $17 nightly. For RVs, sites with full hookups are $23.50, or $22 for electric, water, and cable TV hookups only. If you stay for a week, the seventh day is free. KOA cardholders get a 10% discount.

Open: Year-round.

Directions: From Interstate 75, take exit 97 west and travel one-quarter mile.

Contact: Cordele KOA, 373 Rockhouse Road East, Cordele, GA 31015; 229/273-5454.

Trip notes: Cordele is 30 minutes from Andersonville, a Civil War POW camp, and Plains, home of former President Jimmy Carter. It is also near Lake Blackshear and the Flint River. Cordele is the watermelon capital of Georgia, and the site of many festivals in the spring, summer, and fall.

14 Cordele RV Park

Location: Cordele, map 8, grid A3.

Campsites, facilities: There are 12 tent sites with water and electric hookups, and 90 RV sites, most with full hookups. Some sites have picnic tables. Restrooms have hot showers and flush toilets. A coin laundry, swimming pool, playground, and clubroom

are provided. Pets are permitted.

Reservations, fees: Reservations are accepted, and no deposit is required. Tent sites are $12 per night, and RV sites are $16.

Open: Year-round.

Directions: From Interstate 75, take exit 97 and turn east on Rockhouse Road. After half a mile, turn right on Floyd Road.

Contact: Cordele RV Park, 191 Floyd Rd., Cordele, GA 31015; 229/271-3111.

Trip notes: The fishing pond at the campground is stocked with catfish, bluegill, and bass. The campground is 30 miles from the Andersonville Civil War POW camp, and from the Cotton Museum in Vienna.

15 Southern Gates RV Park and Campground

Location: Arabi, map 8, grid B3.

Campsites, facilities: There are 27 tent sites, all with good shade and hookups for electric and water. In a separate section, the 23 RV sites have shade and full hookups. All are pull-through sites. The campsites include picnic tables and fire rings. Restrooms have flush toilets and hot showers. Firewood and ice are available at the campground, and groceries are available 10 miles away in Arabi. The campground has a swimming pool, clubroom, playground, and sanitary disposal station. Cable TV is available. The buildings are wheelchair accessible. Leashed pets are permitted. You must clean up after your pets.

Reservations, fees: Reservations are accepted. Fees range from $10 for tents to $16–21 for RVs.

Open: Year-round.

Directions: From Interstate 75, take the Arabi exit, turn west and follow the signs.

Contact: Southern Gates

RV Park and Campground, 138 Campsite Rd., Arabi, GA 31712; 229/273-6464.

Trip notes: The campground is close to the Andersonville Civil War POW historic site, and to Plains, the home of former President Jimmy Carter. The campground has two ponds for year-round fishing, and is near Lake Blackshear's swimming beach.

16 Knights Inn RV Park

Location: Ashburn, map 8, grid C3.

Campsites, facilities: There are 77 campsites suitable for tents or RVs. Two-thirds of the sites have full hookups, and the rest have water and electric only. Pull-through sites are available. Restrooms have hot showers and flush toilets. A sanitary disposal station, coin laundry, tennis courts, swimming pool, and playground are provided. Ice, groceries, and supplies are available at the campground. Pets are permitted.

Reservations, fees: Reservations are accepted, and no deposit is required. Campsites are $9.95 per night.

Open: Year-round.

Directions: From Interstate 75, take exit 84/Highway 159 and go west about 100 yards to the campground.

Contact: Knights Inn RV Park, P.O. Box 806, Ashburn, GA 31714; 229/567-3334.

Trip notes: There is a public golf course within five miles, and Lake Blackshear is about 25 miles from the campground.

17 Amy's South Georgia RV Park

Location: Tifton, map 8, grid E4.

Campsites, Facilities: There are 86 campsites at this park. Sixty of them are pull-through sites with full hookups and are reserved for RVs. The other sites have water and electric hookups, and can be used by either tents or RVs. Picnic tables are provided, and some sites have cooking grills. Fire rings are provided except in drought years, when fires are prohibited. Restrooms have hot showers and flush toilets. A coin laundry, swimming pool, playground, and activity room are provided. Ice, LP gas, and some supplies are available at the campground. Leashed pets are permitted. You must clean up after your pet.

Reservations, fees: Reservations are accepted, and held with a credit card. Cancellation must be made at least 72 hours in advance or the credit card will be charged for one night's fee. The rate for water and electric sites is $16.50, and sites with full hookups are $18–21 per night.

Open: Year-round.

Directions: From Interstate 75, take exit 60 (South Central/Union Road) and turn west. The campground is on the right, 1.1 miles from the interstate.

Contact: Amy's South Georgia RV Park, 4632 Union Rd., Tifton, GA 31794; 229/386-8441.

Trip notes: The campground is about five miles from the Georgia Agrirama.

18 The Pines Campground

Location: Tifton, map 8, grid E4.

Campsites, Facilities: There are 34 RV sites at this campground, all with full hookups and all pull-through sites. Both 30- and 50-amp hookups are available. Picnic tables are provided. Primitive tent camping is also allowed, and there is room for 5–7 tents. Restrooms have hot showers and flush toilets. One of the restrooms is wheelchair accessible. A coin laundry and meeting room are provided. Supplies and a restaurant are about 100 yards from the campground. Leashed pets are permitted.

Reservations, fees: Reservations are accepted at 229/382-3500. No deposit is required. Tent sites rent for $10 per night. RV sites rent for $15.

Open: Year-round.

Directions: From Valdosta, take Interstate 75 north to exit 61 and turn west on Omega Road. The campground is on the left, about 100 yards from the interstate.

Contact: The Pines Campground, 18 Casseta Road, Tifton, GA 31794; 229/382-3500.

Trip notes: The campground is primarily a stopover for travelers on Interstate 75. There are few amenities, but it is just a mile from the Georgia Agrirama, a living history museum depicting life in the 1800's.

19 Reed Bingham State Park

Location: Adel, map 8, grid G4.

Campsites, facilities: There are 46 tent and RV sites at this campground, all with water and electric hookups. Cable and satellite TV hookups are available. Picnic tables, fire rings, and cooking grills are provided. Restrooms have hot showers and flush toilets. A boat ramp, dock, playground, coin laundry, and sanitary disposal station are provided. Leashed pets are permitted.

Reservations, fees: Reservations are accepted at 800/864-7275 or 770/389-7275 (within the Atlanta area). The deposit of one night's stay is non-refundable, but your reservation date can be moved once. Rates are $15–17 per night. Like all of Georgia's

state parks, there is a $2 per day parking fee, or you can purchase an annual Georgia Park-Pass for $25. Campers pay for just one daily pass for their entire stay.

Open: Year-round.

Directions: From Interstate 75, take Highway 37 west six miles.

Contact: Reed Bingham State Park, Rt. 2, Box 394 B-1, Adel, GA 31620; 229/896-3551.

Trip notes: The 375-acre lake offers boating, fishing (for bass, crappie, catfish, and bream), and water-skiing year-round. Hiking is available on the 3.5-mile Coastal Plains Nature Trail and the half-mile Gopher Tortoise Nature Trail. There is a beach in the swimming area. The threatened gopher tortoise can be found in the park, along with indigo snakes and waterfowl. The park is near the Banks Lake National Wildlife Refuge, the Georgia Agrirama in Tifton, and the Jefferson Davis Memorial State Historic Site in Fitzgerald.

20 Pebble Ridge RV Park

Location: Adel, map 8, grid G4.

Campsites, Facilities: There are 30 campsites suitable for tents or RVs, all with full hookups. All sites are pull-through. RV sites, all with full hookups. Both 30- and 50-amp service is available. Pull-through sites are available. Restrooms have hot showers and flush toilets. A clubhouse with fireplace is provided. Leashed pets are permitted.

Reservations, fees: Reservations are accepted at 229/896-2819. Deposits are not required. Sites cost $10 per night, $55 per week, and $190 per month.

Open: Year-round.

Directions: From Tifton, take Interstate 75 south to exit

39/Highway 37 west, and turn right. Turn right onto Evergreen Church Road at the sign for Reed Bingham State park. Make the first left onto Reed Bingham State Park Road. The campground is on the left, immediately after the turn.

Contact: Pebble Ridge RV Park, Rt. 2, Box 394, Adel, GA 31620; 229/896-2819 or 229/896-7434.

Trip notes: The campground is a quarter mile from Reed Bingham State Park, which offers fishing, hiking trails, swimming, playgrounds, and picnicking. Most of the guests at this park rent by the month.

21 Spence Field

Location: Moultrie, map 8, grid H3.

Campsites, facilities: There are 500 developed campsites for tents or RVs, all with water and electric hookups. A primitive area is also available for approximately 100 tents. Restrooms have hot showers and flush toilets. A sanitary disposal station is provided. Leashed pets are permitted.

Reservations, fees: Reservations are accepted at 229/890-5426. Reservations are required for the Sunbelt Expo. There is a four-night minimum stay required during the Expo, and the deposit of the full amount is not refundable. The fee for primitive sites is $10, developed sites are $15.

Open: Year-round.

Directions: The campground is about seven miles south of Moultrie on Highway 133.

Contact: Spence Field, City of Moultrie, Attn: George Price, P.O. Box 3368, Moultrie, GA 31776; 229/890-5425.

Trip notes: The campground is on an old abandoned airbase, and there are few amenities. It is the site of the annual Sunbelt Expo, one of the largest farming shows in the country. During the Expo, which normally runs the third week of October, only attendees may stay at the campground. Although reservations aren't required the rest of the year, call ahead to find out if the restrooms will be open. If there aren't enough campers to warrant it, the restrooms are closed. The nearest fishing is at Reed Bingham State Park, about 18 miles away. There are no hiking trails at the campground, but there are plenty of walking areas on the old base.

22 General Coffee State Park

Location: Douglas, map 9, grid D2.

Campsites, facilities: There are 50 campsites that can be used for either tents or RVs, all with water and electric hookups. All are pull-through sites, and most have shade. In addition, there are group sites available and five cabins. Picnic tables, fire rings, and cooking grills are available. Restrooms have hot showers and flush toilets. Communal patios are available, and a coin laundry, playground, clubroom, and swimming pool are provided. Ice, firewood, and some gifts are available. The campground also has a sanitary disposal station. The buildings are wheelchair accessible. Pets are permitted except in the cabins, and must be kept on a six-foot maximum length leash.

Reservations, fees: Reservations are accepted at 800/864-7275 or 770/389-7275 (within the Atlanta area). The deposit is non-refundable, but the date can be moved once. Site fees are $13–15 per night. Like all of Georgia's state parks, there is a $2 per day parking fee, or you can purchase an annual Georgia ParkPass for $25. Campers pay for just one daily pass for their entire stay.

Open: Year-round.

Directions: From Douglas, go east on Highway 32 six miles to the park.

Contact: General Coffee State Park, 46 John Coffee Rd., Nicholls, GA 31554; 912/384-7082.

Trip notes: The park has two trails totaling just over four miles. The lake offers fishing for bream, catfish, and bass. Green fly orchids bloom in the summer. Wildlife in the area includes deer, gopher tortoises, raccoons, and wild turkeys.

23 Lazy Acre Mobile Home and RV Park

Location: Waycross, map 9, grid G6.

Campsites, facilities: The campground has 40 RV sites, all with full hookups and. All are pull-through sites. Group sites are available. Restrooms have hot showers and flush toilets. Groceries and supplies are available within walking distance. Cable TV hookups are available, and a sanitary disposal station is provided. Pets are permitted.

Reservations, fees: Reservations are accepted. The campground does not publish its rates.

Open: Year-round.

Directions: From Waycross, take US 1 south to the campground.

Contact: Lazy Acre Mobile Home and RV Park, 2102 Memorial Dr., Waycross, GA 31501; 912/283-0410.

Trip notes: The campground is six miles north of the Okefenokee Swamp.

24 Laura S. Walker State Park

Location: Waycross, map 9, grid G7.

Campsites, facilities: There are 44 campsites available for either tents or RVs. Two are pull-through sites, and 15 have shade. No sites have hookups. There are also 16 cabins at the park. Picnic tables and cooking grills are provided at each site. Restrooms have hot showers and flush toilets. A coin laundry, ice, firewood, limited grocery items, and gifts are available at the camp store. The nearest supply store outside of the campground is six miles away. A sanitary disposal station, boat ramp, swimming pool, and playground are provided. Boat motors are restricted to 10 horsepower between 11 A.M. and 6 P.M. The facilities are wheelchair accessible. Pets are not allowed in the cabins, but are allowed in the campground. Dogs must be on leash at all times.

Reservations, fees: Reservations are accepted at 800/864-7275 or 770/389-7275 (within the Atlanta area). The deposit is nonrefundable, but the date can be moved once. Like all of Georgia's state parks, there is a $2 per day parking fee, or you can purchase an annual Georgia ParkPass for $25. Campers pay for just one daily pass for their entire stay. All tent sites are $15, regular RV sites are $17, and premium RV sites on the lake are $18 per night.

Open: Year-round.

Directions: Take Highway 177 southeast from Waycross and follow the signs.

Contact: Laura S. Walker State Park, 5653 Laura Walker Rd., Waycross, GA 31503; 912/287-4900; email: lswalker@gate.net.

Trip notes: Just nine miles from the Oke-fenokee National Wildlife Refuge, the park is a good location to experience the swamp. Either go during the late fall and winter months, or bring plenty of mosquito repellent. Bass, bream, catfish, chain pickerel, and perch can be caught in the 120-acre lake, which also offers swimming, kayaking, and rafting. There is a 1.2-mile nature trail at the park, where wildflowers can be found blooming along the trail in the spring and summer. The park is 43 miles from the Okefenokee National Wildlife Refuge. Wildlife that can be found at the park and campground includes alligators, turtles, deer, squirrels, rabbits, gopher tortoises, and snakes.

25 Adamson's Fish Camp and Beards Bluff Campground

Location: Altamaha River, map 10, grid A1.

Campsites, Facilities: There are 20 sites for tents and RVs, all with water and electricity. Pull-through sites are available. Thirteen cabins range from sleeping areas to fully equipped with kitchens and bathrooms. Two primitive camping areas are also available. The developed sites have picnic tables, fire pits, and grills. The restrooms have hot showers and flush toilets. The grocery store sells food, ice, tackle, bait, and canister gas for stoves, and free firewood is available. A coin laundry, playground, and boat ramp are provided. Marine gas is available. The store and one of the cabins are wheelchair accessible. Controlled pets are permitted.

Reservations, fees: Reservations are recommended, and required in the winter. Campsite fees are $10–18, and cabins are $20–55 except in the winter, when cabin rates are discounted to $20–50.

Open: Year-round.

Directions: Take Highway 301 south from Interstate 16 through Glennville. Ten miles past Glennville, cross a small bridge over Beard's Creek. Just after the bridge, turn right onto a dirt road next to a historical marker. When the road forks, take the right fork to the campground, about five miles from the highway.

Contact: Adamson's Fish Camp and Beards Bluff Campground, Rt. 3, Box 5155, Glennville, GA 30427; 912/654-3632.

Trip notes: The historical marker on Highway 301 marks the site of Fort Telfair, which was built in 1790 on the bank of Beard's Creek to protect the settlers from the Creeks. The fort succumbed to the widening of the creek long ago, and the marker is the only sign remaining except for underwater, where divers can explore remnants of the fort. Kayaks, canoes, and kiwis (small kayaks) are available for rent. A shuttle service will drop you at the river as far north as Lumber City, and pick you up as far south as Brunswick, which allows for trips from an hour or two to all day. Three nature trails, varying from one-half to two miles in length, take hikers through cypress groves to several lakes, providing a chance to glimpse wild turkeys, hogs, and deer. Bald eagles nest by the river, along with kites. Fish are plentiful, primarily catfish, bass, bream, shell crackers, gar, shad, and eel. The area is home to the endangered indigo snake and gopher tortoise. When the river is low, numerous sandbars appear and are available for primitive camping.

26 Happy Acres Resort

Location: Lake Grace, map 10, grid D1.

Campsites, facilities: There are 20 tent sites with water and electric hookups, and 110 RV sites, all with full hookups and all pull-through sites. Some sites have shade. Most sites have picnic tables. There are also five mobile homes available, as well as RV storage. Restrooms have hot showers and flush toilets. A sanitary disposal station, coin laundry, swimming pool, and clubroom are provided. Ice, LP gas, and some groceries are available at the campground. Leashed pets are permitted.

Reservations, fees: Reservations are accepted, and no deposit is required. Tent sites are $7 per night, and sites with full hookups are $12. Coast to Coast, Passport America, and RPI discounts apply.

Open: Year-round.

Directions: Take US 84 through Jesup to Highway 203, and turn right. After five miles, turn right onto Odum Road, and travel two miles to the campground.

Contact: Happy Acres Resort, 5441 Odum Road South, Screven, GA 31560; 912/586-6781.

Trip notes: Fishing is available in the lake for bass, bream, catfish, and crappie. There are hiking trails in the area. The campground is 35 miles from the Okefenokee Swamp, and 50 miles from Jekyll Island, St. Simons Island, and Sea Island. The campground caters to mostly retired couples and might not be the best choice for families with small children.

27 Pine Lake Campground

Location: Jesup, map 10, grid D2.

Campsites, facilities: There are 35 campsites suitable for tents or RVs, all with hookups. Pull-through sites and shade are available. Picnic tables are provided. RV storage is available. Restrooms have hot showers and flush toilets. A playground and clubroom are provided. Cable TV hookups are available. Pets are permitted.

Reservations, fees: Reservations are accepted, and no deposit is required. Campsites are $10 per night.

Open: Year-round.

Directions: From Jesup, take US 341 south 6.5 miles, turn right on Gardi Road, and follow the signs.

Contact: Pine Lake Campground, 555 Gardi Rd., Jesup, GA 31546; 912/427-3664.

Trip notes: There is a small fish pond stocked with bass, bream, catfish, perch, and crappie. There are five miles of seldom-used roadway for biking and horseback riding. The campground is two miles from horse stables, which provide boarding services and horse rental, 39 miles from Brunswick.

28 Semimole Sportsman Lodge Marina and Campground

Location: Donalsonville, map 11, grid A1.

Campsites, facilities: All of the 20 tent sites offer shade and water and electric hookups. Of the 26 RV sites, all have shade, and 10 have full hookups. Pull-through sites are available. There are also 10 primitive sites, group sites, and nine cabins. Picnic tables are provided. RV storage is available. Restrooms have showers and flush toilets. Ice, firewood, and cable TV hookups are available. A sanitary disposal station is on the property. Pets are permitted.

Reservations, fees: Reservations are accepted at 877/258-1080, and the deposit is refundable up to 48 hours before your scheduled arrival. Tent sites are $8, sites with water and electric are $15, and sites with full hookups are $17.

Open: Year-round.

Directions: From Bainbridge, go north on Highway 38 16 miles and turn left into the campground.

Contact: Seminole Sportsman Lodge, Rt. 3, Box 215-A, Donalsonville, GA 31745; 229/861-3862, fax 229/861-3501.

Trip notes: The campground is close to Lake Seminole and Seminole State Park, so has easily accessible fishing and hiking.

29 Seminole State Park

Location: Donalsonville, map 11, grid B1.
Campsites, facilities: There are 50 campsites suitable for tents and RVs, all with water and electric hookups. Picnic tables and fire rings are provided. Pull-through sites are available. Rental cabins are available. Restrooms have hot showers and flush toilets. A sanitary disposal station, miniature golf, boat ramp, and dock are provided. Ice and gifts are available at the campground and park. Leashed pets are permitted.
Reservations, fees: Reservations are accepted at 800/864-7275 or 770/389-7275 (within the Atlanta area). The deposit of one night's fee is non-refundable, but your reservation can be moved once to another date. Fees range from $13–17. Like all of Georgia's state parks, there is a $2 per day parking fee, or you can purchase an annual Georgia Park-Pass for $25. Campers pay for just one daily pass for their entire stay.
Open: Year-round.
Directions: From Donalsonville, take Highway 39 south 16 miles and follow the signs to the park and campground.
Contact: Seminole State Park, 7870 State Park Dr., Donalsonville, GA 31745; 229/861-3137.
Trip notes: Lake Seminole is a 37,500-acre reservoir credited with being among the best lakes in the country for fishing.

Canoes and paddleboats are available to rent. There is a sand beach in the swimming area. There is a 2.2-mile nature trail in the park. Wildlife you may see includes the endangered gopher tortoise, waterfowl, and deer.

30 Wingate's Lunker Lodge and Bass Island Campground

Location: Lake Seminole, map 11, grid B3.
Campsites, facilities: There are 80 campsites suitable for tents or RVs. One-third of the sites have full hookups, and the rest have water and electric hookups. Most sites have cable TV available. Picnic tables, fire rings, and some cooking grills are provided. There are also cabins and mobile homes for rent. RV storage is available. Restrooms have hot showers and flush toilets. A coin laundry, boat ramp, dock, and playground are provided. Ice, supplies, groceries, and marine gas are available at the campground. There is a restaurant on-site. The restrooms are wheelchair accessible. Pets are permitted.
Reservations, fees: Reservations are accepted, and the deposit is refundable with advance notice. Site fees are $10–23 per night, depending on hookups.
Open: Year-round.
Directions: From Bainbridge, take Highway 97 south 15 miles to the Highway 97 Spur, and turn right. The campground is three miles down on the left.
Contact: Wingate's Lunker Lodge and Bass Island Campground, 139 Wingate Rd., Bainbridge, GA 31717; 229/246-0658.
Trip notes: Lake Seminole has been rated

the third best lake in the nation. It offers fishing for bass, bluegill, crappie, catfish, and shell cracker. Fishing and lake tour guides are available for rent. Hiking and biking are available in a 255-acre area cut with roads around the lake.

31 Sugar Mill Plantation RV Park

Location: Thomasville, map 12, grid A1.
Campsites, facilities: There are 30 tent sites at this campground, all with water and electric hookups, and 125 RV sites, all with full hookups. Thirty of these are pull-through sites. Most campsites have shade. Group sites are available. RV storage is available. Picnic tables are provided at all sites. Restrooms have hot showers and flush toilets. A coin laundry, cable TV, three clubrooms, and sanitary disposal station are provided. LP gas and firewood are available. Leashed pets are permitted, but cannot be left tied up outside of your tent or camper.
Reservations, fees: Reservations are accepted. Fees are $19 per night, $114 per week, and $135 per month, plus electric charges.
Open: Year-round.
Directions: From Thomasville, take US 84 east to US 19 and turn north. After seven miles, turn left on McMillan Road.
Contact: Sugar Mill Plantation RV Park, 4857 McMillan Rd., Ochlocknee, GA 31773; 229 /227-1451, fax 229/227-0999.
Trip notes: Fishing for catfish and bass is available at the campground, as well as hiking in the 900+ acres of undeveloped property. The campground is nine miles from Thomasville, and 50 miles from Albany and Valdosta.

32 City of Roses RV Park

Location: Thomasville, map 12, grid B1.
Campsites, facilities: There are 12 tent or camper sites with water and electric hookups, and 60 RV sites with full hookups. Some shade is available. Some sites have picnic tables. RV storage is available. Restrooms have hot showers and flush toilets. A sanitary disposal station, coin laundry, and clubroom are provided. Cable TV hookups are available. The buildings are wheelchair accessible. Leashed pets are permitted. You must clean up after your pet.
Reservations, fees: Reservations are accepted, and no deposit is required. Tent camping is $10, and sites with full hookups are $20. AAA, AARP, and Good Sam discounts apply.
Open: Year-round.
Directions: From Interstate 10, take US 319 north to Thomasville, and stay on Business 319 into town. Turn right onto Business 84/3/38 and head east. Turn right onto East Pine Tree Boulevard, then left onto Old Boston Road.
Contact: City of Roses RV Park, 277 Old Boston Rd., Thomasville, GA 31792; 229/228-7275.
Trip notes: The campground is 15 miles from the Florida border. There are 73 plantations in the area, some open to the public for touring. Most of the campers here are renting by the month and are either retired or working temporary jobs in the area.

33 Valdosta Oaks Campground

Location: Valdosta, map 12, grid A6.

Campsites, facilities: There are 20 tent sites with water and electric hookups, and 35 pull-through RV sites with full hookups. Most sites have shade. Restrooms have hot showers and flush toilets. A coin laundry and playground are provided. Some sites have picnic tables. Pets are permitted.

Reservations, fees: Reservations are not accepted. The fee is $14 per night for all sites.

Open: Year-round.

Directions: From Interstate 75, take exit 22 and go west. The campground is less than one-tenth of a mile from the interstate.

Contact: Valdosta Oaks Campground, 4598 N. Valdosta Rd., Valdosta, GA 31602; 229/247-0494.

Trip notes: The campground is three miles from Langdale Park, which has hiking trails along the Withlacoochie River. Fishing, kayaking, rafting, and canoeing are available at the river. Wild Adventures, a wild animal theme park, is 11 miles from the campground.

34 River Park Mobile Home and RV Park

Location: Valdosta, map 12, grid B6.

Campsites, facilities: There are 57 RV sites, all with full hookups. All are pull-through sites. Some sites have shade. There is also a primitive tent area. Water is available. Picnic tables are provided for the developed campsites. Restrooms have hot showers and flush toilets. A sanitary disposal station, coin laundry, and swimming pool are provided. Cable TV hookups are available. The facilities are wheelchair accessible. Pets are permitted.

Reservations, fees: Reservations are accepted, and no deposit is required. Primitive tent sites cost $10, sites without cable TV are $15, and sites with cable TV hookups are $17.

Open: Year-round.

Directions: From Florida, take Interstate 75 north and take exit 18/St. Augustine Road, turning left. The campground will be on the right.

Contact: River Park Mobile Home and RV Park, 1 Suwanee Dr., Valdosta, GA 31602; 229/244-8397.

Trip notes: The campground is near the Withlacoochee River, which offers kayaking, rafting, and paddleboats. It is eight miles from Wild Adventures, a wildlife preserve and amusement park.

35 Pride Country Lakes

Location: Quitman, map 12, grid C3.

Campsites, facilities: There are 70 campsites at this campground. Ten of the sites have full hookups and are reserved for RVs. The rest have water and electric hookups and can be used by tents or RVs. Most are pull-through sites. A few sites have shade. Some sites have picnic tables and/or fire rings. RVs must be 40 feet or less in length. Cabins are also available. RV storage is available. Restrooms have hot showers and flush toilets. A sanitary disposal station, coin laundry, boat ramp, dock, swimming pool, playground, and recreation room are provided. The facilities are wheelchair accessible. Pets are permitted.

Reservations, fees: Reservations are accepted, and no deposit is required. Tents cost $10 per night, and campers and RVs cost $17 for water and electric or $20 for full hookups. Cabins rent for $40–50 per night. Coast to Coast, RPI, AOR, and United Campers Club of America discounts apply.

Open: Year-round.

Directions: From Quitman, take US 221 south for 6.5 miles. At the sign, turn right onto Hickory Head Road. The campground will be on the left 1.8 miles from the highway.

Contact: Pride Country Lakes, 1877 Hickory Head Rd, Quitman, GA 31643; 229/263-5350.

Trip notes: There are two private lakes in the campground, stocked with catfish, crappie, and bass. Fishing is also available in Stanley Bay. There is one marked trail a little over a mile in length, plus 200-acres of land. Wildlife seen in the area includes armadillos, bobcats, deer, wild turkeys, bears, and alligators. The campground is 22 miles from Thomasville, where the Lapham-Patterson House State Historic Site can be toured, and about half an hour from outlet shopping and The Parks at Chehaw, a wild animal park.

36 Eagle's Roost Campground

Location: Lake Park, map 12, grid C7.

Campsites, facilities: This large campground has 140 RV sites. Most have full hookups, and pull-through sites are available. Most have shade. There are also 30 tent sites in a separate section, all with water and electric hookups. There are 25 primitive sites and 60 group sites. Restrooms have flush toilets and hot showers. RV storage and cable TV are available, and the campground store sells ice, LP gas, and groceries. A swimming pool, playground, clubroom, and coin laundry are on the premises, along with a sanitary disposal station. Pets are permitted. They must be walked on leash in a designated area and cannot be tied outside.

Reservations, fees: Reservations are accepted with a credit card. Rates are $19 per night for 30-amp and $22 for 50-amp sites.

Open: Year-round.

Directions: From Valdosta, take Interstate 75 south to exit 5/Highway 376, and go east. Turn immediately right onto Mill Store Road. The entrance is one-half mile down on the left.

Contact: Eagle's Roost Campground, 5465 Mill Store Rd., Lake Park, GA 31636; 229/559-5192, fax 229/559-0141.

Trip notes: The campground is centrally located for activities in south Georgia, such as the Wild Adventures park (13 miles), the Agrirama (45 miles), and the Thomasville Plantations and Rose Gardens (45 miles). It is near fishing. It is fairly close to Interstate 75 but still has an abundant amount of wildlife, including deer, alligators, eagles and other birds, raccoons, opossums, armadillos, and squirrels.

37 Stephen C. Foster State Park

Location: Okefenokee Swamp, map 13, grid B6.

Campsites, Facilities: There are 66 campsites suitable for tents or RVs, all equipped with water and electric hookups. Pull-through sites are available. Picnic tables and fire rings are provided. Primitive camping and rental cabins are available. Restrooms have hot showers and flush toilets. Ice, supplies, and groceries are available at the campground. A sanitary disposal station, boat ramp, and dock are provided. The buildings are wheelchair accessible. Leashed pets are permitted.

Reservations, fees: Reservations are accepted at 800/864-7275 or 770/389-7275 (within the Atlanta area). The deposit of one night's fee is non-refundable, but your reservation can be moved once to another date. Campsite fees are $13–15, except between March and May when they're $16–18 per night. Like all of Georgia's state parks, there is a $2 per day parking fee, or you can purchase an annual Georgia ParkPass for $25. Campers pay for just one daily pass for their entire stay.

Open: Year-round.

Directions: From Fargo, take Highway 177 northeast to the park and campground.

Contact: Stephen C. Foster State Park, Rt. 1, Box 131, Fargo, GA 31631; 912/637-5274.

Trip notes: The park is at the western entrance to the Okefenokee National Wildlife Refuge. Guided tours are available, and motorboats, canoes, and johnboats are available for rent. There is an elevated boardwalk through the area. The park is located within a wildlife refuge. Wildlife in the park includes 223 species of birds, 41 species of mammals, 54 species of reptiles, and 60 species of amphibians. There is a large alligator population, so keep close tabs on small children and pets. My friend Allan noticed that every time his youngest child wandered more than 10 feet away from him, nearby alligators would start heading in his direction. When Allan would walk towards his son, the alligators would change direction.

38 Okefenokee RV Campgrounds

Location: Okefenokee Swamp, map 13, grid B8.

Campsites, Facilities: There are 52 RV sites, all with full hookups. Both 30- and 50-amp hookups are available. Pull-through sites are available. Picnic tables and fire rings are provided. Restrooms have hot showers and flush toilets. Ice, groceries, and a small deli are at the campground. A playground, shuffleboard court, and video game room are provided, and a swimming pool was in construction at press time. The buildings are wheelchair accessible. Leashed pets are permitted.

Reservations, fees: Reservations are accepted at 866/300-3119. Deposits are not required. Sites with 30-amp service rent for $15 per night. Sites with 50-amp service rent for $17.

Open: Year-round.

Directions: From Waycross, go south on US 1 to Homeland, and turn right on Bowery Lane. The campground is on the left just after the railroad tracks, about three blocks from the highway.

Contact: Okefenokee RV Campground, 400 Bowery Lane, Homeland, GA 31537; 912/496-3258.

Trip notes: The campground is five miles from the St. Mary's River, and seven from the swamp. Canoe tours of the swamp from two hours to two days in length can be arranged at the campground. Fruit trees and vines grow throughout the campground, and campers can pick fresh apples, peaches, pears, grapes, and pomegranates.

39 Kingfisher Wilderness Campground

Location: Okefenokee Swamp, map 13, grid B8.

Campsites, Facilities: There are 15 campsites suitable for tents or small RVs less than 16 feet in length. Fire rings are provided, and most sites have some shade. Cabins are planned for 2003. Restrooms have hot showers and flush toilets. A lighted cook shed with picnic tables is provided. Free firewood is available at the campground. Leashed pets are permitted.

Reservations, fees: Reservations are accepted at 912/496-2186. Deposits are not required. Sites cost $8 per person per night, up to 10 people. For groups over 10, sites cost $6 per person.

Open: Year-round.

Directions: From Waycross, take US 1 south 23 miles. Turn right onto dirt road County Road 99 at the small brown sign for Kingfisher Landing. The campground is a quarter mile down on the right.

Contact: Kingfisher Wilderness Campground, Route 3 Box 970, Folkston, GA 31537; 912/496-2186; email: camp2001@planttel.net; website: www.okecamp.com.

Trip notes: The campground is half a mile from the Okefenokee National Wildlife Refuge, which offers fishing for warmouth, bream, largemouth bass, catfish, and jack fish. Neighboring Kingfisher and Beyond offers canoe rentals and shuttle service, which can be arranged at the campground.

40 Trader's Hill Recreation Area

Location: Folkston, map 13, grid B8.

Campsites, facilities: There are 24 RV sites with water and electric hookups. Tent camping is allowed in a large primitive area. RV sites have picnic tables, and there are some in the primitive area. Restrooms have hot showers and flush toilets. A sanitary disposal station, boat ramp, and dock are provided. Pets are permitted, but due to the number of alligators in the area, they should be kept inside or leashed at all times.

Reservations, fees: Reservations are accepted, and no deposit is required. The fee for tent camping is $5 per night. RV sites are $10.

Open: Year-round.

Directions: From Folkston, go south on Highway 121 about four miles, then turn left at the sign onto a dirt road.

Contact: Trader's Hill Recreation Area, Board of County Commissioners, 100 Third St., Folkston, GA 31537; 912/496-3412.

Trip notes: The campground is on the St. Marys River, which has bass, bream, catfish, and crappie. There are two nature trails.

41 Okefenokee Pastimes

Location: Okefenokee Swamp, map 13, grid B8.

Campsites, facilities: There are 12 tent sites and 12 RV sites at this campground. Five of the RV sites have full hookups, and the rest have water and electric. Both 30- and 50-amp hookups are available. Picnic tables are provided. Fire rings are provided in the tent section. There are also four cabins. Restrooms have hot showers and flush toilets. A sanitary disposal station and coin laundry are provided. Ice and limited groceries are available at the campground. Pets are permitted in the campground but not in the cabins.

Reservations, fees: Reservations are accepted. The deposit is refundable with a three-day notice of cancellation prior to your scheduled arrival date, less a $1 service charge. The fee for tents is $15 per night, $18 for RVs.

Open: The campground is closed from mid-July through mid-August.

Directions: The campground is seven miles south of Folkston on Highway 121.

Contact: Okefenokee Pastimes, RR 2, Box 3090, Folkston, GA 31537; 912/496-4472; website: www.okefenokee.com.

Trip notes: Fishing is available in the swamp and in the St. Marys river for bream, sunfish, bass, and catfish. There are nature trails on the property and across the road in the wildlife refuge. The campground rents boats, canoes, kayaks, mountain bikes, and even guides for touring the swamp, and provides a shuttle service. The campground also has a gallery with the work of 30 southeastern artists. Due to the alligator population in the area, keep a close watch on pets and small children.

42 Hidden River Campground

Location: St. George, map 13, grid E7.

Campsites, facilities: There are 11 RV sites at this campground, all pull-through sites and all with water and electric hookups. Some shade is available. Primitive tent camping is also available in the 40-acre wooded area. Restrooms have hot showers and flush toilets. A sanitary disposal station and swimming pool are provided. Leashed pets are permitted.

Reservations, fees: Reservations are ac-

cepted. The deposit is refundable with three days notice of cancellation. All sites cost $15 per person, plus $15 for a site with hookups.

Open: Year-round.

Directions: From Interstate 10, take the MacClenny/Highway 121/23 exit and go north seven miles. Turn left on Highway 185. After 8.5 miles, turn left onto Reynolds Bridge Road.

Contact: Hidden River Campground, 885 Reynolds Bridge Rd., St. George, GA 31646; 912/843-2603.

Trip notes: The campground is on the St. Marys River, which offers fishing, kayaking, rafting, and canoeing. The wooded area contains marked trails for hiking and horseback riding. The campground is 40 minutes from the Okefenokee Swamp. This is a clothing-optional campground.

43 St. Marys River Area

Location: Okefenokee Swamp, map 13, grid F7.

Campsites, Facilities: Primitive camping is allowed along the St. Marys Canoe Trail on any sandbar that is not posted. Camping is also allowed under bridge overpasses and at Camp Pinckney Landing. No facilities are provided.

Reservations, fees: Reservations are not accepted. There is no fee.

Open: Year-round.

Directions: The put-in point for the canoe trail is five miles north of MacClenny, Florida on Highway 23. From Waycross, take US 23/US 1 south to Folkston, and turn right onto Highway 23. Continue on Highway 23 south to the St. Marys River at the state line. Camp Pinckney Landing is the end of the St. Marys Canoe Trail, half a mile past the US 1 bridge over the river. From Waycross, take US 23/US 1 south to Folkston, and continue to the river.

Contact: Folkston-Charlton County Chamber of Commerce, P. O. Box 756, Folkston, GA 31537; 912/496-2536.

Trip notes: The water level on the St. Marys River varies depending on rainfall and drought conditions, and rises and falls somewhat due to the tidal effect from the Atlantic Ocean. There are several canoe outfitters and shuttle services along the river, or you can leave one vehicle at Camp Pinckney and one at the put-in point. This is leave-no-trace, wilderness camping. All trash must be packed out, and be sure your fire (if one is used) is out and ashes scattered before leaving your campsite. Fishing on the St. Marys River is generally good for bass, unless you are relying on catching fish for your dinner. There are no supplies available along the canoe trail.

COASTAL GEORGIA

Jekyll Island Beach

COASTAL GEORGIA

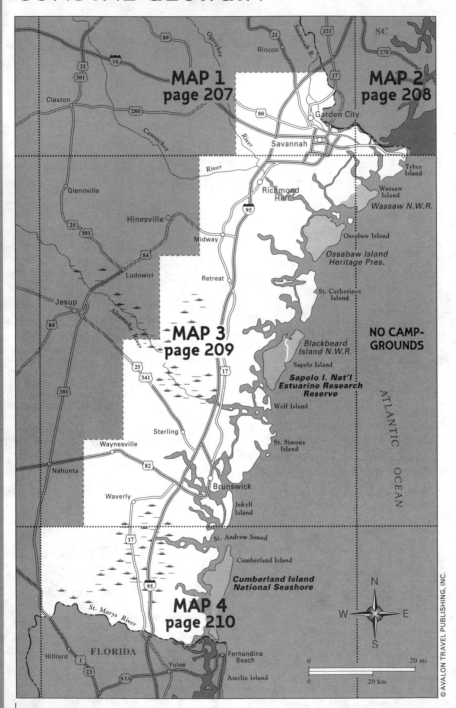

MAP 1
page 207

MAP 2
page 208

MAP 3
page 209

MAP 4
page 210

NO CAMP-
GROUNDS

SC

Rincon

Garden City

Savannah

Richmond Hill

Hinesville

Midway

Claxton

Glennville

Ludowici

Jesup

Retreat

Waynesville

Nahunta

Waverly

Sterling

Brunswick

Hilliard

Yulee

FLORIDA

Fernandina
Beach

Amelia Island

Tybee
Island

Wassaw
Island

Wassaw N.W.R.

Ossabaw Island

Ossabaw Island
Heritage Pres.

St. Catherines
Island

Blackbeard
Island N.W.R.

Sapelo Island

Sapelo I. Nat'l
Estuarine Research
Reserve

Wolf Island

St. Simons
Island

Jekyll
Island

St. Andrew Sound

Cumberland Island

Cumberland Island
National Seashore

ATLANTIC OCEAN

Ogeechee

Savannah R.

Canoochee

River

River

Altamaha River

St. Marys River

N
W   E
S

0   20 mi
0   20 km

© AVALON TRAVEL PUBLISHING, INC.

MAP 1

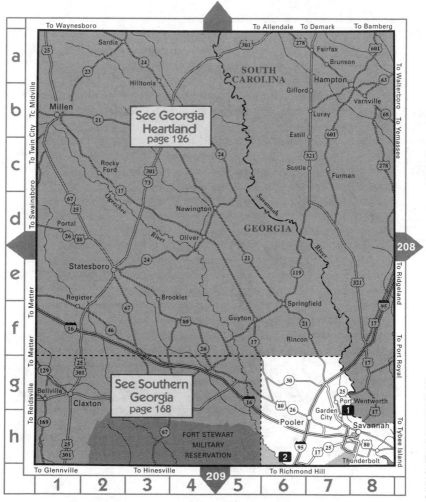

To Waynesboro • To Allendale • To Demark • To Bamberg

Sardis
Hilltonia
SOUTH CAROLINA
Fairfax
Brunson
Hampton
Gifford
varnville

Millen
See Georgia Heartland page 126
Luray
Estill

Rocky Ford
Scotia
Furman

Ogeechee River
Newington
Oliver
GEORGIA
Savannah River

Statesboro
Register
Brooklet
Springfield
Guyton
Rincon

See Southern Georgia page 168
Port Wentworth
Garden City
Savannah
Bellville
Claxton
Pooler
FORT STEWART MILITARY RESERVATION
Thunderbolt

To Glennville • To Hinesville • To Richmond Hill

To Midville • To Twin City • To Swainsboro • To Metter • To Metter • To Reidsville

To Walterboro • To Yemassee • To Ridgeland • To Port Royal • To Tybee Island

208 • 209

MAP 2

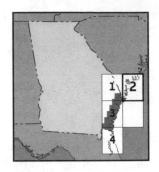

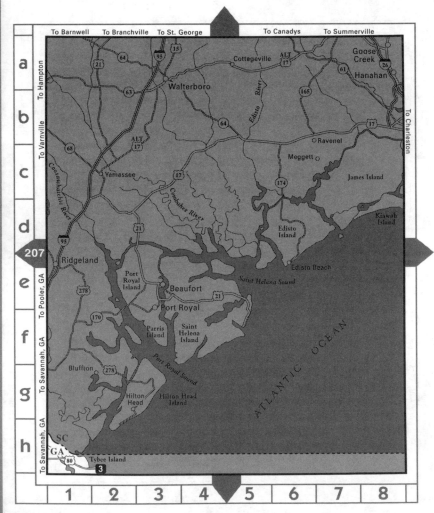

To Barnwell   To Branchville   To St. George   To Canadys   To Summerville

a   Cottageville   ALT 17   Goose Creek
               21   64   95   15   Hanahan   26
To Hampton   61
               63   165
               Walterboro

b   64   Edisto River   17   To Charleston
To Varnville   17
               68   ALT 17   Ravenel

c   Yemassee   17   Meggett
To Coosawhatchie River   174   James Island
               Combahee River

d   95   21   Kiawah Island
207   Edisto Island

e   Ridgeland   Port Royal Island   Edisto Beach
To Pooler, GA   278   Beaufort   Saint Helena Sound
                                  Port Royal   21

f   170   Parris Island   Saint Helena Island   ATLANTIC OCEAN
To Savannah, GA

g   Bluffton   278   Port Royal Sound
               Hilton Head   Hilton Head Island

h   SC
               GA   80   Tybee Island   3
To Savannah, GA

1   2   3   4   5   6   7   8

© AVALON TRAVEL PUBLISHING, INC.

MAP 3

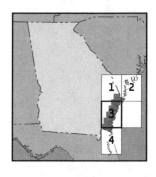

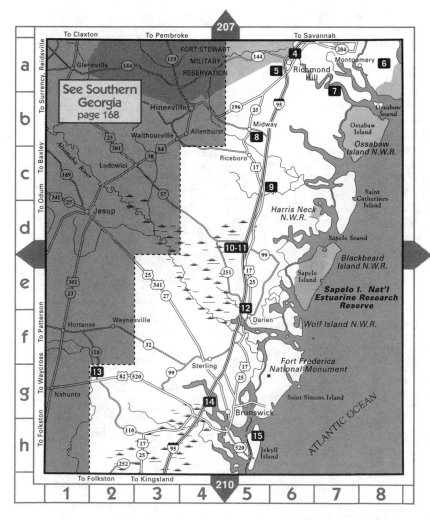

MAP 4

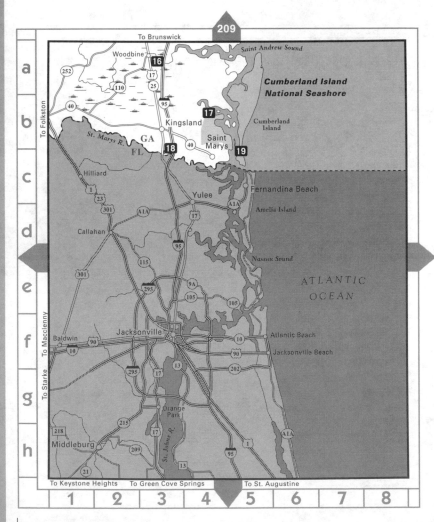

To Brunswick

209

To Folkston

To Macclenny

To Starke

a
Woodbine
252
16
17
110
25

b
40
17
95
Kingsland
St. Marys R.
GA
Cumberland Island
National Seashore
Saint Andrew Sound
Cumberland
Island

c
FL
18
40
Saint
Marys
19
Hilliard
Yulee
Fernandina Beach

d
1
23
301
A1A
17
Amelia Island
Callahan
95

e
115
Nassau Sound
301
295
9A
ATLANTIC
OCEAN
105
105

f
Baldwin
90
Jacksonville
10
Atlantic Beach
10
90
Jacksonville Beach

g
295
17
13
202

h
218
215
Orange Park
Middleburg
17
209
St. Johns R.
1
A1A
21
13
95

To Keystone Heights   To Green Cove Springs   To St. Augustine

1   2   3   4   5   6   7   8

© AVALON TRAVEL PUBLISHING, INC.

COASTAL GEORGIA

1 Almar Inn and Mobile Home Park

Location: Savannah, map 1, grid H7.

Campsites, facilities: There are 12 RV sites, all with full hookups. Shade is available. There are no restrooms. A coin laundry is provided, and cable TV and phone hookups are available. Quiet pets are permitted.

Reservations, fees: The campground does not publish its rates.

Open: Year-round.

Directions: From Savannah, go north on Highway 21, and turn right on Highway 307. After one mile, turn right onto Highway 25. The campground will be on the right within one-half mile.

Contact: Almar Inn and Mobile Home Park, 35 Main St., Garden City, GA 31408; 912/964-9917.

Trip notes: This is primarily a mobile home park, but one-third of the sites are reserved for RVs. It is off the beaten path in a residential community, about 25 miles from the ocean. It is 12 miles from fishing in the Savannah River or Crystal Lake.

2 Bellaire Woods Campground, Ltd.

Location: Savannah, map 1, grid H6.

Campsites, facilities: The campground has 26 tent sites, and four primitive sites. There are also 140 RV sites, 99 with full hookups. Most sites have shade, and 60 are pull-through sites. RVs are restricted to less than 45 feet. Group sites are available. Picnic tables, fire rings, and cooking grills are provided. Restrooms have hot showers and flush toilets. A coin laundry, swimming pool, playground, clubroom, boat ramp, dock, and sanitary disposal station are provided. Boats are restricted to 16 feet in length. Ice, LP gas, firewood, VCR tapes, limited groceries, and gifts are available at the campground store. The buildings are wheelchair accessible. Leashed pets are permitted, and you must clean up after your pet.

Reservations, fees: Reservations are accepted at 800/851-0717, and the $10 deposit is not refundable. Site fees are $24–30 per night.

Open: Year-round.

Directions: From Interstate 95, take exit 94 and go west on Highway 204, which becomes Fort Argyle Road. The campground is just over two miles from the interstate.

Contact: Bellaire Woods Campground, Ltd., 805 Fort Argyle Rd., Savannah, GA 31419; 912/748-4000.

Trip notes: The lake is stocked with bass, catfish, and bream. Kayaking and rafting are available at the nearby river. The campground is about 15 miles from the historical section of Savannah. It's also near the ruins of Fort Frederica, General Oglethorpe's fort built to guard against the Spanish, and Christ Church, the first church in Georgia.

3 River's End Campground

Location: Tybee Island, map 2, grid H2.

Campsites, facilities: There are 26 sites suitable for tents or RVs with water and electric hookups. There are 23 additional primitive sites with no hookups, and 71 RV sites with full hookups. Pull-through sites are available, as are sites with shade. Picnic tables are provided, and some sites have fire rings. There are eight cabins. Restrooms have hot showers and flush toilets. A coin laundry, swimming pool, and game room are provided. Ice, propane, supplies, and groceries are available at the campground. Leashed pets are permitted. You must pick up after your pet.

Reservations, fees: Reservations are accepted at 800/786-1016. The deposit is refundable with a 24-hour notice for campsite reservations and a seven-day notice for cabin reservations. Primitive sites are $20 per night. For sites with water and electric hookups, the charge for tents is $27, and $28 for pop-up campers. Sites with full hookups are $32–34. The cabins are $99–109 per night. Good Sam and AARP discounts apply.

Open: Year-round.

Directions: From Interstate 95, take US 80 east to Tybee Island. Two miles after getting to the island, turn right on Polk Street. The campground will be on the left.

Contact: River's End Campground, P.O. Box 988, Tybee Island, GA 31328; 912/786-5518.

Trip notes: Fishing, swimming, and walking are accessible at the beach. The campground is 15 miles from Savannah.

◪ Waterway RV Campground

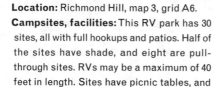

Location: Richmond Hill, map 3, grid A6.

Campsites, facilities: This RV park has 30 sites, all with full hookups and patios. Half of the sites have shade, and eight are pull-through sites. RVs may be a maximum of 40 feet in length. Sites have picnic tables, and

there is a screened room with a cooking grill. Restrooms have hot showers and flush toilets. Ice, LP gas, and supplies are available at the campground, and groceries are available 1.5 miles away. The campground has a coin laundry, clubroom, and tanning salon, and movies are available for rent. A boat ramp and docks are available. One of the restrooms is wheelchair accessible. Leashed pets are permitted. Owners who pick up after their pets are welcome.

Reservations, fees: Reservations are accepted. Sites cost $26.50 per night.

Open: Year-round.

Directions: Take the Highway 144/Richmond Hill exit off Interstate 95, and turn east. Turn left onto US 17. The campground is located at the Kingsferry Bridge.

Contact: Waterway RV Campground, P.O. Box 1337, 70 Highway 17, Richmond Hill, GA 31324; 912/756-2296.

Trip notes: The campground is 10 miles from Savannah, and 30 to the ocean, so it's a good location if closer campgrounds are full. It is seven miles to historic Fort McAllister, used during the Civil War. The campground is on the Ogeechee River, which offers fresh- and saltwater fishing, blue crabs, and kayaking. There is plenty of shopping in the area, from malls to flea markets. Wildlife in the area includes deer, alligators, and eagles.

◫ Savannah South KOA

Location: Savannah, map 3, grid A6.

Campsites, facilities: There are 127 sites suitable for tents and RVs. Five of the sites have water and electric only, and the rest have full hookups. Most are pull-through sites. Shade is available. Picnic tables are provided. There are also five cabins. RV storage is available. Restrooms have hot showers and flush toilets. A coin laundry, swimming pool, playground, and clubroom are provided. CableTV hookups are available. Up to three pets are permitted per campsite or cabin.

Reservations, fees: Reservations are accepted at 800/562-8741. The deposit is refundable with 24 hours notice before your scheduled arrival. Campsites are $25, and cabins range from $30–35. KOA discounts apply.

Open: Year-round.

Directions: Take exit 87 off Interstate 95 and turn south on US 17. The campground is one-half mile down on the left.

Contact: Savannah South KOA, P.O. Box 309, Richmond Hill, GA 31324; 912/756-3396.

Trip notes: The campground contains a 35-acre private lake stocked with bream, bass, catfish, and crappie, which attracts a variety of waterfowl in addition to alligators. No gas motors are permitted on the lake, but row boats can be rented. The campground is 20 miles from the historic district in downtown Savannah.

6 Skidaway Island State Park

Location: Savannah, map 3, grid A8.

Campsites, Facilities: There are 88 campsites suitable for tents or RVs, all with water and electric hookups. All are pull-through sites. Picnic tables and fire rings are provided. Restrooms have hot showers and flush toilets. A sanitary disposal station, playground, swimming pool, and boat ramp are provided. Ice is available at the campground. The buildings are wheelchair accessible.

Leashed pets are permitted.

Reservations, fees: Reservations are accepted at 800/864-7275. Within the Atlanta area, call 770/389-7275. The deposit of one night's fee is non-refundable, but your reservation can be moved once to another date. Site fees are $16–18. Like all of Georgia's state parks, there is a $2 per day parking fee, or you can purchase an annual Georgia Park-Pass for $25. Campers pay for just one daily pass for their entire stay.

Open: Year-round.

Directions: Take Interstate 16 to Savannah, then exit onto Interstate 516, which runs into DeRenne Avenue. Turn right on Waters Avenue, then follow the signs to Diamond Causeway and the park.

Contact: Skidaway Island State Park, 52 Diamond Causeway, Savannah, GA 31411-1102; 912/598-2300.

Trip notes: Both fresh- and saltwater fishing is available. There are several trails totaling over four miles in length, and one of them is wheelchair accessible. Wildlife in the area includes deer, waterfowl, migratory birds, and alligators.

7 Fort McAllister State Park

Location: Savannah, map 3, grid A7.

Campsites, facilities: There are 65 campsites suitable for tents or RVs, all with water and electric hookups. Pull-through sites are available. Primitive camping is also available. Restrooms have hot showers and flush toilets. A sanitary disposal station, boat ramp, and dock are provided. The facilities are wheelchair accessible. Leashed pets are permitted.

Reservations, fees: Reservations are

accepted at 800/864-7275. Within the Atlanta area, call 770/389-7275. The deposit of one night's fee is not refundable, but the reservation can be moved once to another date. The fee for tents is $13, and $15 for trailers. Discounts for senior citizens and disabled veterans apply. Like all of Georgia's state parks, there is a $2 per day parking fee, or you can purchase an annual Georgia Park-Pass for $25. Campers pay for just one daily pass for their entire stay.

Open: Year-round.

Directions: From Richmond Hill, take Highway 144 south for one mile to Spur 144 and follow the signs.

Contact: Fort McAllister State Park, 3894 Fort McAllister Rd., Richmond Hill, GA 31324; 912/727-2339.

Trip notes: The park has the best preserved Confederate earthworks remaining. There is a museum of Civil War artifacts. Fishing is available for freshwater fish. There are two hiking trails totaling about 4.5 miles.

8 Martin's Glebe Plantation Campground

Location: Midway, map 3, grid B5.

Campsites, facilities: One section of the campground has 20 tent sites, while a separate RV area has 42 pull-through sites, 41 with full hookups. The RV sites have shade. Picnic tables are provided. Restrooms have hot showers and flush toilets. A sanitary disposal station, small playground, and coin laundry are provided. Firewood, ice, bait, tackle, and rental boats are available. Leashed pets are permitted, and you must clean up after your pooch.

Reservations, fees: Reservations are accepted. Sites are $14 a night, $80 a week, or $200 a month, plus seasonal fees for air conditioning and heating.

Open: Year-round.

Directions: From Interstate 95, take US 84, exit 76, west to the entrance.

Contact: Martin's Glebe Plantation Campground, 529 Glebe Rd., Midway, GA 31320; 912/884-5218, fax 912/884-5233.

Trip notes: The campground is located 27 miles from Savannah and 35 miles from Tybee Island. With 70 acres of fishing ponds, many of the campers who come here are interested in bass (available year-round), bream (May through September), or catfish (April through September). No fishing license is required to fish in the ponds. The campground is also near the Midway Colonial Museum and the Fort Morris State Historic Site.

9 Riverfront RV Park

Location: Savannah, map 3, grid C5.

Campsites, Facilities: There are 58 RV sites, all with full hookups. Both 30- and 50-amp hookups are available. About half of the sites are pull-through. RV storage is available. Rest rooms have hot showers and flush toilets. A coin laundry, boat dock, fishing pier, and swimming pool are provided. The restrooms are wheelchair accessible. Leashed pets are permitted. You must clean up after your pet.

Reservations, fees: Reservations are accepted at 912/884-4678. No deposit is required. Sites rent for $18–20 nightly.

Open: Year-round.

Contact: Riverfront RV Park,

39 Sawgrass Lane, Riceboro, GA 31323; 912/884-4678.

Directions: From Savannah, take Interstate 95 south to exit 67 and turn left onto US 17. Turn right onto the unmarked gravel road at the McDonald's, which is Sawgrass Lane.

Trip notes: The campground is equidistant between Savannah and Darien. The South Newport River offers fishing in the brackish water for flounder, mullet, catfish, and trout. There is a nature trail along the marsh area at the campground, where a variety of birds and alligators can be seen. The Desert Storm Museum at Fort Stewart is about 18 miles west of the campground in Hinesville. The beach is 35–45 minutes away.

10 Lake Harmony RV Park

Location: Townsend, map 3, grid D5.

Campsites, facilities: There are 20 tent sites and 50 RV sites at this campground. All RV sites have full hookups and are pull-through sites. Picnic tables and some fire rings are provided. RV storage is provided. Restrooms have hot showers and flush toilets. A coin laundry, boat dock, swimming pool, playground, and clubroom are provided. Ice, bait, and tackle are available at the campground. The buildings are wheelchair accessible. Leashed pets are permitted, but cannot be left unattended. You must clean up after your pet.

Reservations, fees: Reservations are accepted at 888/767-7864. The deposit is refundable if you cancel at least 24 hours in advance of your scheduled arrival. Tent sites are $15 per night, and RV sites are $20.

Open: Year-round.

Directions: Take exit 58 off Interstate 95 and

go west on Highway 57 0.6 miles. The entrance will be on your left.

Contact: Lake Harmony RV Park, Rt. 3, Box 3128, Townsend, GA 31331; 912/832-4338.

Trip notes: The campground has an 18-acre lake stocked with bass and bluegill. Paddleboats and row boats are available for rent. The campground is 30 miles from both Jekyll and St. Simons Islands, both of which have miles of bike trails. It is 10 miles from the outlet shopping in Darien, and 42 miles from Savannah.

11 McIntosh Lake RV Park

Location: Eulonia, map 3, grid D5.

Campsites, facilities: There are 42 RV sites at the campground, and eight sites for tents. Each site has a picnic table and fire ring. Restrooms have hot showers and flush toilets. Ice, LP gas, and firewood are available at the campground, and other supplies are available 1.5 miles away. A coin laundry and sanitary disposal station are provided. Buildings are wheelchair accessible. Pets are permitted.

Reservations, fees: Reservations are accepted. The campground does not publish its rates.

Open: Year-round.

Directions: From Interstate 95, exit west nine-tenths of a mile at exit 11.

Contact: McIntosh Lake RV Park, Rt. 3, Box 3112, Townsend, GA 31331; 912/832-6215.

Trip notes: Fishing for bass and bream is available in the lake.

12 Tall Pines Campground and RV Park

Location: Darien, map 3, grid E5.

Campsites, facilities: There are four tent sites and 40 RV sites. Pull-through sites are available. All of the RV sites have full hookups. Picnic tables are provided, and RV storage is available. Restrooms with hot showers and flush toilets are provided. A coin laundry is on the premises, and the campground is next to a supply store with ice, gas, and groceries. Leashed pets are permitted.

Reservations, fees: Reservations are accepted. The nightly rate is $20, or $225 per month.

Open: Year-round.

Directions: Take exit 49 east off Interstate 95.

Contact: Tall Pines Campground and RV Park, P.O. Box 559, Darien, GA 31305; 912/437-3966.

Trip notes: The campground is next to an 80-shop outlet center. It is located between St. Simons Island and Sapelo Island along the coast, and abundant salt- and freshwater fishing are available nearby in the ocean and rivers. Kayaking is popular in the Altamaha River. While in the area, tour Sapelo Island and the Fort Frederica National Monument. Historic Darien is 1.5 miles away. Wildlife is plentiful in the area, and it's not unusual to see deer, wild turkeys, and ducks. You are less likely to see alligators and wild hogs. Jim Fowler of *Wild Kingdom* fame is opening a large wild animal theme park five miles from the campground.

⒔ Satilla River Vacation Land

Location: Waynesville, map 3, grid G2.

Campsites, facilities: The campground has 30 tent sites. All have shade. There are also unlimited primitive tent sites along the river and on the sandbars. In a separate section, there are 75 RV sites, 40 with full hookups. All are pull-through sites, and all have shade. Picnic tables and fire grills are provided. RV storage is available. Restrooms have hot showers and flush toilets. Supplies, ice, firewood, and groceries are available at the campground. A coin laundry, playground, boat ramp, swimming pool, and clubroom are provided. A sanitary disposal station is on the premises. Leashed pets are permitted.

Reservations, fees: Reservations are accepted at 888/788-7010, and no deposit is required. Daily rates are $14 for water and electric hookups, and $16 for full hook-ups. The monthly rate for a site with full hookups is $240.

Open: Year-round.

Directions: From US 82, go east on Highway 259 for just over one mile.

Contact: Satilla River Vacation Land, Rt. 1, Box 210-B, Waynesville, GA 31566; 912/778-3111.

Trip notes: This family-oriented campground is located on an old Indian village, complete with mount. There is easy river access for fishing, boating, canoeing, and kayaking. Swimmers can choose between the river, any of the lakes, or the pool. The campground is 25 miles from the Okefenokee Swamp, and 30 miles from the coast.

⒕ Blythe Island Regional Park

Location: Brunswick, map 3, grid G4.

Campsites, facilities: There are 26 tent sites with water and electric hookups. There are also 70 RV sites, half with full hookups and half with water and electric only. Pull-through sites are available. All sites have shade, picnic tables, and fire rings. RV storage is available. Restrooms have hot showers and flush toilets. A sanitary disposal station, coin laundry, boat ramp, dock, and playground are provided. Ice is available at the campground. Leashed, quiet pets are permitted. You must clean up after your pet.

Reservations, fees: Reservations are accepted at 800/343-7855. The deposit is refundable with 24 hours notice. Tent sites are $20 per night, and RV sites are $21–23.

Open: Year-round.

Directions: Coming from the north, take exit 36 off Interstate 95 and turn left onto US 341. After three miles, turn right onto US 303. The campground is four miles down on the left. Coming from the south, take exit 29 off Interstate 95 and turn west onto US 17. Turn right onto US 303. The campground is about four miles down on the right.

Contact: Blythe Island Regional Park, 6616 Blythe Island Highway, Brunswick, GA 31523; 912/261-3805.

Trip notes: Fishing is available in the private lake for bass, catfish, and bream. There is a sand beach in the swimming area.

15 Jekyll Island Campground

Location: Jekyll Island, map 3, grid H5.

Campsites, facilities: The campground has 57 tent sites and 158 RV sites. All sites have shade. Two-thirds of the RV sites have full hookups, and the rest have water and electric only. Primitive sites are also available. Pull-through sites and RV storage are available. Picnic tables are provided, and fire rings at sites with full hookups. The restrooms have hot showers and flush toilets. The supply store sells ice, LP gas, firewood, groceries, and gifts. A coin laundry and clubroom are on the premises, and cable TV hookups are available. The buildings are wheelchair accessible. Leashed pets are permitted, but you may not leave your pet unattended.

Reservations, fees: Reservations are accepted, and the required deposit is not refundable. Primitive campsites are $12 per night, sites with water and electric hookups are $17, and sites with full hookups are $20. There is an additional $3 entrance fee for the island.

Open: Year-round.

Directions: Take the Jekyll Island Causeway onto the island, and turn left on Beach View Drive to the campground.

Contact: Jekyll Island Campground, 1197 Riverview Dr., Jekyll Island, GA 31527; 912/635-3021.

Trip notes: Jekyll Island is a developed vacation area with fishing, golf, tennis, bicycle rental and paths, horseback riding, and swimming. The campground is about two miles from the historic district on the island, and about 20 miles from the St. Simons lighthouse and Fort Frederico. Kayaking is available nearby. Besides deer and migratory birds, loggerhead turtles and dolphins are frequently seen.

16 King George RV Resort

Location: Woodbine, map 4, grid A3.

Campsites, Facilities: There are 40 RV campsites, half with full hookups and half with water and electric only. All are pull-through sites. Picnic tables are provided.

Restrooms have hot showers and flush toilets. A coin laundry, swimming pool, clubroom, and screened room are provided. Ice is available. Pets are permitted.

Reservations, fees: Reservations are accepted, and no deposit is required. Sites with water and electric hookups are $18 per night; sites with full hookups are $20. Passport America, Coast to Coast, and RPI club discounts apply.

Open: Year-round.

Directions: From Interstate 95, take exit 7 and turn west on Harriets Bluff Road. Take the first left onto Old Still Road.

Contact: King George RV Resort, 5200 Old Still Rd., Woodbine, GA 31569; 912/729-4110.

Trip notes: Though primarily a membership campground, vacant sites are usually available for overnight travelers. The campground is one-quarter mile from the Crooked River, and five miles from the St. Marys River, both good for fishing. It is 12 miles from the St. Marys ferry to Cumberland Island, open only to campers on foot.

🅗 Crooked River State Park

Location: St. Marys, map 4, grid B4.

Campsites, facilities: There are 60 campsites suitable for tents or RVs, all with water and electric hookups. Picnic tables and fire rings are provided. Pull-through sites are available. Some cabins are also available. Restrooms have hot showers and flush toilets. Ice, supplies, and groceries are available at the campground. A sanitary disposal station, swimming pool, miniature golf, boat ramp, and dock are provided. Leashed pets are permitted.

Reservations, fees: Reservations are accepted at 800/864-7275. Within the Atlanta

area, call 770/389-7275. The deposit is non-refundable, but your reservation date can be moved once. Site fees are $14–16 per night. Like all of Georgia's state parks, there is a $2 per day parking fee, or you can purchase an annual Georgia ParkPass for $25. Campers pay for just one daily pass for their entire stay.

Open: Year-round.

Directions: From St. Marys, go west on Highway 40 to Spur 40, and turn right to the park and campground.

Contact: Crooked River State Park, 3092 Spur 40, St. Marys, GA 31558; 912/882-5256.

Trip notes: Fishing is available in the river for freshwater game fish. There is a short, 1.5-mile nature trail, and the ruins of an old sugar mill inside the park.

🅘 Country Oaks Campground and RV Park

Location: Kingsland, map 4, grid B3.

Campsites, facilities: This RV park has 44 sites, all with full hookups. Eleven are pull-through sites, and most have some shade. Group sites and RV storage are available. Picnic tables and fire rings are available. Restrooms have hot showers and flush toilets. A coin laundry and clubroom are provided. Ice, LP gas, firewood, and limited supplies are available at the campground. Pets are permitted, and you must clean up after your pet.

Reservations, fees: Reservations are accepted. The fee is $19 for 30-amp service, and $21 for 50-amp service.

Open: Year-round.

Directions: Take exit 1 off Interstate 95 and turn west. Turn left onto Carlton Cemetery Road, one-third mile from the interstate.

Contact: Country Oaks Campground and RV Park, 6 Carlton Cemetery Rd., Kingsland, GA 31548; 912/729-6212, fax 912/729-1302; email: oaksrv@eagnet.com.

Trip notes: The fishing pond has catfish and bream all year. There is a short nature trail, and kayaking and rafting are just eight miles away at the St. Marys River. The campground is near Cumberland and Jekyll Islands.

19 Cumberland Island National Seashore

Location: Cumberland Island, map 4, grid B5.

Campsites, facilities: There are two camping options on the island. Sea Camp is a developed campground of 16 sites that accommodate up to 3 tents per site, with picnic tables, fire rings, cooking grills, and food cages. Restrooms have cold showers and flush toilets. Drinking water is available. When you get off the ferry, you can use the large wheeled carts provided to help you transport your gear to the campground. A dock is provided at Sea Camp, if you come by private boat. The backcountry camping areas have no amenities except for a hand pump for unpurified water. There are four backcountry campsites which each accommodate about 20 campers, with room to spread out. The sites are three, five, seven, or 10 miles from the dock, and you won't know which site you are getting until you arrive.

Reservations, fees: Reservations can be made up to six months in advance at 912/882-4335 or 888-817-3421, or can be faxed to 912/673-7747. Call as soon as your visit dates are firmed up, as the few campsites fill up rapidly. The camping fee for Sea Camp is $4 per person per day, and $2 for the backcountry areas. In addition, the day use fee is $4 per 7-day visit, and the ferry trip is $12 for adults, $7 for children, and $9 for senior citizens round-trip. Golden Age Passport discounts apply except for the ferry charge.

Open: Year-round.

Directions: From Interstate 95, take Highway 40 to the downtown St. Marys waterfront, and follow the signs to the ferry parking.

Contact: Cumberland Island National Seashore, P.O. Box 806, St. Marys, GA 31558; 912/882-4336; website: www.nps.gov/cuis/.

Trip notes: A trip to Cumberland Island is an incredible adventure. Nearly the entire island is protected as a national seashore, and amenities for visitors are few. Without a bicycle, a day-trip visitor will not be able to see much, but you can't bring a bicycle on the main ferry. Bikes are only allowed in certain areas of the island, such as the main road and along the beach, but not in the wilderness areas. To charter a private boat that would allow you to transport a bike, call Lang Seafood at 912/882-4452. The charge for up to four campers is $95, plus $10 per bike. When camping, plan to spend at least four nights to have a chance to hike some of the trails and experience the island. Camping is limited to seven days. If you are camping in the backcountry area, you'll need to purify the water, either by boiling, chemical treatment, or running through a water filter. Backcountry campers need to bring rope to hang their food. Campers at Sea Camp are provided with a locking cage to protect their food from squirrels and raccoons. If you bring a cooler, bring rope to tie it shut and attach it to a picnic table, as the raccoons drag off unsecured coolers.

The wildlife on Cumberland Island is a large part of its attraction for many visitors. While on the island, look for the endangered loggerhead sea turtles that lay their eggs in the sand before heading back to sea. You will probably also see the wild horses the island is famous for, as well as armadillos, deer, and countless varieties of birds. Less visible are the alligators, wild boars, bobcats, and rattlesnakes, all of which exist in large numbers on the island. Watch for right whales offshore as well.

ALABAMA

NORTHWEST ALABAMA

ALABAMA COTTONFIELDS

ALABAMA REGIONS

ALABAMA REGIONS

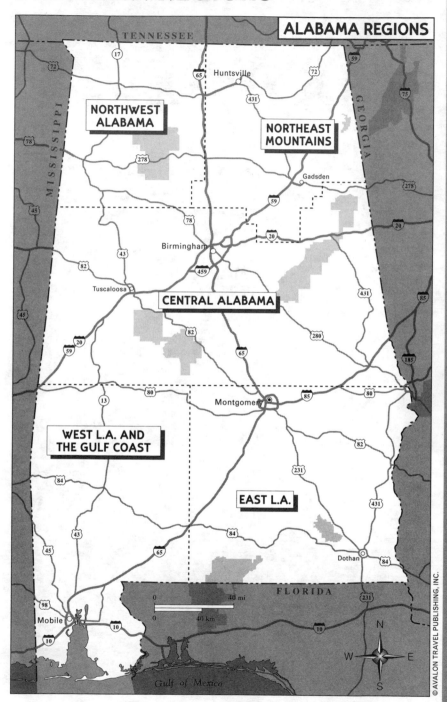

NORTHWEST ALABAMA

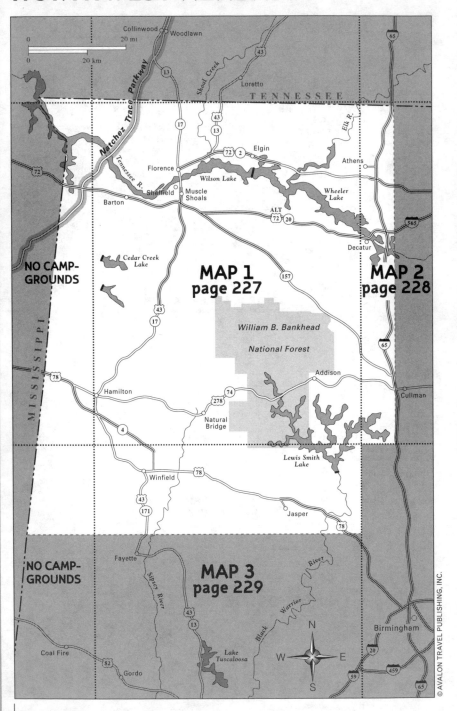

MAP 1
page 227

MAP 2
page 228

MAP 3
page 229

NO CAMP-GROUNDS

NO CAMP-GROUNDS

William B. Bankhead

National Forest

TENNESSEE

MISSISSIPPI

Collinwood
Woodlawn
Loretto
Elgin
Athens
Florence
Wilson Lake
Muscle Shoals
Sheffield
Barton
Wheeler Lake
Decatur
Cedar Creek Lake
Addison
Cullman
Hamilton
Natural Bridge
Lewis Smith Lake
Winfield
Jasper
Fayette
Birmingham
Coal Fire
Gordo

Natchez Trace Parkway
Tennessee R.
Shoal Creek
Elk R.
Sipsey River
Black Warrior River
Lake Tuscaloosa

0   20 mi
0   20 km

N
W   E
S

MAP 1

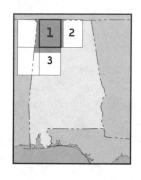

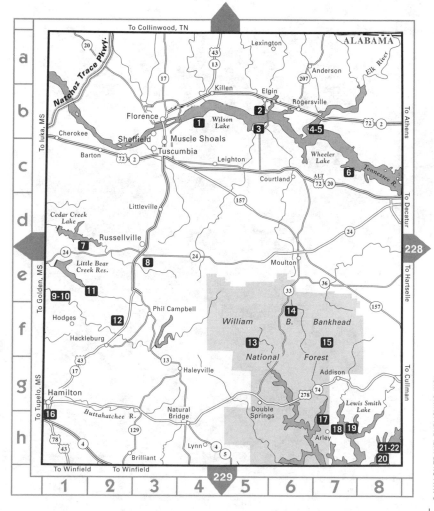

© AVALON TRAVEL PUBLISHING, INC.

MAP 2

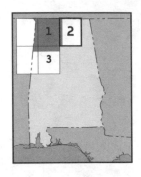

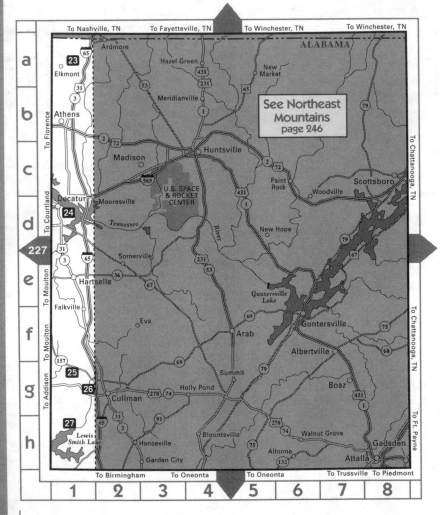

See Northeast Mountains page 246

To Nashville, TN   To Fayetteville, TN   To Winchester, TN   To Winchester, TN

ALABAMA

a
Ardmore
23 65
Elkmont
31
3

b
Athens
To Florence
Hazel Green
431
231
Meridianville
1
53
New Market
65
79

c
Madison
Huntsville
2 72
Paint Rock
Scottsboro
565
U.S. SPACE & ROCKET CENTER

d
Decatur
To Courtland
24
Mooresville
Tennessee
River
431
1
Woodville
New Hope
79
67
To Chattanooga, TN

227
31
3 65
Somerville
231
53
Guntersville Lake
To Moulton

e
Hartselle
36
67
Falkville

f
To Moulton
Eva
Arab
69
Guntersville
Albertville
75
68
To Chattanooga, TN

g
157
25
26
Cullman
278 74
Holly Pond
Summit
79
Boaz
431
1
To Ft. Payne

h
27
Lewis Smith Lake
Hanceville
31
3
91
Blountsville
278
74
Walnut Grove
Altoona
132
Gadsden
Attalla
65
Garden City
75

To Birmingham   To Oneonta   To Oneonta   To Trussville   To Piedmont

1   2   3   4   5   6   7   8

MAP 3

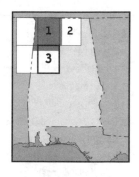

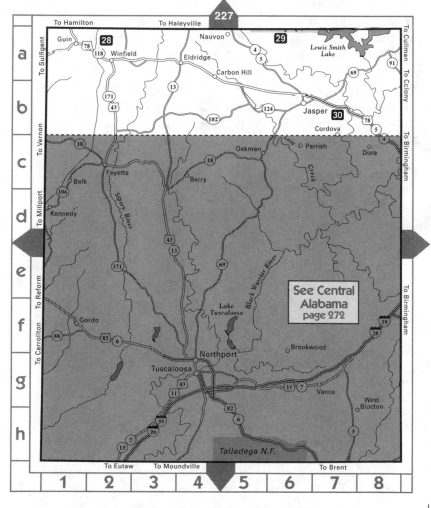

NORTHWEST ALABAMA

❶ Rockpile/Wilson Dam Campground

Location: Tennessee River, map 1, grid B3.

Campsites, Facilities: There are 23 primitive campsites, all fronting the river. Picnic tables and fire rings are provided. Restrooms have hot showers and flush toilets. A boat ramp and sanitary disposal station are provided. Leashed pets are permitted.

Reservations, fees: Reservations are not accepted. The fee is $11 per night. Golden Age and Golden Access discounts apply.

Open: Year-round.

Directions: From Florence, take US 72/Highway 133 south about three miles. After crossing Wilson Dam, turn right and follow the signs.

Contact: Rockpile Campground, TVA, P.O. Box 1010, SB1H, Muscle Shoals, AL 35662; 256/386-2006.

Trip notes: The river offers excellent fishing. There are three miles of biking and jogging trails, and five miles of hiking trails. The campground is four miles from both the Helen Keller home and the home of W.C. Handy, the "Father of the Blues."

❷ Doublehead RV Park and Campground

Location: Wilson Lake, map 1, grid B5.

Campsites, facilities: There are a total of 30 campsites suitable for tents or RVs. All sites have water and electric hookups. Picnic tables and cooking grills are provided. Restrooms have hot showers and flush toilets. Some cabins and a lodge are also available. A sanitary disposal station is provided. The facilities are wheelchair accessible. Leashed pets are permitted.

Reservations, fees: Reservations are accepted at 800/685-9267. The deposit is refundable if cancellation is made seven days in advance. All campsites are $15 per night; cabins are $150–275 per night.

Open: Year-round.

Directions: From Birmingham, go north on Interstate 65 to US 72, and turn west. After 30 miles, turn south on Highway 101. The campground is located 100 yards north of Wheeler Dam on Highway 101.

Contact: Doublehead RV Park and Campground, 145 County Road 314, Town Creek, AL 35672; 256/685-9267; email: info @doublehead.com; website: www.double head.com.

Trip notes: Fishing is available at the lake, and professional fishing guides are available. There is a 2.5-mile gravel walking path. Watercraft rentals include canoes, pontoon boats, paddleboats, fishing boats, and Jet Skis. Horseback riding and clay shooting are available. Cabin guests also have access to swimming pools, playgrounds, and a sand beach in the swimming area on the lake.

❸ Joe Wheeler State Park

Location: Rogersville, map 1, grid B5.

Campsites, Facilities: There are 116 campsites suitable for tents or RVs. All have full hookups. Picnic tables are provided. Restrooms have hot showers and flush toilets. There are 40 primitive camping sites also available. Group sites and RV storage are available. A boat dock, boat ramp, coin laundry, clubroom, playground, golf course, and tennis courts are provided. Twenty six cabins and a resort lodge are also

available. The campground store sells ice, firewood, limited supplies, and groceries. The facilities are wheelchair accessible. Leashed pets are permitted.

Reservations, fees: Reservations are accepted at 800/ALA-PARK (800/252-7275). The deposit is refundable, if the reservations are cancelled at least 72 hours in advance. Site fees range from $11 for primitive sites to $17.60 for improved sites with full hookups.

Open: Year-round.

Directions: From Interstate 65, take US 72 west two miles past Rogersville, and follow the signs.

Contact: Joe Wheeler State Park, 201 McLean Dr., Rogersville, AL 35652; 256/247-1184; website: www.dcnr.state.al.us/parks/state_parks_index_1a.html.

Trip notes: This is one of the most beautiful parks in the state system. Fishing is available in the lake for bass, bream, crappie, sauger, and catfish. There are two hiking trails that wind through the park, the longest 1.5 miles in length.

4 Lucy's Branch Wilderness Campground

Location: Wheeler Lake, map 1, grid B6.

Campsites, Facilities: The campground has a large wooded area with 50 primitive tent sites, all with good shade. Fire pits are provided. Restrooms have flush toilets. A boat launch is provided. Leashed pets are permitted.

Reservations, fees: Reservations are not required. The fee is $10 per night.

Open: Year-round.

Directions: From Birmingham or Decatur, take Interstate 65 north to exit 351/Athens, and turn west onto US 72. After 16 miles, turn left just before the Elk River Bridge at the sign for Bay Hill Village. Follow the signs to the campground.

Contact: Lucy's Branch Wilderness Campground, 6120 Snake Road, Athens, AL 35611; 256/729-6443.

Trip notes: Lucy's Branch was named for a Native American woman who lived along the branch, which fed into the Tennessee River. When the TVA dammed the river, it formed Wheeler Lake. The waterfront is lined with large rocks, and the water is deep enough that only experienced swimmers should swim in the lake. Fishing is available either along the lakeshore or by boat, and bass tournaments are held each year. Though there are no hiking trails per se, the campground and neighboring RV park and marina have walking trails along the 1.5-mile waterfront. The marina rents pontoon boats, ski boats, and jet skis, and also houses a restaurant. Nearby Athens hosts a fiddler's convention in October.

5 Bay Hill Village RV Park

Location: Wheeler Lake, map 1, grid B6.

Campsites, Facilities: There are 168 RV sites, most with full hookups and all with water and electric hookups. Both 30- and 50-amp service is available. All the sites are level and paved. Shaded sites are available. Picnic tables, fire pits, and cooking grills are provided. Restrooms have hot showers and flush toilets. A boat launch, coin laundry, playground, and swimming pool are provided. The restrooms are wheelchair accessible. Leashed pets are permitted.

Reservations, fees: Reservations are not required. The fee is $19 per night, $100 per week, and $250 per month.

Open: Year-round.

Directions: From Birmingham or Decatur, take Interstate 65 north to exit 351/Athens, and turn west onto US 72. After 16 miles, turn left just before the Elk River Bridge at the sign for Bay Hill Village. Follow the signs to the campground.

Contact: Bay Hill Village RV Park, 5381 Village Drive, Athens, AL 35611; 256/729-6443.

Trip notes: The campground is at the widest part of the lake, and offers family activities on holidays. The waterfront is lined with large rocks, and there is a sand beach in the swimming area. Fishing is available either along the lakeshore or by boat, and bass tournaments are held each year. There are no hiking trails per se, but walking trails from the campground to the marina and neighboring Lucy's Branch Wilderness Campground total 1.5 miles. The marina rents pontoon boats, ski boats, and jet skis, and also houses a restaurant. The town of Athens hosts a fiddler's convention in October.

6 TVA Mallard Creek

Location: Tennessee River, map 1, grid C7.

Campsites, facilities: There are 56 campsites suitable for tents or RVs, all with water and electric hookups. Two of the sites are pull-through, and most have shade. Picnic tables, fire rings, and cooking grills are provided. Restrooms have hot showers and flush toilets. Ice and some groceries are available at the campground. A boat ramp, dock, sanitary disposal station, and playground are provided. The restrooms are wheelchair accessible. Leashed pets are permitted.

Reservations, fees: Reservations are not accepted. The rate is $15 per night. Golden Age and Golden Access discounts apply.

Open: The campground is open from March through mid-November.

Directions: From Decature, take Highway 20 east. Two miles past Hillsboro, turn left on

County Road 400. After four miles, turn right at the sign for the recreation area onto County Road 443.

Contact: TVA Mallard Creek Campground, P.O. Box 1010, SB1H, Muscle Shoals, AL 35662; 256/386-2006.

Trip notes: The Tennessee River offers world-class fishing for bream, catfish, and crappie, water skiing, and a large swimming area with a sand beach. Though there aren't any hiking trails as such, there is a three-mile walking path through the overflow area.

7 Slickrock Campground

Location: Russellville, map 1, grid D1.

Campsites, facilities: There are 53 campsites suitable for tents or RVs. All sites have water and electric hookups. Four are pull-through sites. RVs are restricted to 45 feet or less. Picnic tables, fire rings, and cooking grills are provided. Restrooms have hot showers and flush toilets. A sanitary disposal station is provided. Ice, some groceries, and LP gas are available in the campground store. A boat ramp, dock, and playground are provided. The buildings are wheelchair accessible. Leashed pets are permitted.

Reservations, fees: Reservations are not accepted. The fee is $12 per night.

Open: The campground is open from March through October.

Directions: From Decatur, take Highway 24 west through Belgreen, and turn onto County Road 21 west. Turn north on County Road 33 to the campground.

Contact: Slickrock Campground, P.O. Box 670, Russellville, AL 35653; 256/332-9809 or 256/332-4392; fax 256/332-4372.

Trip notes: The campground is located on Cedar Creek Lake. Fishing for bass, crappie, and catfish is available in the lake, which has a sand beach in the swimming area. The campground is 25 miles from the Bear Creek Canoe Run, which is a 34-mile portion of Bear Creek, from Red Bay to Pickwick Lake. The canoe trail is best from May to October. The water level is generally lower in the summer and fall. During the spring flood months, the leisurely one-mile-per-hour flow can become much faster and more dangerous. Deer, wild turkeys, and geese are abundant in the area.

8 Elliott Branch Campground

Location: Russellville, map 1, grid E3.

Campsites, facilities: There are 30 campsites with water and electric hookups, all suitable for tents or RVs. Seven of the sites are pull-through, and all have shade. RVs must be 45 feet or less. Picnic tables, fire rings, and cooking grills are provided. Cabins are planned to be added to the park in 2001. Restrooms have hot showers and flush toilets. A sanitary disposal station is provided. The campground store sells ice, LP gas, and limited groceries. A boat ramp and dock are provided. The buildings are wheelchair accessible. Leashed pets are permitted in the campground, but not in the cabins.

Reservations, fees: Reservations are not accepted. The fee is $12 per night.

Open: The campground is open from March through October.

Directions: The campground is two miles south of Highway 24 on County Road 88.

Contact:. Elliott Branch Campground, P.O. Box 670, Russellville, AL 35653; 256/332-4392, or 256/332-9804.

Trip notes: The campground is located on Little Bear Creek Reservoir. Fishing is available for bass, crappie, and catfish. There is

a sand beach in the swimming area. The campground is located 17 miles from the Bear Creek Canoe Run, which is a 34-mile portion of Bear Creek, from Red Bay to Pickwick Lake. The canoe trail is most enjoyable from May to October. The water level is generally lower in the summer and fall. During the spring flood months, the leisurely one-mile-per-hour flow can become much faster and more dangerous. Deer, wild turkeys, and geese are abundant in the area.

9 Horseshoe Bend Campground

Location: Big Bear Creek Reservoir, map 1, grid E1.

Campsites, facilities: There are 26 campsites suitable for RVs or tents, all with water and electric hookups, and five with full hookups. All of the sites have shade, and two are pull-through sites. RVs are restricted to 45 feet or less. Picnic tables, fire rings, and cooking grills are provided. Restrooms have hot showers and flush toilets. Ice, some groceries, and limited supplies are available at the campground store. A boat ramp is available. A sanitary disposal station is provided. The facilities are wheelchair accessible. Leashed pets are permitted.

Reservations, fees: Reservations are not accepted. The fee is $11 per night.

Open: The campground is open from April through October.

Directions: From Russellville, go west about 7.5 miles on Highway 24 past Belgreen, and turn south on Country Road 88. Turn left on County Road 16, then right on Horseshoe Bend Road to the campground.

Contact: Horseshoe Bend Campground, P.O. Box 670, Russellville, AL 35653; 256/332-4392.

Trip notes: This US Army Corps of Engineers campground is located on Big Bear Creek

Reservoir. The lake is stocked with bass, crappie, and catfish, and there is a sand beach in the swimming area. The campground is 16 miles from the Bear Creek Canoe Run, which is a 34-mile portion of Bear Creek, from Red Bay to Pickwick Lake. The canoe trail is most enjoyable from May to October. The water level is generally lower in the summer and fall. During the spring flood months, the leisurely one-mile-per-hour flow can become much faster and more dangerous. Deer, wild turkeys, and geese are abundant in the area.

🔟 Piney Point Campground

Location: Big Bear Creek Lake, map 1, grid E1.
Campsites, facilities: There are 19 campsites suitable for tents or RVs, all with water and electric hookups. Four of the sites are pull-through, and all have shade. RVs are restricted to 45 feet or less. Picnic tables, fire rings, and cooking grills are provided. Restrooms have hot showers and flush toilets. A sanitary disposal station, fishing pier, and boat ramp are provided. Ice is available at the campground. The restrooms are wheelchair accessible. Leashed pets are permitted.
Reservations, fees: Reservations are not accepted, and no deposit is required. Campsites are $12 per night. Some are available on a monthly basis.
Open: The campground is open from April through October.
Directions: From Russellville, take US 43 south to Highway 172 and turn right. At Atwood, turn right onto County Road B-25. The campground is on the right, just before Bear Creek Dam.
Contact: Piney Point Campground, P.O. Box

670, Russellville, AL 35653; 256/356-9580, or 256/332-4392.
Trip notes: Big Bear Creek Lake is stocked with bass, crappie, and catfish. There is a sand beach in the swimming area. Wildlife in the area includes deer, wild turkeys, and geese. The campground is about 30 miles from the Bear Creek Canoe Run.

🔟🔟 Williams Hollow Campground

Location: Russellville, map 1, grid E1.
Campsites, facilities: There are a total of 30 sites suitable for RVs or tents. Sixteen of the sites have water and electric hookups, and 14 are primitive with no hookups. All have shade. Picnic tables, fire rings, and cooking grills are provided. Restrooms have hot showers and flush toilets. Ice, some supplies, and some groceries are available at the campground. A sanitary disposal station and a boat ramp are provided. Leashed pets are permitted.
Reservations, fees: Reservations are not accepted. Primitive campsites are $7.50 per night; sites with hookups are $11.
Open: The campground is open from April through September.
Directions: From Russellville, take Highway 24 west towards Red Bay. At Belgreen, turn left onto Highway 187. Turn right onto County Road 52, then left onto County Road 227, and follow the signs. The campground is about 15 miles from Russellville.
Contact: Williams Hollow Campground, P.O. Box 670, Russellville, AL 35653; 256/332-4392.
Trip notes: The lake is stocked with bass, crappie, and catfish. There is a sand beach in the swimming area. Wildlife in the area includes deer, wild turkeys, and geese.

12 Dismals Canyon Campground

Location: Bear Creek, map 1, grid F2.

Campsites, facilities: There are 10 tent sites, one with water and electric hookups. Picnic tables, fire rings, and cooking grills are provided. There are also two cabins. Restrooms have hot showers and flush toilets. The campground store sells ice, LP gas, supplies, groceries, and gifts. A 75-foot natural limestone swimming pool is provided, and firewood is free. Pets are permitted.

Reservations, fees: Reservations are accepted. The deposit is refundable if cancellation is made 10 days in advance. Regular sites cost $14 per night. Sites near the waterfall are $35. The cabins are $120–165 per night, plus a refundable damage deposit and cleanup fee.

Open: The campground is open daily from Memorial Day to Labor Day, and weekends starting in March.

Directions: From Russellville, go south on US 43 twelve miles to County Road 8 and turn right. The campground and park will be on your left.

Contact: Dismals Canyon, 901 Highway 8, Phil Campbell, AL 35581; 205/993-4559.

Trip notes: Dismals Canyon is an interesting place to visit. The park contains caves that were used by the Indians, and by Aaron Burr when he went into hiding after killing Alexander Hamilton in a duel. There are two waterfalls. Dismals Branch maintains a constant 50-degree temperature year-round where it runs into Bear Creek, which is a three-mile walk from the campground. The campground is three miles from the Bear Creek Canoe Run, and canoes, rafts, and kayaks are available for rent. The creek offers rapids from Class I–IV.

13 Sipsey Wilderness

Location: Bankhead National Forest, map 1, grid F5.

Campsites, Facilities: There are unlimited primitive campsites in the wilderness. No facilities are provided. Leashed pets are permitted.

Reservations, fees: There are no reservations accepted. The fee is $3 per night.

Open: Year-round.

Directions: The Sipsey Wilderness area encompasses almost 26,000 acres, and there are several parking areas. From Double Springs, take Highway 33 north. Turn left on County Road 6 (which will change to County Road 60) to one of the parking areas.

Contact: Sipsey Wilderness, Bankhead National Forest, P.O. Box 278, Double Springs, AL 35553; 205/489-5111.

Trip notes: The area is remote and you should not backpack or hike here without a compass, topographic map, and provisions including some water and a water filter. There is no potable water in the area, but there are numerous creeks. Follow "Leave No Trace" guidelines while in the wilderness area. What I have learned from working with compasses and topographic maps is that you need to be proficient in both before you need them. Stop by the Bankhead Ranger Station in Double Springs or call the number listed above to get maps before your trip. There are 10 marked trails through the wilderness area, generally rated moderate, suitable for horseback riding as well as hiking.

14 Brushy Lake Recreation Area

Location: Brushy Lake, map 1, grid F6.

Campsites, facilities: There are 13 primitive

tent sites, most with shade. Picnic tables, fire rings, and cooking grills are provided. Restrooms have hot showers and toilets. A boat ramp is provided. Boat motors must be electric only. Pets are permitted, but must be kept on leash at all times.

Reservations, fees: Reservations are not accepted. The camping fee is $5 per night.

Open: Year-round, but there is no water in the winter in the restrooms.

Directions: From Interstate 65, take US 278 west to Double Springs, and turn north on Highway 33. Turn right on County Road 70, and follow the signs.

Contact: Brushy Lake Recreation Area, Bankhead National Forest, P.O. Box 278, Double Springs, AL 35553; 205/489-5111.

Trip notes: This Forest Service campground in the Bankhead National Forest has fewer amenities than some. Fishing is available in the lake, as well as kayaking and rafting.

15 Owl Creek Horse Camp

Location: Bankhead National Forest, map 1, grid F7.

Campsites, Facilities: Primitive tent camping is available. Fire rings and hitching rails are provided. A pond provides water for horses but no drinking water is available. Dogs are permitted, but not recommended.

Reservations, fees: Reservations are not accepted. The fee is $3 per night.

Open: Year-round.

Directions: From Double Springs, go north on Highway 33 to Forest Service Road 249 and turn right. At the T-junction with Forest Service Road 268, turn left and look for the sign.

Contact: Owl Creek Horse Camp, Bankhead National Forest, P.O. Box 278, Double Springs, AL 35553; 205/489-5111.

Trip notes: There are about 30 miles of horse

trails available. Stay on the trails marked with the metal diamonds. Follow the "Leave No Trace" guidelines, packing out all trash and scattering your horse's droppings.

16 US 78 Campground

Location: Hamilton, map 1, grid H1.

Campsites, facilities: There is a large primitive camping area with access to fresh water, and 14 RV sites, all with full hookups and all pull-through sites. Some RV sites have picnic tables. Restrooms have hot showers and flush toilets. A sanitary disposal station and coin laundry are provided. The restrooms are wheelchair accessible. Pets are permitted.

Reservations, fees: Reservations are accepted, and no deposit is required. RV sites cost $10, and primitive camping is also available.

Open: Year-round.

Directions: From Jasper, take US 78 north towards Hamilton. South of Hamilton, 78 becomes a restricted access highway. Turn left at exit 14/County Road 35, and turn left at the campground sign within site of the highway.

Contact: US 78 Campground, 3194 County Road 55, Hamilton, AL 35570; 205/921-2718.

Trip notes: The campground is five miles from Lake Marian, which is stocked with bass and catfish, and is four miles from hiking trails.

17 Houston Recreation Area

Location: Lake Lewis Smith, map 1, grid H7.

Campsites, facilities: There are 86 tent sites, most with shade. Electric and water hookups are available at the campsites. Picnic tables, fire rings, and cooking grills are provided. Restrooms have hot showers and flush toilets. A boat ramp and sanitary disposal station are provided. The restrooms are wheelchair accessible. Leashed pets are permitted.

Reservations, fees: Reservations are not accepted. The fee is $10 per night.

Open: The campground is open from April through September.

Directions: From Double Springs, take US 278 east to County Road 63 and turn right. Turn right on County Road 67 and follow the signs.

Contact: Houston Recreation Area, Bankhead National Forest, P.O. Box 278, Double Springs, AL 35553; 205/489-5111.

Trip notes: Fishing, kayaking, and boating are available on the lake, and there is a sand beach in the swimming area. There are several hiking trails through the area. Wildlife in the area includes deer and wild turkeys.

18 Hidden Cove Resort

Location: Lewis Smith Lake, map 1, grid H7.

Campsites, Facilities: The eight tent sites have water and electric hookups, and the 76 RV sites have full hookups. Most of the tent sites have shade. Picnic tables and fire rings are provided at most sites. RV storage is available. Restrooms have hot showers and flush toilets. A coin laundry, boat ramp, dock, playground, fitness room, reading room, and swimming pool are provided. Wood and ice are available. Leashed pets are permitted, except in the rental RVs.

Reservations, fees: Reservations are accepted for the rental RVs. The deposit of one night's fee is refundable if cancellation is made at least 48 hours in advance. The campground is a member of the Coast to Coast

Resorts club. For more information on this RV club, see www.coastresorts.com/. Rental RVs are available for $42 per day for members. Non-members pay $10 more. Both tent and RV sites are $6 for members, and $18 for non-members.

Open: Year-round.

Directions: From Cullman, take US 278 west to Addison, and turn left onto County Road 41. At Arley, turn left onto County Road 77. After one mile, take the right fork onto County Road 12, which leads into the campground.

Contact: Hidden Cove Resort, 687 County Road 3919, Arley, AL 35541; 205/221-7042.

Trip notes: The campground is on Lewis Smith Lake, which offers water-skiing as well as fishing for bass, crappie, and striper. There are no hiking trails, but the campground covers over 100 acres along the lake. Not all the campers here come for the fishing. Nearly as many come for the peaceful relaxation in this beautiful spot.

19 Corinth Recreation Area

Location: Lake Lewis Smith, map 1, grid H7.

Campsites, facilities: There are 50 campsites suitable for tents or RVs, all with full hookups. Five of the sites are pull-through, and most have shade. Picnic tables, fire rings, and cooking grills are provided. Restrooms have hot showers and flush toilets. A boat ramp and sanitary disposal station are provided. The buildings and some campsites are wheelchair accessible. Leashed pets are permitted.

Reservations, fees: Reservations are not accepted. The fee is $21 per night for hookups; primitive sites are $12.

Open: March through October.

Directions: Take Highway 278 east of

Double Springs about six miles, then follow the signs.

Contact: Corinth Recreation Area, Bankhead National Forest, P.O. Box 278, Double Springs, AL 35553; 205/489-5111, entrance station 205/489-3165.

Trip notes: The recreation area includes Lake Lewis Smith, creeks, and rivers, and offers recreational activities on each, including fishing, boating, kayaking, and paddleboats. Wildlife you may see includes deer and wild turkeys.

20 Arrowhead Park

Location: Lewis Smith Lake, map 1, grid H8.
Campsites, facilities: There are 20 RV sites, all with full hookups. Primitive tent camping is also available in a large area. Restrooms have hot showers and flush toilets. A coin laundry and boat ramp are provided, and dry storage for boats is available. Leashed pets are permitted.
Reservations, fees: Reservations are accepted. The deposit is refundable if the reservation is cancelled in advance. Primitive campsites are $8, and RV sites are $12.
Open: Year-round.
Directions: Go north from Birmingham on Interstate 65, and turn west on Highway 69. After seven miles, turn right on County Road 222, then left onto County Road 941.
Contact: Arrowhead Park, 761 County Road 941, Crane Hill, AL 35053; 256/747-2519.
Trip notes: There is a sand beach in the swimming area. Fishing is available in the lake, and there are hiking trails throughout the area. Wildlife you may see includes deer and wild turkeys.

21 Hames Marina and RV Park

Location: Smith Lake, map 1, grid H8.
Campsites, facilities: There are 20 primitive tent sites with piped water, and 28 large RV campsites with full hookups. There are also two cabins. Picnic tables and fire rings are provided. Restrooms have hot showers and flush toilets. The campground store sells ice, some groceries, bait, and supplies. A coin laundry and sanitary disposal station are provided. Both 30- and 50-amp service is available. Cable TV hookups are available, and a one-acre play area with volleyball net is provided. The restrooms are wheelchair accessible. Leashed pets are permitted.
Reservations, fees: Reservations are accepted, and a deposit of one night's fee is required. The deposit is refundable if the reservation is cancelled in advance. Primitive sites are $10 per night, and RV sites are $15–20 per night.
Open: Year-round.
Directions: From Interstate 65, take exit 299/Highway 69 southwest towards Jasper. Turn right on County Road 223, and continue at the intersection to County Roads 248 and 233.
Contact: Hames Marina and RV Park, 850 County Road 248, Cullman, AL 35057; 256/287-9785.
Trip notes: The campground has a small pond stocked with bream and bass. There are several hiking and biking trails along the lake and the creek that feeds into it. In the spring, when the creek is high, kayaking and rafting are popular. The campground is approximately 10 miles from the Ave Maria Grotto in Cullman.

22 Bremen Lakeview Resorts

Location: Smith Lake, map 1, grid H8.

Campsites, facilities: There are 95 sites suitable for tents or RVs. Thirty-five of the sites have full hookups, and the rest have water and electric only. Five are pull-through sites, and most have some shade. Picnic tables, cooking grills, and some fire rings are provided. There are also four cabins and 28 motel rooms available. A sanitary disposal station, coin laundry, playground, swimming pool, clubroom, miniature golf, sports field, boat ramp, and dock are provided. Ice, LP gas, and some groceries are available at the campground. The buildings are wheelchair accessible. Leashed pets are permitted in the campground, but not in the cabins or rooms.

Reservations, fees: Reservations are accepted. The deposit is refundable with advance notice. Campsites are $21 per night, and rooms and cabins are $55–65 per night.

Open: Year-round.

Directions: Take exit 299/Highway 69 from Interstate 65 southwest towards Jasper. At Bremen, turn right on County Road 222. Travel four miles and then turn right on County Road 143. The campground will be on the left, about one mile down the road.

Contact: Bremen Lakeview Resorts, 1940 County Road 143, Bremen, AL 35033; 256/287-0023.

Trip notes: Smith Lake is stocked with bass. There are four nature trails, the longest about one mile in length. Johnboats are available for rent, and water skiing is popular in the lake. The campground is 20 miles from Cullman, home of the Ave Maria Grotto.

23 Mill Creek Park

Location: Elkmont, map 2, grid A1.

Campsites, facilities: There are 10 tent sites and 20 RV sites at this campground. All of the pull-through RV sites all have full hookups. Picnic tables and fire rings are provided. RV storage is available. Both 30- and 50-amp services are available. Restrooms have hot showers and flush toilets. A coin laundry and clubroom are provided. Ice, supplies, firewood, groceries, and gifts are available at the campground. The facilities are wheelchair accessible. Leashed pets are permitted.

Reservations, fees: Reservations are accepted. Deposits are required for certain tent sites, and are refundable if your reservation is cancelled in advance. The fee for all sites is $18. Discounts are honored.

Open: Year-round.

Directions: From Decatur, go north on Interstate 65 to exit 361 and turn west towards Elkmont. After 4.5 miles, turn right at the stop sign in Elkmont onto Veto Road. The campground is three miles from the stop sign.

Contact: Mill Creek Park, 28861 Veto Rd., Elkmont, AL 35620; 256/732-3686; website: www.millcreekrv.com.

Trip notes: Fishing is available in the creek for bream and bass. There are short hiking trails at the campground. Over 100 species of wildflowers bloom between February and November. The campground is 30 miles from the US Space and Rocket Center in Huntsville, and Civil War historical sites are less than a mile away.

24 Jay Landings Marina and RV Park

Location: Wheeler Lake, map 2, grid D1.

Campsites, facilities: There are 30 RV sites at this campground, all with full hookups. Five are pull-through sites. A few sites have shade. Picnic tables and fire rings are provided. RV storage is available, and a sanitary disposal station is provided. Restrooms have flush toilets and hot showers. Ice is available on-site. A coin laundry, cable TV, boat ramp, dock, and marine gas are available. The buildings are wheelchair accessible. Pets are permitted.

Reservations, fees: Reservations are accepted. Campsites are $15 per night, and $75 per week. Monthly guests pay $230 plus electricity, or $260 for waterfront sites.

Open: Year-round.

Directions: From Interstate 65, take exit 340A and go west on Highway 20 eight miles.

Contact: Jay Landings Marina and RV Park, 1600 Highway 20 West, Decatur, AL 35601; 256/350-4722.

Trip notes: The lake is stocked with bass, crappie, and catfish. Pontoon boats and wave runners are available for rent. The campground is three miles from golf courses, and five miles from a water park.

25 Cullman Campground

Location: Cullman, map 2, grid G1.

Campsites, facilities: There are 75 campsites suitable for tents or RVs, all with full hookups. Nearly all are pull-through sites. Some sites have shade. Both 50- and 30-amp hookups are available. Picnic tables are provided, and some sites have cooking grills.

RV storage is available. Restrooms have hot showers and flush toilets. A coin laundry, sports field, and playground are provided. Leashed pets are permitted.

Reservations, fees: Reservations are accepted, and no deposit is required. Sites with 30-amp service are $15, and 50-amp sites are $17 per night. Good Sam and AAA discounts apply.

Open: Year-round.

Directions: Take the Cullman exit (exit 310/Highway 157) off Interstate 65 and turn north on Highway 157. After 1.5 miles, turn left onto County Road 1185. The campground is less than a mile from Highway 157.

Contact: Cullman Campground, 220 County Road 1185, Cullman, AL 35057; 256/734-5853, or 256/734-9794.

Trip notes: The fishing pond is stocked with catfish. There are hiking trails by the creek that runs through the back of the 40-acre campground, but watch out for snakes. The campground is about six miles from the Ave Maria Grotto, 15 miles from Sister Angelica's monastery, which offers tours, and 40 miles from the US Space and Rocket Center. Cullman has a covered bridge park, and there is a large flea market about 12 miles away.

26 Sportsman Lake Campground

Location: Sportsman Lake, map 2, grid G1.

Campsites, facilities: There are 20 primitive tent sites with access to piped water, and four RV sites with water and electric hookups. Some sites have picnic tables. Restrooms have hot showers and flush toilets. A sanitary disposal station and playground are provided. Leashed pets are permitted.

Reservations, fees: Reservations are not accepted. Tent sites are $13; RV sites are $18 per night.

Open: The campground is open from March through October 15.

Directions: Take exit 310/Highway 157 off Interstate 65 and turn east towards Cullman. Turn right on Highway 31. After one mile, turn right onto Sportsman Lake Road.

Contact: Sportsman Lake Campground, 1536 Sportsman Lake Rd., Cullman, AL 35055; 256/734-3052.

Trip notes: The 33-acre lake offers fishing for catfish, bream, and bass. Paddleboats are available. There is a walking trail around the lake. The campground has a wildflower garden and a small amusement park, including a train, rides, and miniature golf. It is five miles from the Ave Maria Grotto.

27 Smith Lake Park

Location: Lewis Smith Lake, map 2, grid H1.

Campsites, facilities: There are a total of 235 campsites. Sixty-one of the sites are for tents only, 85 for RVs only, and the rest can be used by either. The RV sites have full hookups, and most of the other sites have water and electric hookups. Picnic tables are available at most campsites, and there are fire rings at some. There are cooking grills in the pavilions. Pop-up campers and cabins are also available. Restrooms have hot showers and flush toilets. Ice is available at the campground. Amenities include a swimming pool with water slide, playground, miniature golf, and horseshoe area. RV storage is available, and a sanitary disposal station is provided. Leashed pets are permitted.

Reservations, fees: Reservations are accepted. Deposits are refundable in an emergency. Rates are $13 for a tent, $18 for a camper, $20 for a rental pop-up, $20 for sites with sewer hookup, and $35–55 for the cabins.

Open: Year-round.

Directions: From Interstate 65, take exit 304/Good Hope Road and turn west. After five miles, turn at the Smith Lake Park sign.

Contact: Smith Lake Park, 416 County Road 385, Cullman, AL 35055; 256/739-2916.

Trip notes: The lake is stocked with fish, and there is a sand beach in the swimming area. Canoes can be rented nearby. This is a quiet, secluded campground, which caters to families. Wildlife in the area includes deer and wild turkeys.

28 Someplace Else Mobile Home RV Park

Location: Guin, map 3, grid A2.

Campsites, Facilities: There are five RV sites with full hookups at this campground. One of the sites is a pull-through, and three have shade. Picnic tables are provided. Leashed pets are permitted.

Reservations, fees: Reservations are not accepted. Fees vary by season. The campground does not publish its rates.

Open: Year-round.

Directions: From Hamilton, travel south on US 78/278 to Winfield, and turn north on Highway 253. The campground is about three miles from Winfield.

Contact: Someplace Else Mobile Home RV Park, 3161 Highway 253, Guin, AL 35563; 205/487-6092.

Trip notes: This tiny campground offers a quiet, country setting. It is located about a half hour from a natural bridge, and two hours from Ivy Green, Helen Keller's home, and from Elvis' birthplace.

29 Clear Creek Recreation Area

Location: Lake Lewis Smith, map 3, grid A6.

Campsites, facilities: There are 102 sites suitable for tents or RVs, all with water and electric hookups. Ten of the sites are pull-through, and most have shade. Picnic tables, fire rings, and cooking grills are provided. Group sites are available, and a sanitary disposal station is provided. Restrooms have hot showers and flush toilets. A boat ramp and playground are provided. The restrooms are wheelchair accessible. Leashed pets are permitted.

Reservations, fees: Reservations are accepted at 877/444-6777 for some campsites. There is a reservation fee of $8, plus a cancellation fee of $8. Fees range from $18.90–31.50 per night, depending on location.

Open: The campground is open from mid-March through October.

Directions: The campground is about 15 miles north of Jasper on Highway 195.

Contact: Clear Creek Recreation Area, Bankhead National Forest, P.O. Box 278, Double Springs, AL 35553; 205/489-5111, entrance station 205/384-2792.

Trip notes: This Forest Service campground includes fishing areas and trails for hiking and mountain biking. Canoeing and kayaking are popular in the creek. Wildlife in the area includes deer and wild turkeys.

30 Sleepy Holler Campground

Location: Jasper, map 3, grid B7.

Campsites, facilities: There are 120 RV campsites, all with full hookups. Forty of the sites are pull-through, and some have shade. Some sites have picnic tables. There are also four cabins. Restrooms have hot showers and flush toilets. RV storage is available. A coin laundry and playground are provided. Ice, LP gas, and snacks are available at the campground. The buildings are wheelchair accessible. Pets are permitted as long as they are kept leashed, and you must clean up after your pet.

Reservations, fees: Reservations are accepted, and no deposit is required. Campsites range from $15–19 per night. Call for cabin prices.

Open: Year-round.

Directions: From Jasper, head east on US 78 towards Birmingham. The campground will be on the right.

Contact: Sleepy Holler Campground, P.O. Box 1687, Jasper, AL 35502; 205/483-7947.

Trip notes: The campground has two small fishing lakes stocked with catfish and bass, and three miles of trails for hiking. The campground is about 30 miles from Birmingham.

NORTHEAST MOUNTAINS

DeSoto Falls in DeSoto State Park

NORTHEAST MOUNTAINS

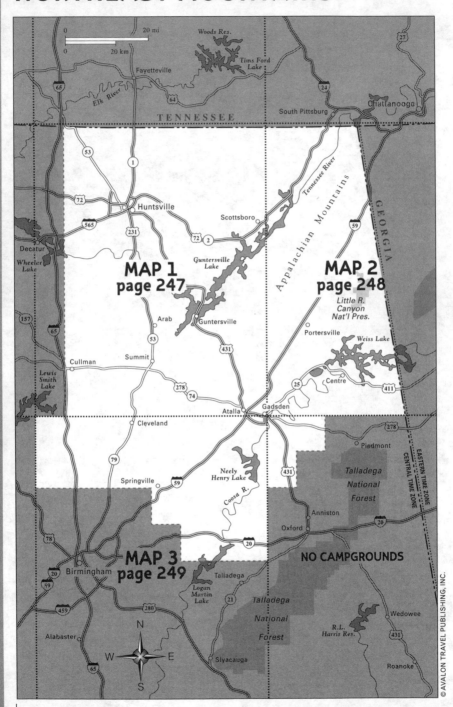

MAP 1

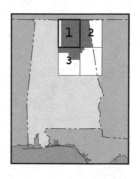

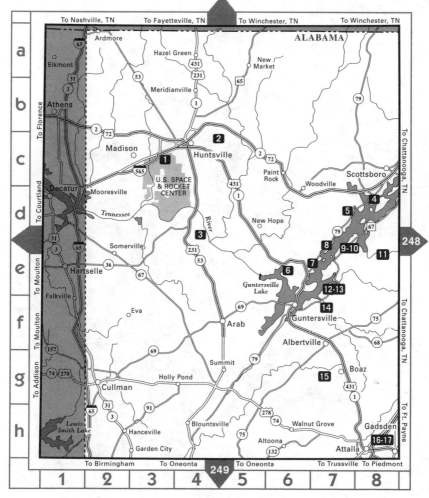

To Nashville, TN   To Fayetteville, TN   To Winchester, TN   To Winchester, TN

ALABAMA

Ardmore

Elkmont

Hazel Green

New Market

Athens

Meridianville

Madison

Huntsville

Paint Rock

Woodville

Scottsboro

U.S. SPACE & ROCKET CENTER

Decatur

Mooresville

Tennessee

New Hope

River

Somerville

Guntersville Lake

Hartselle

Falkville

Eva

Arab

Guntersville

Albertville

Boaz

Summit

Holly Pond

Cullman

Lewis Smith Lake

Hanceville

Blountsville

Walnut Grove

Gadsden

Garden City

Altoona

Attalla

To Birmingham   To Oneonta   To Oneonta   To Trussville   To Piedmont

To Florence
To Courtland
To Moulton
To Moulton
To Addison

To Chattanooga, TN
To Chattanooga, TN
To Ft. Payne

248

249

© AVALON TRAVEL PUBLISHING, INC.

MAP 2

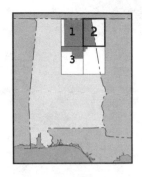

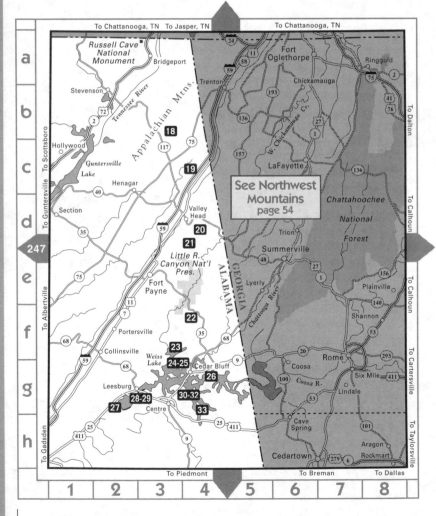

To Chattanooga, TN   To Jasper, TN   To Chattanooga, TN

a
Russell Cave National Monument
Bridgeport
24
11   58   Fort Oglethorpe
Ringgold
193   Chickamauga
75   2

b
Stevenson
72   Tennessee River
Trenton
136   W. Chickamauga Cr.
27   1
41   76
To Dalton

c
Hollywood
2
Guntersville Lake
Henagar
117   75
18
157
LaFayette
136
Chattahoochee
To Calhoun

d
Section
40
35
59
Valley Head
19
20
21
Little R. Canyon Nat'l Pres.
Trion
Summerville
48
National Forest
See Northwest Mountains page 54
247

e
75
Fort Payne
Lyerly
Chattooga River
1
27
156
Plainville
140
To Calhoun

f
68
11
7
Portersville
22
35
68
68
Shannon
53

g
Collinsville
59
68
Weiss Lake
23
24-25
Cedar Bluff
26
9
20
Coosa
Coosa R.
Rome
100
Six Mile
293
411
Lindale
To Cartersville

h
Leesburg
27
28-29
Centre
30-32
33
25
25   411
53
Cave Spring
Cedartown
279   6
101
Aragon
Rockmart
To Taylorsville

To Gadsden
To Albertville
To Scottsboro
To Guntersville

ALABAMA   GEORGIA
Appalachian Mtns.

To Piedmont   To Breman   To Dallas

1   2   3   4   5   6   7   8

© AVALON TRAVEL PUBLISHING, INC.

MAP 3

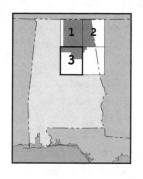

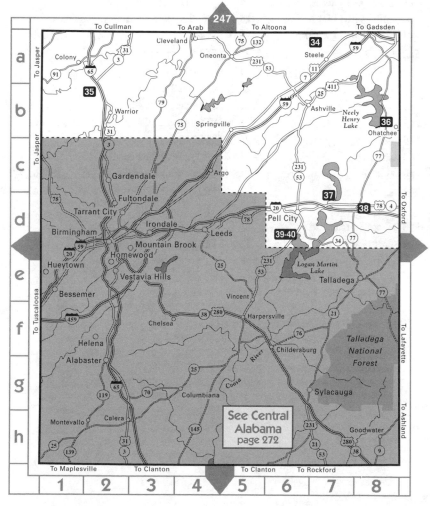

To Cullman   To Arab   **247**   To Altoona   To Gadsden

a

Cleveland   75   132   **34**

Colony   31   Oneonta   Steele   59

To Jasper   91   65   3   231   53   11

b

7

35   25   411

79   Warrior   59   Ashville   Neely Henry Lake   **36**

31   75   Springville   Ohatchee

To Jasper

c

3

Gardendale   Argo   231   77

53

78   Fultondale

d

Tarrant City   Irondale   78   20   Pell City   38   78   4

Birmingham   Leeds   **37**

59   Mountain Brook   **39-40**   To Oxford

Hueytown   Homewood   34   77

20   25

e

Vestavia Hills   Logan Martin Lake   Talladega

Bessemer   Vincent   231   53

To Tuscaloosa

f

459   38   280   Harpersville   21   77

Chelsea   76   Talladega National Forest

Helena   Childersburg

Alabaster   River

To Lafayette

g

25   Coosa   Sylacauga

65   70

119   Columbiana

Montevallo   Calera   **See Central Alabama page 272**   231   Goodwater

To Ashland

h

25   139   31   145   21   280   38   9

3   53

To Maplesville   To Clanton   To Clanton   To Rockford

1   2   3   4   5   6   7   8

NORTHEAST MOUNTAINS

◉ US Space and Rocket Center Campground

Location: Huntsville, map 1, grid C3.

Campsites, facilities: There are 27 RV sites, all with full hookups. Five of the sites are pull-through, and most have shade. Picnic tables and cooking grills are provided. The restrooms have hot showers and flush toilets. A coin laundry and sanitary disposal station are provided. Leashed pets are permitted.

Reservations, fees: Reservations are accepted. The deposit is refundable if the cancellation is made in advance. The rate is $14 per night.

Open: Year-round.

Directions: Heading north on I-65, take exit 340 and turn east on Highway 565. Travel 15 miles, then turn right at exit 15 onto Tranquility Base Road, just past the sign for the US Space and Rocket Center, and follow the signs.

Contact: US Space and Rocket Center Campground, One Tranquility Base, Huntsville, AL 35807; 256/830-4987.

Trip notes: The US Space and Rocket Center covers 500 acres and includes biking and hiking trails. There is a mock-up of the space shuttle used for training. There are 150 artifacts from our exploration of space, hands-on exhibits, a prototype of the moon buggy, rides, a launch pad, an IMAX movie, and an underwater tank used for weightlessness training. Allow six hours to tour the Center. The cost of entry to the center is $14.95 for adults, $10.95 for children 3–12. It is open from 9A.M. to 5P.M. from Labor Day until Memorial Day, and stays open until 6P.M. during the summer.

◉ Monte Sano State Park

Location: Huntsville, map 1, grid C4.

Campsites, facilities: There are 20 tent sites and 89 RV sites at this campground. Twenty-two of the RV sites have full hookups, and four are pull-through. All sites have shade. Picnic tables, fire rings, and cooking grills are provided. There are also 14 cabins. Restrooms have hot showers and flush toilets. A coin laundry, tennis courts, and playground are provided. The campground store sells ice, supplies, and firewood. A sanitary disposal station is provided. The facilities are wheelchair accessible. Leashed pets are permitted.

Reservations, fees: Reservations are not accepted for individual campsites. Campsites with water and electric hookups are $14 per night, and sites with full hookups are $15.

Open: Year-round.

Directions: From Huntsville, take US 431 east towards Gadsden, and turn left at the sign onto Montesano Boulevard. The park will be on your right, about a mile from the highway.

Contact: Monte Sano State Park, 5105 Nolen Ave., Huntsville, AL 35801; 256/534-6589 or 256/534-3757, fax: 256/539-7069; website: www.dcnr.state.al.us.

Trip notes: Of the park's 27-mile trail system, 20 miles of trails are shared by both hikers and mountain bikers. The upper trails are for hiking only. There are also wheelchair-accessible trails along former roadways. The park contains caves and rock formations suitable for climbing (by permit only). The park includes the Von Braun Planetarium, and is six miles from the US Space and Rocket Center.

3 Ditto Landing Campground

Location: Huntsville, map 1, grid D4.

Campsites, facilities: The campground has 26 sites suitable for tents or RVs, all with water and electric hookups. Picnic tables and cooking grills are provided. There is an additional area for about 12 primitive sites. Restrooms have hot showers and flush toilets. A sanitary disposal station, coin laundry, tennis courts, boat ramp, dock, and playground are provided. Ice, snacks, and marine gas are available at the campground. The facilities are wheelchair accessible. Pets are permitted.

Reservations, fees: Reservations are accepted at 800/552-8769. A deposit is required, but is refundable if cancellation is made at least 24 hours in advance. The rate for sites with hookups is $12; primitive sites are $10.

Open: Year-round, call the campground for exact dates.

Directions: From Huntsville, take US 231 south 12 miles, turn left at the Tennessee River Bridge onto Hobbs Island Road, and follow the signs.

Contact: Ditto Landing Campground, 293 Ditto Landing Rd., Huntsville, AL 35803; 256/883-9420.

Trip notes: The campground is on the Tennessee River, which offers fishing for bass, crappie, and catfish, canoeing, and kayaking. It is 12 miles from the US Space and Rocket Center.

4 Goose Pond Colony Campground

Location: Lake Guntersville, map 1, grid D8.

Campsites, facilities: There are 116 campsites suitable for tents or RVs. Thirty-seven sites have full hookups, and two are pull-through. Most sites have shade. Picnic tables are provided. There are also 10 primitive sites and 11 cabins. Group sites and RV storage are available. Restrooms have hot showers and flush toilets. Ice, LP gas, and firewood are available. A swimming pool, clubroom, boat ramp, dock, playground, and sanitary disposal station are provided. The buildings are wheelchair accessible. Leashed pets are permitted.

Reservations, fees: Reservations are not accepted. Sites are $15–17 per night, depending on proximity to the water.

Open: Year-round.

Directions: The campground is located just off Highway 79, four miles south of Scottsboro.

Contact: Goose Pond Colony Campground, 417 Ed Hembree Dr., Scottsboro, AL 35769; 256/259-2884, or 800/268-2884.

Trip notes: Located on Lake Guntersville on the Tennessee River, fishing is available year-round for bass, bream, crappie, and catfish. Water skiing is permitted in the lake. There is a two-mile trail for hiking. The 365-acre resort includes two golf courses, lakefront cottages, a full service marina, meeting facilities, and a seafood restaurant. Wildlife in the area includes deer, great blue herons, and other waterbirds.

5 Clay Marina

Location: Tennessee River, map 1, grid D7.

Campsites, facilities: There are 28 RV sites at this campground, all with full hookups. Pull-through sites are available. Most sites have some shade. RV storage is available. Restrooms have hot showers and flush toilets. A coin laundry, boat ramp, and dock are provided. Ice, snacks, and bait are available at the campground. The facilities are wheelchair accessible. Pets are permitted.

Reservations, fees: Reservations are accepted. The deposit is refundable with 72 hours notice. Campsites cost $15 per night.

Open: The campground is open from March through October.

Directions: The campground is on Highway 79 between Guntersville and Scottsboro, 4.5 miles north of the Highway 79 and US 431 split.

Contact: Clay Marina, 3784 Scottsboro Highway, Scottsboro, AL 35769; 256/582-4709.

Trip notes: The campground is located on Mill Creek and the Tennessee River, which offer fishing for bass, crappie, catfish, and bream. The nearest hiking trails are at Guntersville State Park, about 15 miles away. Kayaking, rafting, and canoeing are popular activities on the river. The campground is 10 miles from Cathedral Caverns, billed the largest caverns in the world, and 20 miles from the outlet shopping in Boaz.

6 Honeycomb Campground

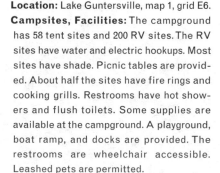

Location: Lake Guntersville, map 1, grid E6.

Campsites, Facilities: The campground has 58 tent sites and 200 RV sites. The RV sites have water and electric hookups. Most sites have shade. Picnic tables are provided. About half the sites have fire rings and cooking grills. Restrooms have hot showers and flush toilets. Some supplies are available at the campground. A playground, boat ramp, and docks are provided. The restrooms are wheelchair accessible. Leashed pets are permitted.

Reservations, fees: Reservations are accepted at 256/582-7529. The deposit of one night's fee is refundable if cancellation is made at least 24 hours in advance. Primitive sites are $15 per night. Sites with hookups are $17 per night or $100 per week.

Open: The campground is open March 1-December 1.

Directions: From Huntsville, take US 431 south approximately 25 miles, and turn right onto Campground Road.

Contact: Honeycomb Campground, 188 Campground Road, Grant, AL 35747; 256/582-7529.

Trip notes: Lake Guntersville offers fishing year-round for bass, bream, crappie, and catfish. There are two short hiking trails, which total 2.75 miles. There is a sand beach in the swimming area. Woods surround the campground.

7 Seibold Campground

Location: Lake Guntersville, map 1, grid E7.

Campsites, facilities: There are 102 campsites, all with water and electric hookups. Either tents or RVs are permitted on any site, but this is primarily an RV campground. Most sites have some shade. RVs may be a maximum of 40 feet in length. Picnic tables and fire rings are provided. RV storage is available. Restrooms have hot showers and flush toilets. A sanitary disposal station, coin laundry, boat ramp, dock, pier, playground, swimming pool, and clubroom are provided. Ramps are available for wheelchair access. Pets are permitted.

Reservations, fees: Reservations are accepted. A deposit is required and is refundable with two days notice of cancellation.

Lakeside campsites are $20 per night, other sites are $17 per night.

Open: The campground is open from March through October.

Directions: From Guntersville, take US 431/Highway 79 north. When the roads fork (less than five miles from Guntersville), stay on Highway 79 for one mile, then turn right onto Seibold Creek Road.

Contact: Seibold Campground, 54 Seibold Creek Rd., Guntersville, AL 35976; 256/582-0040.

Trip notes: Fishing is available at the lake for bass, crappie, and catfish. Water skiing is permitted in the lake. This is a family-oriented campground with on-site security. It's located 15 miles from Cathedral Caverns State Park.

8 Ossa-Win-Tha Resort

Location: Lake Guntersville, map 1, grid E7.

Campsites, facilities: The campground has 30 RV sites, all with full hookups. Pull-through sites are available. All sites have some shade. There are also 12 cabins. Restrooms have hot showers and flush toilets. A boat ramp, dock, playground, and clubroom are provided. Leashed pets are permitted.

Reservations, fees: Reservations are not required. Campsites are $18 per night, and cabins are $50–90 per night.

Open: The campground is open from March through October.

Directions: From Guntersville, go north on US 431/Highway 79, and take Highway 79 when it splits off to the right. The campground is on the right side, two miles from the split.

Contact: Ossa-Win-Tha Resort, 212 Ossa-Win-Tha Rd., P.O. Box 203, Guntersville, AL 35976; 256/582-4595.

Trip notes: Lake Guntersville offers fishing for bass, crappie, bream, and catfish. The name means "Place of the Pines." There is a one-mile walking trail through the woods. Water skiing is permitted in the lake. This campground caters to Christian families and has planned entertainment for kids during the summer season. No alcohol is allowed. Non-denominational services are held on Sunday mornings.

9 South Sauty Creek Resort

Location: Lake Guntersville, map 1, grid E7.

Campsites, facilities: There are 88 sites suitable for either tents or RVs, all with water and electric hookups. Some sites have shade, and all have picnic tables and fire rings. RV storage is available, and a sanitary disposal station is provided. Restrooms have hot showers and flush toilets. Ice, LP gas, supplies, and groceries are available at the campground. A boat ramp, dock, swimming pool, and play area are provided. The campground is next to a café and restaurant. Wet and dry boat storage is available. Leashed pets are permitted.

Reservations, fees: Reservations are accepted, and the required deposit is non-refundable. Campsites cost $18 per night, or $100 per week.

Open: Part of the campground is open year-round.

Directions: From US 431 in Guntersville, turn south on Highway 227. After 15 miles, Highway 227 turns off, and South Sauty Road goes straight ahead. Stay on South Sauty Road for another seven miles to the campground.

Contact: South Sauty Creek Resort, 6845 South Sauty Rd., Langston, AL 35755; 256/582-3367.

Trip notes: This campground is on the lake, which offers water skiing as well as fishing for bass, bream, and catfish. It is 10 miles from Guntersville State Park.

10 Little Mountain Marina Resort

Location: Lake Guntersville, map 1, grid E7.

Campsites, facilities: There are over 200 RV campsites, all with full hookups. Eight of the sites are pull-through, and about half have some shade. Picnic tables and cooking grills are provided. Cabins are available. Restrooms have hot showers and flush toilets. A coin laundry, tennis court, sauna, spa, swimming pool, clubroom, playground, boat ramp, and dock are provided. Ice is available. The facilities are wheelchair accessible. Pets are permitted.

Reservations, fees: Reservations are accepted, and no deposit is required. Campsites are $20 per night, and cottages are $48–59.

Open: Year-round.

Directions: From US 431 in Guntersville, take Highway 227 south 15 miles. When the highway splits, continue straight into South Sauty Road another two miles, and turn left on Murphy Hill Road. The campground will be on the left.

Contact: Little Mountain Marina Resort, 1001 Murphy Hill Rd., Langston, AL 35755; 256/582-8211, or 256/582-1280.

Trip notes: Lake Guntersville offers water skiing, and fishing for bass, bream, and catfish year-round. The state park is five miles from the campground, and contains hiking trails.

11 Buck's Pocket State Park

Location: Grove Oak, map 1, grid E8.

Campsites, facilities: There are 25 tent sites, 15 with water and electric hookups, and 32 RV sites, six with full hookups. Four of the RV sites are pull-through sites. Picnic tables, fire rings, and cooking grills are provided. The primitive camping area has approximately 100 sites. Group sites are available. Restrooms have hot showers and flush toilets. A coin laundry, boat ramp, sanitary disposal station, and playground are provided. Ice is available at the campground. The buildings are wheelchair accessible. Leashed pets are permitted.

Reservations, fees: Reservations are accepted at 800/ALA-PARK (800/252-7275). No deposit is required. Fees are $7.50 for primitive campsites, $12 for sites with water and electric hookups, and $13 for sites with full hookups.

Open: Year-round.

Directions: From Guntersville, go north on Highway 227 about 14 miles, then turn right at the sign onto Couty Road 174. The campground is two miles from Highway 227.

Contact: Buck's Pocket State Park, 393 County Road 174, Grove Oak, AL 35975; 256/659-2000.

Trip notes: Fishing at the lake is available year-round. There are six trails totaling 30 miles in length. Located in the bottom of a canyon, the campground is shaded and peaceful, with wildflowers blooming in the spring, and colorful trees in the fall. Wildlife in the area includes deer and wild turkeys.

12 Lake Guntersville State Park

Location: Lake Guntersville, map 1, grid E7.

Campsites, facilities: There are 364 campsites suitable for tents or RVs, all with water and electric hookups. Full hookups are available at 150 sites. There are also primitive camping sites, a lodge, and 35 cabins. A sanitary disposal station is provided. Restrooms have hot showers and flush toilets. Tennis courts, boat launch, dock, playground, and coin laundry are provided. The campground store sells supplies and some groceries. The cabins are wheelchair accessible. Leashed pets are permitted in the campgrounds, but not in the cabins.

Reservations, fees: Reservations are accepted at 800/ALA-PARK (800/252-7275). The deposit of one night's fee is non-refundable, but you can move the date of your reservation twice. Campsites cost $14 per night. The fee for the cabins is $110 per night.

Open: Year-round.

Directions: From Guntersville, take Highway 227 about six miles north to the park.

Contact: Lake Guntersville State Park, 7966 Alabama Highway 227, Guntersville, AL 35976; 256/571-5455.

Trip notes: This is one of Alabama's "resort" state parks, and includes a hotel, convention center, restaurants, pro shop, nature center, and art gallery in addition to the campground and cottages. There is an 18-hole golf course, fishing and water skiing are available in the lake, and there are 31 miles of marked trails through the park. The swimming area has a sand beach. Besides deer and other wildlife, you may see bald eagles here in the winter. See also the listing for the Town Creek Fishing Center, which is a first-come, first-served campground within the state park.

13 Town Creek Fishing Center

Location: Lake Guntersville, map 1, grid E7.

Campsites, facilities: This campground has 42 sites suitable for tents or campers, all with water and electric hookups. Most sites have shade, and pull-through sites are available. There is also a section for primitive tent camping. Picnic tables and cooking grills are available in the developed sites. The main restrooms have hot showers and flush toilets. The restrooms in the outside primitive area do not have showers. Groceries, ice, marine gas, and bait are available. A sanitary disposal station, boat ramp, and dock are provided. Leashed pets are permitted.

Reservations, fees: Town Creek Fishing Center is part of Guntersville State Park, but you cannot reserve these sites. They are all first-come, first-served. Sites with water and electric hookups are $13, and primitive sites are $7.

Open: The campground is open from March through October.

Directions: From Guntersville, take US 431 north eight miles to Highway 227. After the second bridge (less than a mile), the campground will be on the right.

Contact: Town Creek Fishing Center, 7966 Alabama Highway 227, Guntersville, AL 35976; 256/582-8358.

Trip notes: Lake Guntersville offers excellent crappie fishing, and also contains bass, bream, and catfish. Canoes and johnboats are available for rent, and water skiing is permitted.

14 Riverview Campground

Location: Lake Guntersville, map 1, grid F7.

Campsites, facilities: The campground has 187 campsites suitable for tents or RVs, all with water and electric hookups. Shade is available. Picnic tables are provided at each site. Restrooms have hot showers and flush toilets. A coin laundry, boat ramp, dock, playground, and sanitary disposal station are provided. Ice and LP gas are available. The facilities are wheelchair accessible. Leashed pets are permitted.

Reservations, fees: Reservations are accepted, and no deposit is required. Campsites cost $15 per night.

Open: The campground is open from March through October.

Directions: From Guntersville, go east on Highway 69 three miles past US 431, and turn right on Cha-La-Kee Road.

Contact: Riverview Campground, 1345 Cha-La-Kee Rd., Guntersville, AL 35976; 256/582-3014.

Trip notes: Fishing for bass and crappie is available both at Lake Guntersville and the Tennessee River. Water skiing is permitted in the lake. There is a sand beach in the swimming area. This is a family-oriented campground. It is 12 miles from the outlet shopping in Boaz.

15 Barclay RV Parking

Location: Boaz, map 1, grid G7.

Campsites, facilities: There are 22 RV sites, all with full hookups. Six are pull-through sites. Both 30- and 50-amp hookups are available. There is some shade, and group sites are available. Picnic tables and cooking grills are provided. No restrooms are provided. Cable TV hookups are available. A grocery store is two blocks away. Pets are permitted.

Reservations, fees: Reservations are accepted, and no deposit is required. The 50-amp, pull-through sites are $16.25 per night. The 30-amp sites are $14.

Open: Year-round.

Directions: From US 431 in Boaz, go west 0.7 miles on Billy Dyar Boulevard. The campground will be on the left in the curve.

Contact: Barclay RV Parking, 104 South Main, Boaz, AL 35957; 256/593-8769.

Trip notes: People come to Boaz for the outlet shopping, and the campground is very near four major outlet centers. It is 12 miles from Lake Guntersville.

16 Noccalula Falls Campground

Location: Gadsden, map 1, grid H8.

Campsites, Facilities: The campground has 30 tent sites, all with some shade and all with electric and water hookups. In a separate section, there are 130 RV sites, 28 of which have full hookups. Six of these are pull-through sites, and all have some shade. Primitive sites are reserved for organized groups such as scout troops. Picnic tables, fire rings, and cooking grills are provided. Cable TV hookups are available. Restrooms have showers and flush toilets. A sanitary disposal station, coin laundry, pool, clubroom, and playground are provided. The campground store sells LP gas, ice, groceries, firewood, and some supplies. Leashed pets are permitted. Please pick up after your pet.

Reservations, fees: Reservations are not accepted. Tent sites are $16 per night, RV sites are $22.

Open: Year-round.

Directions: From Interstate 59, take exit 188 to Highway 211 south. The campground will be on your right.

Contact: Noccalula Falls Campground, 1600 Noccalula Rd., Gadsden, AL 35904; 256/543-7412.

Trip notes: Besides the natural beauty of the 90-foot waterfall, this city park includes a one-mile canyon and nature trail, along with a botanical gardens, pioneer village, passenger train, animal park, museums, and miniature golf. Fishing for bass, crappie, and catfish is available nearby at Lake Gadsden. There are wonderful antique shops within walking distance of the park.

17 Ashley's Lake

Location: Gadsden, map 1, grid H8.

Campsites, facilities: There are six tent sites, four with water and electric hookups. All have some shade. Of the 28 RV sites, 22 have full hookups, and most have some shade. Picnic tables are provided. Group sites and two cabins are available. RV storage is available. Restrooms have hot showers and flush toilets. A coin laundry and cable TV hookups are available. Pets are permitted if kept leashed. Pets must be kept inside your camper or tent at night.

Reservations, fees: Reservations are accepted, and no deposit is required. The fee is $16 per night, $85 per week, or $225 per month.

Open: Year-round.

Directions: From Gadsden, take US 411. The campground is four miles north of the intersection of US 411 and US 431, at the Coosa River bridge.

Contact: Ashley's Lake, 3509 US 411 North, Gadsden, AL 35901; 334/388-2720.

Trip notes: All campsites are on the 18-acre private lake, stocked with bass, crappie, bluegill, and catfish. Hiking is available nearby. Kayaking, rafting, and paddleboats are available on the Coosa River. The campground is one mile outside of Gadsden, and close to a mall, movie theaters, antique shops, and restaurants. It is near Noccalula Falls, the Talladega International Speedway, and the Little River Canyon.

18 Thunder Canyon Campground

Location: Sand Mountain, map 2, grid B3.

Campsites, facilities: The campground has 11 primitive tent sites. Water is available nearby. There are also 36 RV sites. Twenty of the sites have full hookups, and the rest have water and electric only. Picnic tables are available at the RV sites. The campground also offers three cottages and two bunkhouses. Restrooms have hot showers and flush toilets. A coin laundry, swimming pool, playground, recreation hall, and sanitary disposal station are provided. RV storage is available. Pets are permitted in the campground only, and must be leashed at all times.

Reservations, fees: Reservations are accepted. Deposits are not required. Primitive sites are $5, sites with water and electric hookups are $12, and sites with full hookups are $16 per night. The cottages and bunkhouses are $28–64 per night.

Open: The campground is open from May through October.

Directions: Heading south from Chattanooga on Interstate 59, take exit 231/Highway 117 and turn north. Stay on Highway 117 through Ider, then turn right onto Wilson Road/County Road 141. Turn left at the sign into the campground, less than a mile from Highway 117.

Contact: Thunder Canyon Campground, 583 Thunder Canyon Dr., Ider, AL 35981; 256/632-2103.

Trip notes: The campground is located between two mountain streams, both offering bass, catfish, and bream. There are three hiking trails, the longest three miles in length. The campground is 15 miles from DeSoto Falls, and 30 miles from the Little River Canyon.

19 Sequoyah Caverns and Campground

Location: Valley Head, map 2, grid C4.

Campsites, facilities: There are 55 tent sites at this campground, all with water and electric hookups. Most have shade. There are also 50 RV sites in a separate section, about 30 of which are pull-through sites. Four sites have full hookups, and the rest have water and electric only. Group sites are available. Picnic tables are provided, and some sites have fire rings and cooking grills. Restrooms have hot showers and flush toilets. A coin laundry, sanitary disposal station, swimming pool, and playground are provided. Groceries, ice, and firewood are available. The buildings are wheelchair accessible. Leashed pets are permitted. There is a $1 fee per pet, and you must clean up after your pet.

Reservations, fees: Reservations are accepted at 800/843-5098. The deposit is not refundable. The rate for tent sites is $14. RV sites range from $15–16, depending on hookups.

Open: Year-round.

Directions: The campground is 35 miles south of Chattanooga at exit 239/Sulphur Springs off Interstate 59. Go south on Highway 11, about eight miles to the campground.

Contact: Sequoyah Caverns and Campground, 1306 County Road 731, Valley Head, AL 35989; 256/635-0024; website: www.alabamatravel.org/north/scc.html.

Trip notes: The interesting things at this campground are the caverns and waterfalls. The campground is located 18 miles north of DeSoto State Park and the Little River Canyon, which offer hiking and fishing. There is a catch-and-release fishing pond in the park, plus hiking trails. There are a variety of animals at the campground, including buffalos, emus, white fallow deer, sheep, and goats.

20 DeSoto State Park

Location: Fort Payne, map 2, grid D4.

Campsites, facilities: Of the 78 campsites at this state park, 20 have full hookups and are reserved for RVs. Ten of these are pull-through. The remaining 58 campsites are for either tents or RVs, and have water and electric hookups. All campsites have shade. Picnic tables, fire rings, and cooking grills are provided. An additional primitive camping area can accommodate approximately 150 campsites. Restrooms have hot showers and flush toilets. Cabins are available. A coin laundry, tennis courts, boat ramp, dock, swimming pool, and playground are provided. Firewood, ice, groceries, supplies, and gifts are available. Other supplies are less than a mile away. RV storage is available. A sanitary disposal station is provided. Leashed pets are permitted.

Reservations, fees: Resrvations are accepted at 800/ALA-PARK (800/760-4089). The deposit of one night's fee is refundable if cancellation is at least 72 hours in advance. Sites with full hookups are $14 per night, and sites with water and electric hookups are $12. Primitive campsites are $7.50 per night.

Open: Year-round.

Directions: From Interstate 59, take exit 218/Fort Payne/Highway 35 and turn southeast. Continue on Highway 35 through Fort Payne to Lookout Mountain, about 15 miles from the interstate. At the top of the mountain, turn left onto County Road 89. The park and campground are about five miles from the highway.

Contact: DeSoto State Park, 13883 County Road 89, Fort Payne, AL 35967; 256/845-4089; email: desotostpk@mindspring.com; website: www.mentone.com/desoto.

Trip notes: There are eight miles of hiking trails in the park, where over 900 species of wildflowers bloom in the spring and summer. The peak is from April to June. The campground is 10 miles from the Little River Canyon National Preserve. Fishing, kayaking, and rafting are available on the Little River, whose entire length is at the top of the mountain. The area near 104-foot DeSoto Falls is dammed, creating an additional lake for swimming, fishing, and boating. Other points of interest in the area include cave tours of Sequoyah Caverns, and the Alabama Fan Club in Fort Payne, a museum dedicated to the country music group.

21 Knotty Pine Resort

Location: Fort Payne, map 2, grid D4.

Campsites, Facilities: The campground has a large wooded area for primitive tent camp-ing, and eight fully furnished cabins for rent. Restrooms have hot showers and flush toilets. Supplies, groceries, and a coin laundry are available within 1.5 miles.

Reservations, fees: Reservations are accepted at 256/845-5293. The deposit of one night's fee is refundable with 72 hours notice. Campsites are $8 per night per person. The cabins rent for $50-90 per night. If you stay for a week, the seventh night is free.

Open: Year-round.

Directions: From Gadsden, take Interstate 59 north to exit 218/Fort Payne/DeSoto State Park, and turn right. Following the signs to the state park, after about 15 miles turn left onto County Road 89. Drive into the state park, and turn left at the Country Store. Travel another 1.5 miles to the campground.

Contact: Knotty Pine Resort, 1492 County Road 618, Fort Payne, AL 35967; 256/845-5293.

Trip notes: Though the campground doesn't have any amenities, it is surrounded by DeSoto State Park, which offers hiking, boating, and fishing, all within seven miles. Since the management feeds the wildlife, you will probably see deer, turkeys, skunks, rabbits, and raccoons during your stay. There is a 1000-foot ski slope within 10 miles which offers natural and manmade snow in the winter.

22 Adams Outdoors

Location: Lookout Mountain, map 2, grid F4.

Campsites, Facilities: There are five tent sites and one RV site at this small campground. All sites have water and electric hookups and shade. There are also four log cabins and seven huts. Picnic tables and fire rings are provided. Restrooms have hot showers and flush toilets. A swimming pool and softball field are provided. The restrooms and some of the cabins are wheelchair accessible. Pets are permitted.

Reservations, fees: Reservations are accepted. The deposit is refundable with a two-week notice of cancellation. The fee for camping is $12. Cabins are $35–90 per night, and huts are $25.

Open: The campground is open from mid-March through December.

Directions: From Interstate 59, take the Fort Payne/Highway 35 exit south. At the top of Lookout Mountain, turn left onto County Road 89. After 4.5 miles, turn right onto Gray Road. After a half mile, turn right onto Mitchell Road.

Contact: Adams Outdoors, 6102 Mitchell Rd. NE, Fort Payne, AL 35967; 256/845-2988.

Trip notes: Fishing is available in a small pond, the Little River, and Lake Weiss. There are short hiking trails at the campground that lead to two waterfalls, and 50 miles of hiking/horseback riding trails in the Little River Canyon Nature Preserve nearby. There are also eight miles of trails at adjacent DeSoto State Park. You can rent kayaks or rafts at the campground for trips down class one rapids, and up to class four rapids are available with your own equipment. The rapids are best in early spring. The manager of the campground teaches rappelling near DeSoto Falls. Other activities in the area include cave tours of Sequoyah Caverns, and the Alabama Fan Club in Fort Payne, a museum dedicated to the country music group.

23 Big Oak Campground

Location: Lake Weiss, map 2, grid F3.

Campsites, facilities: There are 45 campsites suitable for tents or RVs. All have water and electric hookups, and some have shade. Picnic tables are provided. Restrooms have hot showers and flush toilets. A sanitary disposal station, coin laundry, boat ramp, and two piers are provided. Groceries, ice, LP gas, and bait are available at the campground. Leashed pets are permitted.

Reservations, fees: Reservations are not accepted. Tent sites are $10 per night, and camper sites are $12.

Open: Year-round.

Directions: From Rome, Georgia, take Georgia 20 west to Alabama, where it becomes Alabama Highway 9. About seven miles into Alabama, turn right onto Highway 35 left onto Highway 273, and follow the signs.

Contact: Big Oak Campground, 830 County Road 732, Cedar Bluff, AL 35959; 256/526-8723.

Trip notes: The lake offers water skiing, fishing and swimming. The campground is five miles from the Little River Canyon and Little River Falls area, which have hiking trails.

24 Driftwood Family Campground

Location: Lake Weiss, map 2, grid G3.

Campsites, facilities: There are 16 tent sites with water and electric hookups, most with some shade. There are 121 RV sites with full hookups. Pull-through sites are available. Picnic tables are provided. Restrooms have hot showers and flush toilets. A boat ramp, nine docks, sports field, and playground are provided. Ice, LP gas, bait, supplies, and groceries are available at the campground. Leashed pets are permitted.

Reservations, fees: Reservations are accepted. The deposit is not refundable, but they will give credit for another visit. Sites are $12.50–15, depending on air-conditioning use.

Open: Year-round.

Directions: From Rome, Georgia, take US 411 west towards Gadsden, Alabama. At Leesburg (before Gadsden), turn right on Highway 68/273. Turn right onto County Road 48, then left onto County Road 600. The campground is 12 miles from Leesburg.

Contact: Driftwood Family Campground, 500 County Road 600, Cedar Bluff, AL 35959; 256/526-8069.

Trip notes: The campground is surrounded on three side by the lake, which offers fishing, a beach in the swimming area, and boating. Approximately half of the sites are used by long-term campers.

25 J.R.'s Marina, Inc.

Location: Lake Weiss, map 2, grid G3.

Campsites, facilities: There are 10 tent sites with water and electric hookups, and 10 RV sites with full hookups. Some sites have picnic tables. Rental mobile homes and motel rooms are also available. Restrooms have hot showers and flush toilets. Groceries, ice, LP gas, marine gas, and bait are available. Three boat ramps and six docks are provided. A boat shop with mechanic and a small café are on-site. The facilities are wheelchair accessible. Pets are permitted.

Reservations, fees: Reservations are not accepted. Tent sites are $10, RV sites are $15, motel rooms are $40–50, and mobile homes are $50 per night.

Open: Year-round.

Directions: From Rome, Georgia, take Georgia 20 west to Alabama, where it becomes Alabama Highway 9. At Cedar Bluff, turn north onto Highway 68. After two miles, turn left on County Road 44 and follow the signs.

Contact: J. R.'s Marina, Inc., P.O. Box 69,

Cedar Bluff, AL 35959; 256/779-6461.

Trip notes: Lake Weiss is called the "Crappie Capital of the World," but it also contains bass, bream, catfish, and stripers. Water skiing is permitted in the lake. Hiking is available at the Little River Canyon National Preserve, about 15 miles from the campground. There is a swimming area near one of the docks.

26 Riverside Motel and RV Park

Location: Lake Weiss, map 2, grid G4.

Campsites, facilities: There are 30 tent sites at this campground. Half the sites are primitive, and half have water and electric hookups. There are also 30 RV sites. Six of the sites have full hookups, and the rest have water and electric. All sites have cable TV hookups. Some sites are on the water. Picnic tables are provided for the sites with hookups. There are also cabins and motel rooms available. RV storage is available. Restrooms have hot showers and flush toilets. A sanitary disposal station, two boat ramps, six docks, and a swimming pool are provided. Ice, LP gas, groceries, and bait are available at the campground. Some buildings are wheelchair accessible. Leashed pets are permitted if you clean up after your pet. There is a $25 deposit required per pet if you are staying in the motel.

Reservations, fees: Reservations are accepted at 800/292-9324. The deposit is refundable if cancellation is made more than 48 hours in advance of your scheduled arrival date. Tent sites are $8–14 per night, depending on hookups. Lakeside RV sites are $20; other sites are $16. The cabins are $55–65 per night, and the motel rooms are $35–55.

Open: Year-round.

Directions: From Rome, Georgia, take Georgia 20 west to Alabama, where it becomes Alabama Highway 9. Turn left onto County Road 131 two miles east of Cedar Bluff. The campground will be on the right at the lake, about one mile from Highway 9.

Contact: Riverside Motel and RV Park, 1210 County Road 131, Cedar Bluff, AL 35959; 256/779-6117.

Trip notes: Fishing, water skiing, kayaking, and canoeing are available in the lake. The historic Cornwall Furnace, part of a Confederate iron works operational during the Civil War, is three miles from the campground. It is said to be the best preserved Civil War-era iron works in the country,

27 Pine Cone Marina and Campground

Location: Lake Weiss, map 2, grid G2.

Campsites, facilities: There are nine primitive tent sites, five on the water. There are also 52 RV sites. Nine of the sites have full hookups, and the rest have water and electric. Three are pull-through sites. Picnic tables and fire rings are provided. There are three cabins. RV storage is available, and a sanitary disposal station is provided. Restrooms have hot showers and flush toilets. A boat ramp, dock, and sports fields are provided. Ice, groceries, bait, and some supplies are available at the campground. The bathrooms are wheelchair accessible. Leashed pets are permitted.

Reservations, fees: Reservations are accepted. The deposit is refundable with notice. The fee for tent sites is $13 per night, RV sites are $15.

Open: The campground is open from March through November.

Directions: The campground is located between Gadsden and Leesburg, at the junction of US 411 and County Road 106/Pine Cone Street.

Contact: Pine Cone Marina and Campground, 470 Pine Cone St., Leesburg, AL 35983; 256/526-8611.

Trip notes: Fishing is available at the lake for crappie, bream, bass, and catfish. Hiking is available within 2.5 miles at Little Rock City, and at Shinbone Ridge, 35 miles away. The campground director teaches rappelling and rock climbing. There is a sand beach in the swimming area of the lake. Lake Weiss covers an area of 33,000 acres, and has 470 miles of shoreline. Water skiing is permitted in the lake.

28 Bailey's Campground

Location: Lake Weiss, map 2, grid G3.

Campsites, facilities: There are 22 sites suitable for tents or campers, all with water and electric hookups. Shade is available. Picnic tables are provided. Restrooms have hot showers and flush toilets. A sanitary disposal station, boat ramp, and dock are provided. Ice, groceries, LP gas, and bait are available at the campground. The buildings are wheelchair accessible. Pets are permitted.

Reservations, fees: Reservations are not accepted. Campsites cost $15 per night.

Open: Year-round.

Directions: In Centre, take the US 411 Bypass off US 411 for 0.25 miles, then turn left on County Road 22. The campground is two miles from the Bypass.

Contact: Bailey's Campground, 4645 County Road 22, Centre, AL 35960; 256/927-5227.

Trip notes: The campground is located on 38,000-acre Lake Weiss, which offers fishing, swimming, and water-skiing.

29 Bay Springs Marina and Restaurant

Location: Lake Weiss, map 2, grid G3.

Campsites, facilities: There are six tent sites and six RV sites. All sites have water and electric hookups and shade. Some sites have picnic tables. Mobile homes are also available for rent. Restrooms have hot showers and flush toilets. A sanitary disposal station, boat ramp, and dock are provided. There is a restaurant on the property, and marine gas is available. The buildings are wheelchair accessible. Pets are permitted in the campground but not in the mobile homes.

Reservations, fees: Reservations are accepted. The deposit is refundable with 24 hours notice on cancellations. All campsites cost $10 per night, and the mobile homes are $50–65.

Open: Year-round.

Directions: From Rome, Georgia, take US 411 southwest into Alabama and through Centre. Turn right onto County Road 379 at the sign for the campground.

Contact: Bay Springs Marina and Restaurant, 145 County Road 379, Centre, AL 35960; 256/927-8322.

Trip notes: Lake Weiss bills itself as the "Crappie Capital of the World," and the fishing is particularly good in the spring and fall. Besides crappie, you might catch bass, catfish, and bream. Water skiing is permitted in the lake. Hiking and rock climbing are available about 30 miles away at Little Rock City.

30 Pruett's Fish Camp and Cabins

Location: Lake Weiss, map 2, grid G4.

Campsites, facilities: There are 10 RV sites, half with full hookups and half with water and electric only. Some shade is available. Some sites have picnic tables. There are also 23 cabins and five motel rooms. Restrooms have hot showers and flush toilets. A sanitary disposal station is provided. Groceries and restaurants are next door.

Reservations, fees: Reservations are accepted at 800/368-6238. The deposit is refundable if the reservation is cancelled 30 days in advance. The rate for camping is $20 per night. Cabins are $75–150 per night, and the motel rooms are $35.

Open: Year-round.

Directions: From Gadsden, take Interstate 759 to US 411 and turn north. After 30 miles, turn left on the Chestnut bypass. After 3.5 miles, turn left on County 22. The campground is another 3.5 miles from the bypass, and will be on the right after you cross the lake.

Contact: Pruett's Fish Camp and Cabins, 5360 County Road 22, Centre, AL 35960; 256/475-3950.

Trip notes: Fishing, water skiing, and swimming are available in the lake.

31 Pruett's Campground

Location: Lake Weiss, map 2, grid G4.

Campsites, Facilities: There are 52 RV sites with full hookups, some with shade. A boat ramp and pier are provided. Pets are permitted, but no large dogs.

Reservations, fees: Reservations are not accepted. The fee is $15 per night.

Open: Year-round.

Directions: From Gadsden, take Interstate 759 to US 411 and turn north. After 30 miles, turn left on the Chestnut bypass. After 3.5 miles, turn left on County 22. Turn left onto County Road 30, 3.5 miles from Centre.

Contact: Pruett's Campground, 404 County Road 30, Centre, AL 35960; 256/475-3487.

Trip notes: Most of the campers here are retired and are renting for a month or longer. Fishing and water-skiing are popular activities in the lake.

32 Cowan Creek Grocery and Campground

Location: Lake Weiss, map 2, grid G4.

Campsites, facilities: There are four tent sites with water and electric hookups. Picnic tables are available. Restrooms have flush toilets, and showers are available in a separate building. A boat ramp and 600 foot fishing pier are provided. Groceries and ice are available at the store. The store and showers are wheelchair accessible. Pets are permitted.

Reservations, fees: Reservations are not accepted. Campsites are $10 per night.

Open: Year-round.

Directions: From Gadsden, take Interstate 759 to US 411 and turn north. After 30 miles, turn left on the Chestnut bypass. After 3.5 miles, turn left on County 22. The campground is on the lake, about 3.5 miles from the bypass.

Contact: Cowan Creek Grocery and Campground, 5330 County Road 22, Centre, AL 35960; 256/475-3670.

Trip notes: Fishing is available in the lake for crappie, bass, catfish, and bream. There is

a swimming area near the boat ramp. Water skiing is permitted in the lake.

33 John's Grocery and Campground

Location: Lake Weiss, map 2, grid G4.

Campsites, facilities: There are five tent sites with water and electric hookups, and 45 RV sites. Twenty of the sites have full hookups, and the rest have water and electric only. Pull-through sites are available. Some sites have shade. Picnic tables and cooking grills are provided. RV storage is available. A sanitary disposal station, coin laundry, boat ramp, dock, playground, and clubroom are provided. Groceries, video rentals, supplies, ice, LP gas, bait, and marine gas are available. The bathhouse is wheelchair accessible. Leashed pets are permitted.

Reservations, fees: Reservations are accepted. The deposit is refundable if the cancellation is made at least two days in advance of your scheduled arrival. Lakeside sites are $25 per night, and sites off-water are $20.

Open: Year-round.

Directions: From Gadsden, take Interstate 759 to US 411 and turn north. Five miles east of Centre, turn left on County Road 31. The campground is at the intersection of County Roads 16, 22, and 31, two miles from US 411.

Contact: John's Grocery and Campground, 6480 County Road 22, Centre, AL 35960; 256/475-3234.

Trip notes: The campground is located on Lake Weiss, known for crappie, bass, catfish, and bream. There is a swimming area at the campground. Water skiing is permitted in the lake. The campground is 15 minutes from Cave Springs, which has antique and gift shopping, and is 40 minutes from the outlet malls of Boaz.

34 Horse Pens 40

Location: Chandler Mountain, map 3, grid A7.

Campsites, facilities: There are about 150 campsites suitable for tents or RVs, all with water and electric hookups. Picnic tables are available. There are also primitive sites available. A dump station is provided. Restrooms have hot showers and flush toilets. Groceries and some supplies are available, and there is a restaurant on-site. A playground is provided. Some of the restrooms are wheelchair accessible. Leashed pets are permitted.

Reservations, fees: Reservations are not required. The fee for primitive sites is $10, and $15 for sites with water and electricity.

Open: Year-round.

Directions: From Birmingham, take Interstate 59 north to exit 174 (Steele), turn left, and follow the signs.

Contact: Horse Pens 40, 1211 28 St. South, Birmingham, 35205; 800/421-8564.

Trip notes: The two fishing ponds on the property are stocked with catfish, bass, and bream. Hiking and mountain biking are permitted throughout the 120-acre property, both on developed trails and old roads. The campground's name refers to a 40-acre area on the property where Native Americans used to pen their horses.

35 Rickwood Caverns State Park

Location: Warrior, map 3, grid B2.

Campsites, Facilities: There are eight tent sites at this campground. Four sites have water hookups, and four have water and electric. There are also nine RV sites with water and electric hookups. Picnic tables are provided. Restrooms have hot showers and flush toilets. Snacks and gifts are available at the campground. A sanitary disposal station, swimming pool, and playground are provided. Leashed pets are permitted.

Reservations, fees: Reservations are accepted at 800/ALA-PARK (800/252-7275). The deposit of one night's fee is non-refundable, but you can move the date of your reservation twice. You can also call the campground directly at the number below for reservations. Site fees are $14 per night.

Open: The campground is open year-round, but the caverns are open only from March through October.

Directions: From Birmingham, take I-65 north to exit 284, Hayden Corner, and turn left onto Highway 160. Follow the highway for four miles and turn at the sign into the park and campground.

Contact: Rickwood Caverns State Park, 370 Rickwood Park Rd., Warrior, AL 35180; 205/647-9692.

Trip notes: The caverns at this park extend for over a mile and descend as far as 175 feet underground. At the end, there is a 60-foot deep lake with transparent, blind fishes and amphibians. Weekend tours of the caverns are offered in the spring and fall, but are offered daily throughout the summer. There are two hiking trails that total about two miles. Children can ride the miniature train that runs about a half mile around the campground and park.

36 Willow Point Marina and Campground

Location: Henry Neely Lake, map 3, grid B8.

Campsites, facilities: There are 50 tent sites and 70 RV sites at this campground. All sites have water and electric hookups, nearly all are waterfront sites, and some have shade. One is a pull-through site. Picnic tables and fire rings are available. Some sites have patios. Restrooms have hot showers and flush toilets. Firewood, ice, LP gas, and groceries are available at the campground store, and the marina sells marine gas. A dock, two boat ramps, sanitary disposal station, and sports field are provided. The buildings are wheelchair accesible. Pets are permitted, but the campground does not permit certain breeds of dogs, including chows, pit bulls, German shepherds, Dobermans, and Rottweilers.

Reservations, fees: Reservations are accepted at 800/566-9906. The deposit of the first night's fee is refundable with advance notice of cancellation. The normal rate is $20 per night. During holidays or when races are taking place at the Talladega International Speedway, the site fees increase to $30 per night with a two-night minimum stay.

Open: Year-round.

Directions: The campground is located on Highway 77, which is a 30-mile connector between Interstates 59 and 20. From Interstate 20, take the exit 168/Talladega/Lincoln to Highway 77 north. From Interstate 59, take the exit 181/Attalla/Rainbow City to Highway 77 south.

Contact: Willow Point Marina and Campground, 138 Willow Point Dr., Ohatchee, AL 36271; 256/892-2717.

Trip notes: The campground is located on the Henry Neely Lake, and 60 of the sites are waterfront. Fishing for bass, bream, and crappie is available in the lake, as well as kayaking and canoeing. There is a sand beach in the swimming area. The campground is across the road from a horse ranch that provides rental horses and boarding. It is 18 miles from the Talladega International Speedway.

37 Safe Harbor Campground

Location: Riverside, map 3, grid D7.

Campsites, Facilities: There are 32 RV sites in this campground, all pull-through sites. Twenty-three of the sites have full hookups. Some picnic tables are available. RV storage, cable TV hookups, and a sanitary disposal station are available. A boat dock and ramp are provided. Leashed pets are permitted.

Reservations, fees: Reservations are accepted. Fees are $12–15 per night, $70 per week, or $225 per month.

Open: Year-round.

Directions: The campground is one-half mile east of Interstate 20 off exit 162.

Contact: Safe Harbor Campground, P.O. Box 324, Riverside, AL 35135; 205/338-2591.

Trip notes: Fishing is available for bass, crappie, catfish, and bream at Logan Martin Lake. Hiking is available at nearby Cheaha Mountain. The campground is five miles from the Talladega International Speedway.

38 Dogwood RV Park

Location: Lincoln, map 3, grid D8.

Campsites, facilities: There are 140 campsites suitable for tents or RVs, but, as the name suggests, this is primarily an RV park. Most of the sites have full hookups, and the rest have water and electric only. Most campsites have picnic tables, and fire rings are available. Most campsites have cable TV hookups. RV storage is available, and a sanitary disposal station is provided. Restrooms have hot showers and flush toilets. A coin laundry, swimming pool, and playground are provided. Ice, LP gas, and some snacks are available at the campground. Pets are permitted, but must be kept leashed and inside your camper.

Reservations, fees: Reservations are accepted, and no deposit is required. Site fees are $20–35 per night, with the higher rate effective during race weekends.

Open: Year-round.

Directions: From Interstate 20, take exit 168/Highway 77 and turn north. The campground will be on the right, less than a mile from the interstate.

Contact: Dogwood RV Park, 76626 Alabama Highway 77, Lincoln, AL 35096; 205/763-7454.

Trip notes: The campground is two miles from the Talladega International Speedway, eight miles from the fishing at Logan Martin Lake, and 20 miles from the hiking trails of Cheaha State Park.

39 Lakeside Landing RV Park and Marina

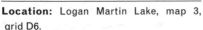

Location: Logan Martin Lake, map 3, grid D6.

Campsites, facilities: There are 200 campsites, all with full hookups. Although Lakeside is primarily an RV campground, tent campers are welcome here. Nearly all the sites are pull-through, and half have shade. Picnic tables are provided. RV storage and group sites are available. Restrooms have

hot showers and flush toilets. Patios and cable TV hookups are available. A coin laundry, boat ramp, dock, sanitary disposal station, and clubroom are provided. Ice, LP gas, and some supplies are available on-site. Leashed pets are permitted.

Reservations, fees: Reservations are accepted. The fee is $18 per night. Good Sam discounts apply.

Open: Year-round.

Directions: From Interstate 20, take Highway 231 south 5.5 miles.

Contact: Lakeside Landing RV Park and Marina, 4600 Martin St. South, P.O. Box 817, Cropwell, AL 35054; 205/525-5701.

Trip notes: The campground is located at Logan Martin Lake, and fishing is available for bass, crappie, catfish, and bream. The campground is convenient to shopping, theaters, and restaurants.

40 Logan Landing Campground

Location: Logan Martin Lake, map 3, grid D6.

Campsites, facilities: There are 145 RV sites, most with full hookups, and the remainder have water and electric only. Picnic tables and cooking grills are provided. Restrooms have hot showers and flush toilets. RV storage is available. A sanitary disposal station, coin laundry, boat ramp, fishing pier, swimming pool, and playground are provided. Pets are permitted.

Reservations, fees: Reservations are only accepted for holidays and race weekends. The deposit is refundable with one week's notice. Rates are $15 for sites with water and electric hookups, and $18 for full hookups.

Open: Year-round.

Directions: From Birmingham, take Interstate 20 east to exit 158. Take US 231 south across the dam. Turn left at the sign for the campground.

Contact: Logan Landing Campground, 1036 Paul Bear Bryant Rd., Alpine, AL 35014; 256/268-0045.

Trip notes: The campground is on a private, 14-acre lake stocked with bass, crappie, and bream. There are several trails on the property, the longest about two miles in length. The swimming area has a sand beach. Paddleboats are available for rent, and pontoon boat tours are also available. The campground is 12 miles from DeSoto Caverns, and 20 miles from the Talladega International Speedway.

CENTRAL ALABAMA

BALD ROCK

CHEAHA STATE PARK

CENTRAL ALABAMA

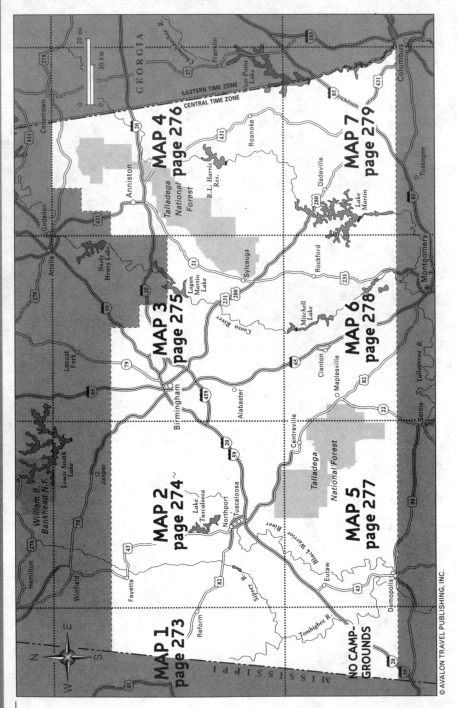

MAP 1
page 273

MAP 2
page 274

MAP 3
page 275

MAP 4
page 276

MAP 5
page 277

MAP 6
page 278

MAP 7
page 279

NO CAMP-
GROUNDS

GEORGIA

MISSISSIPPI

EASTERN TIME ZONE
CENTRAL TIME ZONE

Talladega
National
Forest

R.L. Harris
Res.

Lake
Martin

Roanoke

Dadeville

Sylacauga

Rockford

Clanton

Maplesville

Centreville

Eutaw

Demopolis

Selma

Montgomery

Tuskegee

Columbus

Gadsden

Attalla

Anniston

Neely
Henry Lake

Locust
Fork

Birmingham

Jasper

Lewis Smith
Lake

William B.
Bankhead N.F.

Hamilton

Winfield

Fayette

Reform

Northport

Tuscaloosa

Lake
Tuscaloosa

Alabaster

Logan
Martin
Lake

Mitchell
Lake

Coosa River

Black Warrior River

Sipsey R.

Tombigbee R.

Tallapoosa R.

Talladega
National Forest

Chattahoochee R.

West Point
Lake

Franklin

Cedartown

Roanoke

20 mi

20 km

© AVALON TRAVEL PUBLISHING, INC.

MAP 1

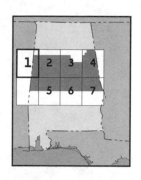

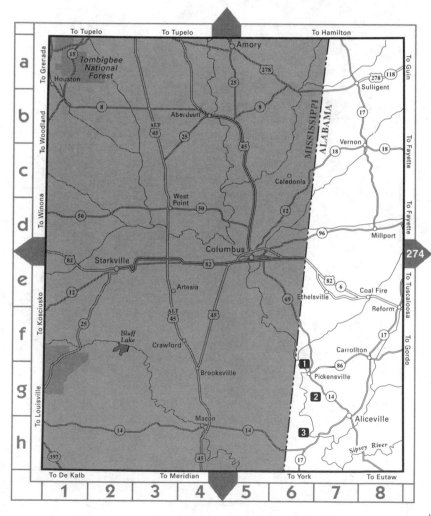

© AVALON TRAVEL PUBLISHING, INC.

MAP 2

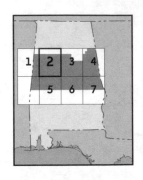

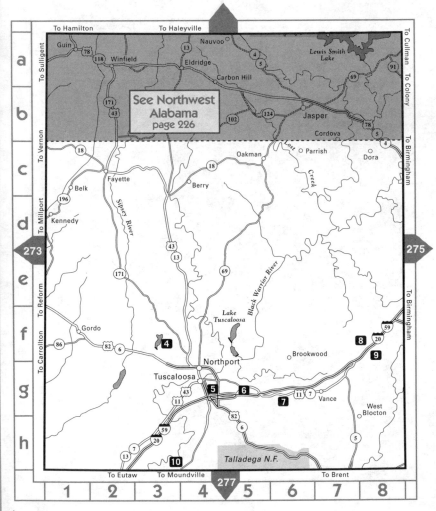

MAP 2

To Hamilton   To Haleyville
To Sulligent

Guin
78
118 Winfield
Nauvoo
13
Eldridge
4
5
Lewis Smith Lake
91
69
Carbon Hill
To Cullman
To Colony

See Northwest Alabama page 226

171
43
102 124
Jasper
Cordova
78
5
To Vernon
18
Oakman
Lost   Parrish
Dora
4
To Birmingham

18
Fayette
Belk
Berry
Creek
196
Kennedy
Sipsey River
43
13

273   **275**

171
69
Black Warrior River
To Reform
To Millport

To Birmingham

Lake Tuscaloosa
Gordo
86 82 6
4
Brookwood
8
59
20
Northport
9
Tuscaloosa
43
5
6
11 7
Vance
7
11
West Blocton
59
82
6
20
7
5
13
10
Talladega N.F.
To Carrollton

To Eutaw   To Moundville

277

To Brent

© AVALON TRAVEL PUBLISHING, INC.

1 2 3 4 5 6 7 8

a b c d e f g h

MAP 3

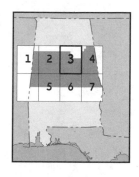

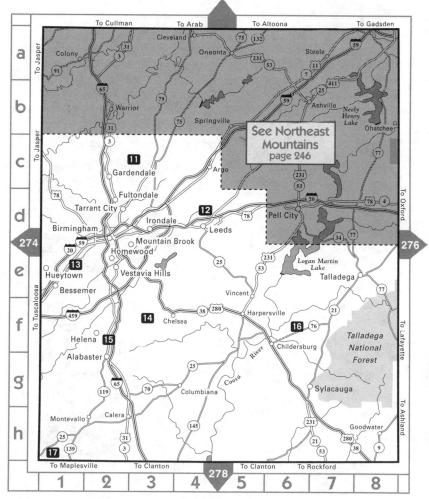

To Cullman — To Arab — To Altoona — To Gadsden

a
To Jasper
Colony
Cleveland
Oneonta
Steele
132
75
31
3
91
231
53
11
7
411
59

b
65
79
Warrior
25
59
Ashville
Neely Henry Lake
Ohatchee
31
75
Springville
See Northeast Mountains page 246

c
To Jasper
3
11
Gardendale
Argo
231
53
77
78

d
Fultondale
Tarrant City
12
20
78
Pell City
4
Irondale
78
Birmingham
Leeds
59
20
Mountain Brook
34
77

e
13
Homewood
25
Logan Martin Lake
Hueytown
Vestavia Hills
231
53
Talladega
Bessemer
Vincent
77

f
459
14
Chelsea
38
280
Harpersville
21
16
76
Talladega National Forest
Helena
15
Childersburg

g
Alabaster
River
65
70
25
Coosa
Columbiana
Sylacauga
119

h
Montevallo
Calera
145
231
Goodwater
25
31
280
9
17
139
3
21
53
38
To Maplesville — To Clanton — To Clanton — To Rockford

To Jasper · To Tuscaloosa · To Lafayette · To Ashland · To Oxford

274 **276** **278**

1 2 3 4 5 6 7 8

© AVALON TRAVEL PUBLISHING, INC.

MAP 4

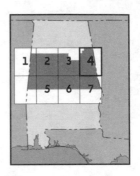

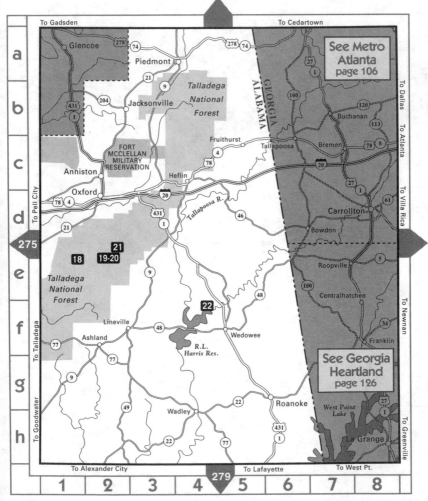

To Gadsden · To Cedartown

See Metro Atlanta page 106

Glencoe · Piedmont · Talladega National Forest

Jacksonville

FORT MCCLELLAN MILITARY RESERVATION

Anniston · Oxford · Heflin

Fruithurst · Tallapoosa · Bremen · Buchanan

Carrollton

Bowdon

Roopville

Centralhatchee

Talladega National Forest

Tallapoosa R.

18 **19-20** **21**

22

Lineville · Ashland · Wedowee

R.L. Harris Res.

See Georgia Heartland page 126

West Point Lake

Wadley · Roanoke · La Grange

Franklin

To Pell City · To Talladega · To Goodwater · To Alexander City · To Lafayette · To West Pt. · To Greenville · To Newnan · To Villa Rica · To Atlanta · To Dallas

GEORGIA ALABAMA

275 · 279

MAP 5

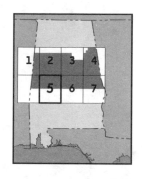

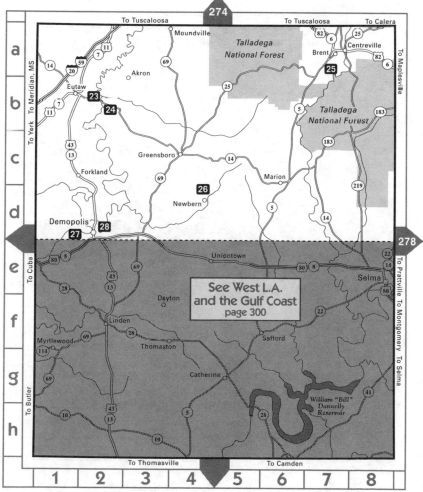

MAP 6

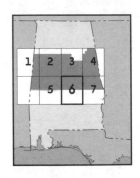

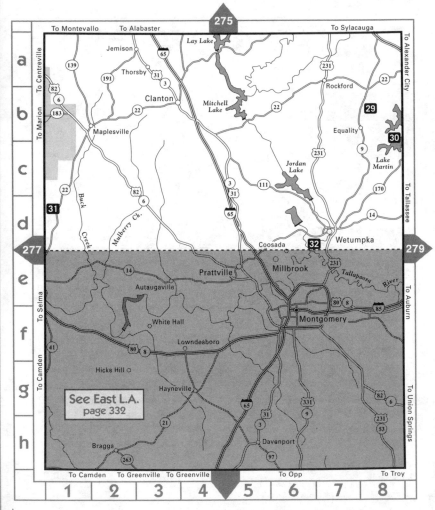

MAP 7

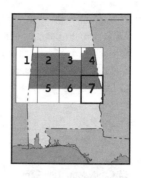

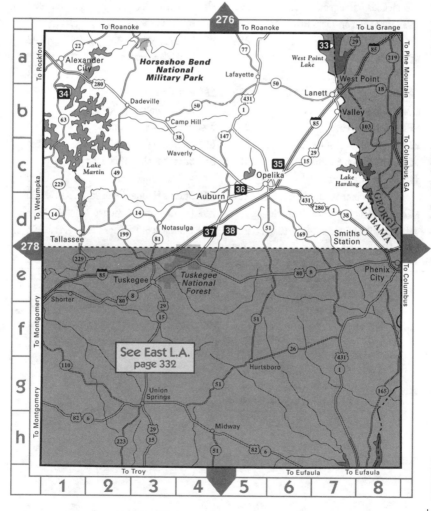

© AVALON TRAVEL PUBLISHING, INC.

CENTRAL ALABAMA

◼ Pickensville Campground

Location: Tenn-Tom Waterway, map 1, grid G6.

Campsites, facilities: The campground has 176 campsites for either tents or RVs, all with water and electric hookups. Picnic tables, fire rings, and cooking grills are provided. Restrooms have hot showers and flush toilets. A sanitary disposal station, coin laundry, boat ramp, and playground are provided. The restrooms are wheelchair accessible. Leashed pets are permitted.

Reservations, fees: Reservations are accepted through the National Recreation Reservation Service (NRRS) at 877/444-6777, website: www.reserveusa.com. The full amount is payable in advance. Campsites are $14 per night.

Open: Year round.

Directions: From Tuscaloosa, take US 82 west to Highway 86 and turn left. The campground is 2.5 miles west of Pickensville on Highway 86.

Contact: Pickensville Campground, US Army Corps of Engineers, 3606 W. Plymouth Rd., Columbus, MS 39701-9504; 662/327-2142.

Trip notes: Fishing is available for bass, walleye, sauger, crappie, and catfish.

◼ Marina Cove Campground

Location: Carrollton, map 1, grid G7.

Campsites, facilities: There are 20 campsites suitable for tents or RVs. All have water and electric hookups. About half the campsites have picnic tables. RV storage is available, and a sanitary disposal station is provided. Restrooms have hot showers and flush toilets. A coin laundry, boat ramp, dock, and ac-

tivity field are provided. Ice, LP gas, marine gas, groceries, and supplies are available at the campground. The buildings are wheelchair accessible. Leashed pets are permitted.

Reservations, fees: Reservations are not accepted. The fee is $12 per night.

Open: Year-round.

Directions: From Pickensville, take Highway 14 south a half mile and turn right on Lock and Dam Road. Follow the signs to the marina and campground.

Contact: Marina Cove Campground, 595 Marina Parkway, Carrollton, AL 35447; 205/373-6701.

Trip notes: The campground is on the Tenn-Tom Waterway. Fishing is available for bass and crappie, and there are several miles of hiking trails. Rafting and canoeing are popular on the river.

◼ Cochrane Campground

Location: Tenn-Tom Waterway, map 1, grid H6.

Campsites, Facilities: There are 60 campsites for either tents or RVs, all with water and electric hookups. Picnic tables, fire rings, and cooking grills are provided. Restrooms have hot showers and flush toilets. A sanitary disposal station, coin laundry, boat ramp, and playground are provided. The restrooms are wheelchair accessible. Leashed pets are permitted.

Reservations, fees: Reservations are accepted through the National Recreation Reservation Service (NRRS) at 877/444-6777, website: www.reserveusa.com. The full amount is payable in advance. Campsites are $14 per night.

Open: Year-round.

Directions: From Tuscaloosa, take Interstates 20/59

west to exit 40/Highway 14, and turn right. At Aliceville, turn left onto Highway 17. The campground is 10 miles south of Aliceville on Highway 17.

Contact: Cochrane Campground, US Army Corps of Engineers, 3606 W. Plymouth Rd., Columbus, MS 39701-9504; 662/327-2142.

Trip notes: Fishing is available for bass, walleye, sauger, crappie, and catfish.

⁴ Lake Lurleen State Park

Location: Tuscaloosa, map 2, grid F3.

Campsites, facilities: There are 64 campsites suitable for tents or RVs, all with water and electric hookups. There are an additional 27 sites with full hookups. Restrooms have hot showers and flush toilets. Supplies are available at the camp store. The restrooms are wheelchair accessible. Leashed pets are permitted.

Reservations, fees: Reservations are accepted at 800/ALA-PARK (800/252-7275). The deposit of one night's fee is non-refundable, but you can move the date of your reservation twice. Campsites are $15.05 per night.

Open: Year-round.

Directions: From Tuscaloosa, go west on US 82 and follow the signs. The campground is about 10 miles west of the city.

Contact: Lake Lurleen State Park, 13226 Lake Lurleen Rd., Coker, AL 35452; 205/339-1558.

Trip notes: Bass, crappie, bream, and catfish are available in the lake. There are four hiking trails through the park which total five miles. Boat and canoe rentals are available. There is a sand beach in the swimming area. A boat ramp is provided.

⁵ South Plaza RV and Mobile Park

Location: Tuscaloosa, map 2, grid G4.

Campsites, Facilities: This campground has 18 RV sites, all with full hookups. RV storage is available. Both 30- and 50-amp services are available. A play area is provided. No motorcycles are permitted. Pets are allowed, but no large dogs.

Reservations, fees: Reservations are not accepted. The fee for a campsite is $20 per night.

Open: Year-round.

Directions: From Birmingham, take Interstate 20/59 to Interstate 359, and turn towards Tuscaloosa. At exit 1, go straight across at the light onto 11th Avenue. The campground is on the left about two blocks from the interstate.

Contact: South Plaza RV and Mobile Park, 3801 11th Ave., Tuscaloosa, AL 35401; 205/759-2691.

Trip notes: Though mainly for monthly renters, the campground is available for travelers when there is a vacancy.

⁶ Geer Brother's Sunset 2 Campground

Location: Tuscaloosa, map 2, grid G5.

Campsites, Facilities: There are 33 RV sites, all with full hookups. Ten are pull-through sites, and eight have shade. RV storage is available. Restrooms have hot showers and flush toilets. Patios, LP gas, cable TV, and firewood are available. Both 30- and 50-amp hookups are available. The facilities are wheelchair accessible. Leashed pets are permitted if you clean up after them.

Reservations, fees: Reservations are accepted. Fees are $20 per night. Weekly fees range from $90 for 30-amp service to $110 for 50-amp service.

Open: Year round.

Directions: From Tuscaloosa, take Interstates 20/59 east to exit 76, and turn left onto Skyland Boulevard/Highway 11. The campground is one-eighth of a mile from the interstate.

Contact: Geer Brother's Sunset 2 Campground, 5001 JVC Rd., Cottondale, AL 35453; 205/553-9233.

Trip notes: The campground is 40 miles from the Vision Land Amusement Park, and seven miles from the Paul Bear Bryant Museum and University of Alabama Stadium.

7 Candy Mountain Campground

Location: Coaling, map 2, grid G6.

Campsites, facilities: There are 45 RV sites with full hookups. Pull-through sites are available, and some sites have shade. Primitive and group camping are also offered, plus four cabins. Restrooms have hot showers and flush toilets. A sanitary disposal station, coin laundry, swimming pool, playground, and game room are provided. A supply store, bar, restaurant, and pirate ship with sleeping quarters are planned for 2002. The buildings are wheelchair accessible. Indoor pets are permitted.

Reservations, fees: Reservations are accepted, and no deposit is required. Tent sites are $15 per night, and RV sites are $17. Primitive camping is free to physically or mentally challenged individuals.

Open: Year-round.

Directions: From Birmingham, take exit 86 off Interstate 59 and turn left onto Highway 11. After 3.9 miles, turn right onto County Road 59. The campground will be on the left.

Contact: Candy Mountain Campground, P.O. Box 694, Coaling, AL 35449; 205/553-5428.

Trip notes: There are four fishing ponds stocked with catfish, bass, crappie, and bream. Hiking trails around the ponds are being developed for 2002. The campground is on an artificial mountain with twin waterfalls that drop into a pool, with caves behind the falls under the mountain.

8 McCalla Campground

Location: Birmingham, map 2, grid F8.

Campsites, facilities: There are 11 tent sites and 73 RV sites at this campground. Half of the RV sites have full hookups and are pull-through sites, and the others have water and electric only. Most campsites have some shade. There are also five cabins. Picnic tables and fire rings are provided. RV storage is available, and a sanitary disposal station is provided. Restrooms have hot showers and flush toilets. Both 30- and 50-amp services are available. A coin laundry, swimming pool, playground, game room, and miniature golf are provided. Ice, LP gas, groceries, and supplies are available at the campground. The buildings are wheelchair accessible. Pets are permitted.

Reservations, fees: Reservations are accepted, and no deposit is required. Tent sites are $17 per night. Sites with water and electric hookups are $21–24, and sites with full hookups are $22–25. Cabins are $29–37 per night.

Open: Year-round.

Directions: From Birmingham, go south on Interstate 59 to exit 100, and turn west on Highway 216. The campground is on the left within one-fourth mile.

Contact: McCalla Campground, 22191 Highway 216, McCalla, AL 35111; 205/477-4778.

Trip notes: The campground is eight miles from both the Tannehill Ironworks Historical State Park and the city of Birmingham.

9 Tannehill Ironworks Historical State Park

Location: Birmingham, map 2, grid F8.

Campsites, facilities: There are about 300 campsites at this campground, 40 with full hookups, and the rest with water and electric hookups. Campsites are suitable for either tents or RVs. There are also about 40 primitive sites and four cabins. Picnic tables are provided. Restrooms have hot showers and flush toilets. A coin laundry and small playground are provided. LP gas, ice, groceries, and some supplies are available at the campground. The buildings are wheelchair accessible. Pets are permitted.

Reservations, fees: Reservations are not accepted. Primitive sites are $9 per night, sites with water and electric hookups are $14, and sites with full hookups are $17. Senior discounts apply.

Open: Year-round.

Directions: From Birmingham, take Interstates 20/59 south, then turn east at exit 100/Highway 216, and follow the signs for about two miles to the park.

Contact: Tannehill Ironworks Historical State Park, 12632 Confederate Parkway, McCalla, AL 35111; 205/477-5711.

Trip notes: The park contains two furnaces used during the Civil War, a museum, and an old grist mill. Fishing for rainbow trout is available in the creek. There are 2.5 miles of hiking trails. Swimming is available in the creek, and a bubbling spring makes a wading pool for younger children. There is a water park about 12 miles away, and outlet shopping within 15 miles. The University of Alabama is 20 miles from the park.

10 Moundville Archaeological State Park

Location: Moundville, map 2, grid H3.

Campsites, facilities: There are 30 tent or RV sites at this campground. All sites have water and electric hookups, and five have full hookups. Five of the sites are pull-through, and most have shade. Some picnic tables, fire rings, and cooking grills are provided. There is also a primitive camping area with five sites, all with fire rings. Picnic tables are available in the primitive area, but not at the sites. Restrooms have hot showers and flush toilets. A boat ramp and sanitary disposal station are provided. Leashed pets are permitted.

Reservations, fees: Reservations are not accepted. The fee is $10 per night ($8 for seniors 55 and older) in the developed campground, and $8 for the primitive campsites. Campers pay for one admission to the park per person for their entire stay. Admission to the park is $4 for adults, $2 for seniors and students.

Open: The campground is open year-round. The park is closed Thanksgiving Day, Christmas Eve, Christmas Day, New Year's Eve, and New Year's Day.

Directions: From Tuscaloosa, take Highway 69 south to the campground and park, one-half mile north of Moundville.

Contact: Moundville Archaeological Park, One Mound State Parkway, P.O. Box 66, Moundville, AL 35474; 205/371-2234, or 205/371-2572; website: www.ua.edu/mndville.htm.

Trip notes: The campground is located inside the archaeological park, a 320-acre National Historic Landmark operated by the University of Alabama. The park includes 26 prehistoric Mississippian-era (1000-1500 AD) Native American mounds. Moundville was the site of a large and powerful Indian community 800–1000 years ago, which was the cultural, religious, and agricultural center of the Southeast. The park's museum contains exhibits featuring many of the spectacular artifacts unearthed at the site. Two small ponds at the park provide fishing for bass, bream, and catfish. A short (.75-mile) nature trail and wooden boardwalks provide some hiking.

11 Gardendale Kampground

Location: Gardendale, map 3, grid C2.
Campsites, Facilities: There are 34 sites that accommodate both tents and RVs, all with full hookups. Almost all sites are pull-through. Some sites have picnic tables. Restrooms have hot showers and flush toilets. A coin laundry and small playground are provided. Pets are permitted, if kept inside your tent or rig.
Reservations, fees: Reservations are accepted. No deposit is required. The fee for tent sites is $12, and $19 for RVs.
Open: Year-round.
Directions: From Interstate 65, take exit 272/US 31 for one mile, then turn east on Moncrief Road.
Contact: Gardendale Kampground, 2128 Moncrief Rd., Gardendale, AL 35071; 205/631-7364.
Trip notes: The campground is across the street from a city park, which has a larger playground and tennis courts.

12 Holiday Travel Park

Location: Birmingham, map 3, grid D4.
Campsites, Facilities: The campground has two areas for tents. There are 20 developed tent sites, some with water and some with water and electric hookups. Primitive tent camping is also available. Some of the tent sites have shade. There are 48 RV sites, half with full hookups and half with water and electric only. All of the RV sites are pull-through. Restrooms have hot showers and flush toilets. A coin laundry, sanitary disposal station, and miniature golf are provided. RV storage is available. Leashed pets are permitted. You must clean up after your pet.
Reservations, fees: Reservations are accepted at 205/640-5300. The deposit of one night's fee is refundable if cancellation is made at least seven days in advance. Primitive sites cost $13 per day, sites with water and electric rent for $20, and sites with full hookups are $22. Senior citizen discounts apply.
Open: Year-round.
Directions: Take Interstate 20 east from Birmingham to exit 144B/Moody/Odenville, and turn right. One block from the interstate, turn left onto Old Ashville Road, which leads into the campground.
Contact: Holiday Travel Park, 900 Old Ashville Road, Leeds, AL 35096; 205/640-5300.
Trip notes: The Little Catawba River cuts through the campground. Fishing is catch and release only, as the fish cannot be eaten due to runoff from industrial and farming areas. The campground is about 18 miles from the Talladega International Speedway, and about 12

miles from the Whistle Stop Café, from the movie Fried Green Tomatoes.

13 M & J RV Park

Location: Birmingham, map 3, grid E1.
Campsites, facilities: There are 72 RV sites with full hookups, six of them pull-through sites. A few sites have some shade. There are no restrooms. Small and medium dogs are permitted.
Reservations, fees: Reservations are accepted, and no deposit is required. Campsites cost $14–20 per night.
Open: Year-round.
Directions: From Interstate 20, take exit 118 and go south on Valley Road for 0.6 miles. Turn left on Aronov Drive. After a little over a mile, turn right on US 11. The campground is at mile marker 128.
Contact: M & J RV Park, P.O. Box 28104, Birmingham, AL 35228; 205/788-2605.
Trip notes: The campground doesn't have any amenities, but it is next to a city park which offers a swimming pool, playground, fishing pond, and tennis courts. It is less than four miles from a public golf course.

14 Oak Mountain State Park

Location: Pelham, map 3, grid F3.
Campsites, Facilities: The campground has 40 tent sites and 85 RV sites. Fifty-eight of the RV sites have full hookups, and 15 are pull-through sites. Most sites have some shade. Picnic tables, fire rings, and cooking grills are provided. RV storage is available. Ten fully-equipped cabins are also available. Backpacking on the backcountry trails is also permitted. Restrooms have hot showers and flush toilets. A sanitary disposal station, coin laundry, tennis courts, and playground are provided. The campground store sells ice, firewood, and some supplies. Leashed pets are permitted, except in the cabins.
Reservations, fees: Reservations are accepted at 800/ALA-PARK (800/252-7275). The deposit of one night's fee is non-refundable, but you can move the date of your reservation twice. Fees range from $9.50 for tent sites to $13 for RVs, plus $2 for sewage connections.
Open: Year-round.
Directions: Take exit 246/Highway 119 from Interstate 65, turn east, and follow the signs. The campground is less than two miles from the interstate.
Contact: Oak Mountain State Park, P.O. Box 278, Pelham, AL 35124; 205/620-2527.
Trip notes: This is the largest of Alabama's state parks; it calls itself the "Southernmost part of the Appalachian Chain." The views from the top of Oak Mountain are reminiscent of those in the Smokies. Two 85-acre lakes offer fishing for bass, bream, and catfish. Johnboats and paddleboats are available for rent. Seven trails total over 51 miles, including hiking, horse, and bike trails. The Treetop Nature Trail is an elevated walkway with a view of permanently injured birds housed at the Wildlife Rehabilitation Center. The Peavine Falls trail is a short but steep trail that leads to the 50-foot falls, which are great in wet years and can dry completely in drought years. BMX races are held throughout the summer. In addition to the horse trails, guided group rides are available. There's a petting zoo for the kids, and swimming is available at the 74-acre lake with a sand beach. Tennis courts and an 18-hole championship golf course are available. The park has a large deer population.

15 Birmingham South KOA

Location: Birmingham, map 3, grid F2.

Campsites, Facilities: There are six tent sites and 100 sites reserved for RVs. All sites have full hookups, and over half are pull-through sites. Most sites have shade. RV storage is available. Some sites have patios. Group sites are available, and there are six cabins. Picnic tables, fire rings, and cooking grills are provided. Restrooms have hot showers and flush toilets. The campground store sells ice, LP gas, groceries, and gifts. A spa, playground, pool, and clubroom are provided. Cable TV hookups are available at no charge. Movies are available for rent. Activities on site include basketball, horseshoes, badminton, and volleyball. The facilities are wheelchair accessible. Pets are permitted on leash only. Pets must be walked in a fenced "Piddle Parlor," and you must pick up after your pet. Pets are not allowed in the buildings.

Reservations, fees: Reservations are accepted at 800/KOA-4788 (800/562-4788), and the deposit is refundable if cancelled one day in advance of your scheduled arrival. Site fees are $25 per night, $26 for sewage hookup. Weekly renters pay for six days.

Open: Year-round.

Directions: From Birmingham, take exit 242/Highway 52 off Interstate 65, and turn right. Drive one-half mile to Highway 33, and turn right.

Contact: Birmingham South KOA, 222 Highway 33, Pelham, AL 35123; 205/664-8832.

Trip notes: The campground is 15 miles from Oak Mountain State Park and its amenities, including fishing and miles of hiking trails. Other activities within three miles include scuba diving, roller skating, ice skating, golf, horseback riding, fishing, and hiking. The campground is 20 miles from the Birmingham Zoo, Birmingham Botanical Gardens, and Birmingham Race Course.

16 DeSoto Caverns Park Campground

Location: Birmingham, map 3, grid F6.

Campsites, facilities: There are five tent sites at the campground. There are also 16 RV sites in a separate section, all with full hookups. Six of these are pull-through sites. Most sites have some shade. Some sites have picnic tables and cooking grills. Group sites are available, and a sanitary disposal station is provided. Restrooms have hot showers and flush toilets. Ice, firewood, and some gifts are available at the campground. A playground is provided. The restrooms are wheelchair accessible. Leashed pets are permitted.

Reservations, fees: Reservations are accepted at 800/933-2283, only during race and festival weekends. The deposit is refundable if cancellation is received a week prior to your reservation date. Tent sites are $14, sites with full hookups are $19.

Open: Year-round.

Directions: From Birmingham, take US 280 south to Childersburg, turn left onto Highway 76, and follow the signs. The park is located five miles east of Childersburg.

Contact: DeSoto Caverns Park Campground, 5181 DeSoto Caverns Parkway, Childersburg, AL 35044-5663; 256/378-7252; fax 256/378-3678; website: www.cavern.com/desoto/.

Trip notes: The campground is located next to the DeSoto Caverns Park. The main room of the cavern is longer than 200 yards and higher than a 12-story building. Other attractions at the caverns include miniature golf, gemstone panning, cave wall climbing, and bow and arrow shooting ranges. The campground is 20 miles from the Talladega International Speedway.

⓱ Brierfield Ironworks Historical State Park

Location: Brierfield, map 3, grid H1.

Campsites, facilities: There are 50 campsites with water and electric hookups suitable for tents or RVs. Primitive camping is also available. Some sites have picnic tables, and some have fire rings. There are also two cabins. Restrooms have hot showers and flush toilets. A coin laundry, sanitary disposal station, swimming pool, shooting range, and playground are provided. Ice is available. Most of the facilities are wheelchair accessible. Leashed pets are permitted.

Reservations, fees: Reservations are accepted only for the cabins. Primitive campsites are $7.50 per night, and other sites are $12. The cabins are $50–60 per night.

Open: Year-round.

Directions: From Birmingham, go south on Interstate 65 to exit 228 and turn right on Highway 25 through Montevallo. Six miles south of Montevallo, turn east on County Road 62, then left onto Furnace Parkway.

Contact: Brierfield Ironworks Historical State Park, 240 Furnace Parkway, Brierfield, AL 35035; 205/665-1856.

Trip notes: The park contains the ruins of a Civil War ironworks factory. There is one short hiking trail. Fishing is available at the Cahaba River about 15 miles away.

⓲ Lake Chinnabee

Location: Talladega National Forest, map 4, grid E1.

Campsites, facilities: Primitive camping is available. Picnic tables, fire rings, and cooking grills are provided. Water is available. Pit toilets are provided. Leashed pets are permitted.

Reservations, fees: Reservations are not accepted. The fee is $8 per night.

Open: The campground is open from mid-April through October.

Directions: The recreation area is three miles from Cheaha State Park. From Interstate 20, take US 431 south to Highway 281, and turn right. Pass Cheaha State Park, and then turn right on County Roads 42/385 to Lake Chinnabee.

Contact: Lake Chinnabee, Talladega National Forest, 1001 North St., Talladega, AL 35160; 256/362-2909.

Trip notes: Fishing is available in the Lake Wedowee, and there are many hiking trails in the area. Many of the trails are connecting loops, and wilderness camping is available for backpackers anywhere in the recreation area. The Chinnabee Silent Trail is 12 miles round trip, and is rated strenuous because of its change in elevation. The trail leads past several waterfalls and the lake, and ties into the Pinhoti Trail (see Resources for more information on the Pinhoti Trail). Because of hunting in this area, you must wear orange from mid-October through January. Hiking or backpacking here during hunting season is not recommended.

19 Cheaha State Park

Location: Delta, map 4, grid E2.

Campsites, facilities: There are 73 developed campsites at this campground, all suitable for tents or RVs. All sites have full hookups, and 28 are pull-through. All sites have some shade. RVs must be 45 feet or less. Picnic tables and cooking grills are provided. There is also primitive camping available in a wooded area, and 15 cabins. Restrooms have hot showers and flush toilets. A coin laundry, pool, and playground are provided. Limited supplies, including some groceries, ice, and firewood, are available at the campground store. No gasoline motors are allowed on the lake. The buildings are wheelchair accessible. Leashed pets are permitted.

Reservations, fees: Reservations are accepted at 800/ALA-PARK (800/252-7275). The deposit of one night's fee is non-refundable, but you can move the date of your reservation twice. There is a two-night minimum for reservations, except for holiday weekends, when there is a three-night minimum. The fee is $16.50 per night for the developed campsites, $11 for semiprimitive, and $8.80 for primitive camping.

Open: Year-round.

Directions: From Birmingham, travel east on Interstate 20 to exit 191 and turn south on US 431. After four miles, turn right on Highway 281, and take it south to the park.

Contact: Cheaha State Park, 19644 Highway 281, Delta, AL 36258; 256/488-5111.

Trip notes: The lake is stocked with fish, and paddleboats are available for rent during the warmer months. There are four hiking and biking trails, all a mile or less in length, plus the park is surrounded by the Talladega National Forest, which has many miles of hiking trails. Wildlife in the area includes deer and wild turkeys.

20 Cheaha Wilderness Area

Location: Talladega National Forest, map 4, grid E2.

Campsites, facilities: Primitive camping is available anywhere in the wilderness area. There are no campsites, and you must leave no trace of your stay. Leashed pets are permitted.

Reservations, fees: Reservations are not accepted, but you must fill out a card at the trailhead with your planned destination and the number of people in your party. There are no camping fees, but some of the parking areas charge a daily fee of $3.

Open: Year-round.

Directions: Many of the trailheads into the wilderness area have parking areas, or you can park at the Cheaha Trail entrance at Cheaha State Park. From Interstate 20, take US 431 south to Highway 281, and turn right to the park.

Contact: Cheaha Wilderness Area, Talladega National Forest, 1001 North St., Talladega, AL 35160; 256/362-2909.

Trip notes: There are 30 miles of trails through the 7000-acre wilderness area. Familiarize yourself with wilderness camping techniques before you go, as this is a "leave no trace" area. You'll need a topographic map and compass. Because of hunting in this area, you must wear orange from mid-October through January. Hiking or backpacking here during hunting season is not recommended.

21 Turnipseed Hunter Campground

Location: Talladega National Forest, map 4, grid E2.

Campsites, facilities: There are eight primitive campsites at this campground. Picnic tables, fire rings, and cooking grills are provided. Water is available. Pit toilets are provided. Leashed pets are permitted.

Reservations, fees: Reservations are not accepted. The campground is free now, but the US Forest Service is considering whether to charge $5 a night.

Open: Year-round.

Directions: The campground is three miles past the Cheaha State Park on Scenic Drive.

Contact: Turnipseed Hunter Campground, Talladega National Forest, 1001 North St., Talladega, AL 35160; 256/362-2909.

Trip notes: There are 50 miles of hiking trails in the forest, including the Chinnabee Silent Trail, which ties into the Pinhoti Trail (see Resources for more information on the Pinhoti Trail). This challenging six-mile trail (12 miles round trip) leads to several waterfalls. There is also a four-mile trail to Lake Chinnabee, and several other trails of varying lengths. Some of the loop trails intersect and could create an interesting backpacking trip. Get a map to the trails from the Forest Service (address above). The half-mile Bald Rock Trail is wheelchair accessible. The campground is three miles from Cheaha State Park. Because of hunting in this area, you must wear orange from mid-October through January. Hiking or backpacking here during hunting season is not recommended.

22 Bartlett's Lakeside Marina

Location: Wedowee, map 4, grid F4.

Campsites, facilities: This campground has 75 sites suitable for both tents and RVs. Most have full hookups, and the rest have water and electric. Pull-through sites are available. There are also three cabins. Picnic tables are provided, and some cooking grills and fire rings are available. Restrooms have hot showers and flush toilets. A coin laundry, sanitary disposal station, boat ramp, and playground are provided. The campground store sells supplies, groceries, ice, LP gas, and bait. RV storage is available. The buildings are wheelchair accessible. Leashed pets are permitted.

Reservations, fees: Reservations are accepted. The required deposit is refundable with three-day advance notice. Campsites cost $15 per night.

Open: Year-round.

Directions: From Birmingham, take Interstate 20 east to exit 191, and turn south on US 431. The campground is about 20 miles from the interstate.

Contact: Bartlett's Lakeside Marina, 21143 Highway 431, Wedowee, AL 36278; 256/357-2033.

Trip notes: Most sites here are rented monthly to full-time RVers, open sites are available to vacationers. Fishing (for bass, catfish, bream, and crappie) and water-skiing in the Big and Little Tallapoosa Rivers are the major draws to this area. Canoes are available for rent, and there is a sand beach in the swimming area.

23 Jennings Ferry Campground

Location: Black Warrior River, map 5, grid B2.

Campsites, Facilities: The campground has 29 sites suitable for tents or RVs. Picnic tables, fire rings, and cooking grills are provided. Pit toilets and a boat ramp are provided. Leashed pets are permitted.

Reservations, fees: Reservations are not accepted. There is no fee.

Open: Year-round.

Directions: The campground is four miles east of Eutah on Highway 14.

Contact: US Army Corps of Engineers, 384 Resource Management Dr., Demopolis, AL 36732; 334/289-3540.

Trip notes: This is a no-frills campground in an area where fishing, boating, and water-skiing are the main sources of recreation.

24 Old Lock #7 East

Location: Black Warrior River, map 5, grid B2.

Campsites, Facilities: This campground has primitive camping only with room for approximately 100 campsites. There are a few picnic tables throughout the area. Pit toilets are provided, as is a boat ramp. Leashed pets are permitted.

Reservations, fees: Reservations are not accepted. There is no fee to camp here.

Open: Year-round.

Directions: From Greensboro, go west on Highway 14 and follow the signs. The campground is approximately seven miles east of Eutah.

Contact: US Army Corps of Engineers, 384 Resource Management Dr., Demopolis, AL 36732; 334/289-3540.

Trip notes: Boating, fishing, and water-skiing on the Black Warrior River are the main reasons to camp in this area.

25 Lake Payne Recreation Area

Location: Lake Payne, map 5, grid A7.

Campsites, facilities: There are 11 sites reserved for tents only, and 15 sites suitable for either tents or RVs. Water is available. Most sites are along the lake. They are working on adding hookups to the campsites, and plan to be finished by 2003. Picnic tables are provided. Some sites have cooking grills. There are also primitive sites available. Restrooms have flush toilets and cold showers. A boat ramp is provided. There is a no-wake rule on the lake. Leashed pets are permitted.

Reservations, fees: Reservations are not accepted. The camping fee is $4 plus a $3 day-use fee.

Open: Year-round.

Directions: Take Highway 5 from Centreville, turn right on Highway 25, and watch for the Forest Service park signs.

Contact: Lake Payne Recreation Area, US Forest Service, Oakmulgee Ranger District, 1 Forest Dr., Brent, AL 35034; 205/926-9765.

Trip notes: The lake offers fishing for bass, bream, and catfish. There are two trails, totaling less than two miles. There is a sand beach in the swimming area. This campground plans to do major improvements over the next few years, and parts of the campground will be closed periodically. Because funding for the campground has been an issue in the past, expect rates to increase when the improvements are completed.

26 Old Lock #5

Location: Black Warrior River, map 5, grid D4.

Campsites, Facilities: This campground has primitive camping only. There is room for approximately 20 campsites. Some picnic tables are available. Restrooms have vault toilets and no showers. A boat ramp is provided. Leashed pets are permitted.

Reservations, fees: Reservations are not accepted. There is no fee to camp here.

Open: Year-round.

Directions: From Greensboro, go south 10 miles on Highway 69, and turn right on County Road 16, which dead ends into the campground.

Contact: US Army Corps of Engineers, 384 Resource Management Dr., Demopolis, AL 36732; 334/289-3540.

Trip notes: Boating, fishing, and water-skiing on the Black Warrior River are the main reasons to camp in this area.

27 Foscue Park

Location: Tombigbee River, map 5, grid D1.

Campsites, Facilities: There are 45 campsites suitable for tents or RVs, all with water and electric hookups. A coin laundry, boat ramp, and playground are provided. Leashed pets are permitted.

Reservations, fees: Reservations are accepted through the National Recreation Reservation Service (NRRS) at 877/444-6777, website: www.reserveusa.com. The full amount is payable in advance. Waterfront campsites are $14 per night, and the other are $12.

Open: Year-round.

Directions: From Demopolis, take US 80 west and follow the signs.

Contact: US Army Corps of Engineers, 384 Resource Management Dr., Demopolis, AL 36732; 334/289-5535 or 334/289-3540.

Trip notes: Fishing is available in the river. There is a one-mile exercise trail, but the main focuses at this park are boating, fishing, and water-skiing.

28 Forkland Park

Location: Black Warrior River, map 5, grid D2.

Campsites, Facilities: There are 42 campsites suitable for tents or RVs, all with water and electric hookups. Picnic tables, fire rings, and cooking grills are provided. Restrooms have hot showers and flush toilets. A coin laundry, boat ramp, dock, and playground are provided. Leashed pets are permitted.

Reservations, fees: Reservations are accepted through the National Recreation Reservation Service (NRRS) at 877/444-6777, website: www.reserveusa.com. The full amount is payable in advance. Campsites are $12–$14 per night.

Open: Year-round.

Directions: Take US 43 north of Demopolis 12 miles and follow the signs.

Contact: US Army Corps of Engineers, 384 Resource Management Dr., Demopolis, AL 36732; 334/289-5530 or 334/289-3540.

Trip notes: The area is best known for boating, water-skiing, and fishing.

29 Lakeway RV

Location: Lake Martin, map 6, grid B8.

Campsites, facilities: There are 19 RV sites, all with full hookups. Picnic tables are provided. There are no restrooms. A coin laundry is provided, and there is a pub and grill at the campground. Pets are permitted.

Reservations, fees: Reservations are accepted, and no deposit is required. Campsites are $15 per night.

Open: Year-round.

Directions: From Birmingham, go south on US 280 through Sylacauga, and turn right onto Highway 9. Travel south about 16 miles to the campground.

Contact: Lakeway RV, P.O. Box 176, Equality, AL 36026; 334/541-2010.

Trip notes: About half of the campers here rent monthly. The campground is four miles from Lake Martin, Alabama's largest lake, where boat rentals, fishing, and swimming are available.

30 Real Island Marina and Campground

Location: Lake Martin, map 6, grid C8.

Campsites, facilities: There are 51 RV sites at this campground. Water and electric hookups are provided, and pull-through sites are available. All sites have some shade. Picnic tables, fire rings, and cooking grills are provided. Restrooms have hot showers and flush toilets. Group sites, furnished campers, and two cabins are also available. Patios and cable TV hookups are available. A boat ramp, dock, and sanitary disposal station are provided. Boat storage is available. Ice, LP gas, and supplies are available at the campground. The buildings are wheelchair accessible. Leashed pets are permitted.

Reservations, fees: Reservations are accepted, and no deposit is required. Campsites are $30 per night, and $230 per month.

Open: Year-round.

Directions: From Montgomery, take US 231 north 41 miles to Highway 9 and turn right. Turn right on Highway 55, then right on County Road 2, to Real Island Road.

Contact: Real Island Marina, 2700 Real Island Rd., Equality, AL 36026; 334/857-2741.

Trip notes: The campground is located on Lake Martin, and fishing is available for crappie, bream, and catfish. There is a sand beach in the swimming area, and paddleboats and pontoon boats for rent. The area has a great deal of mountain laurel, which blooms in May. Wildlife in the area includes deer, wild turkeys, and bobcats.

31 Paul Grist State Park

Location: Selma, map 6, grid D1.

Campsites, facilities: There are six primitive tent sites and six RV sites. There is piped water in the tent section, and full hookups in the RV section of the campground. Picnic tables and fire rings are provided. Restrooms have hot showers and flush toilets. Ice and snacks are available at the campground store. A playground, boat ramp, and pier are provided. The buildings are wheelchair accessible. Leashed pets are permitted.

Reservations, fees: Reservations are not accepted. Credit cards are not accepted. The fee for tents is $8, and $15 for RVs.

Open: Year-round.

Directions: From Selma, take Highway 22 north 15 miles 10 miles, and turn left on County Road 222. At the dead end, turn right on County Road 37, then right into the park.

Contact: Paul Grist State Park, 1546 Grist Rd., Selma, AL 36701; 334/872-5846, or 800/ALA-PARK (800/252-7275).

Trip notes: Fishing for bass, bream, and catfish is available in the lake, and there is a sand beach in the swimming area. There are five interconnected hiking trails. The longest is about three miles in length. Johnboats, canoes, and paddle boats are available for rent.

32 Fort Toulouse–Jackson Park

Location: Montgomery, map 6, grid D7.
Campsites, facilities: There are 39 RV sites at this campground, all with water and electric hookups. All sites have some shade. Picnic tables, fire rings, and cooking grills are provided. Restrooms have hot showers and flush toilets. A boat ramp, clubroom, and sanitary disposal station are provided. Firewood and some gifts are available. The facilities are wheelchair accessible. Leashed pets are permitted.
Reservations, fees: Reservations are accepted for groups only. The fee is $11 per night for tent sites; full hookups are $14. Senior discounts apply.
Open: Year-round.
Directions: From Wetumpka, take US 231 south three miles and turn onto West Fort Toulouse Road.
Contact: Fort Toulouse–Jackson Park, 2521 West Fort Toulouse Rd., Wetumpka, AL 36093; 334/567-3002; fax 334/514-6625.
Trip notes: Fishing, kayaking, and rafting are available on the river at the campground. Hiking is available at the campground and other parks nearby. The campground is four miles from Jasmine Hill Gardens, and eight miles from the Coosa River Rapids area.

33 Amity Campground

Location: West Point Lake, map 7, grid A7.
Campsites, facilities: There are 96 campsites suitable for tents or RVs. All but three have water and electric hookups. Most sites have shade. Picnic tables and fire rings are provided. Restrooms have hot showers and flush toilets. A sanitary disposal station, coin laundry, tennis court, boat ramp, dock, and playground, are provided. The buildings are wheelchair accessible. Leashed pets are permitted. You must clean up after your pet.
Reservations, fees: Reservations are accepted through the National Recreation Reservation Service (NRRS) at 877/444-6777, website: www.reserveusa.com. The full amount is payable in advance. Primitive sites are $12 per night. Sites with water and electric hookups are $18.
Open: The campground is open from April through mid-September.
Directions: From LaGrange, Georgia, take Interstate 85 south to exit 79/US 29 and turn north. US 29 becomes State Line Road, then County Road 212. Turn right onto County Road 393.
Contact: Amity Campground, 1001 County Road 393, Lanett, AL 36863; 334/499-2404.
Trip notes: Fishing is available in the lake for bass, crappie, catfish, and carp. There are two short hiking trails, totaling about 1.5 miles in length. The campground is seven miles from the powerhouse at West Point Dam, which offers tours, a visitor center, and a short film.

Wind Creek State Park

Location: Lake Martin, map 7, grid B1.

Campsites, facilities: There are 642 campsites. Of these, 231 have full hookups and are reserved for RVs. The rest are suitable for either tents or RVs, and have water and electric hookups. Picnic tables, fire rings, and cooking grills are provided. Group sites are available. Restrooms have hot showers and flush toilets. A coin laundry, boat ramp, dock, clubroom, and playground are provided. RV and boat storage are available. A sanitary disposal station is provided. The campground store sells ice, supplies, groceries, and firewood. The buildings are wheelchair accessible. Leashed pets are permitted. You must clean up after your pet.

Reservations, fees: Reservations are accepted at 800/ALA-PARK (800/252-7275). The deposit of one night's fee is non-refundable, but you can move the date of your reservation twice. The base rate for tents is $14; $16 for RVs. There are additional charges of $3 for waterfront sites from April through October, and $3 for sewage hookups. Senior citizen discounts apply.

Open: Year-round.

Directions: From US 280 at Alexander City, go south on Highway 63. Turn left on Highway 128. The park is about seven miles south of Alexander City.

Contact: Wind Creek State Park, 4325 Highway 128, Alexander City, AL 35010; 256/329-0845.

Trip notes: The campground is located on Lake Martin, which is stocked with bass, crappie, and bream. There is a sand beach in the swimming area. Paddleboats are available for rent. There are two main hiking trails with short side trails that total about six miles. Look for wildflowers along the trails in the spring and summer. Wildlife in the park includes deer and wild turkeys.

Baker's Mobile Home Park and Campground

Location: Opelika, map 7, grid C6.

Campsites, facilities: The campground has six sites suitable for tents or RVs, all with full hookups and some shade. A sanitary disposal station is provided. Restrooms have hot showers and flush toilets. The restrooms are wheelchair accessible. Leashed pets are permitted.

Reservations, fees: Reservations are accepted, with a non-refundable deposit. All campsites are $12 per night.

Open: Year-round.

Directions: From Interstate 85, take US 280 west and turn right on US 431 north. Turn left onto Old 431, which is also Old LaFayette Parkway.

Contact: Baker's Mobile Home Park and Campground, 2000 Old LaFayette Parkway, Opelika, AL 36801; 334/745-5165.

Trip notes: This small campground is about one mile from the Lazy Lost Lake, where fishing is available.

Starr's Mobile Home Park

Location: Auburn, map 7, grid C5.

Campsites, facilities: There are 20 RV sites at this campground, all with full hookups. Shade is available. There are no restrooms. A swimming pool is provided. Pets are permitted.

Reservations, fees: Reservations are accepted. The deposit is refundable with cancellation 10 days in advance of your scheduled arrival. Campsites are $12 per night, and $60 per week.

Open: Year-round.

Directions: The campground is located on Highway 29 east of Auburn, and west of Opelika.

Contact: Starr's Mobile Home Park, 1425 Opelika Rd., Auburn, AL 36830; 334/887-5321.

Trip notes: The campground is about 10 miles from Chewacla State Park, which offers fishing and hiking, and about a half mile from a public golf course.

37 Leisure Time Campground

Location: Auburn, map 7, grid D4.

Campsites, Facilities: There are 60 sites suitable for tents or RVs. All have hookups and shade, and half are pull-through sites. Picnic tables and cooking grills are provided. Restrooms have flush toilets and hot showers. A coin laundry and cable TV hookups are available. Ice is available at the campground, and supplies are within walking distance. The facilities are wheelchair accessible. Leashed pets are permitted.

Reservations, fees: Reservations are accepted, and no deposit is required. Fees are $18 per night, $97 per week, and $290 per month. Good Sam, AARP, and AAA discounts apply.

Open: Year-round.

Directions: From Interstate 85, take exit 51 and turn south. The campground is next to the Auburn softball complex about two-tenths of a mile from the interstate.

Contact: Leisure Time Campground, 2670 South College St., Auburn, AL 36832; 334/821-2267.

Trip notes: The campground is near Chewacla State Park, which offers fishing, boating and hiking. It's just three miles from Auburn University. Although few amenities are available at the campground, it is next door to a water park, and go-karts, miniature golf, and a softball complex are all nearby.

38 Chewacla State Park

Location: Auburn, map 7, grid D5.

Campsites, Facilities: There are 36 RV sites with full hookups, and six primitive tent sites. Picnic tables and cooking grills are provided for the RV sites, and fire pits in the primitive camping area. There are also five cabins. Restrooms have hot showers and flush toilets. Supplies and groceries are available about three miles from the park. A coin laundry and picnic pavilions are provided. Wood is available for sale at the campground. Leashed pets are permitted in the campground, but not in the cabins.

Reservations, fees: Reservations for the cabins and RV sites are accepted at 334/887-5621. No reservations can be made for the primitive sites. The deposit of one night's fee is non-refundable. RV sites are $16.50 per night, and tent sites are $9.90. Cabins range from $48–65. Senior citizens receive a 15% discount.

Open: Year-round.

Directions: From Opelika, take Interstate 85 south to exit 51/Auburn University/Chewacla State Park, and turn left. Turn left on the first road, which dead ends into the park after two miles.

Contact: Chewacla State Park, 124 Shell Toomer Parkway, Auburn, AL 36830; 334/887-5621.

Trip notes: The lake is not stocked with fish, but being creek-fed, contains bass, crappie, catfish, and bream. Paddleboats, canoes, and fishing boats are available for rent. No gasoline motors are allowed on the lake. The eight hiking trails are interconnected for a total of about ten miles. The swimming area has both low and high diving boards. The park contains mainly hardwood trees, and is particularly pretty in the fall. There is a 30-foot waterfall at the dam.

WEST L.A. AND
THE GULF COAST

DAUPHIN ISLAND

WEST L.A. AND THE GULF COAST

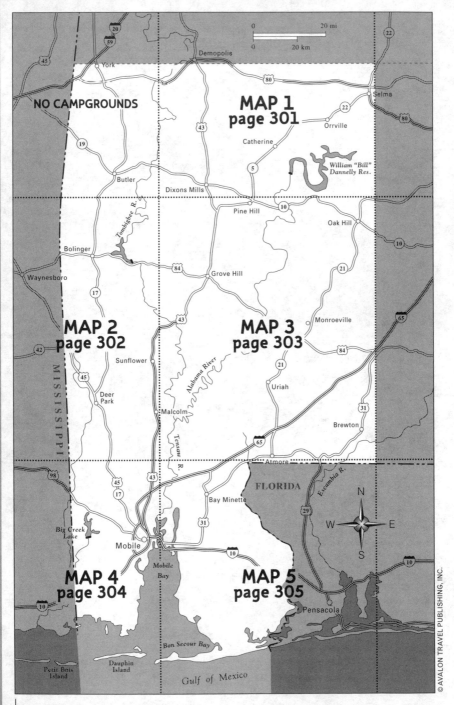

NO CAMPGROUNDS

MAP 1
page 301

MAP 2
page 302

MAP 3
page 303

MAP 4
page 304

MAP 5
page 305

William "Bill"
Dannelly Res.

MISSISSIPPI

FLORIDA

Gulf of Mexico

Mobile
Bay

Bon Secour Bay

Demopolis
York
Selma
Orrville
Catherine
Butler
Dixons Mills
Pine Hill
Oak Hill
Bolinger
Grove Hill
Waynesboro
Monroeville
Sunflower
Uriah
Deer
Park
Malcolm
Brewton
Atmore
Bay Minette
Big Creek
Lake
Mobile
Pensacola
Petit Bois
Island
Dauphin
Island

Tombigbee R.
Alabama River
Tensaw R.
Escambia R.

N
W   E
S

© AVALON TRAVEL PUBLISHING, INC.

MAP 1

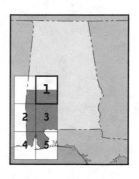

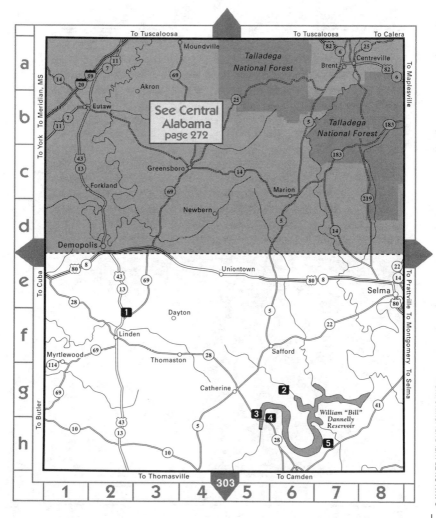

© AVALON TRAVEL PUBLISHING, INC.

MAP 2

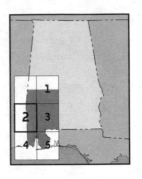

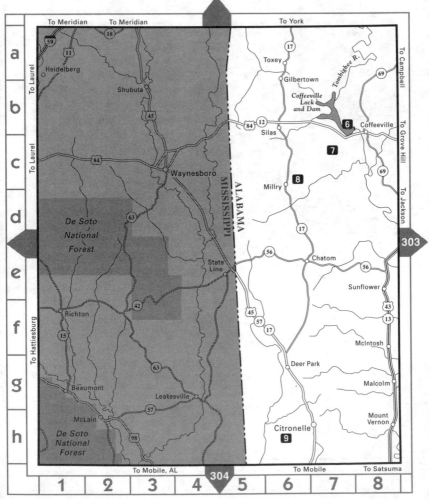

© AVALON TRAVEL PUBLISHING, INC.

MAP 3

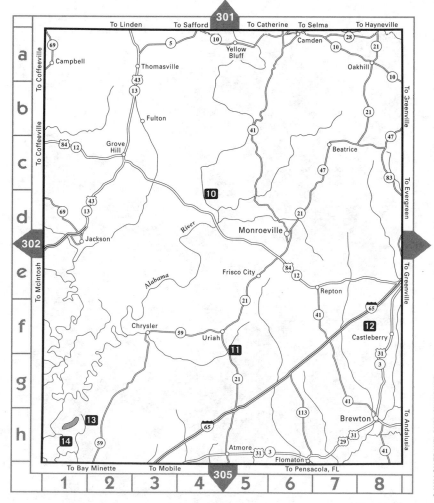

© AVALON TRAVEL PUBLISHING, INC.

MAP 4

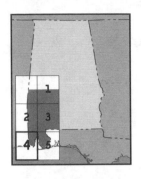

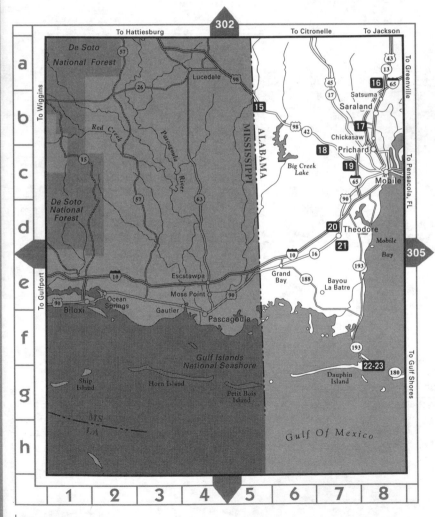

To Hattiesburg To Citronelle To Jackson

302

De Soto National Forest

Lucedale

57

26

98

15

43

13

45

65

16

17

Satsuma

Saraland

To Wiggins

Red Creek

98

42

17

Chickasaw

Prichard

18

MISSISSIPPI ALABAMA

Pascagoula River

Big Creek Lake

19

65

Mobile

15

De Soto National Forest

57

63

90

20 Theodore

Mobile Bay

305

10

16

21

To Pensacola, FL

193

10

Escatawpa

Grand Bay

188

Bayou La Batre

To Gulfport

90

Biloxi

Ocean Springs

Moss Point

90

Gautier

Pascagoula

To Greenville

193

Gulf Islands National Seashore

22-23

180

Dauphin Island

To Gulf Shores

Ship Island

Horn Island

Petit Bois Island

MS LA

Gulf Of Mexico

© AVALON TRAVEL PUBLISHING, INC.

1 2 3 4 5 6 7 8

MAP 5

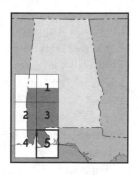

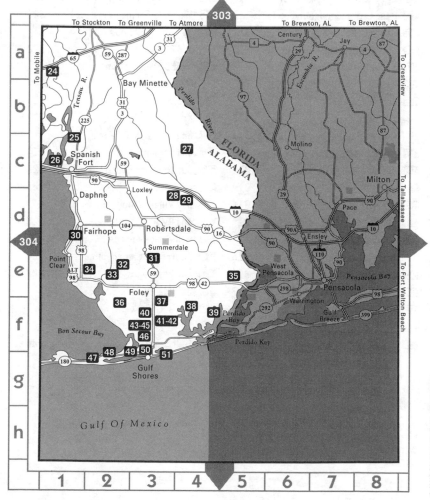

WEST L.A. AND THE GULF COAST

◼ Chickasaw State Park

Location: Gallion, map 1, grid F2.

Campsites, facilities: There are five developed tent sites and an unlimited number of primitive sites at this campground. The developed sites have access to water, and two have electric hookups as well. There are also eight sites reserved for RVs that have water and electric hookups. Picnic tables and cooking grills are provided. Restrooms have flush toilets but no showers. A sanitary disposal station, wading pool, and playground are provided. Supplies are available within one mile. Leashed pets are permitted.

Reservations, fees: Reservations are not accepted. The fee for tents is $8, and $10 for RVs.

Open: Year-round.

Directions: The campground is four miles north of Linden, or 11 miles south of Demopolis, on US 43.

Contact: Chickasaw State Park, 26955 US Highway 43, Gallion, AL 36742; 334/295-8230.

Trip notes: The campground is on 520 acres of mostly virgin timber, and has six miles of hiking trails through the woods. Some trails are off-limits from November through January because of handicapped hunting. Wildlife in the area includes deer and wild turkeys.

◼ Chilatchee Creek Campground

Location: Alberta, map 1, grid G6.

Campsites, Facilities: The campground has 47 sites for either tents or RVs. All have water and electric hookups, and most have shade. Picnic tables, fire rings, and cooking grills are provided. Six primitive camping sites are available. Restrooms have hot showers and flush toilets. A coin laundry, boat dock, boat ramp, and playground are provided. Supplies are available five miles from the park. A sanitary disposal station is available. Leashed pets are permitted in the campground.

Reservations, fees: Reservations are accepted through the National Recreation Reservation Service (NRRS) at 877/444-6777, website: www.reserveusa.com. The full amount is payable in advance. Waterfront sites are $14 per night. Other developed sites are $12, and primitive sites are $8.

Open: Year-round.

Directions: From Selma, take Highway 22 southwest to Alberta. Turn left on County Road 29, and follow the signs to the campground.

Contact: Chilatchee Campground, US Army Corps of Engineers, Dannelly Resource Office, 1226 Power House Rd., Camden, AL 36726-9106; 334/573-2562; website: www.reserveusa.com.

Trip notes: Fishing and hiking are available in the park. Wildlife in the area includes deer, wild turkeys, and bobcats. You probably won't see the bobcats living here, but deer are frequently seen. An overlook provides a nice view of the river and the surrounding area.

◼ Mills Ferry Campground

Location: Lake Dannelly, map 1, grid H5.

Campsites, facilities: There are 58 campsites suitable for either tents or RVs. Picnic tables, fire rings, and cooking grills are provided. Restrooms have hot showers and flush toilets. A sanitary disposal station, coin laundry, boat ramp, dock, and playground are provided. The buildings are wheelchair accessible. Leashed pets are permitted.

Reservations, fees: Reservations are accepted through the National Recreation Reservation Service (NRRS) at 877/444-6777, website: www.reserveusa.com. The full amount is payable in advance. Waterfront sites are $14 per night, and all other sites are $12.

Open: Year-round.

Directions: From Camden, take Highway 28 north 10 miles to the Alabama River, and turn right at the US Army Corps of Engineers sign.

Contact: Mills Ferry Campground, Mills Ferry Resource Center, 1256 Powerhouse Rd., Camden, AL 36726; 334/682-4244.

Trip notes: Fishing is available on Lake Dannelly and the Alabama River. There is one short hiking trail near the campground, with others in the area. Kayaking and canoeing are popular on the river, and water-skiing on the lake.

❹ East Bank Park Campground

Location: Camden, map 1, grid H5.

Campsites, Facilities: There are 58 RV campsites, all with full hookups. Three of the sites are drive-through, and most have shade. Picnic tables, fire rings, and cooking grills are provided. Restrooms have hot showers and flush toilets. A coin laundry, boat ramp, dock, and playground are provided, along with a sanitary disposal station. Leashed pets are permitted.

Reservations, fees: Reservations are accepted through the National Recreation Reservation Service (NRRS) at 877/444-6777, website: www.reserveusa.com. The full amount is payable in advance. The sites are $12 if not on the water, $14 otherwise.

Open: Year-round.

Directions: From Camden, take Highway 28 west nine miles.

Contact: US Army Corps of Engineers, Dannelly Resource Office, 1226 Power House Rd., Camden, AL 36726-9106; 334/682-4191; website: www.reserveusa.com.

Trip notes: Fishing for catfish, crappie, bream, and bass are available at the river at the campground. There are hiking trails in the park.

❺ Roland Cooper State Park

Location: Camden, map 1, grid H7.

Campsites, facilities: There are 13 tent sites, and 41 RV sites with full hookups. All have shade. Two are pull-through sites. Picnic tables, fire rings, and cooking grills are provided. Primitive camping is also available, as well as five cabins. RV storage is available, and a sanitary disposal station is provided. Restrooms have hot showers and flush toilets. A coin laundry, boat ramp, dock, and playground are provided. Ice is available at the campground. Leashed pets are permitted in the campground, but not in the cabins or cabin area.

Reservations, fees: Reservations are accepted for 15 of the campsites at 800/ALA-PARK (800/252-7275). The deposit of one night's fee is non-refundable, but you can move the date of your reservation twice. Rates range from $8 for tent sites to $14 for full hookups. The cabins are $43–63 per night, depending on time of year.

Open: Year-round.

Directions: Take Highway 41 five miles north of Camden, and follow the signs.

Contact: Roland Cooper State Park, 285 Deer Run Dr., Camden, AL 36726; 334/682-4838.

Trip notes: The campground is located on the Bill Dannelly Reservoir. Fishing is available in the river for crappie, bass, catfish, and bream. There is a short (.5-mile) hiking trail. Wildlife in the area includes deer, wild turkeys, and red foxes.

6 Service Park

Location: Tombigbee River, map 2, grid B7.
Campsites, Facilities: There are two tent sites and 32 sites suitable for either tents or RVs. The dual-use sites have water and electric hookups. Picnic tables are provided. Restrooms have hot showers and flush toilets. A sanitary disposal station, coin laundry, boat ramp, and playground are provided. The restrooms are wheelchair accessible. Leashed pets are permitted.
Reservations, fees: Reservations are accepted through the National Recreation Reservation Service (NRRS) at 877/444-6777, website: www.reserveusa.com. The full amount is payable in advance. Waterfront campsites are $14 per night, and other sites are $12.
Open: Year-round.
Directions: From Grove Hill, travel west on US 84. The campground is on Highway 84 between US 42 and Highway 17, three miles west of Coffeeville.
Contact: US Army Corps of Engineers, 384 Resource Management Dr., Demopolis, AL 36732; 251/754-9338, or 334/289-3540.
Trip notes: This campground is on the Tombigbee River and is subject to flooding, so call before planning to camp here. Fishing, boating, and water-skiing are available on the river.

7 Bladon Springs State Park

Location: Bladon Springs, map 2, grid C7.
Campsites, Facilities: There are 10 RV sites, all with full hookups. Picnic tables and cooking grills are provided. Restrooms have flush toilets. A playground is provided. Leashed pets are permitted.
Reservations, fees: Reservations are accepted at 251/754-9207. No deposit is required. Sites cost $12 per night.
Open: Year-round.
Directions: From Evergreen, take US 84 west through Coffeeville and over the Tom Bigbee River. Three miles after you cross the river, turn left onto County Road 6. Travel four miles to the campground.
Contact: Bladon Springs State Park 2139 Bladon Road, Bladon Springs, AL 36901; 251/754-9207.
Trip notes: There are old hiking trails in the state park, but they were not being maintained at press time. Wildlife you may see in the campground includes deer and wild turkeys. This is a quiet park. The artesian springs the park is named for are tapped for drinking water.

8 Washington County Campground

Location: Millry, map 2, grid C6.
Campsites, facilities: The campground has 12 sites suitable for tents or RVs, all with water and electric hookups. Most sites have good shade. Picnic tables and cooking grills are provided. Restrooms have hot showers and flush toilets. A sanitary disposal station, boat ramp, and playground are provided. Ice and snacks are available at the campground. Some of the buildings are wheelchair accessible. Pets are permitted.
Reservations, fees: Reservations are accepted, and no deposit is required. The fee for tents is $7.50 per night, and $10 for RVs.
Open: The campground is open from January through November.
Directions: From Mobile, travel north on US 45 ap-

proximately 40 miles to Deer Park, and turn right on Highway 17. Take Highway 17 about 30 miles to Millry, and turn right on Highway 36. After two miles, turn left on Lake Road at the sign for the J Emmett Public Fishing area.

Contact: Washington County Campground, Rt. 1, Box 17AA, Millry, AL 36558; 251/846-2512.

Trip notes: The lake is stocked with catfish, bass, bluegill, and shell cracker. Deer and Canada geese are the most commonly seen wildlife in the park. It is a wildlife preserve basically in the middle of nowhere. No hunting is allowed in the area.

9 Citronelle Lakeview RV Park

Location: Citronelle, map 2, grid H6.

Campsites, facilities: There are 10 tent sites and 38 RV sites at this campground. Twenty-eight sites have full hookups, and seven are pull-through. Picnic tables and fire rings are provided, and cooking grills are available at the pavilions. Group sites and RV storage are available. Restrooms have flush toilets and hot showers. Firewood, ice, and video tape rentals are available at the campground store. Delivery of LP gas is available. A boat ramp and dock are provided. Boat motors on the lake are restricted to electric only. A sanitary disposal station is provided. The restrooms are wheelchair accessible. Leashed pets are permitted. You must clean up after your pet.

Reservations, fees: Reservations are accepted. Camp sites are $17.50 per night or $100 per week.

Open: Year-round.

Directions: From Mobile, take US 45 north 30 miles. Turn west on County Road 96. The campground is approximately six miles from Highway 45.

Contact: Citronelle Lakeview RV Park, 17850 Municipal Park Dr., Citronelle, AL 36522; 251/866-9647.

Trip notes: Fishing is available in the 100-acre lake for bass, catfish, bream, and perch. A hiking trail was under construction at the time of this writing. Paddleboats are available for rent. Swimming is available at the lake, and the campground is adjacent to an 18-hole public golf course.

10 Isaac Creek Campgound

Location: Claiborne Lake, map 3, grid D4.

Campsites, Facilities: The campground has 55 sites, all available for either tents or RVs. All have water and electric hookups, and most have some shade. Five are pull-through sites. All sites have picnic tables, fire rings, and cooking grills. Restrooms have hot showers and flush toilets. A coin laundry, boat ramps, docks, a sanitary disposal station, three playgrounds, and activity fields are provided. The buildings are wheelchair accessible. Leashed pets are permitted.

Reservations, fees: Reservations are accepted through the National Recreation Reservation Service (NRRS) at 877/444-6777, website: www.reserveusa.com. The full amount is payable in advance. Waterfront sites are $14 per night. All other sites are $12 per night. Golden Age and Golden Access discounts apply.

Open: Year-round.

Directions: From Monroeville, take Highway 41 north to County Road 17/13. Turn left, and follow the signs. The campground is about 20 miles from Monroeville.

Contact: US Army Corps of Engineers, Dannelly Resource Office, 1226 Power House Rd., Camden, AL 36726-9106; 251/282-4254; website: www.reserveusa.com.

Trip notes: The Alabama River Heritage Museum is located in the park. Fishing is available for catfish, crappie, bream, and bass all year. There are two hiking trails, the longest being the Cypress Trail at two miles in length. Biking is permissible on the paved roadways. Wildlife is plentiful, including deer, squirrels, turkeys, hummingbirds, and wild hogs.

Claude D. Kelley State Park

Location: Atmore, map 3, grid F5.
Campsites, Facilities: There are seven tent sites, all with some shade and all with water and electric hookups. There are 12 RV sites, all with shade. Five of the RV sites have full hookups, and three are pull-through sites. There are also group sites, unlimited primitive sites, and one cabin for rent. Picnic tables, fire rings, and cooking grills are provided. Restrooms have hot showers and flush toilets in the developed campground. A playground is provided. A sanitary disposal station is provided. Ice and firewood are available. A boat ramp and dock are provided. The buildings are wheelchair accessible. Leashed pets are permitted.
Reservations, fees: Reservations are accepted for the cabin, but the campground is first-come, first-served. The deposit of one night's site fee is required, and is refundable. Site fees are $6–12 per night, depending on hookups. The cabin is $41.60 per night.
Open: Year-round.
Directions: From Evergreen, take Interstate 65 south to take Highway 21 north. The park is about 10 miles from the interstate.
Contact: Claude D. Kelley State Park, 580 H.

Kyle Rd., Atmore, AL 36502; 251/862-2511, fax 251/862-2511.

Trip notes: The park was built in the 1930s by the CCC, and the original buildings are somewhat rustic. Fishing is available at the 25-acre lake for bass, bream, and catfish. Paddleboats, johnboats, and canoes are available for rent. There are three hiking trails vary from two to 3.5 miles in length. A variety of wildflowers bloom in the spring and summer, and a profusion of dogwoods offer both spring and fall color. Wildlife seen in the park includes deer, turkeys, squirrels, raccoons, and bobcats.

Country Sunshine RV Park

Location: Castleberry, map 3, grid F8.
Campsites, facilities: There are two tent sites with hookups, both with shade and both pull-through sites. In a separate section, there are 11 RV sites, all pull-through sites with full hookups. Three of them offer some shade. Picnic tables, fire rings, and cooking grills are provided. Restrooms have hot showers and flush toilets. Firewood is available. A coin laundry, playground, and sanitary disposal station are provided. RV storage is available. The buildings are wheelchair accessible. Leashed pets are permitted. You must clean up after your pet.
Reservations, fees: Reservations are accepted, and no deposit is required. The fee for tent sites is $10 per night, and $15 for RV sites.
Open: Year-round.
Directions: The campground is located halfway between Montgomery and Mobile. Take exit 83 off Interstate 65 and go east on County Road 6 for 3.5 miles.
Contact: Country Sunshine RV Park, Rt. 2, Box 290, Castleberry, AL 36432; 251/966-5540 or 251/966-5560.

Trip notes: This is a quiet, peaceful campground, which caters to families. There are four fishing ponds within one mile offering catfish, bream, and trout. Nearby restaurants have seafood, Cajun, or country cooking.

13 Hubbard's Landing

Location: Stockton, map 3, grid H2.
Campsites, facilities: This campground has 50 campsites, all with full hookups. Although tents are allowed, this is primarily an RV campground. Picnic tables and some cooking grills are provided. Six cabins are also available. Restrooms have hot showers and flush toilets. The campground store sells ice, supplies, groceries, and bait. A boat ramp and dock are provided, and marine gas is available.
Reservations, fees: Reservations are accepted. A deposit of one night's stay is required, and is refundable with a 10-day notice. No credit cards are accepted. The campground does not publish its rates.
Open: Year-round.
Directions: From Mobile, take Interstate 65 north to exit 34, Highway 59, and head north. North of Stockton, turn left on County Road 96 to the lake and campground.
Contact: Hubbard's Landing, 9100 Hubbard's Landing Rd., Stockton, AL 36579; 251/937-5726.
Trip notes: Freshwater fishing is available in the lake, but no swimming, water-skiing, or Jet Skis are permitted.

14 Upper Bryant Landing

Location: Tensaw Lake, map 3, grid H1.
Campsites, facilities: There are 14 RV sites at this campground, all with full hookups, and half with shade. Picnic tables are pro-

vided. Group sites and cabins are available. Restrooms have hot showers and flush toilets. Ice and some groceries are available at the campground. A sanitary disposal station, boat ramp, and dock are provided. The buildings are wheelchair accessible. Pets are permitted.
Reservations, fees: Reservations are accepted. No deposit is required. The rate is $13 per night for RVs or campers and $9 for tents.
Open: Year-round.
Directions: From Mobile, take Interstate 65 north to exit 34, Highway 59, and head north approximately two miles. Turn left on County Road 21, and follow the signs to the lake and Upper Bryant Landing Road.
Contact: Upper Bryant Landing, 8075 Bryant Landing Rd., Stockton, AL 36574; 251/580-2610.
Trip notes: Fishing is available at the lake for bream, bass, and crappie. Paddleboats are available for rent.

15 Escatawpa Hollow Campground

Location: Escatawpa River, map 4, grid B5.
Campsites, facilities: The 15 primitive tent sites are along the river. The 22 RV sites all have water and electric hookups. Ten of the RV sites are pull-through, and about half have shade. All sites have picnic tables, and some have fire rings or cooking grills. Some sites have patios. Restrooms have hot showers and flush toilets. RV storage is available. A sanitary disposal station, boat ramp, and volleyball court are provided. The buildings are wheelchair accessible. Leashed pets are permitted for overnight travelers, but not for campers staying a week or more.
Reservations, fees: Reservations are accepted. Deposits are required for holiday

weekends, and are refundable if cancellation is made at least one week in advance. The fee is $20 for RVs and $10 for up to two people in tents; fees for additional campers are $5 per adult and $4 per children.

Open: Year-round.

Directions: From Mobile, take Interstate 65 north to exit 3. Travel west on US 98 for 22 miles. US 98 becomes Moffett Road.

Contact: Escatawpa Hollow Campground, 15551 Moffett Rd., Wilmer, AL 36587; 251/649-4233.

Trip notes: Fishing is available in the creek and river for bream, catfish, and goggle-eye bass. There is a short nature trail by the creek, and a sand beach in the swimming area. Kayaking, rafting, canoeing, and tubing are popular on the creek.

16 I-65 RV Campground

Location: Mobile, map 4, grid A8.

Campsites, Facilities: There are 10 primitive tent sites, and 76 RV sites with full hookups at this campground. Most sites have some shade. Sixteen of the sites are pull-through. Picnic tables are provided. Restrooms have hot showers and flush toilets. Ice, LP gas, and groceries are available at the campground store. A large discount store is less than 10 miles away. Food delivery is available. A sanitary disposal station, children's play area, and clubroom are provided. Telephone service is available at weekly or monthly sites. One restroom is wheelchair accessible. Pets are permitted provided they are on an eight-foot maximum length leash, walked in designated areas, and kept in your camper at night. You must pick up after your pet. Pets are not allowed in buildings and must not disturb other campers.

Reservations, fees: Reservations are accepted with a major credit card at 800/287-3208. Cancellations without penalty are allowed provided the reservation is cancelled 24 hours prior to the scheduled arrival (48 hours prior for holiday periods). Sites cost $20-21 depending on hookups, and Good Sam and FMCA discounts apply.

Open: Year-round.

Directions: From Mobile, take Interstate 65 north to exit 19 and turn north on US 43. Turn west on Jackson Road to the campground.

Contact: I-65 RV Campground, 730 Jackson Rd., Creola, AL 36525; 251/675-6347; website: www.i65rvcampground.com.

Trip notes: Fishing for bass and bluegill is available at the campground, and hiking trails are nearby. The campground is about 90 miles from the beach at Gulf Shores, and 15 miles from Mobile.

17 Chickasabogue Park

Location: Mobile, map 4, grid B8.

Campsites, facilities: There are 10 tent sites at this campground, and 38 RV sites in a separate section. Twelve RV sites have full hookups, and 28 are pull-through. All sites have shade. Picnic tables, fire rings, and cooking grills are provided. There are seven primitive sites, and group sites are available. Restrooms have hot showers and flush toilets. A coin laundry, boat ramp, dock, clubroom, and playground are provided. Ice, groceries, and firewood are available at the campground store. Other supplies are within two miles. A sanitary disposal station is provided. The buildings are wheelchair accessible. Pets are permitted if kept on leash and if you have proof of current rabies vaccination.

Reservations, fees: Reservations are accepted. The deposit of one night's fee is refundable if the reservation is cancelled at least 24 hours in advance. Primitive sites are $5 per night, tent sites are $9 per night, and RVs sites are $12–15, depending on hookups.
Open: Year-round.

Directions: From Mobile, go north on Interstate 65 to exit 13, and turn left onto US 213 south. Turn left immediately onto Shelton Beach Road, left onto Whistler Street, and left again onto Aldock Road.

Contact: Chickasabogue Park, 760 Aldock Rd., Mobile, AL 36613; 251/457-0541; fax 251/457-0541; email: rjones@mobile-county.net.

Trip notes: This 1,200-acre county park includes a lake that offers fishing for bass, bluegill, sea trout, flounder, and red fish. Canoes can be rented at the park. The swimming area has a sand beach. There are three connected loop trails totaling 11 miles for mountain biking, and additional miles are added to the trails periodically. Though, technically, the trails can be used by both hikers and mountain bikers, this is one of the most popular mountain biking areas in the region. Because of the heavy use by bikers, these aren't recommended as good hiking trails. The park has an 18-hole disc golf course, and a wildlife refuge. The primitive camping sites are all on the water, and some can be reached only by canoe or boat.

18 Brown's RV Park

Location: Gulf, map 4, grid C7.
Campsites, Facilities: There are 38 RV sites, all with full hookups. Pull-through sites are available, and most sites have shade. Both 30- and 50-amp service is available. Picnic tables are provided. Most sites have either a patio or a deck. Restrooms have hot showers and flush toilets. A coin laundry is provided. Cable TV is free to overnight guests. A computer and modem are available in the office. Leashed pets are permitted.

Reservations, fees: Reservations are accepted at 251/342-3383. No deposit is required. Sites rent for $18 per night or $110 per week, which includes cable TV. The monthly rate is $240 without cable, or $255 with. Phone lines are available for long-term guests.

Open: Year-round.

Directions: In Mobile, take Interstate 65 to exit 5B and turn west onto US 98/Moffett Road. Travel 3.5 miles to Howell's Ferry Road and turn left. After one block, turn left onto Dover Street. The campground is .2 miles down Dover Street on the left.

Contact: Brown's RV Park, 1619 Jasper Road, Mobile, AL 36618; 251/342-3383; email brownsrvpark@aol.com; website www.brownsrvpark.com.

Trip notes: It is about 15 miles to either a fishing lake or the Bay. The campground is within walking distance of groceries, a post office, and supplies, and is less then two miles to the Robert Trent Jones golf coarse, the Mitchell House, and the Mobile Museum of Art. It is convenient to all of the attractions in the Mobile area. There aren't a lot of amenities, but the resident manager stays onsite, and the campground is a quiet, friendly play to stay.

19 Ace's RV Park

Location: Mobile, map 4, grid C7.
Campsites, facilities: There are 40 RV sites, all with full hookups. Ten are pull-through sites. Shade is available. Picnic tables are provided. RV storage is available. A coin laundry is provided. Pets are permitted.

Reservations, fees: Reservations are accepted, and no deposit is required. Campsites are $20 per night, and you can get a $5 discount by asking at any Alabama visitors' center. Weekly and monthly discounts are available.

Open: Year-round.

Directions: From Mobile, take Interstate 65 south to Interstate 10 east across the bay. Take exit 35, and turn west on US 98/Moffett Road one block to the campground.

Contact: Ace's RV Park, 3815 Moffett Rd., Mobile, AL 36618-1200; 251/460-4633; email: acesrvpark@aol.com; website: www.acesrvpark.com.

Trip notes: This campground is convenient to many attractions in Mobile, including Bellingrath Gardens, Robert Trent Jones Golf Course, Hank Aaron Baseball Stadium, the Mobile Convention and Civic Center, Gulf Fairgrounds, Dauphin Island, the beach, tournament tennis complexes, and Battleship Park. The campsites are level and landscaped.

20 I-10 Kampground

Location: Gulf, map 4, grid D7.

Campsites, Facilities: The campground has 25 tent sites, most with water and electric hookups. There are 164 RV sites, all with full hookups. Both 30- and 50-amp service is available. Some sites have shade. Pull-through sites are available. Some sites have picnic tables. Restrooms have hot showers and flush toilets. Ice and some groceries are available at the campground. A coin laundry and swimming pool are provided. Cable TV is available. Leashed pets are permitted.

Reservations, fees: Reservations are accepted at 251/653-9816. No deposit is required. Tent sites are $14 per night, and RV sites cost $21. Rates are discounted $2 for

Good Sam, AAA, Golden Age, AARP, and KOA members. Cable TV and 50-amp service cost $2 per night each, and there is a lodging tax of $1.

Open: Year-round.

Directions: From Mobile, take Interstate 10 west to exit 13/Theodore-Dawes Road and turn left. The campground is half a mile down on the left.

Contact: I-10 Kampground, 6430 Theodore-Dawes Road, Theodore, AL 36582; 251/653-9816.

Trip notes: The campground is 16 miles from the attractions in downtown Mobile, and six miles from Bellingrath Gardens. The best fishing in the area is at Dolphin Island, about 25 miles away.

21 Shady Grove Campground

Location: Mobile, map 4, grid D7.

Campsites, facilities: There are 90 RV sites at this campground, all with full hookups. Both 30- and 50-amp services are available. Picnic tables are provided. Restrooms have hot showers and flush toilets. A coin laundry is provided, and cable TV hookups are available. The buildings are wheelchair accessible. Pets are permitted, but must not be left outside.

Reservations, fees: Reservations are accepted, and no deposit is required. Campsites are $16 per night for a 30-amp hookup, $17 for a 50-amp.

Open: Year-round.

Directions: From Mobile, take Interstate 65 south to Interstate 10 east across the bay. Take exit 15A/US 90 west about four miles. The campground will be on the left.

Contact: Shady Grove Campground, 6171 Highway 90 West, Theodore, AL 36582; 251/653-0835.

Trip notes: The majority of campers here are monthly

renters. The campground is two miles from the Mobile International Speedway, and near to Bayou La Batre, home of the Bubba Gump Shrimp Company from *Forrest Gump.*

22 US Coast Guard Recreational Facility

Location: Dauphin Island, map 4, grid G8.
Campsites, facilities: The campground has 100 primitive tent sites, and five RV sites with full hookups. Picnic tables and cooking grills are provided. There are also 13 cabins. Restrooms have hot showers and flush toilets. A coin laundry, playground, and video arcade are provided. Groceries and ice are available at the campground. Two of the cabins are wheelchair accessible.
Reservations, fees: Reservations are accepted. A deposit of the full fee is required and is refundable if cancellation is received at least five days in advance. Primitive sites are $5 per night, and RV sites are $13. The cabins are rented for a minimum of two days for $100.
Open: Year-round.
Directions: From Mobile, take Interstate 10 to exit 17/Highway 193 south to the island. Turn left on Bienville Boulevard. Turn right on Agassiz Street.
Contact: US Coast Guard Recreational Facility, P.O. Box 436, Dauphin Island, AL 36528; 251/861-7113.
Trip notes: The campground is restricted to active and retired military personnel and their families. The island is a layover point for migratory birds, and there are special events for birdwatchers in the winter months. The Dauphin Island Audubon Bird sanctuary has several hiking and biking trails. There

are tennis courts, a public golf course, and a swimming pool on the island, and a sea life museum with hands-on exhibits.

23 Dauphin Island Campground

Location: Dauphin Island, map 4, grid G8.
Campsites, facilities: There are 15 tent sites with water and electric hookups. There are also 135 RV sites, about half with full hookups and the rest with water and electric service only. Shade is available. Picnic tables and some fire rings are provided. Restrooms have hot showers and flush toilets. A coin laundry and playground are provided. Ice, LP gas, some groceries, and limited supplies are available at the campground. The buildings are wheelchair accessible. Leashed pets are permitted.
Reservations, fees: Reservations are accepted, and no deposit is required. Tent sites are $15 per night, and RV sites are $22–26 per night.
Open: Year-round.
Directions: From Mobile, take Interstate 10 to exit 17/Highway 193 south to the island. Turn left onto Bienville Boulevard. After 2.5 miles, the campground will be on the right.
Contact: Dauphin Island Campground, 109 Bienville Blvd., Dauphin Island, AL 36528; 251/861-2742.
Trip notes: The campground is located across the street from a boat ramp, and saltwater fishing is available. It is next to Dauphin Island Audubon Bird Sanctuary, which is open to the public. There are six miles of biking and jogging trails on the island. The campground has a private path and boardwalk to the beach.

24 Mobile North River Delta KOA

Location: Mobile, map 5, grid A1.

Campsites, facilities: There are 42 campsites at this campground. Fifteen sites have water and electric hookups and can be used by tents or RVs. The rest have full hookups. All are pull-through sites. There are four cabins for rent. Picnic tables are provided. Some sites have fire rings, and the cabins have cooking grills. Restrooms have hot showers and flush toilets. A coin laundry, sanitary disposal station, swimming pool, playground, boat ramp, and dock are provided. Ice, LP gas, supplies, groceries, bait, and fishing supplies are available at the campground. The restrooms are wheelchair accessible. Leashed pets are permitted in the campground and cabins.

Reservations, fees: Reservations are accepted. The deposit is refundable with a two-week advance notice prior to your scheduled arrival. The fee for tent sites is $17, RV sites are $19, and cabins rent for $30 per night.

Open: Year-round.

Directions: From Mobile, go north on Interstate 65 to exit 22 and turn left on the service road. Turn left on Sailor Road, then right onto Dead Lake Road.

Contact: Mobile North River Delta KOA, 2350 Dead Lake Rd., Creola, AL 36525; 251/675-0320.

Trip notes: The campground is on Dead Lake and also has a small fishing pond stocked with perch, bream, bass, and catfish. Paddleboats are available for rent. Wildlife in the area includes alligators and snakes.

25 Historic Blakeley State Park

Location: Gulf, map 5, grid C1.

Campsites, Facilities: There are 36 campsites suitable for tents or RVs. Picnic tables and fire rings are provided. Cabins are also available. Restrooms are pit toilets. A small boat ramp (for hand-carried boats) is provided. There is no drinking water available. Leashed pets and horses are permitted. Keep a close watch on small pets due to the alligators.

Reservations, fees: Reservations are accepted at 800/ALA-PARK (800/252-7275). The deposit of one night's fee is non-refundable, but you can move the date of your reservation twice. The fee is $10 per night.

Open: Year-round.

Directions: From Mobile, take Interstate 65 south to Interstate 10 east across the bay. Take exit 35A and turn left on US 98. At the top of the hill in Spanish Fort, turn right onto US 31, then left at the next light onto Highway 225. The park will be on the left, 4.5 miles from US 31.

Contact: Historic Blakeley State Park, 33707 State Highway 225, P.O. Box 7279, Spanish Fort, AL 36577-7279; 251/626-0798; email: Blakeley@dibbs.net.

Trip notes: Blakeley is believed to be the site of the last battle of the Civil War, as the battle was fought after the war was over but before the soldiers learned of the outcome. The Tensaw River offers canoeing, as well as fishing for bass, bream, catfish, and mullet. There are 10.5 miles of hiking, biking, and horseback riding trails. Wildlife in the area includes deer, a variety of birds, and a healthy population of alligators.

26 Meaher State Park

Location: Mobile Bay, map 5, grid C1.

Campsites, facilities: The campground has 12 sites for tents or RVs, all with water and electric hookups. Picnic tables and cooking grills are provided. Pit toilets and a sanitary disposal station are provided. A playground, boat launch, fishing pier, and 1,300-foot boardwalk are available. Leashed pets are permitted.

Reservations, fees: Reservations are accepted, if the entire amount is paid in advance. The deposit is refundable with two week's notice. Campsites are $13–15 per night.

Open: Year-round.

Directions: From Mobile, take Interstate 65 south to Interstate 10 east across the bay. Take exit 35A and turn left onto US 98. The park is a couple of miles from the interstate, between the last two bridges on the right.

Contact: Meaher State Park, 5200 Battleship Parkway E., P.O. Box 7826, Spanish Fort, AL 36577; 251/626-5529.

Trip notes: This campground doesn't have a lot of frills, but it is located on Mobile Bay, and the main draw is salt- and freshwater fishing. There are two short nature trails. The campground is located about four miles from the USS *Alabama.*

27 Styx River Water World Camp Park

Location: Loxley, map 5, grid C4.

Campsites, facilities: There are 20 tent sites, and, in a separate section, 25 RV sites. The RV sites have water and electric hookups, and 10 are pull-through. RVs must be 30 feet or less in length. There are 30 primitive campsites. RV storage is available, and a sanitary disposal station is provided. Picnic tables, fire rings, and cooking grills are provided. Restrooms have hot showers and flush toilets. Firewood and ice are available. A playground and swimming pool are provided. Pets are permitted only in the primitive sites and must be leashed at all times.

Reservations, fees: Reservations are accepted. The deposit is refundable if your reservation is cancelled, but not for no-shows. The campground does not publish its rates.

Open: The RV section is open year-round.

Directions: From Mobile, take Interstate 10 east across the bay to exit 53/Wilcox Road. Turn east on Wilcox Road and travel eight miles to the campground.

Contact: Styx River Water World Camp Park, 24875 Water World Rd., Rt. 3, Box 340, Robertsdale, AL 36567-5017; 251/580-4157.

Trip notes: The campground is adjacent to a 54-acre water park, and discount tickets are available. River and lake fishing for bass, bream, and catfish is available. There is a one-mile nature walk along the Styx River. Canoes and inner tubes are available for rent. Wildlife in the area includes deer, bears, otters, and water birds. The campground is 25 miles from Gulf Shores, and about halfway between Pensacola and Mobile.

28 Hilltop RV Park

Location: Gulf, map 5, grid D4.

Campsites, facilities: There are 75 RV sites, all with full hookups. Most are pull-through sites, and most sites have picnic tables. RV storage is available. Restrooms have hot showers and flush toilets. A coin laundry and recreation building are provided. Pets are permitted.

Reservations, fees: Reservations are accepted, and no deposit is required. Campsites are $18 per night, or $90 per week.
Open: Year-round.
Directions: From Mobile, take Interstate 65 south to Interstate 10 east across the bay. Take exit 53/Wilcox Road, and travel south a half mile to the campground.
Contact: Hilltop RV Park, 23420 County Road 64, Robertsdale, AL 36567; 251/960-1129.
Trip notes: This campground is adults-only for weekly renters. Children are accepted for overnight stays only, but this is not a good choice for families with kids since there is nothing for them to do, and no one for them to do it with. Children must not be left unattended at any time. There is a small fish pond at the campground, stocked with bream and bluegill. The campground is within two miles of the Styx River, popular with canoeists. A water park and a shooting range are within two miles, and the campground is about half an hour from Gulf Shores, which offers beaches, bungee jumping, miniature golf, and shopping.

29 Wilderness RV Park

Location: Gulf, map 5, grid D4.
Campsites, facilities: There are 70 RV sites at this campground. All sites have full hookups, and all are pull-through sites. Most have some shade, and most have picnic tables. Restrooms have hot showers and flush toilets. Ice, LP gas, and snacks are available at the campground. A sanitary disposal station, coin laundry, swimming pool, clubroom, library, TV room, and hot tub are provided. Pets are permitted, but they must be kept leashed, and you must clean up after your pet.
Reservations, fees: Reservations are accepted, and no deposit is required. Campsites are $18 per night.
Open: The campground is closed the first two weeks of August.
Directions: From Mobile, take Interstate 65 south to Interstate 10 east across the bay. Take exit 53/Wilcox Road, and travel south a third of a mile, and turn left on Patterson Road.
Contact: Wilderness RV Park, 24280 Patterson Rd., Robertsdale, AL 36567; 251/960-1195.
Trip notes: This campground is primarily for members only, but vacant sites are rented to drop-ins. It has a small lake and small fishing pond, stocked with bass, catfish, and bream. It is within a half-hour drive of the USS *Alabama*, Bellingrath Gardens, Seville Square in Pensacola, Gulf Shores beaches, and outlet shopping in Foley.

30 East Park Plaza Mobile Home Park

Location: Gulf, map 5, grid D1.
Campsites, facilities: There are 26 RV sites at this campground. All have full hookups, and shade is available. There are no restrooms.
Reservations, fees: Reservations are not accepted. Campsites are $14 per night.
Open: Year-round.
Directions: From Mobile, take Interstate 65 south to Interstate 10 east across the bay. Take exit 35 and turn south on US 98. The campground is six miles south of the interstate, at mile marker 43.
Contact: East Park Plaza Mobile Home Park, 111 North Ingleside, Fairhope, AL 36532; 251/928-7619.
Trip notes: The campground is 45 minutes to the beach, and 10 minutes from the USS *Alabama*.

31 American RV Park

Location: Summerdale, map 5, grid E3.

Campsites, facilities: There are 28 RV sites at this campground, all with full hookups. No restrooms are provided. Cable TV hookups are available. Pets are permitted.

Reservations, fees: Reservations are not accepted. Campsites are $10 per night, and $200 per month.

Open: Year-round.

Directions: From Mobile, take Interstate 65 south to Interstate 10 east across the bay. Take exit 44 and turn south on Highway 59 towards Loxley. The campground is on Highway 59, about 20 miles from Loxley, roughly halfway between Loxley and Gulf Shores.

Contact: American RV Park, 208 North Highway 59, Summerdale, AL 36580; 251/989-6522.

Trip notes: The majority of the campers here rent monthly, but there are usually sites for vacationers. The campground is about 30 minutes from the Gulf of Mexico.

32 Escapees Rainbow Plantation

Location: Robertsdale, map 5, grid E2.

Campsites, facilities: There are 98 RV sites, all with full hookups. RVs are restricted to 40 feet or less. Restrooms have hot showers and flush toilets. A coin laundry, swimming pool, sanitary disposal station, and clubroom are provided. Supplies are available within four miles. The buildings are wheelchair accessible. Leashed pets are permitted.

Reservations, fees: Reservations are not accepted. The fee is $15 per night.

Open: Year-round.

Directions: From Interstate 10, take exit 44 south 14 miles to County Road 28, and turn west. Travel 4.5 miles to the campground.

Contact: Escapees Rainbow Plantation, 14301 County Road 28, Summerdale, AL 36580; 251/988-8132; website: www.escapees.com.

Trip notes: This campground is a member of the Escapees Club, a network for full-time RVers. It is open to the public only when there are adequate vacancies. The campground is near Gulf Shores beaches, where fishing boats can be chartered.

33 Southwind RV Park

Location: Gulf, map 5, grid E2.

Campsites, facilities: There are 120 RV sites at this campground, all with full hookups. All are pull-through sites. About half of the sites have some shade. Both 30- and 50-amp service is available. There are also three cabins, and four efficiency apartments. RV storage is available. Restrooms have hot showers and flush toilets. A coin laundry and clubroom are provided. Cable TV hookups are available. Supplies and groceries are available within a mile. The restrooms are wheelchair accessible. Pets are permitted, provided you clean up after your pet.

Reservations, fees: Reservations are not accepted. Fees are $18 per night or $98 per week.

Open: Year-round.

Directions: From Mobile, take Interstate 65 south to Interstate 10 east across the bay. Take exit 35 and turn south on US 98. At Magnolia Springs, turn left on County Road 9 and head north. The campground will be on the left.

Contact: Southwind RV Park, 12863 County Road 9 North, Magnolia Springs, AL 36555; 251/988-1216.

Trip notes: The campground is one mile from Weeks Bay, where fishing is available for trout, red fish, bass, bream, and flounder. Hiking is available in the Weeks Bay Bog Walk, which backs up to the campground. The Weeks Bay Estuary is part of a national estuarine research reserve system. In addition to fishing and hiking, the estuary contains hummingbird and butterfly gardens and an interpretive center, and offers bird and wildlife photography opportunities. The campground is seven miles from Foley, home of the second largest outlet mall in the country. The campground caters to seniors and has many organized activities in the winter months. Because of this, it might not be the best choice for families with young children.

34 Safe Harbor RV Resort and Marina

Location: Gulf, map 5, grid E2.
Campsites, facilities: There are 20 acres available for primitive camping. Piped water is available. The campground also has 115 RV sites with full hookups, including cable TV. Most are pull-through sites, and all have shade. RVs must be 45 feet or less. Picnic tables and fire rings are provided in the developed campsites. Group sites are available. There are also six cabins available and RV storage. Restrooms have hot showers and flush toilets. A coin laundry, boat ramp, dock, playground, and play room are provided. Ice, supplies, LP gas, and marine gas are available. Pets are permitted, both in the campground and the cabins.
Reservations, fees: Reservations are accepted at 800/928-4544. No deposit is

required. Tent sites are $10 per night; sites with full hookups are $20. The cabins are $125 per week.
Open: Year-round.
Directions: From Mobile, take Interstate 65 south to Interstate 10 east across the bay. Take exit 35 and turn south on US 98. The campground is on the north side of US 98, just past Fairhope.
Contact: Safe Harbor RV Resort and Marina, 11401 US Highway 98, Fairhope, AL 36532; 251/928-2629.
Trip notes: There are four fishing ponds stocked with catfish and bass, and fishing for bass, mullet, and flounder is also available at the river. There is also a swimming area at the river. The campground is across the street from the Weeks Bay Estuary, which has hiking trails.

35 Pop's RV

Location: Gulf, map 5, grid E5.
Campsites, facilities: There are 25 RV sites, all with full hookups. Restrooms have hot showers and flush toilets. A coin laundry, sanitary disposal station, driving range, and putting green are provided. Supplies are available at a store next door. Leashed pets are permitted.
Reservations, fees: Reservations are accepted, and no deposit is required. Campsites cost $10 per night for one or two nights, and $9 per night for three or more nights.
Open: Year-round.
Directions: The campground is one mile from the Florida state line on US 98.
Contact: Pop's RV, P.O. Box 868, Lillian, AL 36549; 251/962-3066.
Trip notes: The campground is near to fishing and swim-

ming on the Gulf, and has a driving range and practice green.

36 Magnolia Springs RV

Location: Gulf, map 5, grid F2.

Campsites, Facilities: The campground has 38 RV sites, all with full hookups. Most sites have shade. Picnic tables are provided, and RV storage is available. Restrooms have hot showers and flush toilets. Groceries are available about two miles away. The restrooms are wheelchair accessible. Leashed pets are permitted. You must clean up after your pet.

Reservations, fees: Reservations are accepted at 251/965-4653. At press time, the campground had just changed ownership and was revamping their deposit and fee schedule. Please call for current rates.

Open: Year-round.

Directions: From Mobile, take Interstate 10 east to Highway 59 and turn south. In Foley, turn right onto County Road 26. At the dead-end, turn left onto County Road 49/Magnolia Springs Highway. The campground is two blocks down on the right.

Contact: Magnolia Springs RV, 10831 Magnolia Springs Highway, Magnolia Springs, AL 36555; 251/965-4653; email david@magnoliaspringsgolf.com; website www.magnoliaspringsgolf.com.

Trip notes: At press time, the campground and adjacent nine hole, par three golf course had just been purchased, and all of the campsites were being upgraded and paved. Fishing and hiking are available at Weeks Bay, about five miles away. There are boardwalks through the wetlands area at Weeks Bay and the Fish River. The beach is about 15 miles from the campground.

37 Helen's Mobile Home and RV Park

Location: Gulf, map 5, grid F3.

Campsites, facilities: There are 18 RV sites, all with full hookups. Both 30- and 50-amp service is available. Pull-through sites are available. Some sites have shade, and some picnic tables are available. There are no restrooms. Cable TV hookups are available. Leashed pets are permitted. They must be kept inside your camper at night.

Reservations, fees: Reservations are accepted, and no deposit is required. The sites are $12 per night.

Open: Year-round.

Directions: From Foley, go south on Highway 59 past the Riviera Centre outlet mall, and turn left onto County Road 20. Turn left onto Juniper Street after one-half mile.

Contact: Helen's Mobile Home and RV Park, 10340 Juniper St., Foley, AL 36535; 251/943-1227.

Trip notes: The campground is six miles from the Gulf, and across the street from outlet shopping. Golf is available within three miles.

38 Wolf Bay Plantation Harbour RV Resort

Location: Gulf, map 5, grid F4.

Campsites, facilities: There are 98 RV sites at this campground. All have full hookups. Pull-through sites are available. Some sites have shade. Picnic tables are provided. RV storage and patios are available. Restrooms have hot showers and flush toilets. A coin laundry, swimming pool, clubroom, cable TV hookups, and VCR library are provided. Buildings are wheelchair accessible. Pets are permitted.

Reservations, fees: Reservations are accepted, and no deposit is required. Campsites are $25 per night.

Open: Year-round.

Directions: From Mobile, take Interstate 65 south to Interstate 10 east across the bay. Take exit 44/Highway 59 south to County Road 20, and turn east. Stay on County Road 20 as it turns right after 4.5 miles, then make the first left at the sign into the campground.

Contact: Wolf Bay Plantation Harbour RV Resort, 24711 County Road 20, Elberta, AL 36530; 251/987-5131.

Trip notes: This is an RV condo lot, and the resort rents them for the owners for overnight vacationers or monthly renters. Both fresh- and saltwater fishing are available. There is a boardwalk through the wetlands to a pavilion at a creek, and a one-mile footpath. The campground is 10 minutes from the Bay, and five miles from the outlet mall.

39 Pensacola–Perdido Bay KOA

Location: Lillian, map 5, grid F4.

Campsites, facilities: There are 39 tent sites and 100 RV sites at this campground. Fifty-seven sites have full hookups, and both 30- and 50-amp service is available. Half of the RV sites are pull-through. Picnic tables are provided. There are also 11 cabins, each with cooking grills. Group sites and RV storage are available. Restrooms have hot showers and flush toilets. A coin laundry, boat ramp, dock, spa, swimming pool, playground, and clubroom are provided. Cable TV and phone hookups are available. Ice, LP gas, groceries, and some supplies are available at the campground. Some facilities are wheelchair accessible. Leashed pets are permitted. You must clean up after your pet, and pets cannot be left unattended or tied up outside.

Reservations, fees: Reservations are accepted, and a deposit is required. There is a $20 cancellation fee on cabins. Tent sites are $19, and RV sites are $23–25 per night. Cabins are $40–60 per night.

Open: Year-round.

Directions: From Mobile, take Interstate 65 south to Interstate 10 east across the bay. Take exit 44/Highway 59 south to the Gulf Beach Express, and turn left. Turn left onto US 98, travel 14 miles, then turn right on Highway 99/Lillian Road to the campground. The campground is two miles south of US 98.

Contact: Pensacola–Perdido Bay KOA, 33951 Spinnaker Dr., Highway 99, Lillian, AL 36549; 251/961-1717.

Trip notes: The campground is located on Perdido Bay, and fishing is available from a pier. It is close to Gulf State Park and other beach areas.

40 Keller Road RV Park

Location: Foley, map 5, grid F3.

Campsites, facilities: There are 40 RV sites at this campground, all with full hookups. Six of the sites are pull-through, and 13 have shade. No restrooms are provided. Cable TV and a clubroom are available. Small pets are permitted. You must clean up after your pet.

Reservations, fees: Reservations are accepted. The $50 deposit is not refundable. Rates are $12 per night and

$60 per week, utilities included. The monthly rate is $125 plus utilities.

Open: Year-round.

Directions: From Mobile, take Interstate 65 south to Interstate 10 east across the bay. Take exit 44/Highway 59 south approximately 4.5 miles past Foley, and turn west on Keller Road.

Contact: Keller Road RV Park, 19723 Keller Rd., Foley, AL 36535; 251/955-6260.

Trip notes: This campground is primarily a long-term park, but they usually have a few sites open for vacationers. It is near salt and freshwater fishing, and five miles from Gulf Shore Beaches.

41 Boggy Branch RV Park and Campground

Location: Gulf Shores, map 5, grid F3.

Campsites, facilities: There are 12 RV sites at this campground, all with full hookups. Pull-through sites are available. There is also a large area for primitive camping. Piped water is available. The RV sites have picnic tables, fire rings, and cooking grills. RV storage is available. Restrooms have hot showers and flush toilets. A coin laundry and playground are provided. The facilities are wheelchair accessible. Small pets (under 15 pounds) are permitted.

Reservations, fees: Reservations are accepted, and no deposit is required. Tent sites are $5–15 per night, and RV sites are $15 per night. Senior discounts apply.

Open: Year-round.

Directions: From Mobile, take Interstate 65 south to Interstate 10 east across the bay. Take exit 44/Highway 59 south to Gulf Shores, and turn left onto County Road 8. The camp-

ground will be on your left, about 0.25 miles from the highway.

Contact: Boggy Branch RV Park and Campground, P.O. Box 543, Gulf Shores, AL 36547; 251/955-5203.

Trip notes: The campground has a pond stocked with catfish, bream, and bass, and another stocked with tilapia. There are trails through the 28-acre wooded property for hiking and biking. The campground is three miles from the beach, 10 minutes from a water park, and five minutes from an amusement park, which offers miniature golf, rides, and bungee jumping. There are three golf courses nearby, the closest about a half mile away.

42 Sun Runners RV Park

Location: Gulf, map 5, grid F3.

Campsites, facilities: The campground has 10 tent sites, all with water and electric. There are also 45 RV sites. Five of the sites have water and electric hookups, and the rest have full hookups. Pull-through sites are available. Most of the campsites have some shade, and most have picnic tables. The tent sites also have fire rings and cooking grills. RV storage is available. Restrooms have hot showers and flush toilets. A sanitary disposal station, coin laundry, and meeting room are provided. Most sites have cable TV hookups. The bathrooms are wheelchair accessible. Leashed pets are permitted.

Reservations, fees: Reservations are accepted. The deposit is refundable if cancellation is made at least 48 hours in advance. All sites cost $14 per night.

Open: Year-round.

Directions: From Mobile, take Interstate 65 south to Interstate 10 east across the bay.

Take exit 44/Highway 59 south to Gulf Shores, and turn left onto County Road 8. The campground is on County Road 8, a half mile from Highway 59.

Contact: Sun Runners RV Park, 19436 Highway 8, Gulf Shores, AL 36542; 251/955-5257.

Trip notes: The campground is four miles from the beach in a 17-acre wooded area. Fishing and swimming are available at the beach.

43 Gulf Breeze RV Resort

Location: Gulf, map 5, grid F3.

Campsites, facilities: There are 200 RV sites, all with full hookups, including cable TV. About half are pull-through sites, and some have shade. RVs must be 40 feet or less. Picnic tables and cooking grills are provided. RV storage is available. There are also five mobile homes and two travel trailers for rent. Restrooms have hot showers and flush toilets. A coin laundry, spa, family room, sports fields, fitness room, hot tub, playground, and two swimming pools are provided. Ice, LP gas, and some groceries are available at the campground. The buildings are wheelchair accessible. Leashed pets are permitted in the campground area only.

Reservations, fees: Reservations are accepted. The deposit of one night's fee is refundable if cancellation is made at least 48 hours in advance. Campsites are $22, and the mobile homes and travel trailers are $55 per night.

Open: Year-round.

Directions: From Mobile, take Interstate 65 south to Interstate 10 east across the bay. Take exit 44/Highway 59 south. About seven miles south of Foley, turn right onto Oak Road. The campground will be on the left.

Contact: Gulf Breeze RV Resort, 19800 Oak Road West, Gulf Shores, AL 36542; 251/968-8462 or 251/968-8884.

Trip notes: There is a small lake at the campground stocked with bass. Paddleboats are available. Gulf State Park is five miles away, and the beach is about four miles away. The campground is a short distance from an amusement park, a water park, and outlet shopping.

44 Bay Village Mobile Home and RV Park

Location: Gulf, map 5, grid F3.

Campsites, Facilities: There are 40 RV sites, all with full hookups and all pull-through sites. Some sites have shade. Picnic tables are provided, and RV storage is available. Both 30- and 50-amp service is available. Restrooms have hot showers and flush toilets. A coin laundry and clubhouse are provided. Cable TV is available. Leashed pets are permitted, but they must be kept inside your camper except when walked. You must clean up after your pet.

Reservations, fees: Reservations are accepted at 251/968-5613. The deposit of one night's fee is refundable if cancellation is made at least 24 hours in advance. Sites with 30-amp service are $22 per night, $95 per week, or $225 per month. Sites with 50-amp service are $25 per night, $125 per week, or $250 per month.

Open: Year-round.

Directions: Take Interstate 10 east from Mobile to exit 44/Loxley, and turn south on Highway 59. Stay on Highway 59 past Foley, and turn right onto County Road 6. The campground is .7 miles from the highway on the left.

Contact: Bay Village Mobile

Home and RV Park, 5975 Easy Street, Gulf Shores, AL 36542; 251/968-5613.

Trip notes: County Road 6 is just four miles north of the beach, so the campground is within minutes of fishing. Charters are available for deep sea fishing at the Bay. The campground is just 15 minutes from the attractions and hiking trails of Gulf State Park, and just 25 minutes from Fort Morgan State Park. The campground has five acres devoted to mobile homes, and five to the campground. Most campers rent by the month, particularly in the winter.

45 Hallmark RV Park

Location: Gulf, map 5, grid F3.

Campsites, Facilities: There are 25 RV sites, all with full hookups and shade. Pull-through sites are available. Most sites have picnic tables. Some sites have grills. Both 30- and 50-amp service is available. Primitive tent camping is also available. Restrooms have hot showers and flush toilets. A coin laundry and large recreation room are provided. Patios are available. The restrooms are wheelchair accessible. Leashed pets are permitted, but they must be kept inside your camper.

Reservations, fees: Reservations are accepted at 251/968-6494. The deposit of one night's fee is refundable if cancellation is made at least one week in advance. Primitive sites are $15 per night, and RV sites are $17. If you stay for a week, the seventh night is free.

Open: Year-round.

Directions: Take Interstate 10 east from Mobile to exit 44/Loxley, and turn south on Highway 59. Turn right onto County Road 6 about 25 miles south of Loxley. The campground is three miles from the highway on the left.

Contact: Hallmark RV Park, 5584 County Road 6, Gulf Shores, AL 36542; 251/968-6494.

Trip notes: County Road 6 is just four miles north of the beach, so the campground is within minutes of fishing. Charters are available for deep sea fishing at the Bay. The campground is within walking distance of a restaurant, 15 minutes from the attractions and hiking trails of Gulf State Park, and just 25 minutes from Fort Morgan State Park. A large outlet mall is about five miles from the campground.

46 Southport Campground

Location: Gulf, map 5, grid F3.

Campsites, facilities: There are 50 campsites suitable for tents or RVs, all with water and electric hookups. There are also 62 RV sites with full hookups. Pull-through sites are available, and most sites have some shade. Picnic tables are provided. RV storage is available. Restrooms have hot showers and flush toilets. A sanitary disposal station, coin laundry, fishing pier, and clubroom are provided. Ice and cable TV are available. Small pets are permitted in campers only, not in tents.

Reservations, fees: Reservations are accepted. The deposit of one night's fee is not refundable. Sites with water and electric hookups are $17 per night, and sites with full hookups are $21.

Open: Year-round.

Directions: From Mobile, take Interstate 65 south to Interstate 10 east across the bay. Take exit 44/Highway 59 south. About ten miles south of Foley, turn left at the bridge over the canal onto 28th Street. The campground is at 108 West 28th Street.

Contact: Southport Campground, P.O. Box

2386, Gulf Shores, AL 36547; 251/968-6220.

Trip notes: The campground sits on the Intracoastal Waterway, which contains brackish water with mostly saltwater fish. It is two miles from the beach.

47 Bay Breeze RV Park

Location: Gulf, map 5, grid G2.

Campsites, facilities: There are four tent sites, all with water and electric hookups. There are also 22 RV sites with full hookups. All sites have some shade and a view of the water. Picnic tables are provided. Restrooms have hot showers and flush toilets. A coin laundry, boat ramp, dock, and pier with sun deck are provided. Ice is available. The facilities are wheelchair accessible. Leashed pets are permitted.

Reservations, fees: Reservations are accepted. The deposit is not refundable but future credit is given if you cancel your reservation in advance. Waterfront campsites are $35 per night. All other campsites are $26 per night.

Open: Year-round.

Directions: From Interstate 10, go south 27 miles on Highway 59. After you cross over the canal, turn right on Highway 180 and head west. The campground is at mile marker 14.

Contact: Bay Breeze RV Park, 13175 Highway 180 West, Gulf Shores, AL 36542; 251/540-2362.

Trip notes: Saltwater fishing is available at the campground. It is less than half a mile to the Bon Secour Wildlife Refuge, a 2,300-acre area crisscrossed with hiking trails. The campground is less than five miles from historic Fort Morgan, the Alabama Gulf Coast Zoo, bungee jumping, miniature golf, Waterville USA water park, and outlet shopping.

48 Bayside RV Park

Location: Gulf, map 5, grid F2.

Campsites, facilities: There are 40 RV sites at this campground, all with full hookups. Pull-through sites are available, and cable TV hookups are provided. Shade is available. Picnic tables are provided. There are also two cabins; bring your own linens, and cooking is not allowed. Restrooms have hot showers and flush toilets. A coin laundry, pier, and pier house are provided, and patios are available. A playground and pool are planned to be added. Pets are permitted.

Reservations, fees: Reservations are accepted. Waterfront sites are $25, and other sites are $20–22.50. Cabins rent for $45 per night.

Open: Year-round.

Directions: Take Highway 59 south to Highway 180 and turn west towards Fort Morgan. The campground is at mile marker 11, about 10 miles from Highway 59 on the right.

Contact: Bayside RV Park, 10397 Second St., Gulf Shores, AL 36542; 251/540-2416.

Trip notes: The campground is located on Mobile Bay, and both salt and fresh water fishing is available in the brackish water. It is one mile to the Bon Secour Wildlife Refuge, which has hiking trails, and nine miles from the Fort Morgan Marina.

49 Doc's RV Park

Location: Gulf Shores, map 5, grid F3.

Campsites, facilities: The campground has 75 RV sites, all with full hookups including for cable TV. Both 30- and 50-amp hookups are available. About half the sites have shade. Picnic tables and cooking grills are provided. There are two cabins. RV storage and group sites are available. Restrooms have hot showers and flush toilets. A coin laundry, swimming pool, playground, and clubroom are provided. Leashed pets are permitted. You must pick up after your pet.

Reservations, fees: Reservations are accepted. The deposit of one night's fee is refundable with 48 hours notice. From April through October, site fees are $24 per night. From November through March, the fee is $21 per night. There is a minimum stay of two nights on weekends, or three nights on holiday weekends.

Open: Year-round.

Directions: At Gulf Shores, take Highway 59 south to Highway 180 and turn right. The campground is located two miles west of Highway 59.

Contact: Doc's RV Park, 17595 State Highway 180, Gulf Shores, AL 36542; 251/968-4511; fax 251/968-1109.

Trip notes: The campground is located three miles from the beach, two miles from a golf course, and seven miles from outlet mall shopping.

Luxury RV Resort

Location: Gulf, map 5, grid F3.

Campsites, Facilities: There are 95 RV sites. All are level, concrete sites with full hookups and patios. Most sites have picnic tables. Restrooms have hot showers and flush toilets. A coin laundry, swimming pool, shuffleboard, volleyball, horseshoes, and clubhouse are provided. Cable TV is available. The facilities are wheelchair accessible. Leashed pets are permitted. You must clean up after your pet.

Reservations, fees: Reservations are accepted with a credit card at 800/982-3510. Rates are $25 per night.

Open: Year-round.

Directions: Take Interstate 10 east from Mobile to exit 44/Loxley, and turn south on Highway 59. The campground is on the left, 1.5 miles from the bridge over the intercoastal waterway.

Contact: Luxury RV Resort, 590 Gulf Shores Parkway, Gulf Shores, AL 36542; 251/948-5444.

Trip notes: The campground is about four blocks from the beach, so is within minutes of fishing. Charters are available for deep sea fishing at the Bay. The campground is within walking distance of restaurants and a water park. It is 15 minutes from the attractions and hiking trails of Gulf State Park, and just 25 minutes from Fort Morgan State Park. A large outlet mall is about five miles from the campground.

51 Gulf State Park

Location: Gulf, map 5, grid F3.

Campsites, facilities: There are 468 campsites, all suitable for RVs or tents, all with water and electric hookups. Over 200 of the sites also have sewer hookups. Picnic tables and cooking grills are provided. There are also 21 wheelchair-accessible cabins. A coin laundry, sanitary disposal station, fishing pier, tennis courts, and playground are provided. Leashed pets are permitted.

Reservations, fees: Reservations are accepted at 800/ALA-PARK (800/252-7275). The deposit of one night's fee is non-refundable, but you can move the date of your reservation twice. Campsites cost $10.80-25 per night. The cabins are $55–111 per night.

Open: Year-round.

Directions: From Gulf Shores, take Highway 59 south to Highway 135, turn left, and follow the signs to the state park and campground.

Contact: Gulf State Park, 20115 State Highway 135, Gulf Shores, AL 36542; 251/948-6353.

Trip notes: The attraction in this part of Alabama is the beach, and this 6,150-acre park includes a 2.5-mile stretch along the Gulf. Fishing is available either from the 825-foot pier, the longest on the Gulf, or the 500-acre lake. Nature trails and the beach offer hiking opportunities. There is also an 18-hole championship golf course and pavilions.

EAST L.A.

MONTGOMERY

EAST L.A.

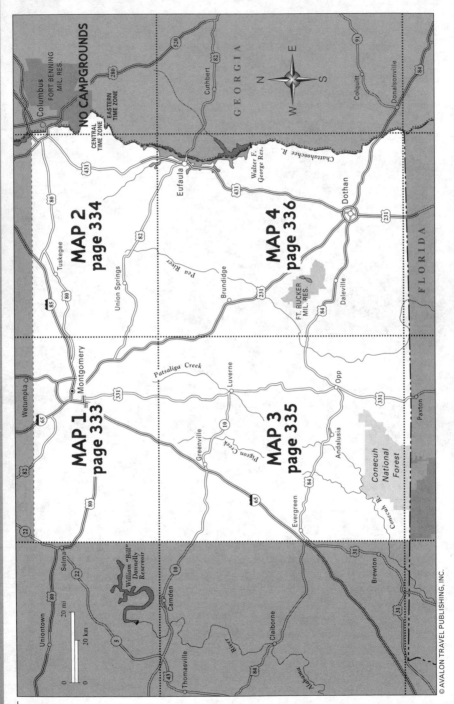

© AVALON TRAVEL PUBLISHING, INC.

MAP 1

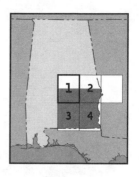

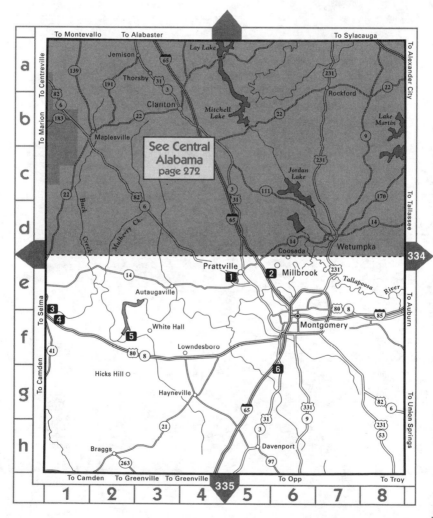

To Montevallo   To Alabaster   To Sylacauga
To Alexander City

a
To Centreville
Jemison
Lay Lake
139
65
231
Rockford
22
Thorsby   31
191
3

b
To Marion
82
6
183
Clanton
Mitchell Lake
22
22
9
Lake Martin
Maplesville
22

c
See Central Alabama page 272
3
111
Jordan Lake
231
170
To Tallassee

d
22
Buck
82
6
65
31
14
14
Wetumpka
334
Coosada
Mulberry Ck.

e
14
Prattville
1
2 Millbrook
231
Tallapoosa River
Autaugaville
80 8
85
To Auburn

f
To Selma
3
4
White Hall
5
Montgomery
80 8
Lowndesboro

g
41
Hicks Hill
6
82 6
To Union Springs
Hayneville
331
9
231
53

h
21
65
31
3
Davenport
Braggs
263
97
To Troy

To Camden To Greenville To Greenville 335 To Opp

1   2   3   4   5   6   7   8

© AVALON TRAVEL PUBLISHING, INC.

MAP 2

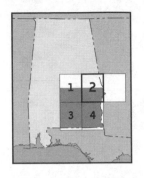

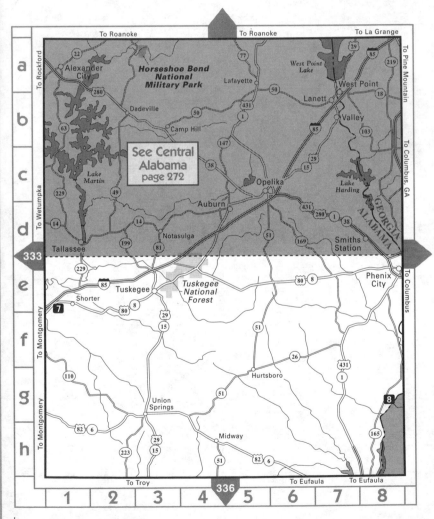

MAP 3

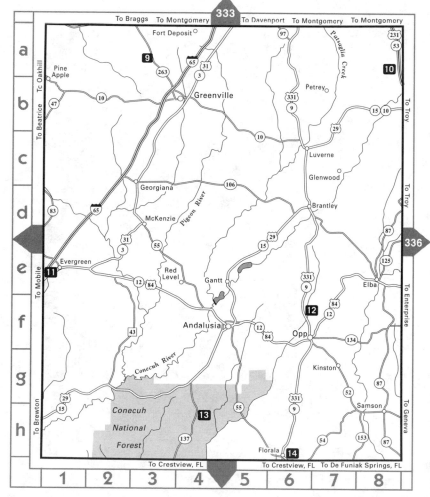

MAP 4

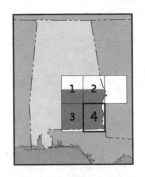

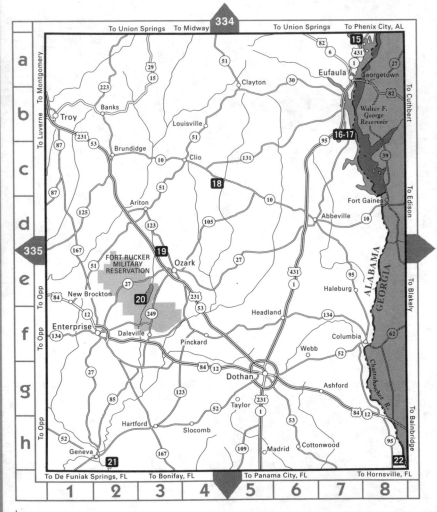

© AVALON TRAVEL PUBLISHING, INC.

EAST L.A.

1 Kountry Air

Location: Prattville, map 1, grid E5.

Campsites, facilities: There are 12 RV sites at this campground, all with full hookups. Picnic tables and cooking grills are provided. Restrooms have hot showers and flush toilets. LP gas and limited supplies are available at the campground.

Reservations, fees: Reservations are not accepted. The fee is $10.50 per night for two people, $1.50 more for each extra person.

Open: Year-round.

Directions: From Montgomery, take Interstate 65 to exit 179/Cobbs Fort Road and turn west. Turn left onto Highway 6/US 82 after 15 miles.

Contact: Kountry Air, 2133 US Highway 82 W., Prattville, AL 36067; 334/365-6861.

Trip notes: The majority of the campers here rent monthly, but overnight guests are permitted when a vacancy exists.

2 K & K Campground

Location: Montgomery, map 1, grid E6.

Campsites, facilities: This campground has nearly 100 RV sites, all with full hookups. All are pull-through sites, and none have shade. RV storage is available. A coin laundry and swimming pool are provided, and limited groceries are available at the campground. Pets are permitted.

Reservations, fees: Reservations are not accepted. Sites are $20.75 per night.

Open: Year-round.

Directions: From Montgomery, take Interstate 65 north about 10 miles to exit 179/Cobbs Ford Road, and turn right. Take the first right onto the Service Road.

Contact: K & K Campground, 1810 Service Road East, Millbrook, AL 36054; 334/285-5251.

Trip notes: This campground is convenient to the interstate for vacationers passing through the area.

3 Selma Flea Market and Campground

Location: Selma, map 1, grid E1.

Campsites, facilities: There are 16 RV sites, all with full hookups. RV storage is available. There are no restrooms. Pets are permitted.

Reservations, fees: Reservations are accepted, and no deposit is required. Sites are $12 per night.

Open: Year-round.

Directions: The campground is located at the intersection of River Road and Highway 80 Truck Route.

Contact: Selma Flea Market and Campground, 606 River Rd., Selma, AL 36703; 334/875-0500.

Trip notes: The campground is mostly used either by people setting up for the flea market or by construction workers renting by the month. Selma was the site of several pivotal events in the fight for civil rights, and the campground is a short drive from historic sites.

4 Six Mile Creek Campground

Location: Alabama River, map 1, grid F1.

Campsites, facilities: The 31 campsites in this campground are used by both tents and RVs. All sites have water and electric hookups. Picnic tables, fire rings, and cooking grills are provided. Restrooms have hot showers and flush toilets. A coin laundry, boat ramp, dock, sanitary disposal station, and basketball courts are provided. The buildings are wheelchair accessible. Leashed pets are permitted.

Reservations, fees: Reservations are accepted through the National Recreation Reservation Service (NRRS) at 877/444-6777; website: www.reserveusa.com. The full amount is payable in advance. Campsites are $12–14 depending on location.

Open: Year-round.

Directions: From Selma, take Highway 41 south six miles to County Road 139 and turn right. Follow the signs to the campground.

Contact: Six Mile Creek Campground, 100 Resource Management Dr., Hayneville, AL 36040; 334/872-9554, or 334/875-6228.

Trip notes: Fishing is available in the Alabama River for bass, catfish, crappie, and bream. There is no swimming area near the campground. Kayaking and rafting are popular on this slow river, but you will not find white water. Pontoon boats are also popular. The campground is about eight miles from Selma and its attractions, and 20 miles from Cahaba, the first capital of the state, and home to many fine antebellum homes.

5 Prairie Creek Campground

Location: Hayneville, map 1, grid F2.

Campsites, facilities: This campground has 19 sites with water and electric hookups, all suitable for tents or RVs. Picnic tables, fire rings, and cooking grills are provided. There are also 40 primitive tent sites. Restrooms have hot showers and flush toilets. A coin laundry, sanitary disposal station, and boat dock are provided. Leashed pets are permitted.

Reservations, fees: Reservations are accepted through the National Recreation Reservation Service (NRRS) at 877/444-6777, website: www.reserveusa.com. The full amount is payable in advance. Waterfront sites are $14 per night. The other developed sites are $12 per night. Tent sites are $10.

Open: Year-round.

Directions: From Benton, go east on US 80 about 3.5 miles, then turn left onto County Road 40 at the sign for Prairie Creek and Lock and Dam Park. After the railroad crossing, 40 turns right at a T-junction. Turn right, then turn left at the levee and follow the signs to the campground.

Contact: Prairie Creek Campground, 100 Resource Management Dr., Hayneville, AL 36040; 334/872-9554.

Trip notes: Fishing is available in Prairie Creek and the Alabama River for bass, catfish, crappie, and bream. Although you can't swim at this Army Corps of Engineers campground, there is a beach and swimming area at historic Holy Ground Battlefield Park, about six miles away. Kayaking and canoeing are popular on the river.

6 Montgomery KOA

Location: Montgomery, map 1, grid F6.

Campsites, Facilities: There are a total of 135 campsites. Twenty-nine of the sites have full hookups and are reserved for RVs, and the rest have water and electric only and can be used by either tents or RVs. About half are pull-through sites. RV storage is available, and a sanitary disposal station is provided. Some sites have picnic tables. There is also one cabin. Restrooms have hot showers and flush toilets. A coin laundry, swimming pool, and playground are provided. Leashed pets are permitted.

Reservations, fees: Reservations are accepted at 800/KOA-5032 (800/562-5032). No deposit is required. The rate for tents is $20 per night. Full hookup sites cost $27, and RV sites with only water and electric cost $26.

Open: Year-round.

Directions: From downtown Montgomery, take exit 164/US 31 off Interstate 65 and go south one block.

Contact: Montgomery KOA, 250 Fischer Rd., Hope Hull, AL 36043; 334/288-0728.

Trip notes: There is a 10-acre lake at the campground stocked with bass and bream. The campground is eight miles from downtown Montgomery.

⑦ Winddrift Travel Park

Location: Montgomery, map 2, grid E1.

Campsites, facilities: There are 32 campsites suitable for tents or RVs. Two sites have water and electric hookups, and the rest have full hookups and are pull-through sites. Some sites have shade. Campsites near the lake have picnic tables. Restrooms have hot showers and flush toilets. A coin laundry and clubroom are provided. Supplies, groceries, ice, and LP gas are available at the campground. The buildings are wheelchair accessible. Pets are permitted.

Reservations, fees: Reservations are accepted, and no deposit is required. Campsites are $22 per night. Good Sam discounts apply.

Open: Year-round.

Directions: From Montgomery, take Interstate 85 northeast to exit 22, and turn south on US 80, which is Main Street in the town of Shorter. The sign for the campground is about a block off the interstate.

Contact: Winddrift Travel Park, P.O. Box 82, Shorter, AL 30075; 334/724-9428.

Trip notes: Fishing is available for bream, catfish, and bass. The campground is a half mile from the Macon County Dog Track and 20 miles from historical sites in Montgomery.

⑧ Bluff Creek Campground

Location: Lake Eufaula, map 2, grid G8.

Campsites, Facilities: There are 88 campsites suitable for tents or RVs. All have water and electric hookups. Picnic tables, fire rings, and cooking grills are provided. Restrooms have hot showers and flush toilets. A coin laundry, sanitary disposal station, playground, and boat ramp are provided. The buildings are wheelchair accessible. Leashed pets are permitted.

Reservations, fees: Reservations are accepted through the National Recreation Reservation Service (NRRS) at 877/444-6777, website: www.reserveusa.com. The full amount is payable in advance. Reservations must be made at least four days in advance. Sites cost $16 per night. Golden Access discounts apply.

Open: The campground is open from March through November.

Directions: From Eufaula, take US 431 north to Highway 165 and turn right. Travel about 15 miles, and turn right at the sign for the park and campground.

Contact: Bluff Creek Campground, Rt. 1, Box 176, Fort Gaines, GA 31751; 334/855-2746.

Trip notes: Fishing is the main attraction at Lake Eufaula, and the lake is stocked with bass and catfish. There is no designated swimming area because of the alligators in the area, but the local wildlife doesn't deter the water-skiers. There are no good hiking trails at the park, but the campground is about 20 miles from Providence Canyon, also known as the "Little Grand Canyon," which has 10 miles of trails leading through the limestone canyons.

9 Sherling Lakes RV Park

Location: Sherling Lakes, map 3, grid A3.
Campsites, facilities: There are 41 RV sites at this campground. Of these, 26 have full hookups, and 15 have water and electric only. Some sites have picnic tables and fire rings. There is also a primitive camping area. RV storage is available. Restrooms have hot showers and flush toilets. A coin laundry, playground, and clubroom are provided. Ice and snacks are available at the campground. Leashed pets are permitted.
Reservations, fees: Reservations are accepted at 800/810-5253. No deposit is required. Campsites with hookups are $18.75 per night, and primitive campsites are $12. Good Sam discounts apply.
Open: Year-round.
Directions: From Birmingham, go south on Interstate 65 to exit 130, and turn right on Highway 185. After 1.5 miles, turn left on Highway 263. The campground is two miles from Highway 185 on the left.
Contact: Sherling Lakes RV Park, P.O. Box 158, Greenville, AL 36037; 334/382-3638.
Trip notes: Fishing is available in the two lakes for bass, bream, catfish, and crappie. The main hiking trail and its side trails total

over four miles. The campground rents johnboats and motor boats. It is adjacent to the Robert Trent Jones Golf Course.

10 Deer Run RV Park

Location: Troy, map 3, grid A8.
Campsites, facilities: This RV campground has 74 sites with full hookups, all pull-through sites. About half have shade. Group sites and RV storage are available. Picnic tables are provided. Ice, LP gas, and some groceries are available. A coin laundry, swimming pool, playground, and clubroom are provided. Cable TV hookups are available. Leashed pets are permitted. You must clean up after your pet.
Reservations, fees: Reservations are accepted at 800/552-3036. Fees are $20.95 per night, $120 per week, and $325 per month.
Open: Year-round.
Directions: The campground is six miles north of Troy on Highway 231, at mile marker 84.
Contact: Deer Run RV Park, 3736 Highway 231 North, Troy, AL 36081; 334/566-6517.
Trip notes: The campground is 10 miles north of Troy State University, and five miles north of the Pike Pioneer Museum. Deer and wild turkeys are frequently seen in the area.

11 Pine Crest Park

Location: Evergreen, map 3, grid E1.
Campsites, facilities: The campground has 12 RV sites, all with full hookups. Half of the sites are pull-through sites. There are no restrooms. Pets are permitted.
Reservations, fees: Reser-

vations are accepted, and no deposit is required. Campsites are $10.30 per night.

Open: Year-round.

Directions: From Birmingham, take Interstate 65 south to the Evergreen exit (93), and go east on US 84 for one-third of a mile.

Contact: Pine Crest Park, 105 Spring St., Evergreen, AL 36401; 251/578-1442.

Trip notes: The campground is convenient to the interstate.

12 Frank Jackson State Park

Location: Opp, map 3, grid F6.

Campsites, Facilities: There are 29 campsites suitable for tents or RVs, all with full hookups. Picnic tables, fire rings, and cooking grills are provided. Restrooms have hot showers and flush toilets. A boat ramp, dock, and playground are provided. Cable TV hookups are available. The facilities are wheelchair accessible. Leashed pets are permitted.

Reservations, fees: Reservations are accepted at 800/ALA-PARK (800/252-7275). The deposit of one night's fee is non-refundable, but you can move the date of your reservation twice. The fee is $10 for tent sites and $15 for RV sites. Senior citizens discounts apply.

Open: Year-round.

Directions: From Montgomery, go south on US 331. Turn right at the sign for the park on Old Pine Road, then left into the park and campground.

Contact: Frank Jackson State Park, Rt. 3, Box 73-C, Opp, AL 36467; 334/493-6988.

Trip notes: Fishing for bass, catfish, and crappie is available in the 1,000-acre lake. Water skiing is popular in the lake as well, along with some kayaking and canoeing.

There are two miles of hiking trails, and a beach in the swimming area.

13 Open Pond

Location: Andalusia, map 3, grid H4.

Campsites, Facilities: There are 55 sites suitable for tents or RVs. Of these, 32 sites have water and electric hookups. Picnic tables and cooking grills are provided. Restrooms have hot showers and flush toilets. A boat ramp, fishing pier, and sanitary disposal station are provided. The restrooms are wheelchair accessible. Leashed pets are permitted.

Reservations, fees: No reservations are accepted. The fee is $6 for sites with no hookups, and $12 for sites with electric and water hookups.

Open: Year-round.

Directions: From Andalusia, take US 29 south for 9.7 miles to Highway 137, and turn left at the sign for Blue Lake–Open Pond. Continue to follow the signs to the campground.

Contact: Open Pond, Conecuh National Forest, 2946 Chestnut St., Montgomery, AL; 334/832-4470.

Trip notes: The pond is stocked with bass, catfish, bream, and bluegill. Hikers can take the half-mile spur trail to the 20-mile Conecuh Recreation Trail. There is also a short trail around the pond.

14 Florala State Park

Location: Lake Jackson, map 3, grid H6.

Campsites, Facilities: The tent area of this campground has 12 campsites, all with water and electric hookups. The RV area has 23 sites with full hookups, and can be used by either tents or RVs. All sites have picnic tables, fire rings, and cooking grills. Restrooms have hot showers and flush toilets. A playground, boat ramp, fishing pier, and coin laundry are provided. The buildings are wheelchair accessible. Leashed pets are permitted in the campground and on the walkway only.

Reservations, fees: Reservations are accepted at 800/ALA-PARK (800/252-7275). The deposit of one night's fee is non-refundable, but you can move the date of your reservation twice. The fee is based on which area you camp in, regardless of whether you are tent or trailer camping. It's $8 to camp in the tent area, and $14 if camping in the RV area.

Open: Year-round.

Directions: From Opp, take US 331 south. The campground is about a mile north of the Florida state line.

Contact: Florala State Park, P.O. Box 322, Florala, AL 36442-0322; 334/858-6425.

Trip notes: Lake Jackson is considered one of the cleanest in the state, and offers fishing for bass, crappie, and catfish. A one-mile bike and walking path leads from the boat launch and winds through the park. There is a sand beach in the swimming area. Security is provided by camp hosts who live on-site, so the park is a good option for families and single campers. The park has had problems with pet owners in the past and is considering banning pets in the future.

⓯ Lakepoint State Park

Location: Eufaula, map 4, grid A8.

Campsites, Facilities: There are 244 campsites suitable for tents or RVs, all with some shade and all with water and electric hookups. Eighty of the sites have full hookups. Almost 100 are pull-through sites. There are also 29 cabins with heat and air conditioning, many with fireplaces. Restrooms have hot showers and flush toilets. A sanitary disposal station is provided, along with a coin laundry, tennis courts, boat ramp, dock, game room, and playground. A swimming pool is available for motel and cabin guests. The campground store sells ice, LP gas, groceries, and some gifts. Marine gas is available. Most buildings are wheelchair accessible. Leashed pets are permitted, but keep a close watch on your pet (and small children) because of the number of alligators living in the area.

Reservations, fees: Reservations are accepted at 800/ALA-PARK (800/252-7275). The deposit of one night's fee is non-refundable, but you can move the date of your reservation twice. Site fees are $14.30–16.50 per night, depending on location and hookups. The cabins are $79–158 per night, depending on size.

Open: Year-round.

Directions: From Eufaula, take US 431 north six miles and follow the signs to the state park.

Contact: Lakepoint State Park, 104 Lakepoint Dr., Eufaula, AL 36027; 334/687-6676.

Trip notes: Lake Eufaula calls itself the "Bass Capital of the World." The lake has an abundance of largemouth bass, crappie, and catfish. There are three hiking trails winding through the woods which total five miles. The park has an 18-hold golf course, and is adjacent to the Eufaula National Wildlife Refuge, which includes a staffed nature center. The lake supports an abundance of wildlife, including geese and other waterfowl, wild turkeys, deer, alliga-

tors, fox, bobcats, beavers, and otters. The swimming area has a sand beach. The town of Eufaula has many lovely antebellum homes.

16 Hardridge Creek Campground

Location: Lake Eufaula, map 4, grid B7.
Campsites, facilities: There are 77 campsites suitable for tents or RVs. Twenty campsites have full hookups, and the rest have water and electricity. Picnic tables, fire rings, and cooking grills are provided. Restrooms have hot showers and flush toilets. A playground, boat ramp, and sanitary disposal station are provided. The buildings are wheelchair accessible. Leashed pets are permitted.
Reservations, fees: Reservations are accepted through the National Recreation Reservation Service (NRRS) at 877/444-6777, website: www.reserveusa.com. The full amount is payable in advance. Sites with water and electric hookups cost $16 per night. Sites with full hookups are $18.
Open: The campground is open from March through September.
Directions: From Eufaula, take US 431 south to Highway 95 and turn left. Turn left again on Highway 97 and follow the signs.
Contact: Hardridge Creek Campground, Rt. 1, Box 176, Fort Gaines, GA 31751; 334/585-5945.
Trip notes: Lake Eufaula (also known as Lake Walter F. George) straddles the border between Georgia and Alabama, and this is one of many Army Corps of Engineers campgrounds along the shore. The lake is stocked with bass and catfish. There is a sand beach in the swimming area. Eufaula is a good choice for a day trip as it contains beautiful antebellum homes, and is only a half an hour's drive from the campground.

17 White Oak Creek Campground

Location: Lake Eufaula, map 4, grid B7.
Campsites, Facilities: There are 132 campsites suitable for tents or RVs. All have water and electric hookups. Picnic tables, fire rings, and cooking grills are provided. Restrooms have hot showers and flush toilets. A coin laundry, sanitary disposal station, several playgrounds, and a boat ramp are provided. The buildings are wheelchair accessible. Leashed pets are permitted.
Reservations, fees: Reservations are accepted through the National Recreation Reservation Service (NRRS) at 877/444-6777, website: www.reserveusa.com. The full amount is payable in advance. Reservations must be made at least four days in advance. Sites cost $16 per night. Golden Access discounts apply.
Open: Year-round.
Directions: From Eufaula, take US 431 south about seven miles, and turn left onto Highway 95. The campground is two miles down on the left.
Contact: White Oak Creek Campground, Rt. 1, Box 176, Fort Gaines, GA 31751; 334/687-3101.
Trip notes: About 90% of the campsites are on the water. Lake Eufaula, also known as Lake Walter F. George, calls itself the "Bass Capital of the World," and fishing is the most popular tourist activity at the park. There are some short trails in the area and along the lake. Swimming in the lake is at your own risk. There are alligators in the lake, and swimming is not recommended.

18 Blue Springs State Park

Location: Clio, map 4, grid C4.

Campsites, facilities: There are 39 tent sites, all with electric and water hookups. There are also 50 RV sites. Seven have full hookups, and the rest have water and electric hookups only. Six of the sites are pull-through. Picnic tables, fire rings, and cooking grills are provided. Restrooms have hot showers and flush toilets. Primitive camping is also available, as are group sites and RV storage. A sanitary disposal station, tennis courts, swimming pool, and playground are provided. Firewood and ice are available at the campground. The restrooms are wheelchair accessible. Leashed pets are permitted.

Reservations, fees: Reservations are not accepted. Primitive sites are $5, sites with water and electric are $11, and sites with full hookups are $15 per night.

Open: Year-round.

Directions: The campground is six miles east of Clio on Highway 10.

Contact: Blue Springs State Park, 2595 Highway 10, Clio, AL 36017; 334/397-4875.

Trip notes: A small fishing pond in the park is stocked with bass, bream, and crappie. Paddleboats are available for rent. The natural springs pump out an average of 2,200 gallons of water per minute, at a constant temperature of 58 degrees, so the blue in the name must refer to the color of your skin if you dare the water. Wildlife in the area includes deer and armadillos.

19 Ozark Trav-L-Park

Location: Ozark, map 4, grid E3.

Campsites, facilities: There are 60 sites at this campground, all suitable for either tents or RVs. Most sites have full hookups including cable TV. Both 50- and 30-amp hookups are available. Picnic tables, cooking grills, and some fire rings are available. RV storage is available, and a sanitary disposal station is provided. Restrooms have hot showers and flush toilets. A coin laundry, swimming pool, playground, and clubroom are provided. The campground store sells ice, LP gas, supplies, and some groceries. The buildings are wheelchair accessible. Leashed pets are permitted.

Reservations, fees: Reservations are accepted at 800/359-3218, and no deposit is required. Campsites cost $20.95 per night for two people, $1 for each additional person over age 6. Good Sam and AAA discounts apply.

Open: Year-round.

Directions: From Montgomery, go south 70 miles on US 231 to mile marker 47.

Contact: Ozark Trav-L-Park, 4000 US Highway 231 North, Ozark, AL 36360; 334/774-3219.

Trip notes: There are two fishing ponds, stocked with catfish and perch, and a waterfall flowing into a goldfish pond. The campground is near four golf courses.

20 Engineer Beach

Location: Fort Rucker, map 4, grid E3.

Campsites, facilities: There are 18 campsites suitable for tents or RVs, all with water and electric hookups. About half are pull-through sites. Picnic tables and cooking grills are provided. Restrooms have hot showers and flush toilets. A sanitary disposal station and playground are provided. Leashed pets are permitted.

Reservations, fees: Reservations are not accepted. Campsites cost $8 for military personnel, and $10 for civilians that have base clearance.

Open: The campground is open year-round, but the water is cut off between November and February.

Directions: From Enterprise, take Highway 248 and turn right on Andrews Avenue. The campground is on the base at Fort Rucker. Enter through the Ozark Gate on Andrews Avenue, and follow the signs.

Contact: Engineer Beach, Outdoor Recreation Building 2906, Andrews Ave., Fort Rucker, AL 36362; 334/255-4305.

Trip notes: The campground is closed to civilians without access to the military installation.

21 Spring Creek Campground

Location: Geneva, map 4, grid H2.

Campsites, facilities: There are 20 primitive tent sites, and 20 RV sites. Half the RV sites have full hookups, and most are pull-through. All sites have shade. Picnic tables and fire rings are provided, and cooking grills are available. Restrooms have hot showers and flush toilets. There are also group sites and four cabins. A coin laundry, hot tub, swimming pool, playground, and clubroom are provided. LP gas, ice, some supplies, and some groceries are available at the campground. RV storage is available, and a sanitary disposal station is provided. The buildings are wheelchair accessible. Leashed pets are permitted.

Reservations, fees: Reservations are accepted. The deposit of half of your planned stay is refundable if cancellation is made seven days in advance. Tent sites are $30 per night, RV sites are $35, and cabins are $60. The campground is a private club, and you need a membership to enter; membership costs $10 per year.

Open: Year-round.

Directions: The campground is 1.5-miles off County Road 4 on Spring Creek Road in Geneva.

Contact: Spring Creek Campground, 163 Campground Rd., Geneva, AL 36340; 334/684-3891; website: www.springcreek-campground.net.

Trip notes: With a catfish pond on the property, and a creek flowing through the campground, there are plenty of fishing opportunities. The creek is also used for kayaking and rafting. There are walking trails by the creek. Wildlife in the area includes deer, wild turkeys, and armadillos. The campground is 10 miles from the Southeast Alabama Speedway, and about an hour from the Fort Walton and Panama City beaches. This is a nudist campground for adults-only, gay, and lesbian campers.

22 Chattahoochee State Park

Location: Gordon, map 4, grid H8.

Campsites, facilities: The campground has 25 primitive campsites suitable for tents or RVs. There are no hookups, but they are planned for future development. Picnic tables, fire rings, and cooking grills are available. Restrooms have pit toilets and cold showers. A boat ramp and dock are provided. No gasoline motors are permitted on the lake. The bathhouse is wheelchair accessible. Leashed pets are permitted.

Reservations, fees: Reservations are not accepted. The fee is $7 per night.

Open: Year-round.

Directions: From Dothan, take US 84 southeast to Highway 95 and turn south.

The campground is just north of the Florida state line. Turn left at the sign into the park.

Contact: Chattahoochee State Park, 250 Chattahoochee State Park Rd., Gordon, AL 36343; 334/522-3607.

Trip notes: Fishing for bream and bass is available at the lake in the park. Rowboats are available for rent. There are eight hiking trails totaling seven miles in length. Wildlife in the area includes deer and wild turkeys.

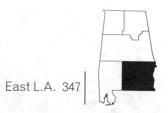

RESOURCE GUIDE

RESOURCES

SOURCES FOR OUTDOOR GEAR

Alabama Outdoors is an outfitter of clothing and gear for outdoor sports, including camping, backpacking, climbing, canoeing, skiing, and travel. It also sponsors outdoor events such as canoe and kayak races, and climbing competitions. It has several stores in Alabama. Its salespeople are excellent sources of information and advice. Check out www.aloutdoors.com or call 800/870-0011.

Camp-Mor is a discount mail order company for outdoor gear. The trick is in knowing what it is you're looking for, and what the price would be elsewhere. The information on its products is rather sketchy at best, the customer service operators are not always knowledgeable, and its discounts can frequently be bettered by sales at other retailers. Check out www.campmor.com or call 888/226-7667.

GORP stands for Great Outdoor Recreation Pages and is a combination outdoor travel agency and source for travel gear and information. Check out www.gorp.com.

L.L. Bean is another retailer that sells a great deal of camping and outdoor gear in addition to clothing. It offers products both through retail stores and mail order, and its telephone order takers are fairly knowledgeable. Check out www.llbean.com, or call 800/441-5713.

Lands' End is primarily a clothing manufacturer, but it also sells high-quality outdoor gear through mail order or its retail stores. Check out www.landsend.com, or call 800/356-4444.

REI (Recreation Equipment, Inc.) is a member co-op supplier of high-quality equipment for a variety of outdoor sports, including camping, hiking, biking, rock climbing, and boating. It started out with a store in Seattle, and covered the rest of the country with mail order. At the time of this writing, there are retail stores in 23 states and more are opening all the time. Check out www.rei.com or call 800/426-4840.

STATE CAMPGROUND INFORMATION

Corps of Engineers (COE) parks either don't require reservations (check the listing), or reservations can be made by calling the National Recreation Reservation Service (NRRS) at 877/444-6777, website: www.reserveusa.com.

Alabama
National Forest Information
- Main Office - 2946 Chestnut Street, Montgomery, AL 36107; 800/879-4496, 334/832-4470

- Bankhead Ranger District - P.O. Box 278, Double Springs, AL 35553; 205/489-5111

- Conecuh Ranger District - Rt. 5, Box 157, Andalusia, AL 36420; 334/222-2555

- Oakmulgee Ranger District - One Forest Drive, Brent, AL 35034; 205/926-9765

- Shoal Creek Ranger District - 450 Highway 46, Heflin, AL 36264; 205/463-2272

- Talladega Ranger District - 1001 North Street, Talladega, AL 35160; 205/362-2909

- Tuskegee Ranger District - 125 National Forest Road 949, Tuskegee, AL 36083; 334/727-2652

State Parks
For reservations in Alabama's state parks, call 800/ALA-PARK(800/252-7275).

Georgia
National Forest Information
- Main Office - 1755 Cleveland Highway, Gainesville, GA 30501-357; 770/297-3000

- Armuchee Ranger District–806 E. Villanow St., Lafayette, GA 30728 706/638-1085

- Brasstown Ranger District–1881 Highway 515, Blairsville, GA 30514 706/745-6928

- Chattooga Ranger District–200 Highway 197 N, Clarkesville, GA 30523 706/754-6221

- Cohutta Ranger District–401 G I Maddox Parkway, Chatsworth, GA 30705 706/695-6736

- Oconee Ranger District–1199 Madison Road, Eatonton, GA 31024 706/485-7110

- Tallulah Ranger District–809 Highway 441 South, Clayton, GA 30525 706/782-3320

- Toccoa Ranger District–6050 Appalachian Highway, Blue Ridge, GA 30513 706/632-3031

State Parks
For reservations in Georgia's state parks, call 800/864-7275, or 770/389-7275 within the Atlanta area.

TOURISM OFFICES

General information on traveling in Alabama can be obtained from the Alabama Bureau of Tourism, 401 Adams Ave., P.O. Box 4927, Montgomery, AL 36103-4927; 800/252-2262, or 334/242-4169 within the state; website: www.state.al.us.

The Georgia Department of Industry, Trade, and Tourism can be reached at 285 Peachtree Center Ave. NE, Suites 1000 & 1100, Atlanta, Georgia 30303-1230; 404/656-3545; website: www.georgia.org/itt/tourism.

THE APPALACHIAN TRAIL (AT)

The Appalachian Trail (AT) starts at Springer Mountain in north Georgia and ends 2,158 miles later at Mount Katahdin in Maine. The trail is managed through cooperation with the National Park Service by the Appalachian Trail Conference, P.O. Box 807, Harpers Ferry, WV 25425-0807; 304/535-6331; website: www.appalachiantrail.org.

The address for the National Park Service office is: Appalachian National Scenic Trail NPS Park Office, Harpers Ferry Center, Harpers Ferry, WV 25425; 304/535-6278; website: www.nps.gov/appa.

Permits are not required to hike or camp on the 78-mile Georgia portion of the trail. Backpacking can be done all along the trail. Three-sided shelters (Adirondack huts) are provided every 10 to 12 miles the length of the trail and campers are required to stay in these shelters.

THE PINHOTI TRAIL

Many people believe the Appalachian Trail should have started in Alabama, where the Appalachian Mountain range begins. The Pinhoti Trail was created to bridge the gap between the start of the Appalachians, and the Appalachian Trail. It stretches for 120 miles in Alabama and 100 miles in Georgia before connecting with the Appalachian Trail at Springer Mountain. For more information on the Pinhoti Trail, check out the article on the Alabama Trails Association's website, at www.alabamatrails.com/at.htm.

INDEX

ABOUT THE AUTHOR

©VICKI EBERLEIN

After moving to the Atlanta area from Florida, **Marilyn Sue Windle** discovered hiking and camping while trying to figure out what people did for fun so far from an ocean. Since then, she has explored the Southeast and the Appalachian Mountains, the canyons of the Southwest, and the wilds of Alaska.

Marilyn worked in information technology before deciding to take the plunge and explore writing as a career. She is the author of *The Atlanta Dog Lover's Companion*. Marilyn writes the newsletter for her local humane society as well as contributes articles to Sierra Club publications. Her articles have appeared in national magazines, regional technical journals, and local newsletters and papers.

Marilyn lives in Atlanta with her dog, Bandit, and cat, Chelsea.

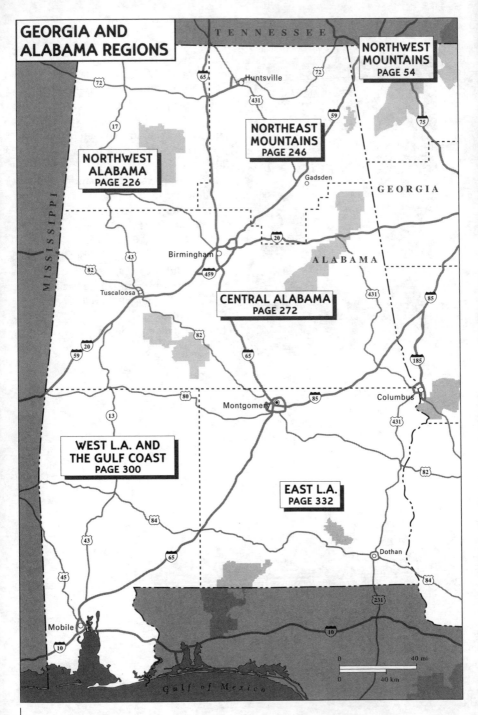

GEORGIA AND ALABAMA REGIONS

TENNESSEE

NORTHWEST MOUNTAINS
PAGE 54

Huntsville

NORTHEAST MOUNTAINS
PAGE 246

NORTHWEST ALABAMA
PAGE 226

Gadsden

GEORGIA

Birmingham

ALABAMA

Tuscaloosa

CENTRAL ALABAMA
PAGE 272

Columbus

Montgomery

WEST L.A. AND THE GULF COAST
PAGE 300

EAST L.A.
PAGE 332

Dothan

Mobile

Gulf of Mexico

0   40 mi
0   40 km

MISSISSIPPI

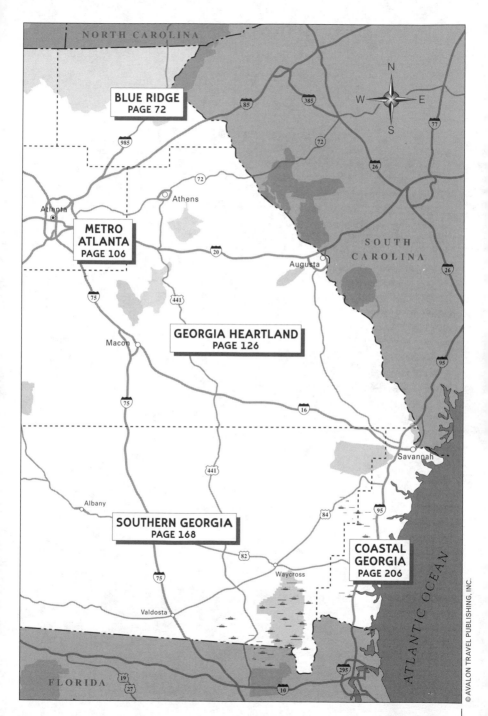

NORTH CAROLINA

BLUE RIDGE
PAGE 72

Athens

Atlanta

METRO
ATLANTA
PAGE 106

SOUTH
CAROLINA

Augusta

GEORGIA HEARTLAND
PAGE 126

Macon

SOUTHERN GEORGIA
PAGE 168

Albany

Savannah

COASTAL
GEORGIA
PAGE 206

Waycross

Valdosta

ATLANTIC OCEAN

FLORIDA

© AVALON TRAVEL PUBLISHING, INC.

Notes

Notes

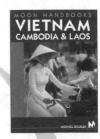